"The authors offer a series of soundings toward an ecclesiology that can be both evangelical and ecumenical, both robust and contemporary. The book is especially important for the way it engages ecclesiology in a dialogue between the church's gospel-shaped identity and the cultural circumstances in which it lives its witness to the gospel."

—George R. Hunsberger, Western Theological Seminary

"We live in an era when there seems to be confusion about the character, nature, purpose, and relevance of the church. *Exploring Ecclesiology* calls for a deeper understanding of the role of the church. Harper and Metzger provide a helpful resource for theologians, pastors, and lay leaders to engage in this much-needed dialogue."

—Soong-Chan Rah, North Park Theological Seminary;
author of *The Next Evangelicalism*

"A thoughtful introduction to ecclesiology that is biblically grounded, historically informed, ecumenically engaged, and culturally relevant. It is a worthy textbook for introducing and furthering current discussion about the church and does so in a way that is accessible, broad-ranging, and practical. *Exploring Ecclesiology* marks an important milestone in the renewal of interest in the doctrine of the church within evangelicalism."

—Kimlyn J. Bender, University of Sioux Falls

"Harper and Metzger unpack some of the most vexing questions and important issues regarding the nature and purpose of the Church. Their clear commitment to speak in an unapologetic manner into the particular ethos of evangelical Christianity will challenge and at times provoke their readers. Theirs is a challenge which needs to be taken seriously as it is grounded in reference to and appreciation of theologians from a wide variety of backgrounds and eras."

—Rev. Dr. Peter M. B. Robinson, Wycliffe College, University of Toronto

"The church—harlot or mother? Experienced as the first by many, this impressive work seeks to encourage the latter judgment by providing an extensive and constructive evangelical theology of the church. Finally, we have an ecclesiology that is not reactionary, separatist, denominationally narrow, impractical, or out of touch with the postmodern world."

—Barry L. Callen, Anderson University

# Exploring Ecclesiology

*An Evangelical and Ecumenical Introduction*

Brad Harper and
Paul Louis Metzger

**BrazosPress**
*a division of Baker Publishing Group*
Grand Rapids, Michigan

Published by Brazos Press
a division of Baker Publishing Group
P.O. Box 6287, Grand Rapids, MI 49516-6287
www.brazospress.com

Printed in the United States of America

Library of Congress Cataloging-in-Publication Data

Harper, Brad.
    Exploring ecclesiology : an evangelical and ecumenical introduction / Brad Harper and
Paul Louis Metzger.
        p. cm.
    Includes bibliographical references and index.
    ISBN 978-1-58743-173-9 (pbk.)
    1. Church. I. Metzger, Paul Louis. II. Title.
BV600.3H443 2009
262—dc22                                                                                    2008047959

A version of chapter 13 appeared as "Christ, Culture, and the Sermon on the Mount Community" by Paul Louis Metzger in *ExAuditu's An International Journal for the Theological Interpretation of Scripture*, 23 (2008): 22–26.

To Mariko, my best friend and precious bride,
With gratitude for the mystery of heart-to-heart life with you,
And to our children, Christopher and Julianne,
For raising me to be a child of God.

Paul


To Robin, Drew, Breegan, and Corey,
For teaching me what it means to love and to live in grace.

Brad

# Contents

# Acknowledgments

The authors would like to acknowledge Multnomah University and Seminary for giving them the time and space to work on this project, the students in their ecclesiology classes for engaging their ideas and helping to refine them, and Rodney Clapp and his team at Brazos Press for consistent counsel and encouragement. Special thanks goes to Halden Doerge, Will Thompson, and James Tucker for their research assistance, helpful suggestions regarding sources and references, and for keen insights on the theology of the church.

Paul wishes to acknowledge Professors Philip Lueck and John Zizioulas and the late Harold O. J. Brown and Colin Gunton for their commitment to being theologians of the church and for their influence on his intellectual development as a churchman; Pastors Samuel Mall, Ron Mancini, Rick McKinley, Barry Morrison, Peter Robinson, Murray Trim, John Wenrich, and the late Roy Jenson and LeRoy Koepke, for the pastoral and missional impressions they have made on his life and thought; and the evangelical Prophet John M. Perkins for his vision of community development centered in Christ's kingdom community. Paul is indebted to his parents and grandparents for raising him in God's household, and to his whole family for sharing life as a household of faith with him.

Brad wishes to thank Pastor Marvin Francine, his spiritual father, for teaching him to hear the voice of Christ in the church; Pastor Michael Andrus, colleague, pastoral mentor, and friend for teaching him that the church, in the midst of all its brokenness, is the place where God most loves to reveal himself; and Pastor Matt Hannan for his leadership in fostering a community of grace where hurting people find hope in the Savior and among his people.

# Introduction

People are into "Jesus" and "spirituality" today, but not "religion" and "church."[1] Many are disillusioned by what they see and hear in church or on television: an obsession with attendance, buildings, and collections;[2] spectacles of prosperity gospel preachers stealing from the poor to get rich; and scandalous reports of priests molesting little children. Christ's church often plays the harlot, just as Israel played the harlot in Hosea's day (see Hos. 1:1–2).

But we must never forget that the church is also our mother. Without the church, we would not have Jesus and the Bible. While the Bible shapes the church's life, the church also birthed the Bible under the guidance of the Spirit. While we are "born again" as children of God through personal relationship with Jesus, those who are born again are born into the church.[3] John Calvin speaks of the church's significance as our mother in the following statement on the visible nature of the church:

> But because it is now our intention to discuss the visible church, let us learn even from the simple title "mother" how useful, indeed how necessary, it is that we should know her. For there is no other way to enter into life unless this mother conceive us in her womb, give us birth, nourish us at her breast, and lastly, unless she keep us under her care and guidance until, putting off mortal flesh, we become like the angels [Matt. 22:30]. Our weakness does not allow us to be dismissed from her school until we have been pupils all our lives. Furthermore, away from her bosom one cannot hope for any forgiveness of sins or any salvation, as Isaiah [Isa. 37:32] and Joel [Joel 2:32] testify. Ezekiel agrees with them when he declares that those whom God rejects from heavenly life will not be enrolled among God's people [Ez. 13:9]. On the other hand, those who turn to the cultivation of true godliness are said to inscribe their names among the citizens of Jerusalem [cf. Isa. 56:5; Ps. 87:6]. For this reason, it is said in another psalm: "Remember me, O Jehovah, with favor toward thy people; visit me with salvation: that I may see the well-doing of thy chosen ones, that I

may rejoice in the joy of thy nation, that I may be glad with thine inheritance" [Ps. 106:4–5; cf. Ps. 105:4, Vg., etc.]. By these words God's fatherly favor and the especial witness of spiritual life are limited to his flock, so that it is always disastrous to leave the church.[4]

So, while it is often the case that we can't live with the church (given its blemishes and brokenness), we can't live without the church either.

Not only is the church our mother, but we as the church are also Christ's bride, a point brought home by the apostle Paul in Ephesians 5:25–32, and the apostle John in Revelation 19:6–9. Luther claimed that the believer is simultaneously blemished and faithless as a harlot on the one hand, and spotless as Christ's bride on the other.[5] The church as Christ's bride is constituted by and constitutes such simultaneously spotted and spotless believers. What drives this book is our firm conviction that for all its warts and wrinkles, the church made up of her various members is God's most beautiful creation as Christ's very own bride, and so well worth living for and writing about. Our hope is that this book will play a part in helping the bride make preparations for the wedding banquet.

To help prepare the church for that day, we believe it is vital that a systematic study of the church be framed by the Bible, historical theology, ecumenical concerns, and cultural considerations. Why? An ecclesiology should be grounded in the Christian scriptures, for they constitute the one completely authoritative witness for the church's theology. A theology of the church should also be historically self-conscious. Theology about the church is best done by those who are cognizant of the church throughout the centuries, for the church did not begin with us. Having said this, it is also important to account for the contemporary church in its various contexts, for the church is a living, growing organism that responds and reacts to the multitude of cultural environments in which it finds itself.

Accounting for these factors, it follows that no one church constitutes the whole church. Just as there are many parts to Christ's body, so there are many churches that form the one true church. As evangelical Protestants writing at the beginning of the twenty-first century, we seek to engage the larger Christian community of our age and throughout the ages from our particular vantage point, entering into dialogue for the mutual benefit of all, going through our distinctive evangelical convictions, not going around them or stopping short at them. Further to the points on the historical and contemporary contexts, it is important that those reflecting on a theology of the church recognize the church and churches throughout church history up to the present time both as products of given cultures and as prophetic voices over against those cultures. Only when the church and its theologians are truly mindful of these biblical, historical, ecumenical, and contemporary factors can the church make itself ready with sensitivity—including hindsight, insight, and foresight—for the marriage supper of the Lamb.

With this approach in mind, we have sought to provide our readers with a fully developed evangelical and ecumenical theology of the church of service to the pastor, theologian, and student, which can be used as a textbook and reference. Thus, the subtitle for our book is "An Evangelical and Ecumenical Introduction." The word *evangelical* means many things to many people. We use the term here to refer to that post–World War II movement in Protestant American Christianity that prizes the "fundamentals of the faith," as they are called, while rejecting a fundamentalist spirit that discourages dialogue with those outside our tradition. Thus, we hold to the "fundamentals of the faith," including belief in Jesus Christ's deity and virgin birth, a high view of scripture's accuracy and authority, and an affirmation of substitutionary atonement, while also prizing personal conversion and relationship with God through Jesus Christ in the Spirit. As evangelical Protestants who affirm these fundamentals while rejecting a fundamentalist spirit, our goal is to represent and embrace those interpretations of the church that reflect the central streams of historic orthodoxy common to the various Christian traditions. Where those traditions disagree, the goal is to present them in dialogue with one another, searching for conclusions that respect the various perspectives. In addition, it is the purpose of this text to allow the best traditions of biblical and historical ecclesiology to speak prophetically and critically to the contemporary church in the West, particularly in the United States. Contemporary issues addressed include individualism, women in ministry, evangelism and social action, consumerism in church growth trends, ecumenism, and the church in a postmodern culture. As a textbook, the main target course for which this book is aimed would be a theology class that contains a component on the theology of the church. It could also be used in courses that compare historic ecclesial traditions and those that consider the relationship of the church to culture.

Why this book? If one were to do a library title search on the topic of the church, it would be clear that there is no shortage of recent publications. However, most recent works appear to be either niche-oriented (addressing a particular ecclesial issue) or confessional, or they lack one of the four basic characteristics listed above (biblical, historical, ecumenical, and cultural) for this proposed volume. For example, Veli-Matti Karkkainen's *An Introduction to Ecclesiology* focuses on ecumenical, historical, and global models. Donald Bloesch's *The Church* provides excellent discussions on ecumenical and historical perspectives but is short on biblical theology. John Stackhouse's edited volume *Evangelical Ecclesiology: Reality or Illusion?* focuses on evangelical perspectives. Moreover, evangelical texts on the church, while traditionally strong on biblical perspectives, often lack true appreciation for ecumenical dialogue and/or serious cultural engagement. Thus, a book of the scope proposed here has the potential not only to be well received in the world of evangelical theology, but also has the potential to provide an effective means for constructive engagement of the broader Christian tradition amidst the diversity of postmodern culture(s).

Now for the outline and structure of the book. Chapters 1 and 3 function as the fundamental theological chapters for the entire work. Chapter 1 focuses consideration on the church as a trinitarian community, and chapter 3 approaches the doctrine of the church from an eschatological kingdom vantage point. Our basic reasoning for choosing these two theological lenses through which to view the various topics that pertain to ecclesiology is twofold: we must give foundational consideration to the church as the community of the Triune God because the church derives its core identity from its relationship with the Triune God to whom the church is united as God's people, Christ's body and bride, and the Holy Spirit's temple; and we must give foundational consideration to the church as the eschatological community of the Triune God because it serves as the primary agent and embodied witness of this God's kingdom. These foundational chapters shape chapters 5, 7, 9, 11, 13, and 15, which are more practical in orientation and address the following themes, and in this order: worship, sacraments/ordinances, service/gifts, order/polity, culture, and mission.

The last item to note in terms of structure is that chapters 1, 3, 5, 7, 9, 11, 13, and 15 are each followed by discussions of culture (chapters 2, 4, 6, 8, 10, 12, 14, and 16). In the even-numbered chapters we flesh out specific instances of the odd-numbered chapters' theological concepts in terms of their cultural import. Thus, for example, chapter 1, "The Church as a Trinitarian Community," gives rise to a discussion of American individualism from a Trinitarian perspective in chapter 2. This cultural component reflects not only one of the characteristic features of the book, but also our conviction expressed more fully in the postscript to the volume that those writing truly meaningful evangelical and nonevangelical ecclesiologies alike in the contemporary, postmodern context must intentionally situate their reflections in concrete cultural settings.

Further to the point on postmodernity, we are mindful that what follows will never serve as a once-and-for-all ecclesiology; at best, it can serve as a handmaiden to the church today as theologians and practitioners continue to prepare the bride for the wedding day, from which future generations can draw as they glean insights from the whole of church history in their own labors of love for the bride. The non-"once-and-for-all" nature of ecclesiology is both problematic and promising: problematic for those who see the church as a static entity, not a dynamic organism that is ever-evolving, and promising for those who see a given ecclesiology's situatedness as providing opportunities and vantage points for further exploration.

Not only is ecclesiology problematic yet promising due to its concrete particularity, and due to the blemished yet beautiful being of the church as noted at the outset of the introduction, but also evangelical ecclesiology is problematic yet promising because it is not a denomination, but rather, a movement. This fact has resulted in a lack of ecclesial distinctives typically found in denominations, as well as a lack of loyalty to any particular ecclesial tradition. Kimlyn Bender addresses both of these problematic issues in the following statement:

> Evangelicalism is marked not so much by an ecclesiology as by ecclesiolae in ecclesia, a fellowship of persons within churches. At its most extreme, it trades the church for Spener's collegia pietatis, a college of piety, though it may also focus on doctrinal non-negotiables. Evangelicalism thus is smaller than churches insofar as it exists within them. It unites persons with shared convictions within traditional churches. Indeed, the ecclesiology of evangelicalism has often been an ecclesiology of division and separation as new denominations emerged from older ones in formal schism due to doctrinal differences or disagreements about the necessity of conversion. Separatism has been a recurrent feature of evangelical ecclesiologies.[6]

In light of Bender's comments, it is worth pausing to ponder how great an influence this separatistic impulse has had on shaping or at least on not resisting the current church shopping scene. Evangelicals do not simply separate based on doctrine or conversion. Personal preferences also play a key part. As John Stackhouse remarks, "Many evangelicals . . . feel free to leave one congregation, or even an entire denominational tradition, to find what to them is most important in a church: usually some combination of the right basic doctrines, good preaching, good programs for the kids, and so on. Indeed, only among evangelicals does one encounter the revealing cliché, 'church shopping.'"[7] We will address the consumerist impulse within evangelicalism at different points in the volume.

As an outgrowth of fundamentalism in the post-WWII period, American evangelicalism's ecclesiological roots are anchored in the fundamentalist-modernist controversy that emerged in the early twentieth century. During this period, the separatism Bender speaks of consisted largely of individual churches leaving their denominations or of the conservatives in certain mainline denominations forming new denominations. The result was a movement of churches and denominations whose fellowship was based on their conservative views of the Bible, Christ, and salvation, yet organized around a variety of ecclesial forms. Thus, one could find fundamentalist, and later, evangelical churches that held to episcopal (Methodist), presbyterian, and congregational/baptistic polities. This diversity of ecclesiologies makes it difficult to define an evangelical ecclesiology. Perhaps this conundrum is no more pointedly exemplified than in the stunning fact that the statement of faith of the National Association of Evangelicals makes no mention of the church![8]

So, as evangelical theologians—if we are to be honest—we have to confess that "evangelical ecclesiology" is problematic in part because it is difficult to define. This challenge can be illustrated by a bit of humor shared among some evangelicals involved in formal dialogue with Roman Catholics. As they put it: "The main difference between us and the Catholics is ecclesiology. They have one and we don't."[9] As Mark Noll comments, the joke is funny because it is at least partially true. Indeed, one evangelical theologian has even floated the idea that "evangelical ecclesiology" may be an oxymoron.[10] Nevertheless, we disagree with those who would claim that evangelicalism does not have an ecclesiology.[11] To be sure, it is an ecclesiology limited, among other things, by the temptation to resort to a kind of lowest-common-denominator approach. For example, evangelicals are less likely than the Catholic or Orthodox churches to claim that there is only one valid form of church polity, since a variety of church government models are represented among professing evangelical churches.

This does not mean, however, that there are no distinctive common denominators to shape an evangelical ecclesiology. The following is a list of ecclesial convictions that evangelicals tend to share, movement-wide: The church is the people of God, body and bride of Christ, temple of the Holy Spirit promised in the Hebrew scriptures, and brought into being by Jesus Christ, who is its head.[12] Its members are those who have experienced salvation through faith in Jesus Christ and who are connected to a local manifestation of the universal church. The sacraments or ordinances of Baptism and the Lord's Supper are to be practiced, and the Word of God is to be taught. Its purpose includes the worship of God, the building up of the body of believers, and the sharing of the good news of Christ with the world in word and deed.

Someone will rightly point out that these convictions could be shared by many traditions. Are there characteristic traits that distinguish evangelical ecclesiology from other traditions or movements? We believe there are, as suggested by the following examples. First, authority—always an issue of ecclesial structure and ethos—is understood as being vested most strongly in the Bible, vis-à-vis the Catholic and Orthodox traditions, where authority is vested heavily in the institution and hierarchy, or the classically Reformed churches, where authority is vested heavily in a creed like the Westminster Confession, or the Pentecostal and charismatic movements, where authority is construed primarily in terms of the direct intervention and personal leading of the Holy Spirit.[13] The result has been that the "main event" in the typical evangelical church service has been the preaching of a sermon engaging a particular biblical text.[14] Second, evangelicals have historically taken a minimalist approach to liturgy. This has been due in large part to the fundamentalist rejection of many of the traditional liturgies of the mainline Protestant churches, since fundamentalists associated them with what they considered to be dead institutional Christianity devoid of heartfelt faith and the life of the Spirit.[15] Third, given the lack of historic liturgy and practice, there has been a strong tendency toward pragmatism in the structure of church worship and ministry.

Church form and practice are often shaped by what works. This has led to a tendency to adopt the forms of popular culture as the basis for everything from church architecture to worship music to evangelistic techniques. It is evangelicals who pioneered the "seeker-sensitive" culture and methodology of the late twentieth century. Thus, in summary, while we recognize the problems of defining an evangelical ecclesiology, we nevertheless contend that there are characteristics particular to the movement, which makes a definition not only possible but also makes evangelical ecclesiology an important contributor to the broader dialogue on ecclesiology. Whether these and other characteristics of evangelical ecclesiology contribute positively or negatively to the discussion will be examined throughout the book.

Having addressed the problematic nature of doing an *evangelical* ecclesiology, we also need to discuss the issues of writing an *ecumenical* ecclesiology. If an evangelical ecclesiology suffers from the lack of distinction that can result from spanning a variety of denominational traditions, an ecumenical approach is susceptible to the same fate. One way to do an ecumenical theology is simply to focus on those items upon which all traditions can agree—the lowest-common-denominator approach—which would result in a pretty short book! The other—which is the direction we have chosen—is to take for granted that the distinctions of the various traditions have the potential to bring richness even in the midst of disagreement, creating a mosaic that, examined up close, may reveal that a few pieces are out of place or misshapen but which nonetheless at a distance becomes an image recognized by all as a beautiful work of art. While we as evangelicals do not accept, for example, the Roman Catholic theology of apostolic succession, we can, however, appreciate the sense of unity it brings to the Catholic Church and could wish that the Roman Catholic commitment to "stick together" in spite of differences were more characteristic of evangelical churches. Or we may not accept the Orthodox view of the Eucharist, but as evangelicals who tend to be individualistic in our worship practices and who often lack any real sense of our connection to the whole church, we can benefit from the Orthodox sense that whenever the church celebrates the Lord's Supper, not only is Christ there, but so too is the entire church, both on earth and in heaven. It is this mosaic-like approach to ecclesiology, we believe, that has the promise of moving the church toward the kind of unity in diversity that must characterize the church of Jesus Christ if it is going to prosper in a culture that is increasingly hostile to organized religion, especially of the Christian variety. Moreover, such mosaic unity in diversity anticipates the fulfillment of the Lord Jesus's prayer in John 17:23: "I in them and you in me—so that they may be brought to complete unity. Then the world will know that you sent me and have loved them even as you have loved me" (TNIV).

The image of a mosaic is attractive to us as a metaphor for the church. As the Lord Jesus's prayer suggests, such mosaic unity in diversity is rooted in the trinitarian communion of the God who puts the various pieces together. And given the eschatological nature of our salvation, we can even now begin to see the beauty of what the church will one day be—even though some pieces are missing—and anticipate its fulfillment by striving to live together in the bond of peace, truth, and love.

Why should we strive for such mosaic unity in diversity? It is because the church—not this or that uniform movement or niche faction—is one body with many parts, created by the one God and Father for his Son as his bride, the one Lord who gives his life for her redemption, a body gifted in a diversity of ways by the one Spirit who calls the church to unity (not uniformity), both to embody and to proclaim the one gospel of God's salvation. The mosaic will be complete on that day when the entire church sits down together at the marriage supper of the Lamb. It is our hope that, in some small way, this book will encourage the whole church to live out more fully in the present that unity which will be completely realized in God's future, and in so doing to invite the whole world to the wedding. Come, Lord Jesus, come!

## STUDY QUESTIONS

1. In your own experience, how have you found people to be disillusioned with the church?
2. How should a person's Christian identity be defined in relation to the church?
3. How do you understand your church background in relationship to other church traditions?

# The Church as a Trinitarian Community

## *The* Being-*Driven Church*

### The Church's Relational Identity, Purpose, and Activity

The church is a trinitarian community. For the church is the creation and covenantal companion of the God who exists as Father, Son, and Holy Spirit in eternal communion. The church belongs to the Triune God. The Father calls the church into being by the Son and indwells it by the Spirit, who unites it to Christ. The church is the people of God (1 Pet. 2:10), the temple of the Holy Spirit (1 Cor. 3:16), and the body and bride of Christ (Eph. 5:29–32). Outside the Trinity, then, there is no church. For the people of God exist by way of the God, who elects it in the beloved and seals it by the Spirit (Eph. 1:1–14). This relationship and sense of belonging determines the church's identity, purpose, and activity, and in that order.

The church's identity is itself communal and relational. It derives this communal being from the Triune God whose being is the three divine persons in communion, and who created it for communion. The God who created everything, including the church, is love (1 John 4:8). In a way similar to the creation story, God births the church as a free and creative expression of that inner-trinitarian love and spreading goodness through the Word and Spirit.[1] This communal state of affairs suggests that while the Christian individual is a temple of the Holy Spirit, the Christian community is the ultimate temple of the Holy Spirit (see 1 Cor. 3 and Rev. 21–22). The Triune God created the church to be God's people and body and bride of Christ in communion one with another, a people who are also constituted in relation to God, to humanity at large, and to the whole of creation.

The church's purpose flows forth from its identity, because the church's communal identity is purposive. The church has its existence in constitutive relation with God, its own, humanity at large, and the world. Moreover, the church exists to love God, its own, the world, and the whole creation because it is loved in covenantal communion with God. This relational orientation signifies that the church is being-driven. A church that begins with a missional purpose before it begins with its identity as communal reality in relation to God is problematic.[2] This orientation is very American but is not biblical. Biblically speaking, the missional purpose flows forth from the church's communal identity and is the inevitable outcome. In fact, communion with God gives rise to missional existence, for God's communal being is co-missional: God ministers in the creation through the sending of the Son and Spirit. The church participates in this missional movement, for the church exists through God's Son and Spirit's advance, bearing witness to God's kingdom in its midst. The church participates in the communal God's life as the Father goes forth into the world through the co-missional Son and Spirit to create and sustain a new humanity and community over whom and through whom God reigns, and in whose midst God dwells. Thus, the church is being-driven—driven into the world by the communal and co-missional God who reigns and dwells in its midst as the one to whom the church belongs.[3]

An illustration of this point will prove helpful. Grandparents in nursing homes and newborn infants are important relationally even though they do not do anything significant. When our children were born, they could not do anything for us. We had to do everything for them—from feeding and burping them to changing their diapers. Even so, we delighted in caring for them—passive as they were—because we loved them. Nursing-home grandparents and newborn babies are vital members of many families. The church is God's family. As those birthed by the Father through the Son in the Spirit, our significance is communal. As those birthed into this world through God, our missional task as we grow as members of this family is to build up this communal dynamic, including inviting others to join our family. We value those who enter the family not ultimately because of God's purposes for the church and what these spiritual newborns can eventually accomplish for the church, but because we are loved by God as the church. Communion with God as members of God's family shapes everything.

The church's relational identity and communal purpose also shapes the church's activity, including its approach to leadership, worship, and outreach. This chapter focuses on the church's identity as a trinitarian community and addresses its missional purpose and activity to the extent that they reflect this theme. Later chapters will bear directly on purpose and activity. We will develop each of our identity claims in conversation with the Bible and the church's own witness past and present, beginning with important images of the church.

## Important Images of the Church's Relational Identity

### Humanity in the Image of the Triune God

The first motif in scripture bearing upon the church is the theme of the image of God.[4] Genesis 1 tells us that the Triune God created humanity in God's image. Ultimately, the church participates in the paradigmatic image of God, who is Christ. It will be good to set forth this theme in terms of its biblical development.

Genesis reveals a God who desires to create. God does not need to create, for God is content as the divine communion of persons. As the Triune God, the Lord Almighty freely fashions a world and a people as an overflowing expression of that holy love experienced in the communion of the divine life. God creates the world through the Word and Spirit, whom Irenaeus of Lyons calls God's "two hands."[5] God's Word engenders life by the Spirit, whom we find in Genesis 1 hovering over the waters. God creates the world and all that is in it through sheer acts of speech, and breathes the spirit of life into humanity.

Genesis 1 tells us that this God creates humanity in the divine likeness. This likeness is fundamentally relational. "Let us make man in our image, in our likeness . . . So God created man in his own image, in the image of God he created him; male and female he created them" (Gen. 1:26–27). As relational, this likeness is totally dependent and in no way autonomous; the human creature is not made to be independent of the Creator. Dietrich Bonhoeffer gets at this in his discussion of Genesis 1 when he writes that the "likeness, the analogy of man to God, is not *analogia entis* [analogy of being] but *analogia relationis* [analogy of relation]. This means that even the relation between man and God is not a part of man; it is not a capacity, a possibility, or a structure of his being but a given, set relationship . . . And in this given relation freedom is given."[6] Bonhoeffer continues on by saying that the human person does not have "this likeness in his possession, at his disposal." It "is a God-given relation,"[7] which continually depends on God for its existence. The likeness between God and humanity is fundamentally relational, one of covenantal communion between God and the human creation, which is initiated, determined, and sustained by God, not human effort.

The divine being is itself communal. The "let us" recorded here in Genesis 1 signifies the three persons of the Godhead, not an angelic counsel to whom God speaks, nor the communicative device known as the "royal we."[8] God creates a relational counterpart that reflects this divine plurality. Just as God is only God as three persons in communion, the man is only fully human in relation to the woman. The man was never meant to be alone (Gen. 2:18). "Man" here is not an individual in isolation, but persons in communion with God and one another. Bonhoeffer points out that according to Genesis 1, man/humanity exists in duality as male and female: "Man is not alone, he is in duality and it is in this dependence on the other that his creatureliness consists."[9]

Human identity is communal because humanity is created in the image of the Triune God. As communal, it is also creative. God creates this communal being to be creative: "Be fruitful and increase in number; fill the earth and subdue it" (Gen. 1:28). Selfless, loving communion is always creative, expansive, and transitive. Self-love, on the other hand, is reductive, recessive, and intransitive.[10] It will prove helpful to elaborate on these claims.

God creates humanity as an overflowing expression of the divine communal love. God's chief aim in creating humanity is to love us and to enter into communion with us.[11] As those created in the image of God, our chief end is to respond to God's love and to invite others into that communion so that they may experience God's goodness and grace and share it with others. There is nothing more glorious than this communal reality, because through it we fulfill God's intention for the creation to participate in God's spreading goodness and glory. When we fail to respond to God's love in faith, we turn in on ourselves and negate the divine and human other as objects of our love. Those who do not respond to God's love turn in on themselves. They become lovers of themselves, rather than lovers of God who also love those around them. In 1 John 4, we find that those who do not love others do not know God's love. God's love produces a chain reaction, where we love because God has first loved us.

The state of affairs to which we speak finds its ultimate fulfillment in the kingdom of which the church is the concrete manifestation on earth. The church's end is to respond to God's love in faith and to invite others into loving communion with God and others. When the church does this, it fulfills its destiny to become the people God intended for the new humanity to be. When the church—Christ's bride—fails to respond to God's love in faith, it turns in on itself rather than upward toward God and outward toward the world in love, denying its predestined identity as God's communal new creation in his eschatological kingdom.

A few pages into the Genesis story, we are told that the indissoluble communion that exists between God and humanity, man and woman, and between humanity and the creation is short-lived. For man and woman determine to express their creativity autonomously from God—wishing to be God (Gen. 3:1–7) rather than express themselves creatively as those who exist in the image of the Triune Creator. Turning their backs on God spells autonomy from each other as Adam blames his wife and will now rule over her (Gen. 3:12, 16).

Their departure from God also spells the cursing of the ground (Gen. 3:17–19) and sets the stage for Cain's murder of Abel (see Gen. 4).

Humanity created in the image of God is a ruined Rembrandt as a result of the fall, a masterpiece severely marred by the fallen world, the flesh, and the devil. Left to itself in this state, there is only dissolution and despair. And yet the divine judgment involves a promise to redeem and transform humanity, and the creation with it. The one through whom and for whom humanity is created will come forth as the paradigmatic or archetypal image of God to restore the masterpiece. God will do this, not simply through the redemption of individuals, but through the redeemed communal life of the church united to Christ.

### The Communal Christ as the Ultimate Image of God

The Triune Creator is revealed to be the Triune Redeemer in the face of the fall and divine judgment. Speaking to the serpent who deceives humanity, God says: "I will put enmity between you and the woman, and between your seed and her seed. He will crush your head, and you will strike his heel" (Gen. 3:15, NASB). The God who exists communally, and who created humanity to be in relation to God, determines to redeem humanity and the whole of creation from the clutches of autonomy, death, and despair. The God who had walked in the Garden, and who had dwelt in their midst, would come in the flesh to pray in the Garden and to offer himself upon the cursed tree from which the man and woman had eaten. As the ultimate image of God (Col. 1:15; Heb. 1:1–3), Jesus would offer himself up to death and rise from the dead so as to reverse the curse and recapitulate or transform the creation. He would make it possible for us to be like God through our participation in his resurrection and ascension. As the Eastern church has so aptly put it: "He became what we are so that we might become what he is."[12] If only our archetypal ancestors had waited to be like God in the way that God had planned for them all along—through union with his Son in the Spirit.[13]

As the archetypal image of God, the incarnate Son of God would come forth to dwell in our midst and share with the church this supreme likeness to the divine. Paul tells us that Jesus is the image of God, and that he is the head of the body—the church (Col. 1:18). As the image of God, Christ does not stand apart from others. Paul indicates that there is a communal character to Christ as the image of God. For he is God with us in bodily form (Col. 2:9), and we have been given fullness in him (Col. 2:10).

For Paul, in Colossians 1, Christ as the image of God in the flesh is a reconciling force, drawing humanity back into peaceful communion with God by taking humanity's brokenness upon himself to redeem and transform it. As such, Christ is the firstborn of the new creation and firstborn from the dead (Col. 1:15, 18). The church is the firstfruits of the new creaturely order, raised with Christ and poured out through the Spirit into the world. So one cannot understand Christ in abstraction from his corporate solidarity with and for the church in the cosmos. He does not stand apart but always exists with and for the church in the world. For its own part, the church exists with and for Christ in the world. The connection between Colossians 1 and Genesis 1 in Paul's thought signifies that Christ is the ultimate image of God. Christ shares this image with the church, and through the church, with humanity.[14]

The creation story serves as the backdrop for Paul's discussion. The only time in the creation story where God says something is not good is in Genesis 2:18, where God says it is not good for man to be alone. Adam is not complete apart from Eve. The same can be said of Christ. Christ *in his humanity* is not complete apart from his bride, the church. Just as it was not good for man created in the image of the Triune God to be alone, it is not good for Christ as the image of the Triune God to be alone. For apart from the church, he could not bear witness to the interpersonal communion of the Triune God in his human state.

The One who would epitomize the image-of-God dynamic in Genesis 1 and 2 through his being in relation to the church is also the One promised in Genesis 3. The promised seed of Genesis 3 would come forth to redeem God's creation and create the church to fulfill God's communal kingdom's mandate: "I will live with them and walk among them, and I will be their God, and they will be my people" (2 Cor. 6:16; cf. Lev. 26:12; Jer. 32:38; Ezek. 37:27). The God who had walked in the garden in the cool of the day (Gen. 3:8) will once again dwell in our midst. The whole of the Hebrew Scriptures points forward to this end.

### The People of the Triune God

God creates humanity for covenantal communion. God comes to us ultimately in Christ to dwell in our midst and to take us to himself to form a people who bear his name. A name expresses identity and character. It also indicates one's source, origin, and relationships: the person or persons to whom one belongs. A nameless God has no people. A people without a name do not belong to anyone. They are without identity and purpose. Those without names must prove themselves to be more than numbers. They must demonstrate their value and worth. On the other hand, those who belong to God do not need to make a name for themselves. God has made a name for them, for those who belong to God bear God's name.

God will not allow humanity to make a name for itself outside of communion with God, but only as God's chosen people. Recall the story in Genesis 11 where God wreaks havoc on the people of Babel, confusing their language because they sought to make a name for themselves. This God is no gluttonous glory grabber, though. In the very next chapter, Genesis 12, God calls

Abram to be his follower, friend, and father of a new people, whose name he will make great (Gen. 12:2). And he promises that through Abraham he will bless all peoples on the earth (Gen. 12:3) by that promised seed, who is Christ (Gal. 3:16, cf. Gen. 3:15; 12:7; 13:15; 24:7).[15]

The God who called Adam and Eve to be fruitful and multiply and fill the earth and subdue it calls Abram (later Abraham) out from among his people to go to a land that God will show him (Gen. 12:1). God renames Abram and leads him and his family on a journey that will take them through the Promised Land and then to Egypt. There, Jacob—renamed Israel—will become a vast people, whom the Egyptians will eventually enslave out of fear.

The God who renames Abram and Jacob is a name-bearing God. While there are many names for God in scripture, "the LORD" stands out. It stands out in Exodus and the New Testament writings of John and Paul. Exodus tells us that God hears his enslaved people's cry and comes down to them. God calls out Moses to go tell Pharaoh to let his people go. Here God reveals himself to Moses and the people as "the LORD," which is his proper name. God had not revealed himself to the patriarchs by this name (Exod. 6:3). But "this is my name forever, the name you shall call me from generation to generation" (Exod. 3:15, TNIV). By this name, God delivers his people from bondage in Egypt, and all peoples from bondage to the curse throughout all generations, including our own.

The name "the LORD," by which God saves his people, is God's triune name. Jesus shares this name with the Father and the Spirit (John 8:58; 17:11–12; Phil. 2:9–11; see also Matt. 28:18–20). In John 8:58, Jesus tells his opponents: "Before Abraham was, I am." They rightly understood him to be referring back to Exodus 3. In Exodus 3, Moses had asked God for his name so that he could tell the Israelites who had sent him. God's response was, "I am who I am. This is what you are to say to the Israelites. 'I AM has sent me to you'" (Exod. 3:14). In the next verse, God tells Moses to say to the Israelites that "the LORD, the God of your fathers—the God of Abraham, the God of Isaac, and the God of Jacob—has sent me to you." Jesus claims to be the named God, the LORD, the God of Abraham, who appeared to Moses in a burning bush as the Angel of the LORD in Exodus 3.

Jesus shares the divine name with the Father and the Spirit, as the Great Commission makes clear: "Therefore go and make disciples of all nations, baptizing them in the name of the Father, and of the Son, and of the Holy Spirit" (Matt. 28:19). Jesus commissions his church to be the missional people of this named God, who will be with them through the mediation of the Spirit until the end of the age (Matt. 28:18–20). Everyone who calls on the name of this God—Jew and Gentile alike—will be saved (Rom. 10:8–13; cf. Joel 2:32). Referring to Jesus, Paul quotes Joel 2:32 in Romans 10:13: "For 'everyone who calls on the name of the LORD will be saved.'" Jesus is the savior of Israel and the church. We belong to "the LORD," who rescued Israel out of bondage in Egypt and the church from slavery to sin.

The God who revealed himself to Pharaoh as "the LORD," and who commanded Pharaoh to let his people go (Exod. 5:1), will not let go of his people. The Father and Son protect Christ's followers in the name that the Father gave the Son (John 17:11–12), so that they may be one like Christ and the Father are one (John 17:11), so that the world might know that God has sent his Son (John 17:20–23). Beginning with Abraham, the father of faith, God's community of faith is the creation and covenantal partner of God through the Son and Spirit. As such, the community of God's people bears God's name.

How we act has a bearing on God's name, for we bear God's name. God's name reveals his identity and character. Thus, if we bear it badly, we reflect badly on God's identity and character. In Romans 2:24, Paul says that God's people were the cause of God's name being blasphemed among the nations. Children who live well honor their parents' names; so too the church that lives well honors God's name. As God's children, and members of God's household, we must seek to bring honor to our Father's name.

### Children of the Triune God

Jesus's opponents in John 5 were stupefied and horrified that he called God his own father. They rightly interpreted him to be saying that he was equal with God. As a result, they sought to stone him (John 5:18). No doubt, more spiritually sensitive recipients of his message took note of Jesus's claim to experience profound intimacy with the Father. The nation of Israel claimed to know God as Father, but it was not common for individual Jews to address God as "Father." Jesus both knows and addresses God as his own Father, and invites us into a similar relationship as members of the church: "Our Father, who art in heaven, hallowed be Thy name" (Matt. 6:9).[16]

It is only through Jesus that the church, and individuals within the church, know God as "Abba"—Daddy Father (Rom. 8:15; Gal. 4:6). For Jesus is the one and only Son of God, who comes forth from the bosom of the Father (John 1:18; 3:16). He alone knows God as Father by nature. We know God as Father by grace—the grace poured out for us in Christ and ministered to us through the Spirit. And so, God is our God and Father through Jesus his one and only Son. The distinction between Christ's sonship and our own forever remains (see John 20:17). But such distinction is no division. In and through Christ, God loves us—his sons and daughters, those who are his church—just as much as he loves his Son (John 17:23).

As God's children, we are brothers and sisters of Christ and one another. Just as there is no division between God and us and Christ and us, there is to be no division between brothers and sisters as members of God's household. For we are God's family. This claim has a profound bearing on the church's approach to matters of ethnic, economic, and ecumenical diversity and divisions, subjects that will receive consideration in the present volume.

### The House and Household of the Triune God

The New Testament views all relational structures (parent–child, husband–wife, brother–sister, and master–slave) through the lens of the church. Jesus revolutionizes our understanding of family by making his community of disciples his primary family, taking precedence over his biological family. On one occasion, when Jesus was told that his mother and brothers had come to see him, Jesus says, "'Who are my mother and my brothers?' he asked. Then he looked at those seated in a circle around him and said, 'Here are my mother and my brothers! Whoever does God's will is my brother and sister and mother,'" (Mark 3:33–35). Family ties in Jesus's day were much stronger than they are today. So, his hearers would have been shocked by this statement. It is not that Jesus disowned his mother and brothers, but that he reframed familial ties so that, for example, his mother would be viewed first and foremost as part of his family of disciples. Thus, at his death, Jesus tells Mary that his disciple John is now her son, and tells John that Mary is now his mother. As a result, she came to live with John, and not one of her other sons (John 19:26–27).

The New Testament views our relational–social structures through the lens of the church. Where there had been disparity, now there is equality. Joseph Hellerman claims that the fundamental family relationship adapted by the early church was that of sibling-to-sibling, and that one of the values reflected in the sibling image was equality. Hellerman writes,

> Those who had the most to gain from the image of the church as family were the poor, the hungry, the enslaved, the imprisoned, the orphans, and the widows. For brother-sister terminology in antiquity had nothing to do with hierarchy, power, and privilege, but everything to do with equality, solidarity and generalized reciprocity.[17]

Such sibling-to-sibling relationships have a bearing on how those in the church treat their children. Our sons and daughters by birth who are also believers are our brothers and our sisters in Christ. Such familial ties mean that we are to treat as brothers and sisters those of other ethnicities and economic levels. Christ levels the playing field in the church. The church becomes the new family unit because it is God's family unit, God's household, and God dwells in its midst. God dwelt in Israel's midst in the person of the Angel of the Lord,[18] who bears God's name (Exod. 23:20–21), and God dwells supremely in our midst through Jesus, who shares God's name (Matt. 28:19–20; John 17:11)—the Word who became flesh, tabernacling with us (John 1:14). Jesus shares God's name with us and makes the church a dwelling place in which God dwells through his Spirit (1 Cor. 3:16).

This idea of "tabernacling" runs throughout scripture.[19] God tabernacles with his people Israel (Exod. 40:34). And as stated above, God also tabernacles as a human in the person of Jesus among his people (John 1:14) through the Holy Spirit, whom he has given to the Son without limit (John 1:32–34; 3:34). Moreover, God tabernacles in us. We are temples of the Holy Spirit (1 Cor. 6:19). The God who tabernacles bodily as Jesus tabernacles bodily in each of us through the Holy Spirit. This is a trinitarian tabernacling. And not only is the individual the temple of the Holy Spirit, but also the church is the temple of the Holy Spirit (1 Cor. 3:16), for the church is the body of Christ (Eph. 4:4–5; 5:29–30; Col. 1:18). Peter tells us that Jesus is the cornerstone of God's temple, and that the church is made up of living stones that are being built up as a spiritual house (1 Pet. 2:4–10).

Jesus makes this all possible by destroying the temple of his own body on the cross and rebuilding it on the third day (John 2:18–25), inaugurating a new order through his resurrection from the dead. Upon his ascension and glorification, streams of living water—the Spirit—descend upon and flow from within those who trust in Christ (John 7:37–39).

No doubt, many have wondered about Jesus's ascent and the Spirit's descent. Would it not have been better for Jesus to stay? Not according to John 14 and 16. According to Jesus, it is a good thing that he goes away. Why? Because he goes to prepare a place for his followers in the Father's house (14:2–3). It is also good that Christ goes because the Father is greater than Christ (v. 28). More can be done through Christ going to the Father than if he were to stay here (v. 12). Jesus's followers can go directly to the Father through him to get great and glorious results—for the Father's sake (vv. 12–14). It is also good that Christ goes because he will ask the Father to send the Spirit (v. 26; 16:7). The Spirit of truth will come to comfort, instruct, and serve as the continued presence of Christ to his followers (see John 14:15–17 and John 16:7–15). In fact, the Father and Son will come to us through the Spirit of truth to make their home with us (14:23; "through the Spirit" follows theologically from the surrounding context). Just as Jesus goes off to prepare a place for us, the Spirit prepares a place for God and Christ in and with us. The Father and the Son send the Spirit to dwell in us, and through the Spirit, they themselves come and dwell in our midst (see John 14, including v. 23). In Jesus, and through Jesus, God truly is with us (Matt. 1:23). And Christ will be with us always, to the end of the age (Matt. 28:20).

Thus, the new tabernacle is better than the old. But the ultimate tabernacle/temple remains future. Christ is preparing a place for his people now. Ultimately, this place is a relational space so that his people can be with him forever (see John 14:3). In the age to come, there will be no need for a temple, for God and the Lamb are *the* temple (Rev. 21:22), and they will dwell in the midst of God's people (Rev. 21:3), which is the holy city of the New Jerusalem (Rev. 21:2) of God's Israel and the church (Rev. 21:12–14), the bride (Rev. 21:2). The Spirit—who is the water of the River of Life flowing down the middle of the great street of the city from the throne of God and the Lamb (Rev. 22:1–2)—and the bride say, "'Come!' And let him who hears say, 'Come!' Whoever is thirsty, let him come; and whoever wishes, let him take the free gift of the water of life" (Rev. 22:17).

### *The Body and Bride of Christ*

The church is Christ's life-giving bride in the Spirit. Unlike with Adam and his bride, whose spirits died when they ate from the tree of the knowledge of good and evil, the nations who walk by the light of the city (Rev. 21:24), which is Christ's bride, find healing from the tree of life, which stands in the city (Rev. 22:2). Outside the Trinity, there is no church; inside the Triune God's church, there is salvation.[20]

God creates a bride for his Son through his Son's death unto life through the Spirit (Eph. 5:25–27). The Spirit who searches the depths of the God who is love (see 1 Cor. 2:10; 1 John 4:8) and who communicates to the Father and Son the love they have for one another unites the church to Christ by pouring forth the divine love into our hearts (Rom. 5:5) through disclosing God's precious promises (see Rom. 8:15–17; 2 Pet. 1:3–4), thereby creating faith (Rom. 10:17). The disclosure of God's love for us in Christ through the Word by the Spirit pierces our hearts and makes us one flesh with Christ by faith.

A good husband loves his wife, nourishing and caring for her as his own body, for they are one flesh. So too Christ nourishes and cares for his body—his bride, the church—for they are one flesh (Eph. 5:28–31) through faith in God's promises of love and favor. Christ cleanses and purifies his bride by the washing of water with the Word (Eph. 5:26). He nurtures and cares for his church by sharing his righteousness with her while taking her unrighteousness to himself. This has been called the "joyful exchange."[21] Here is how Luther describes this joyful exchange:

> Who then can fully appreciate what this royal marriage means? Who can understand the riches of the glory of this grace? Here this rich and divine bridegroom Christ marries this poor, wicked harlot, redeems her from all her evil, and adorns her with all his goodness. Her sins cannot now destroy her, since they are laid upon Christ and swallowed up by him. And she has that righteousness in Christ, her husband, of which she may boast as of her own and which she can confidently display alongside her sins in the face of death and hell and say, "If I have sinned, yet my Christ, in whom I believe, has not sinned, and all his is mine and all mine is his," as the bride in the Song of Solomon (2:16) says, "My beloved is mine and I am his."[22]

For Luther, the bride truly is righteous through her very real union with Christ by the Spirit. Justification by faith through the faithfulness of Christ and outpouring of divine love into human hearts by the Spirit of God means that the bride is truly one with Christ.[23]

Luther's imagery is reflective of the Hebrew Scriptures where the bride in the Song of Solomon stands in stark contrast to the whore of Hosea. Whereas the former looks only to her beloved, the latter goes after other lovers. The former pursues intimacy. The latter seeks after autonomy. God will not abandon us to our autonomy, though, for God is a jealous lover. God has pursued us in his Son and persuaded us by his Spirit to return to him. God has made a people of those who were not his people (see Hos. 1:9–10; 2:23; Rom. 9:25; 1 Pet. 2:10) and has taken the prostitute and purified her of all her unrighteousness to make her his spotless bride—the church (see Eph. 5:26).

As Christ's bride, the church shares in Christ's righteousness. Christ's righteousness creates and completes her. Her righteousness is not her own, but it is hers through faith in Christ. Thus, her righteousness is relational and dialectical (i.e., dynamic, multifaceted, even paradoxical). In fact, the whole of the church's dialectical righteousness bears witness to the church's relational identity as dialectical. How does this kind of dependent righteousness affect the way the church should engage an unrighteous world? The church can never engage the world in a self-righteous manner, but in a gracious manner. Of course, the same would hold true for how Christians are to engage one another. Having drawn attention to important biblical images of the church, discussion will now turn to the dialectical nature of the church's relational identity. Consideration will be given to the church as wholly righteous yet wholly sinful, as one yet many, and as here and not here, now and not yet.

## The Dialectical Nature of the Church's Relational Identity

### Wholly Righteous Yet Wholly Sinful

The Trinity as the one God who is three persons in communion is a dialectical reality. Our union with the Triune God is also dialectical, for while we are sinners, we are also righteous. God's Spirit unites us to Christ, and so we become righteous before God through our relational union with Christ through the Spirit, while remaining unrighteous in ourselves apart from this relational union with the Triune God. This dialectical, relational union is constitutive of the church's identity.

Our righteousness comes from Christ, not ourselves. Christ's righteousness becomes ours, not that we acquire a new capacity, but that we possess him as a new lover. We possess Christ by faith in God's loving promises: "My beloved is mine and I am his." Truly, as those who are the church, we are new creations and spotless, but such newness and purity depend completely on our dynamic interpersonal union with our beloved Christ, not on our works. Luther puts it this way: "No good work can rely upon the Word of God or live in the soul. Just as the heated iron glows like fire because of the union of fire with it, so the Word imparts its qualities to the soul." Christ marries the believer through "the wedding ring of faith." For Luther, Christ marries those who are the church "in faith, steadfast love, and in mercies, righteousness, and justice, as Hosea 2[:19–20] says."[24]

We possess Christ as he gives himself to be had by us. This personal, relational possession ever remains a gift through the outpoured Spirit of love in our lives. No one has grounds to boast when salvation is a gift, no matter one's station in life. For apart from Christ, there is no one righteous, not even one (Rom. 3:9–20). All stand before God condemned apart from his compassionate turn toward us in Jesus—Jew and Gentile alike. The ground is level at the foot of the cross, and so everyone is equal through faith in Christ Jesus through the Spirit of him who makes us one.

Since Christ's righteousness is never ours apart from utter dependence upon Christ, the church is not only a haven for saints, but also a hospital for sinners. The people of God are those who enter God's kingdom as little children completely dependent on God, ever remaining as such even while growing up to complete maturity in Christ (Matt. 18:3). Only children are able to enter into Narnia, and only those who know they are in need of healing seek after a physician to be healed (Mark 2:17). The very first beatitude in the Sermon on the Mount indicates that blessed are the spiritually poor—the spiritually bankrupt,[25] for theirs is the kingdom of heaven (Matt. 5:3). Spiritual bankruptcy is the only way to have one's account paid in full with God. The kingdom of God is short on puffed-up Pharisees and packed full of penitent publicans and prostitutes (see Luke 18:10–14).

The completeness of each person of the Godhead is bound up with the union of the three. In similar fashion, our righteousness—our completeness— is completely dependent on our union with Christ through the Spirit of God. Our righteousness is also completely dependent on the other members of the body. Thus, it is interdependent righteousness. Just as the body is incomplete apart from the head, each of the parts of the body requires the other parts to function properly. Thus, our righteousness depends also on one another. It takes all the parts—people groups, people with their gifts, and the various churches—to make the whole body, and to make the body whole. So, the members of Christ's body share Christ's righteousness by inviting one another to repentance and healing in Christ, not by exclusionary finger-pointing and condemnation. When one grieves due to sin, everyone grieves, and when one rejoices due to victory in righteousness, everyone rejoices. United we stand, divided we fall. The church is whole only when each of its members is whole, and when each and every member works for the good of others in light of the whole.

### One Yet Many

It is a great mystery that Christ and the church are one flesh (Eph. 5:32). Equally mysterious is that the church is one—made up of Jews and Gentiles alike as equals through faith (Eph. 3:4–6). Just as God's atoning work in Christ tore the veil in the temple from top to bottom (Matt. 27:51) so that God's people could become the temple of the Holy Spirit, so Christ's atoning work tore asunder the dividing wall of hostility between Jew and Gentile so that they could become one body (Eph. 2:13–16).

Notice the profoundly trinitarian dynamic in Ephesians 2:14–22. Christ brings peace to the conflict between Jews and Gentiles, and so he is their peace (cf. Micah 5:4–5). He has destroyed the hostility of the flesh (bound up with circumcision and the requirements of the law) in his own death in the flesh on the cross. He has reconciled the two by reconciling them to God through the cross. Through his once-for-all bodily death, he has made the two into one body. It is by this same Jesus that we have access through one Spirit to the Father. Now Gentiles belong to God's household whose foundation is the apostles and prophets and whose cornerstone is Christ. Christ brings into alignment the whole structure so that it grows into God's holy temple. In Christ, God builds together Jews and Gentiles into the place where God dwells by the Spirit. And so, they belong together as members of God's household and as the house in which God dwells.

Through Christ, Gentiles are heirs with Israel, members together of Christ's own body, and sharers together in God's promises in Jesus (Eph. 3:6). And so, Jews and Gentiles (and all other groups) affirm their union with Christ when they are united with one another. Christ died and rose to make Jews and Gentiles one. Christ also died to make male and female and slave and free one, for we are "all one in Christ Jesus" and "Abraham's offspring, heirs according to promise" (see Gal. 3:28–29). Yet, all too often, we do not live by faith with our brothers and sisters, but are instead divided by skin color and ethnicity, social status and economics, gender and personal preference. Still, those who ascend to God in faith will descend to their neighbor in love through the Spirit, who pours out God's love in our hearts.[26]

Paul urges the Ephesians to "maintain the unity of the Spirit in the bond of peace" (Eph. 4:3). The Spirit of peace unifies us in the one who is our peace. He goes on to write, "There is one body and one Spirit—just as you were called to the one hope that belongs to your call—one Lord, one faith, one baptism, one God and Father of all, who is over all and through all and in all" (Eph. 4:4–5). Paul appeals to the common hope and one Triune God. So too must we.

Although Paul's concern for unity in the body does not discount or eradicate particularity, the parts exist for the whole. In Ephesians 4, the apostle writes that there are many parts to the one body (Eph. 4:16). In 1 Corinthians, he speaks to the need to make use of all the parts of the body, and for them to function together (1 Cor. 12:12–31). The Spirit of God is key to the parts actually functioning well together. This same Spirit who mediates the love between Father and Son, who mediates the incarnation of God's Son, and who unites Christ and his church also unites Christ's humanity and his body—the church, including its various parts. The Spirit forms and shapes each part to be the particular one it is intended to be for the diverse outworking of the church as one body. Our unity in and with and through Christ by the Spirit upholds and nurtures the diverse church's various forms of particularity for the sake of the whole.

As Christ's body on earth, we become a divinely appointed means of communicating the person, love, and righteousness of Christ in the flesh here and now. We are Christ's hands and feet by whom God's Spirit communicates Christ to each member of the church. So, when we forgive one another, we experience God's forgiveness. Catholics have recognized this truth and practice it through the liturgy of confession. There is something incredibly powerful about having a fellow believer tell us in the flesh that we are forgiven. Catholics have limited this practice at least sacramentally to the priesthood, and so have limited its profundity.[27] The church as a whole, and not a select ordained few, is a "royal priesthood" (1 Pet. 2:9). And so, we should make public confession to one another and receive forgiveness from one another.

Some Protestants will be quick to point out that "there is one mediator, the man Christ Jesus" (1 Tim. 2:5). While that is certainly true, the very same passage also tells us to make intercession (1 Tim. 2:1–4). Intercession is a form of mediation. It makes sense that the apostle would exhort us to pray, because we are the one mediator's body and bride, and share in his Spirit. While Christ alone is our savior, mediator, and high priest, we bear witness to one another of his saving grace when we forgive in Jesus's name. James calls on us to confess our sins to one another and to pray for one another so that we may be healed (James 5:16). The prayer of faith saves the sick (James 5:15), and the person who brings another back to faith saves him too (James 5:19–20). How we miss out on God's blessings when we fail to hold fast to God's word and be the church—the priesthood of all believers.

The church also misses out on God's blessings when it fails to live in unity. We have already touched on the divisions between Jews and Gentiles and other groups in the church. Divisions spell dysfunction. The same holds true for divisions in the church as a whole. Recall that our righteousness is interdependent. The lack of unity in the body means that the church is not complete, not whole—not living out who we are as Christ's righteous body and bride. This should deeply grieve us. Now just as God is one, so too are we called to be one. And just as when one rejoices, the whole rejoices, and when one grieves, the whole grieves, so too the fact that the church is not whole should grieve every church. For just as we communicate to one another the good news of God's love when we forgive one another, so too we communicate to the world that God has sent his Son when we are one as God is one (John 17:21). Disunity, on the other hand, communicates to the world that God has not sent his Son.

While one does not want to overinstitutionalize the church, it is equally problematic to see the church as completely invisible. If the church is invisible, then it is not visible to the world. While there are wheat and tares and sheep and goats, and while we are to make every effort to make sure we ourselves are not goats, the evangelical emphasis on the invisible church sometimes arises from an individualistic bias that does not account for the interdependent reality of the whole church.[28]

Scripture teaches that the whole church is present at each local assembly. The Baptist theologian Millard Erickson writes that "the individual congregation, or group of believers in a specific place, is never regarded as only a part or component of the whole church. The church is not a sum or composite of the individual local groups. Instead, the whole is found in each place."[29]

The church of God is in Corinth (1 Cor. 1:2), Ephesus, Rome, and the like. This profound reality should cause each local assembly to exist for the whole church. However, the North American church has profound difficulty recognizing and working for the visible unity of the whole church. This is due not only to the emphasis in so many circles on the invisible church, but also to the American affirmation of tolerance as well as the adoption of the free market system for church growth in many quarters. The Christian form of tolerance and the free market system find their origin in the American experiment of the separation of church and state and give rise in part to the separation of churches from one another.[30]

The contributors to *In One Body through the Cross*, a recent proposal for Christian unity, address such tensions as these and call for greater attentiveness on the part of all Christians in North America:

> Congregational and parish life in the United States often proceeds with little sense of contradiction between division from others and life as a realization of the one church of Christ. This unawareness is indeed related to positive developments: greater tolerance and the willingness of many individual Christians to accept members of other churches as brothers and sisters in Christ. But friendly division is still division. We must not let our present division be seen as normal, as the natural expression of a Christian marketplace with churches representing different options for a variety of spiritual tastes. Consumerist values and an ideology of diversity can anesthetize us to the wound of division. Recovering from this ecumenical anesthesia is one of the strongest present challenges to faithfulness.[31]

This ecumenical anesthesia presents a key challenge to faithfulness and reveals our lack of interdependence and completeness. Although Christ is not divided (see 1 Cor. 1:13), the divided church does not bear witness to the one true God.

The fact that we exist by the Triune God should mean that we exist for the church of the Triune God. A mark of the Spirit's presence is that we are one as God is one. Our common confession in the Triune God should lead to common communion. Thus, unity in the truth should lead to a united community. While we should not go around our differences in the pursuit of unity, we should go through them in search of what binds us together in the midst of them. We look forward to the day when our coming, common hope—the Lord Jesus—will make us one. We must live today in view of that day, when we will no longer look through a glass dimly, but face to face (1 Cor. 13:12).[32] One day the whole church will be one, even as it is now one through its union with the ascended Christ through the indwelling presence of the Spirit. Someday, we will become what we are.

### Here and Not Here, Now and Not Yet

Christ is the second Adam, the last Adam, the eschatological human (see 1 Cor. 15:45–49). He has provided purification for sin and has sat down at the right hand of God (Heb. 1:1–3). He purifies us through the Spirit whom the Father has poured out on us and who unites us to Christ. Just as God offered up the willing Christ upon the cross by the Spirit without blemish to make us pure (Heb. 9:14), the risen and ascended Christ pours out the Holy Spirit upon us to complete and perfect us, to make us one with God and with one another. The Spirit is the perfecting member of the Trinity. While Christ institutes our humanity as the firstborn of the new creation, the Spirit constitutes Christ's humanity as the archetype of this eschatological humanity and forms the church as the body and bride of this eschatological human.[33]

And so, Jesus shares that eschatological humanity with the church, which is his people, body, and bride. The church as the eschatological community is the bride of the eschatological man. Christ is what we will be. We shall be like him when we see him as he is. We are called to become what we will be, and what we already are in him.

Although the church is pledged to Christ as his bride through the Spirit, and so according to the biblical world is already married to him, this union will not reach its ultimate consummation until her faith becomes sight at the marriage supper of the Lamb. While one with the ascended Christ now by faith through God's love poured out into its members' hearts through the Spirit, the church will truly consummate her union as one person with Christ, her bridegroom, at the end of the age.[34] The Spirit who unites us to Christ will usher in this eschatological age in its fullness.

Until then, we live in tension. We are here on this earth, yet seated with Christ in the heavens (Col. 3:1–14). We belong to Christ's kingdom, which has been inaugurated, but which will not reach its fulfillment until the end of the age. Christ has all authority, and exercises that authority in and through the church, which is his body (see Eph. 1:20–23). And yet Christ and his church often experience rejection at the hands of this world's authorities (see 1 Pet. 2:4–12). The church must never become attached to this world and its kingdoms, for we are looking forward to an eternal kingdom, and to a city whose foundations are from God (Heb. 11:10).

Our life is now hidden with Christ in God. And yet Christ is also with us in the Spirit here on earth. Thus, while we are resident aliens, we are not orphans (see John 14:18). The Spirit leads us forward. We must keep in step with the Spirit, God's promissory note and perfecting agent preparing us for the day of redemption.

The Spirit who completes the Triune God by uniting the Father and Son does not close God off from the church and world but accomplishes God's turning outward to the church and world in Christ. According to Colin Gunton, the Spirit who, as Basil states, "completes the divine and blessed Trinity" serves

> not as the one who completes an inward turning circle, but as one who is the agent of the Father's outward turning to the creation in his Son. As the one who "completes," the Spirit does indeed establish God's aseity, his utter self-sufficiency. Yet this aseity is the basis of a movement outwards . . . The love of the Father, Son and Spirit is a form of love which does not remain content with its eternal self-sufficiency because that self-sufficiency is the basis of a movement outwards to create and perfect a world whose otherness from God—of being distinctly itself—is based in the otherness-in-relation of Father, Son and Spirit in eternity.[35]

The Holy Spirit's "work is the eschatological work of perfecting through the redemption won by Christ that which was created and fell from its proper being. It is this connection with perfecting that above all characterizes the holiness of the Spirit."[36]

The Spirit who completes the divine life turns outward to create and perfect the church and world. The Spirit completes and perfects us, making us one with God and one another. For its own part, the people of God find completion through union with this outward-turning God and by turning outward toward the world. This outward movement of perfection and perfecting witness in the Spirit gives rise to a church that is truly concerned for the well-being of those outside the church. Such an outwardly directed church witnesses to God's perfecting work of holy love in the Spirit toward and for all creation.

All too often, Christians think of completion and perfection in "members only" terms. Nothing could be further from the truth, though, especially if we reframe our understanding of completion and perfection in light of the Holy Spirit. The Spirit does not close circles but opens the circle, so that all may have access to the Father through the Son, and opens us up toward the world.

Nowhere is this open-circle reality more beautifully envisioned artistically than in Andrei Rublev's icon of the Trinity,[37] which "clearly expresses" the "eternal circle of love which opens to the hospitality of the creature, leading it to the eternal trinitarian Banquet."[38] Here in this icon, "The circle of the infinite tenderness of 'the Three' opens to welcome the viewer, whom the icon leads into sacred space, to communion at the Table of God, at the very heart of the hospitality of God to which man, in turn, is invited and where, with fear and love, he enters into the intimacy of God."[39] Nowhere is this divine hospitality more explicitly depicted biblically than in the closing chapters of Revelation. The God who judges the whore Babylon makes of a whore a holy bride for his Son, and through the Spirit and the bride invites all to come and partake of the marriage feast. And nowhere is this open circle hospitality grasped better theologically than in Robert Jenson's appropriation of Jonathan Edwards's discussion of the church as Christ's bride:

> And the final goal of creation is thus at once God and his creature united in Christ, the totus Christus [the whole Christ] . . . "There was, [as] it were, an eternal society or family in the Godhead, in the Trinity of persons. It seems to be God's design to admit the church into the divine family as his son's wife." "Heaven and earth were created that the Son of God might be complete in a spouse."[40]

The Son will be made complete in a spouse through the Spirit. The bride—the church—is not yet complete either. And so, this is no closed circle. Just as the icon opens up toward the viewer, so God opens up toward the world through the Spirit and bride of Christ and says, "Come!"

## STUDY QUESTIONS

1. How does trinitarian thought shape your understanding of the church?
2. Why is it important to think of the church as a being-driven community, and not simply as a purpose-driven community?
3. Which biblical images of the church do you find most meaningful in your own experience?
4. What would the church look like if we really believed that the church is both a haven for saints and a hospital for sinners?

# 2

# The Trinitarian Church Confronts
# American Individualism

A hallmark of the evangelical Christian tradition is personal relationship with God through Jesus Christ. That God takes us seriously and loves us personally is a profound and precious reality. While God in Christ loves the entire world, Jesus brings God's love home personally to Zacchaeus, whom he finds in a tree (Luke 19:5), to Nathaniel, whom he spots under a tree (John 1:50), and to the Samaritan woman whom he meets at the well (John 4:7). Jesus calls Peter to abandon his fishing nets (Matt. 4:18–20) and summons Matthew from his tax collector's booth (Luke 5:27). Every hair on our heads is numbered (Matt. 10:30), and God leaves the ninety-nine sheep to go after the stray (Luke 15:3–7).

Bertrand Russell—by no means a friend of Christianity—marveled at this characteristic trait of the Christian religion. In *Why I Am Not a Christian*, Russell writes,

> If Christianity is true, mankind are not such pitiful worms as they seem to be; they are of interest to the Creator of the universe, who takes the trouble to be pleased with them when they behave well and displeased when they behave badly. This is a great compliment. We should not think of studying an ants' nest to find out which of the ants performed their formicular duty, and we should certainly not think of picking out those individual ants who were remiss and putting them into a bonfire. If God does this for us, it is a compliment to our

importance; and it is even a pleasanter compliment if he awards to the good among us everlasting happiness in heaven.[1]

This is one reason why we the authors are evangelical Christians. Concern for the individual person is incredibly important to Christianity, and especially to evangelicalism. God's concern for us is both flattering and humbling.

As noted, the individual's profound value to the Creator and Savior is a biblical notion. But this theme has taken on added importance in the modern world as a result of the Enlightenment and rise of fundamentalist-evangelicalism. The Enlightenment, or modern era, arose in part out of concern for safeguarding space for the individual in the face of imperial and ecclesial institutional forces that oppressed the individual person during the medieval period. The same response arose during the fundamentalist period, where conservative Christians rejected what they took to be the oppressive constraints of mainline Protestant liberal institutionalism.[2] The irony here is that the fundamentalist-evangelical movement is both modern and a reaction to modernity.[3]

Having said all this, the fundamentalist-evangelical movement has overreacted to the perceived medieval and modern mainline excesses by failing to situate adequately the individual person in a community of persons. The tendency is for people in the movement to see the temple of the Holy Spirit primarily in individual rather than corporate and/or institutional terms. In like fashion, discussion of spiritual renewal often focuses on the individual rather than on the church body. Listen closely to the words of many praise choruses. The primary focus is often on "I," not "we." Moreover, the way evangelicals often read their Bibles leads them to see most everything in individualistic terms. For example, those within the movement often fail to see that the Epistle to the Romans has much to say about how faith in Jesus is the great equalizer between Jewish and Gentile people before God, much more in fact than it has to say about believing individuals. Consideration of believing individuals in Romans and elsewhere must be set forth against this backdrop of the Bible's communal orientation.[4]

Now, we the authors know what it means to be born from above and to have our hearts strangely warmed. But we do not conceive the born-again encounter as private and individual. Today, the danger exists that people often view the born-again experience in private, individualistic, and even consumerist terms. In *A New Kind of Christian* by Brian McLaren, one of the characters, "Neo," says that the definition of "saved" has been "shrunken and freeze-dried by modernity." Neo calls for

a postmodern consideration of what salvation means, something beyond an individualized and consumeristic version. I may have a personal home, personal car, personal computer, personal identification number, personal digital assistant, personal hot-tub—all I need now is personal salvation from my own personal savior . . . This all strikes me as Christianity diced through the modern Veg-o-matic.[5]

While relationship with Jesus is truly personal, it is by no means private, individualistic, and consumerist. It is public and interpersonal or communal. Prayer requests, sermon titles, and messages often reflect this individualized and consumerized Veg-o-matic imbalance. All too often, sermons tend to follow the "How to Lose Weight and Be Filled with the Holy Spirit" pattern, not the "Take Up Your Cross and Follow Me" paradigm.[6] No doubt, the problem goes back to the fall and its aftermath, where everyone began doing what seemed right in their own eyes. It is just that today we have perfected the art of individualized identity and self-realization.

The problem does not end with the individual Christian. It extends to the individual family. People may claim to be community-oriented by spending time with their families. Unfortunately, the individual nuclear family too often takes precedence over the family of God. One reason why Dr. James Dobson is so powerful a figure now is that he speaks to one of America's greatest national treasures and endangered species—the nuclear family. Pastors can speak on all kinds of subjects at church. But they dare not challenge prevailing notions of success, our use of money, the American nation, and the family. Just about anything else will do. In fact, we often use our money to foster successful ministries that often cater to the American dream of stable and wholesome birth families.

This was brought home to our attention the Christmas of 2005. Many evangelical churches across America decided to close their doors on Christmas Day, because Christmas fell on Sunday. One leading pastor in the area where we live reasoned that his church would have several Christmas Eve services to attend, but that people should be home with their families on Christmas Day. In so doing, this pastor placed the birth family over the born-again family. As a result, many individuals removed from their nuclear families had nowhere to go and no one to talk to on Christmas Day. So much for the emphasis on the individual before God!

Churches often cater to this tendency to overvalue the nuclear family in American culture. Ironically, those churches that cater more to the family—making Christ and the church a predicate of family values—often become more successful churches. And not so ironically, it tends to produce competition between churches where families shop for the best children's ministry with accompanying state-of-the-art children's wing.[7]

We have before us three problems: overemphasis on the individual, the individual family, and the individual church. How shall we respond? The individual is important to God, just not in isolation from the church. The family is important to God, but not to the detriment of God's family. The individual church is important to God, just not in isolation from other churches.

When Christianity places undue emphasis on the individual, it reduces the church to a group of believing individuals or, worse, sees Christian identity as separate from participation in Christian community. But the church is greater than the sum of its parts, and the parts do not stand alone. We are only who we are in relation to others. As stated in chapter 1, "The Church as a Trinitarian Community," God is three persons in communion. The three persons are the being of God, not a divine individual in isolation. As those created in the image of God, we have our personal being in interpersonal communion with God and others. Scripture never refers to the church as a group of believing individuals or autonomous Christians, but as the body of believers, the body and bride of Christ. The risen Christ himself is not simply an individual. He is corporate in that he is one with the church as his body and bride. And so, we are not simply individuals. We are a corporate reality as Christ's body and bride.

The problem is not limited to the individual person. When the church places undue emphasis on the individual nuclear family, it tends to disregard the church as the ultimate family. As a result, it also tends to disregard the single person or the single parent raising a family. However, when we see the church as God's family, and ourselves as part of that family, we realize that our spouses and our children are our brothers and sisters in the Lord. So too we realize that single parents and their children, orphans and widows in their distress, and those who visit our fellowship, are members of our family.

This reality was brought home to one of us when he and his family shared in a Sunday worship celebration with a Jordanian and Egyptian congregation in Oregon. After the service, to our surprise, the people invited everyone over—including us as their guests—to one of their houses to celebrate the birthday of one of their church members. It was such a profound experience. The individual family was part of a larger family, and we were welcomed into their fellowship as part of their family too.

We experienced more intimate conversation with these people we hardly knew that one afternoon than what we normally experience in our own local fellowship of believers. Perhaps one reason is that in the dominant culture we tend to treat one another and our respective families as individuals and individual nuclear units, for identity is ultimately defined in individual terms. Not so for those from Middle Eastern and Asian cultures. Of course, we do not mean to suggest that there are no problematic features in those cultures. All too often, there is insufficient regard for the individual in these cultures. However, our trinitarian faith calls us to affirm the one and the many, for God is triune.

It is important for us to emphasize that members of our church families are members of our nuclear families, and that our nuclear families are part of this larger church family. This would keep us from separating and prioritizing family over church, or vice versa. One of the Jordanian women at the birthday party told us that she had served on the church staff of a largely Caucasian congregation for several years. She was amazed how often people used their nuclear families as a means to the end of not getting involved in church life.[8] In contrast to that either/or perspective, these Middle Eastern Christians were building biological or blood-related family while building Christian community.

Perhaps the problem in the West stems from a contractual model of human identity. The individual subject is the basic unit of human identity, and relationships are based on contractual arrangements made between individual subjects. Men and women enter into marriage contracts as individuals and remain so while fulfilling their commitments to the contractual arrangements of mutual benefits. A marriage can be terminated if either party fails to live by the agreement. A contractual relationship is conditional, based on fulfilling commitments and obligations involving sharing of the respective parties' assets and capacities and mutually satisfying performance of various activities.

This is not how scripture views human identity and marriage. Just as God is indissolubly communal, so too human identity is a relational being. On this view, people make covenants, which express their indissoluble bond as persons in communion. The marriage bond signifies that the two have become one flesh (Eph. 5:31). Biblically speaking, if a marriage were to be terminated, the couple would die. For the two had been one flesh (Eph. 5:31), and their bodies were no longer their own—their bodies belonged to each other (1 Cor. 7:4). It is only as one dies that the other person is free to marry another (Rom. 7:1–3).

The problem of autonomy and contractual relations is not limited to the individual and individual nuclear family. The same problem holds true for churches in relation to one another. If people view relationships in contractual terms, where obligations are met to receive certain benefits, then they will likely look at the church family in contractual terms. In this case, people look for that church that will meet their needs and provide spiritual goods and services. They enter into relations with the church, providing services and financial resources as long as the church meets their expectations. Once expectations are not met, people are tempted to go next door or down the street.

It is very important that we shape people's understanding so that they see that our churches are inviting them to be part of a family, and that family involves risk and loss, not "What's in it for me?" As Rick Warren would say, "It's not about you."[9] It's really about God and all of us, which includes you. It is not about giving people what they want, when they want it, at the least cost to themselves, but about being the people of God, which involves giving and receiving, even at great cost to themselves.

By contrast, when churches focus on being vendors of religious goods and service providers to expectant consumers, churches tend to focus on doing what it takes to make sure their fellowships survive in the religious free market, where only the fittest survive.[10] When the church focuses solely on its own fellowship, it can easily give rise to disregard for other fellowships, and even competition between churches. It is important that each church realizes that Christ is present to each church. Now if Christ is present to each church, and the whole church is the body and bride of Christ, then the whole church is present to each assembly. Thus, each church should exist in an open manner toward the whole. One church in the area where we live includes a prayer request every week in its worship program for other local churches and their leaders. This is a good first step. But other steps are needed, such as churches sharing resources with one another. It would be a profound indication of church unity if affluent churches would put some of their building program money toward assisting less-affluent churches with their facilities. One can learn a lot about churches' hearts based on how they approach their respective building programs.

Individualism and separatism is not limited to how churches relate to one another. It also impacts how the church and individuals within it relate to the world at large. So often, evangelism is reduced to individual proclamation to see that an individual soul is saved, instead of expanded to be an invitation to the individual, and even the individual's community, to enter into God's kingdom community. The community is the place in which our salvation is realized and perfected. In fact, our salvation must be nurtured and realized in community, for our God is communal, and so is our union with God. In fact, entrance into community and communion is salvation.[11]

Such entrance does not involve a retreat from the world, but a new way of being in the world that leads to the redemptive transformation of the world's structures through the creation and cultivation of a new kind of community in the world. The church is Christ's body in the world, and so the church must give itself to the world, just as Christ did. As Dietrich Bonhoeffer claims, the church is the church "only when it exists for others . . . The Church must share in the secular problems of ordinary human life, not dominating, but helping and serving."[12] Just as God gave his Son to save the world, so God gives his church to the world. The church is a microcosm of the world,[13] and of the transformative work God is undertaking through his Son and Spirit to make all things new.

So what would the church look like if it became less individualistic and more trinitarian? It would look something like the Jordanian-Egyptian congregation mentioned earlier. No doubt, it was not a perfect community, but it was profoundly beautiful and unique in a culture where individualism reigns supreme. This community was not centered on the individual or individual family or individual church, but it had a place for all of them at the celebration. The individual and nuclear family had place settings at the dinner table. So too did our family, although we were visiting from another church. This church fellowship also had a heart to share the bounty of the table to those in their community. Perhaps their openness and inclusiveness were due to the fact that they knew the importance of being open and inclusive in a culture where they are often excluded as foreigners and recent immigrants.

We need to sit down together at the birthday-party table of our new identity in Christ more often. All too often, we are a group of individuals, nuclear families, individual churches, a separatistic community set apart from others and the world at large, doing our own thing. The Lord wants to do a new thing in our lives, families, churches, and communities.

What is a trinitarian community? Henri Nouwen and Philip Yancey give us some clues. Developing a point made by Nouwen, Yancey writes:

> Henri Nouwen defines "community" as the place where the person you least want to live with always lives. Often we surround ourselves with the people we most want to live with, thus forming a club or a clique, not a community. Anyone can form a club; it takes grace, shared vision, and hard work to form a community.[14]

Too often, we associate only with our individual friends, but not our brothers and sisters in the Lord. After all, it is our inherent right as Americans to choose! And so, we choose to be with our friends and call that our church family. But the church family is not limited to our friends—those like us. A fellowship exclusively made up of friends—our kind of people—is not a church, but a clique.

Over against the supposedly American freedom to choose whatever we want, and to be with whomever we want, which is actually bondage, because it does not free us for "the other"—the one who is truly different from us— God chose us in Christ, and chose our brothers and sisters in Christ for us. We share a common Father as siblings in Christ through the bond created by the Spirit. God calls us to the family table, to work out our differences with "the other," to share a meal together, and to invite other "others" to the table of the crucified and risen Lord. Christ became other than God, and he became the abandoned other so as to reconcile us to God and one another. Jesus's last supper with his band of social misfits and outcasts was the first supper of the eschatological kingdom family. The supper of the Lord has a way of reshaping us from individuals and nuclear families and churches and insiders in isolation to being inclusive of others so that we might truly become what we already are—the family of God. Christ's own Middle Eastern last supper is truly a birthday celebration for the entire family into which we have been born anew. And so, in light of this celebration that will be consummated again and again in God's eternal home in the coming kingdom, God calls us to expand our circle of friends so that our cliques might be completely transformed into a family circle. Until we do, we will never be complete.

## STUDY QUESTIONS

1. How have you found individualism to be problematic in the American church?
2. Why is personal relationship with Jesus so important to church life?
3. What would the church community look like if we conceived of it as God's ultimate family?
4. How do we move the church from being a social club where people associate only with those like them, toward becoming a true community?

# 3

# The Church as an Eschatological Community

What the church is, in short, is determined by what the church is destined to become.

Stanley Grenz[1]

## From Temporary Community to the Community of God's Future

Several years ago, on a tour of the sites of the life of Martin Luther, a twelve-year-old boy and his father were wandering through the magnificent cathedral in Mainz, a classic Gothic structure, its architecture begging the eyes to look to the heavens. Seeing that his son was quite taken by the majesty of the building, the father asked him for his thoughts. "Dad," he replied, "everything in this building makes me look towards heaven and search for God." What joy his comment would have brought to the architects of this grand medieval church. Indeed, Gothic church architecture illustrates an important theological principle regarding ecclesiology. Just as the boy looked beyond the church building to the God it pointed to, so the church in the world today must look beyond itself, to a God bigger than earth and bigger than the present. To understand its identity and mission, the church must look to its own future. For the Bible's ultimate picture of the church is found at the end of the story. The apostle John in Revelation 21–22 invites us to imagine the church in its consummate form

47

as the New Jerusalem descending from heaven like a bride whose wedding day has finally come, a bride fully prepared for her groom. It is a church purified of all sin, healed from all brokenness, a community that welcomes both the persons and the riches of every human culture. In it, a humanity cured of its own internal animosities, living in perfect harmony with a glorified creation, fulfills its final purpose of an unfettered love relationship with Christ, bringing glory to God the Father.

In the biblical narrative, the people of God are always urged to look forward, imagining their future not simply as a way of ameliorating the pain of their present circumstances, but also to help them understand what kind of people God wants them to be in the present. Thus, for a theology of the church to be truly biblical, it must be one that understands the church as an eschatological community. For many of us who were raised in the American evangelical tradition, eschatology has often focused on the study of charts that graphically depict a particular interpretation of biblical prophecy about the end of the world. Key to this approach is the rise of a renewed nation of Israel (usually said to have been reconstituted in 1948), a nation that would again become the recipient of God's saving grace and the locus of Christ's kingdom rule over the earth—all this as the church faded into a heavenly background.[2] But no matter what one believes about the future of the nation of Israel, the church must never be relegated to the status of a temporary community. It is the community of God's future, which means that a biblical eschatology must always be a study of the future of the church. Conversely, any biblical theology of the church must include a study of its future, or, in eschatological terms, the relationship of the church to the kingdom of God. The relationship between the church and the kingdom is a subject that pours forth from the pages of scripture. The central topic of the teaching of Jesus is the kingdom of God. And it is upon his apostles and their message of the kingdom that he promises to build his church.

Throughout its history the church has struggled to understand its relationship to the kingdom. The fundamental question asks if the promised kingdom is present or still remains a future hope. The gospel writers answered the question paradoxically. The kingdom of God was indeed present in the life and ministry of Jesus and demonstrated its power over death in his resurrection. Nevertheless, the church was still envisioned as a bride waiting for the arrival of her groom. The consensus of twentieth-century scholarship is that the New Testament presents a picture of a kingdom that is here and not here, now and not yet.[3] And the kingdom has created a community that, while not identified with it, is a function of the kingdom's presence and anticipates its consummation at the end of the age. This means that the church is a community both of fulfillment and of hope, realizing the blessings of the future while yet awaiting the fullness of these blessings to be revealed at Christ's second coming. This identity shapes the church, the bride, by calling her to conform now, as much as possible, to her future image as the spotless bride of Christ.

This paradoxical relation to the kingdom raises a number of important questions for the church: What aspects of the kingdom can the church expect to experience in its own existence and mission, now and in the future? What is the church's role in the kingdom of God now? And how does the present/future nature of the kingdom of God guide the church's engagement of culture, including its role in influencing secular government and the shaping of culture's values? These are profound questions that have generated much discussion. It is to these questions that we turn our attention in the following pages. First we will seek to understand the presence of the kingdom in the ministry of Jesus and in the church founded by him as understood in the Synoptics, John, and Acts. Then we will examine the nature and characteristics of this eschatological church, and finally, we will suggest ways in which such a church must engage culture.

### Jesus, the Kingdom, and the Church as an Eschatological Community

Having been anticipated in the pages of the Hebrew Scriptures, it is in the Synoptic Gospels that the topic of the kingdom comes most prominently into focus. The kingdom is the fundamental subject of Jesus's preaching. Indeed, Mark begins his account not with the birth narratives, but with John's annunciation of the coming king and Jesus's declaration that the kingdom is at hand (1:1–15). Similarly, Matthew and Luke record Jesus's first major preaching event as a proclamation of the arrival of the kingdom, as envisioned by Isaiah, and of himself as the one who would inaugurate it.

Of the many passages related to the kingdom and its presence in the preaching of Jesus, one of the most important is found in Matthew 12:22–32. Here, the arrival of the kingdom is cast in imagery reaching all the way back to Genesis 3:15 and the promise of the ultimate defeat of Satan by the seed of Eve. This future blessing of the kingdom has begun in Jesus's casting out of demons by the power of the Holy Spirit (another indication of the presence of the kingdom—cf. Ezek. 36; Joel 2; etc.). Drawing on Exodus imagery and the formation of the people of God, Jesus robs the strong man's house, taking captive for himself Satan's possessions, that is, people. He embarks upon this rescue mission to bring together the kingdom people of God, the church (Matt. 16), which would be made up of those from every tongue and tribe and nation (Matt. 28:19–20). Jesus announces that the work of the kingdom has now begun for this people in the preaching of the gospel, healing, and raising the dead. Thus, the blessings of the future are experienced in the present.

Nevertheless, Jesus's teaching on the arrival of the kingdom contains mixed messages. One of the most poignant examples of the paradox of the preaching of the kingdom is found in Luke 7:18–23. Alone and abandoned in a prison cell for condemning Herod's adulterous marriage, John is struggling with Jesus's ministry. Like the rest of the Jews of this day, John had an expectation of the kingdom that included things that were not happening. Rome and other evil rulers were still in charge, unaffected by Jesus's annunciation of the kingdom, a fact brought home powerfully to John by the fact of his own imprisonment. God was supposed to come in power with the kingdom, wipe away unrighteous rulers, and restore Israel to Davidic glory.[4] Confused, the man who spent his entire life anticipating his God-given job of announcing the arrival of the Messiah/King sends his disciples to ask Jesus if perhaps he has made a mistake. Maybe Jesus is not the one?

Jesus's indirect answer illustrates well the paradox of the kingdom. He tells John's disciples to go back and relate to him the miracles they see. The lame walk, the blind see, the dead are raised, and the gospel is preached to the poor. These miracles are the signs of the kingdom as foretold by the prophets (Isa. 42:7; 61:1). Then, Jesus retorts cryptically, "Blessed is the man who does not fall on account of me." Jesus knows here that his ministry, while clearly fulfilling prophecy, is not living up to all the current expectations. The cataclysmic, apocalyptic elements are not there, nor the restoration of a righteous political system in Israel. Jesus knows this is what the suffering and oppressed Jews are looking for. But he also knows that this aspect of the kingdom promise is not what he came to fulfill . . . yet. So they must not stumble over that. Here Jesus exhorts his followers to recognize the presence of the kingdom of God in the midst of a community that remains broken. Thus, the kingdom and its power become both a realization and a hope.

Contemporary New Testament scholarship has come to understand that the eschatological dualism of John differs from that of the Synoptics. While the Synoptics see the world through the language of the kingdom and its horizontal dualism of this age vs. the age to come, John's dualism is vertical, using the language of above and below. In the incarnation, and later, through the Spirit, God invades human history, bringing the transcendent God into the realm of humanity. This focus results in a significant amount of "realized eschatology." John's approach led such scholars as C. H. Dodd to conclude that, in John, virtually all of the eschatological hope has already taken place with the coming of Christ and the Spirit, so that eternal life is an already present reality in the church rather than a merely future hope. Dodd argues that "all that the church hoped for in the second coming of Christ is already given in its present experience of Christ through the Spirit."[5]

Indeed, John's Gospel does focus a great deal on the present experience of the eschatological blessings. In Christ, God comes to earth to bring life to all people (John 1). Also in John 1, using the eschatological temple imagery of Ezekiel, John pictures Jesus as the new tabernacle (*skene*), fulfilling God's promise to dwell in the midst of his people. And in chapter 4 he is the new temple, replacing both Jerusalem and Gerazim so that the "location" of worship is now found in him. This is the temple to which the Spirit of God and the glory of God has returned, as Ezekiel promised. In John 11, Jesus calls Lazarus from the grave, clarifying for Martha that his identity as the "resurrection and the life" is not simply a matter for the future, but for the present. In John 14, Jesus promises not to leave the community of the disciples as orphans, but, looking forward to the Day of Pentecost, declares that he will return to them in the person of the Paraclete, the Holy Spirit. This does not mean, however, that eschatology in John is entirely realized, that there is no sense of the not-yet as well as the already. For Jesus also tells his disciples that he must go away to prepare a place for them, so that when he returns they can be where he is. Moreover, 1 John 3:2 recognizes that the community of Christ still awaits his coming.

While all of this eschatology is rightly applied to the church, both in Christ's present residence in the church through the Spirit and in his future coming for it, John ties his eschatological vision most clearly to the church in the book of Revelation.[6] The following are several of John's images. First, the eschatological Christ speaks to local churches. Unlike in his letters, where he speaks as the leader of the Johannine community, here John presents the picture of the risen and glorified Christ himself speaking directly to seven local churches. What is important for our purpose here is not the particular content of each of the messages, but the image that in the midst of each local church stands the glorified Christ, the exalted Son of God, witnessing the faithfulness, or lack thereof, of each church to form a community whose values and actions reflect the life and teaching of their risen Lord. He is there to judge, but also to encourage. For it is clear that the churches struggle under both persecution and the lure of an enticing but evil world system. To these suffering churches, Christ extends the promise of future glory if they remain faithful to him.

Another of John's images suggests that the church as the people of God extends beyond the grave, even now. In chapters 4 and 5 we see a majestic crowd of angelic/heavenly creatures worshipping God through the worship of the crucified and risen Lamb in the center of the throne of heaven. Later, in chapter 20, John expands the image by including in this glorious assembly the souls of believers who have died. Here is a prelude to John's understanding of the ultimate destiny of the church. For the church of Jesus Christ is a heavenly community, some of its members even "currently" existing in the very heavenly presence of God himself. The earthly church exists now in union with the heavenly church. Nevertheless, both of these elements of the church still look forward to Christ's final revelation of his bride. For now the earthly church endures as a human community broken by sin, while the heavenly church endures as a purified people who still await their vindication by the resurrection of their bodies. Then, in chapters 19–22, John narrates for us the final moments of the story, where the people of God, through Christ's final victory, become all they are meant to be. In chapter 19, Christ descends to earth to rescue his persecuted bride, transporting her to celebrate with him at the marriage feast of the Lamb. The church then returns to earth in the form of the new Jerusalem, the dwelling place of God. All of this glorious vision is given to the church now, to bring comfort in the midst of a broken and decadent world by assuring it of its future destiny, encouraging it to live in light of that destiny even now.

Finally, John shows us that the church of the eschaton is truly a world church. Pictured in Jewish terms (as the New Jerusalem), it is, nevertheless, a multiethnic, multicultural community. For here we see a community of nations and kings, bringing the treasures of their earthly cultures before Christ in exaltation of his majesty. Jerusalem, the city of the temple of YHWH, represents not the Jewish nation, but the very presence of God in the midst of his people, the church, which he has gathered from every tongue and tribe and nation.[7]

Moving from John to the post-Pentecost story of the church, the book of Acts reveals that the kingdom, which has arrived in the ministry of Jesus, finally creates the church as the eschatological community of God as promised by the Hebrew Scriptures. In Peter's Acts 2 speech, his call to the crowd to embrace Christ is filled with kingdom imagery. They are to repent and be baptized, symbolizing preparation for the coming kingdom by purification. They are promised the Holy Spirit, a key component of kingdom expectations. And Jesus of Nazareth is proclaimed, not only as the promised Messiah, but also as the new David, exalted through his resurrection to the place of ultimate authority.

In summary, historical Christian scholarship has experienced a number of pendulum swings regarding the presence or absence of the kingdom of God relative to the church. But in the twentieth century, a consensus position has emerged among scholars of various Christian traditions. This consensus recognizes the paradox of the biblical narrative—the kingdom of God is here and not here, now and not yet.[8] The gospel of the kingdom Jesus is preaching means that God, in the person of Christ, is attacking the kingdom of Satan and is at work among humanity, reigning as king in the hearts of his people. He demonstrates that the kingdom of God is at work in this present evil age. It has arrived, but has not yet brought this age to an end.

## The Nature of the Eschatological Church in Relation to the Kingdom

The struggle to understand the nature of the kingdom as inaugurated in the ministry of Jesus and yet to be consummated only in the future has resulted in a similar struggle to understand the nature of the church as a community connected to the kingdom of God. What finally emerged as the dialectical nature of the church arose from the tendency to view the church either as a community waiting for the kingdom, or the kingdom of God on earth.

## A Community Waiting for the Kingdom

In his extended sermon known as the Olivet Discourse (Matt. 24–25; Mark 13; Luke 12; 19; 21), Jesus weaves together his vision of the future with his theology of the people of God, the church. One of his main themes, illustrated most dramatically in the story of the virgins waiting for their bridegroom and servants living in expectation of the return of their master, depicts the church as a community (or a bride) in waiting, waiting for her king and his kingdom. Paul also focuses on this theme, consistently describing the church as the community of Christ living in expectation of his parousia. Several examples are found in 1 Corinthians. Paul's advice on marriage, material possessions, and other temporal connections to the world (1 Cor. 7) is given through the lens of this expectation, calling for the establishment of a way of life that will not reflect this-worldly values. Further, chapters 10 and 11 give us a major eucharistic passage on the church as a community living in anticipation of the second coming. The Eucharist is a reenactment of the Last Supper, allowing the church to encounter the crucified Christ in anticipation of his future coming, when Christ will once again drink from the cup with them in his Father's kingdom. In 1 Thessalonians 4–5, Paul pictures the church living in expectation of the second coming, which will arrive like a thief in the night. Peter also uses this imagery of the unexpected thief to encourage the church to wait patiently for the Day of YHWH, which will consummate the kingdom of God.

Having understood itself to be such a community in waiting, the church has struggled with the question of what it means to wait for the kingdom. How should the church wait? What should the church do while it waits? And how should the church endure the hostility of the world while it waits? Before Constantine legitimized the church as the official religion of the empire, the eschatology of the church was influenced by its status as a marginalized and often persecuted sect.[9] Both in the biblical context and in the history of the church, one of the by-products of persecution is an eschatology that focuses on a victorious existence beyond history. This appears variously in the form of the cataclysmic entrance of God from outside history to judge the wicked and reward the righteous, martyrdom as the highest act of spirituality, and the emphasis on the church as a holy community separate from the world around it. All three of these emphases play a role in the eschatology of the early church before Constantine.

The glorification of martyrdom in the theology of the early church illustrates that, under persecution and the threat of death, much of the eschatological thought of the church concerned how believers would endure in the faith so as to enter the kingdom of God. During times of persecution, Christians, especially Christian leaders, were asked if they would recant their confessions of faith and offer incense to the emperor to save their lives. Their refusal to recant, and their subsequent executions, became widely told stories of individual faith in the face of death. In this context martyrdom came to be understood as a sure and instant pathway into the presence of God. Martyrdom became revered and, in the case of some, was even desired.

In the letters of Ignatius of Antioch (ca. 110), we find this idealization of martyrdom. His seven letters to the churches of Asia Minor on the way to his martyrdom in Rome reveal Ignatius's conviction that martyrdom is the surest way to become a true disciple of Jesus. Indeed, as Cyril Richardson comments about Ignatius, "He is clearly impatient to 'get to God.'"[10] While the eschatology of martyrdom is quite individualistic and otherworldly in Ignatius, focusing on the hope of immediate personal and individual union with Christ for the martyr, there are elements of a realized eschatology for the church as well. Ignatius urges believers to meet together in faith as those who are in union with Christ together. When they meet they should always partake of the Eucharist, for it is "the medicine of immortality, and the antidote which wards off death but yields continuous life in union with Jesus Christ."[11]

What the glorification of martyrdom illustrates is that one of the church's historic ways of waiting for the kingdom led to a fundamental disconnection from the world. The marginalized church looked forward to God's return to judge the wicked and reward the righteous. And generally in the early church the expectation was that God's judgment was near. Much of this expectation took the form of premillennialism, the hope of the rule of Christ on a renewed earth for a thousand years before the end of all things.[12] This approach to waiting for the kingdom has ebbed and flowed through the church's history, often depending on the church's own sense of its status as being either integral to society or marginalized by it. Rising to popularity at the end of the nineteenth century, as much of the church in America began to sense itself becoming marginalized by the antisupernaturalism of the Enlightenment, a new kind of premillennialism called dispensationalism saw the church as radically disconnected from the future kingdom of God and thus from eschatology. In classic dispensationalism the kingdom of God is understood to be an earthly and physical kingdom. The Old Testament prophecies of the kingdom, with their earthly imagery, meant that at the second coming Jesus will rule the kingdom from Jerusalem in an Israel restored to Davidic glory. But the church is an entity virtually unforeseen by Old Testament prophecy and in no way a fulfillment of the establishment of the kingdom of God.[13] The church, said William Blackstone in his 1908 classic *Jesus Is Coming*, is a mystery, a reality never spoken of by the Old Testament, which merely awaits the fulfillment of the promises to begin when Christ, the bridegroom, arrives.[14] Thus, the church is not an eschatological community.

In modern times, no major Christian movement, at least in America, has created a stronger discontinuity between ecclesiology and eschatology, between the church and the kingdom, than has the classic dispensational premillennialism of the first half of the twentieth century. Reacting against the liberal postmillennialism of the modernist impulse, dispensationalists rejected any substantive connection between the church and the kingdom of God in the present age. The church was understood as a kind of parenthesis between Israel's rejection of the kingdom as offered to them by Christ and God's renewal of his work with Israel, which is to begin with the pretribulation rapture of the church and the subsequent earthly millennium. One result of this theology was that virtually all eschatological imagery and discussion in the scriptures was understood to be addressing the renewed nation of Israel, not the church. Thus, eschatology and the theology of the kingdom played little role in ecclesiology other than that Christians should actively evangelize and live holy lives in anticipation of the rapture, which could come at any moment. To the extent that the church has conceived of itself as a mystery disconnected from Old Testament promises of the kingdom and has understood the kingdom as primarily a future reality to be waited for rather than a present reality that has taken root in this world, it has tended to disconnect itself from social engagement apart from evangelism.[15] It was in this vein that dispensationalist preachers often warned their listeners not to "polish the brass on a sinking ship" (the world).[16] God was coming to judge the unrighteous world and to remove from it his righteous church. Thus, the church's job, in the popular phrase of early-twentieth-century dispensationalists, was simply to "occupy until I come."

### The Kingdom of God on Earth

The dialectic (tension, paradox) of the kingdom of God as here and not here, now and not yet, results in a dialectical nature of the church as well. It is a community caught between this age and the age to come, on the one hand waiting for a kingdom that remains a future hope, and on the other hand embracing the blessings of a kingdom that has not only created the church, but empowers it for Christ's mission in the world. Christ's vision of the relationship between the church and the kingdom makes it clear that the church is founded upon the power of the kingdom and represents that power on earth. For Jesus promises to Peter and the disciples the keys of the kingdom (Matt. 16:18; 18:18), through which they will declare to the world the terms on which the kingdom may be entered. In this power they would go out, as they already had been sent (Matt. 10:7–8), to teach, heal, and cast out demons. They would stand before government leaders before whom they would witness to Christ and his kingdom (Matt. 10:17–20), perhaps even doing as John the Baptist did with Herod, calling government leaders on the carpet for their immoral behavior and urging them to repent (Mark 6:17–20). In short, the church of Jesus Christ would engage the world in the power of the eschatological kingdom. The theology of Paul also suggests this kind of cultural engagement, contending that as the sin of the first Adam affected the entire human race, the righteousness and redemption of the second Adam would have a universal effect as well, calling into being not simply a new community of persons, but a new creation (2 Cor. 5:17) through a redemption of cosmic proportions (Rom. 8:19–22).

Taking seriously Christ's proclamation that the kingdom had arrived in him, the church, at various points in its history, has understood itself to represent the kingdom of God on earth, seeking to transform society into the image of the kingdom. After Constantine, expectations of a coming kingdom took on new forms that would have been impossible during the centuries of the church's persecution and marginalization before him. Constantine's favor and patronage resulted in a shift in the church's eschatology in the mid-fourth century, moving from an emphasis on the cataclysmic inbreaking of God for judgment and salvation to a more immanent picture of God's salvation within human history. In the works of Eusebius of Caesarea (d. 339), for example, this shift becomes obvious. Eusebius sees God's work of salvation not primarily in the eschaton, but in the establishment of the church as the official religion of the empire. In the church, through his servant Constantine, God has brought the blessings of the eternal kingdom. In Eusebius we see the seeds of eschatology as the Christianization of the world through the church. Brian Daley writes of him,

> As the earthly kingdom takes on, for Eusebius, more and more characteristics of the Kingdom of promise, the future hopes of the church become simply a two-dimensional backdrop for the theatre of human history, where human actors corrupt or realize God's gift of salvation, build Christ's ideal society or hinder its coming. For his de-emphasis of eschatology as well as for his reading of the past, Eusebius has been called with some justice "the first political theologian in the Christian church."[17]

Perhaps a more accurate appraisal of Eusebius is not that he deemphasized eschatology, but that he partially collapsed eschatology into ecclesiology—the hopes of the future become realized in the church and even in the world through the church's work. This perspective takes on monumental significance and influence in perhaps the most important work of theology before the Middle Ages, Augustine's *City of God*.

Augustine, who early on held to a millennialism in the spirit of Irenaeus and others, later rejected that view, opting for a more symbolic interpretation instead. While the kingdom of God in its ultimate form remains future, the kingdom is truly present now in the church. Augustine writes,

> We must understand in one sense the kingdom of heaven in which exist together both he who breaks what he teaches and he who does it, the one being least, the other great, and in another sense the kingdom of heaven into which only he who does what he teaches shall enter. Consequently, where both classes exist, it is the church as it now is, but where only the one shall exist, it is the church as it is destined to be when no wicked person shall be in her. Therefore the church even now is the kingdom of Christ, and the kingdom of heaven.[18]

The millennial kingdom is not to be conceived of as a future earthly reign of Christ, but as the present reign of Christ in the lives of believers who have experienced the resurrection from a life of sin through baptism. This ecclesialization of eschatology played a key role in the tendency for the kingdom to be identified with the Roman church throughout the Middle Ages.

The early church's vision of itself as an eschatological community was largely affected by its status as a marginalized and often persecuted community. Similarly, the ascendancy of the church to a place of social acceptance and power after the conversion of Constantine revolutionized its eschatological vision throughout the Middle Ages and beyond. Simply stated, the massive fact of the Middle Ages is the rise of the church as an institution to a place equal to and sometimes greater than the institution of the state. While the early church could not reasonably hope for an immediate and large-scale change of the culture and society in which it lived, conceiving of itself instead as a refugee community looking for its true home beyond death and hoping for the cataclysmic inbreaking of God to judge the world, the church of the Middle Ages saw itself as an earthly empire. It was God's instrument to bring the kingdom to earth now. Through the political connections of the papacy and, even more importantly, the power of the church to dispense or withhold salvation, even to or from entire countries, the church was able to control legal systems, often making the law of the church the law of the land. This imperial symbiosis between church and state, designed to bring the kingdom of God to earth, was most aptly illustrated in the name of this medieval alliance—the Holy Roman Empire.

As we move from the Middle Ages to the modern period, we find in America another example of the church understanding itself as the kingdom of God on earth. The theology of the kingdom of God in America includes a rich and varied tradition of millennial perspectives ranging from biblical and scholarly approaches to the radical popular millenarianism of dozens of American utopian communities. It is a tradition that sees the development of an American mythos of being "chosen of God" that extends from Cotton Mather's *Magnalia Christi Americana* to Martin Luther King's "I Have a Dream" speech. The variety of perspectives in the American eschatological landscape raises questions similar to those raised in the early and medieval churches—is the kingdom present or future, transcendent or immanent, and what is the relationship of the church to the kingdom of God and to society in terms of engagement vs. disengagement, and optimism vs. pessimism?

In his classic work *Errand into the Wilderness*, historian Perry Miller notes that though some of the early colonists came to America to escape religious persecution in Europe, a major theme in the transcontinental migration was the sense that the settlers were on a divine mission. With God's help they would create a new society with a government that would operate according to the principles of true Christianity and provide for and defend the establishment of the church. John Winthrop led his band of believers to America not with the idea of finding prosperity for the oppressed classes, but to enter into a covenant with God. According to Perry Miller, the Massachusetts Bay Company came to set up a government which would have "at the very beginning of its list of responsibilities, the duty of suppressing heresy, of subduing or somehow getting rid of dissenters—of being in short, deliberately, and consistently intolerant."[19]

The idea was that if people kept their bargain with God, he would prosper American society. The errand into the wilderness was to make America God's "city on a hill" which would be recognized throughout the world. The overriding conviction of these early American settlers was that God would work through the true church in America to reform the world and bring about his kingdom on earth. Historian Ernest Tuveson, commenting on millennial themes in the writings of the early American Puritan Increase Mather, wrote:

> There is the implication that the pioneers of New England were separated out from the pioneer nation of the Reformation to advance that Reformation; as the millennialist doctrine developed, it came to seem "manifest" that this separated community . . . was not only *a* special instrument in God's plan, but *the* agency he had ordained.[20]

In these themes of America as the place of the millennial kingdom and of the church as God's tool for progressively establishing it are revealed a strong American conviction that the kingdom of God is an immanent reality to be developed by the power of God through the historical process. They were taken up and expanded most notably by the colonial era's greatest theologian, Jonathan Edwards, and his disciple, Samuel Hopkins. At the height of the First Great Awakening Edwards spoke in glowing terms about the prospects for the establishment of the millennial kingdom through the church in the near future. In 1742, Edwards wrote:

> 'Tis not unlikely that this work of God's Spirit, that is so extraordinary and wonderful, is the dawning, or at least a prelude, of that glorious work of God, so often foretold in Scripture, which in the progress and issue of it, shall renew the world of mankind . . . And there are many things that make it probable that this work will begin in America.[21]

But by 1747, disappointments began creeping into Edwards's vision. He noted that the church was not continuing to prosper and to reform society at the pace that it had a few years earlier. Edwards shifted from viewing the millennium as an imminent inevitability to seeing it as a future utopian hope.

This note of pessimism reflected a small chink in the armor of the post-millennial optimism of the early Edwards and foreshadows the full-blown pessimism that would characterize American premillennialism in the early twentieth century. What we see here with Edwards, as we saw in the transition from the early church to the church of the Middle Ages, is that the more eschatology is collapsed into ecclesiology, the more likely the church is to engage society with the hope of reforming it. Conversely, the more eschatology becomes separated from the church, the more pessimistic the church becomes about social reform.

In the postmillennialism of colonial America, tempered by the writings of Hopkins and the later Edwards, the kingdom of God was immanent within the historical process.[22] It would not arrive suddenly by the cataclysmic second coming of Christ, but by God's sovereign and gradual work through the church. God had begun a work of reformation in the church in Europe and had brought the pure elements of that church to America to establish a new community that would exemplify and promote the standards of the kingdom of God. Later, this sense of the immanence of the kingdom through the work of the church would be challenged by a growing premillennial perception, conceiving of the kingdom much more in terms of transcendence—as a reality that could never be developed through the church, but only brought suddenly by the power of God at the end of human history.[23]

Throughout its history, the church has best understood the relationship between the church and the kingdom of God when it has maintained the biblical dialectic between the two. In recent decades representatives of the most nondialectical views have become more balanced. In the Roman Catholic Church, the medieval synthesis that virtually collapsed the kingdom into the church has given way to a more moderated approach. Moving beyond the triumphalist perspective of the medieval church, which so closely connected the kingdom with the visible church on earth, Vatican II portrays the church as a pilgrim people, a community already on its way to the future and in possession of the promises of the future in incipient form, yet also one that hopes for the final realization of its identity in the future. The church already possesses a holiness that is real, but incomplete. It is nourished by the real presence of Christ who, by his body and blood, makes the church a partaker in his glorious life.

> The promised and hoped for restoration, therefore, has already begun in Christ. It is carried forward in the sending of the Holy Spirit and through him continues in the church in which, through our faith, we learn the meaning of our earthly

life, while we bring to term, with hope of future good, the task allotted to us in
the world by the Father, and so work out our salvation.[24]

On the other end of the spectrum, the traditional dispensational premillennialism of the first half of the twentieth century in American theology has
given way to what proponents call "progressive dispensationalism," a view
that maintains a clear separation between church and kingdom but has come
to understand that the kingdom has indeed been inaugurated in Christ, Christians are members of the kingdom now, and that the power of the kingdom
is manifest in the church.[25]

## The Function of the Eschatological Church in Relation to the Kingdom

Given the dialectical relationship between the church and the eschatological
kingdom, the church must ask, What, then is the function of the church vis-
à-vis the kingdom of God? Beyond embracing the values of the kingdom for
its own existence, how does the church conceive of its role in living out the
values and the demands of the kingdom in the world? The following categories
suggest several ways in which the church should understand its eschatological
function.

### The Church Is the Doorway to the Kingdom

First, the church is the doorway to the kingdom. This connection is, perhaps,
most clearly attested in Jesus's response to Peter's confession in Matthew 16
and Luke 9. In Matthew, Peter confesses Jesus not only as Messiah, but also
as the royal Son of King YHWH. Jesus responds that he will build his church
upon Peter (and the other apostles), who recognize him as Messiah/King. And
all those who follow the disciples in this confession, becoming members of the
church, also find entrance into the kingdom. The church does not exist as an
individual entity, unrelated to the arrival of the kingdom, but as the doorway
to the kingdom. The leaders and members are given the keys to open the door
of the kingdom to all who enter the "doors" of the church. For on the Day
of Pentecost, Peter contends that entrance into the new community of Christ
followers means entrance into the community of the promised kingdom (Acts
2:14–39).

Early in the life of the church, its leaders began to discuss the idea that
to enjoy the blessings of the kingdom, one must be a member of the church,
the community of the King. In his *On the Unity of the Church*, Cyprian of
Carthage (d. 258) teaches that the church is the only way to eternal blessings.
Those who separate themselves from the church, even if they have confessed
the true faith under the threat of death, cannot receive the blessings of heaven.

Speaking even of those martyred for the faith who are, nevertheless, outside the unity of the church, Cyprian contends:

> What peace, then, do the enemies of the brethren promise to themselves? What sacrifices do those who are rivals of the priests think that they celebrate? Do they deem that they have Christ with them when they are collected together, who are gathered together outside the church of Christ? Even if such men were slain in confession of the Name, that stain is not even washed away by blood: the inexpiable and grave fault of discord is not even purged by suffering. He cannot be a martyr who is not in the church; he cannot attain unto the kingdom who forsakes that which shall reign there.[26]

Thus, for Cyprian, there is no access to the kingdom of God for those who are outside the one church, even if they have confessed Christ. Here we see the beginnings of the idea that the church, as an institution, unified by a specific and recognized group of bishops, is the one and only doorway to the salvation that awaits the faithful beyond this life. This connection between the church and the salvation of the kingdom would come to full flower in the Roman Catholic Church of the Middle Ages.

In spite of the problems inherent in this medieval institutionalization of the church,[27] recognized by Catholic theologians as well as Protestant,[28] it is nevertheless important to recognize the importance of its emphasis on the communitarian nature of the church in light of its eschatological identity. As the eschatology of the early church held it together in the face of persecution, so the institutionalized eschatology of the medieval church never let people forget that the security and enticements of worldly power could not bring them into the kingdom of God—only membership in the church could do that.

One of the benefits of the Roman Catholic view is its focus on the idea that eschatological salvation begins by membership in the eschatological community. To say it another way, a biblical theology of salvation argues that salvation creates a community, "a people for God's own possession," not just saved individuals. In contrast to the Catholic emphasis on membership in the eschatological community in order to enjoy the blessings of the kingdom, modern Protestant evangelicals have tended to focus on the message of Jesus as the doorway to eschatological salvation. Protestants generally have opted for the view popularized by John Calvin that the church is primarily understood as the community of all persons everywhere who have faith in Christ, visible only to God since they are not gathered in any one church or denomination.[29] One of the dangers of disconnecting one's enjoyment of the blessings of the kingdom from one's membership in the visible church is a tendency to conceive of salvation in terms of one's personal relationship with Jesus apart from the church which keeps us from seeing salvation as ultimately communal.

To be a citizen of the kingdom of God comes through personal connection with the King himself. And to be fully connected to the King is to be connected to his body, the church. For many of the blessings of the kingdom are experienced only through the grace dispensed by God to the members of that community to be shared with one another.[30] The church is the doorway to the kingdom.

### The Church Bears Witness to the Kingdom

Second, the church bears witness to the kingdom. The book of Acts makes it clear that the apostolic church understood one of its fundamental functions to be that of being a witness to the kingdom of God. Indeed, in his last words to the disciples at his ascension, Jesus emphasizes this task. In a passage laden with kingdom expectations (Acts 1:3–8), Jesus proclaims that the disciples will be witnesses to Messiah/King Jesus, to whom all authority has been given (Matt. 28:19). For these disciples, to be Christ's witnesses was to be witnesses of the kingdom. Later we see Philip preaching the good news of the kingdom in Samaria (Acts 8:12). Finally, Paul becomes the preacher of the kingdom of God to the Gentiles (Acts 19:8; 20:25; 28:23, 31). What all this means is that when the church proclaims Christ in the world, it is not simply pointing people to him, as if the message of the gospel were fully expressed in calling people to embrace Christ individually. In proclaiming the kingdom, the church points to Christ as king over an eschatological community, calling upon all persons to believe in Christ, thus becoming members of the community that celebrates his kingship now, living under his kingly authority until his rule is finally a de facto reality over all creation. Moreover, the church becomes a living witness to the kingdom by living out its values in community. Biblical scholar George Eldon Ladd writes,

> If Jesus' disciples are those who have received the life and fellowship of the Kingdom, and if this life is in fact an anticipation of the eschatological Kingdom, then it follows that one of the main tasks of the church is to display in this present evil age the life and fellowship of the age to come.[31]

Throughout the church's history, the way it bears witness to the kingdom is always a function of its view of how closely church and kingdom are related. For example, dispensationalism's emphasis on eschatological futurism led to a general tendency toward the rejection of human culture as both a morally declining and irremediable entity, one that would play no part at all in the establishment of the kingdom of God. G. L. Alrich, in the popular periodical *Our Hope*, argued that since the world was obviously in moral decline, and since the kingdom of God would come only by supernatural means, there is no reason to try to reform society. "Remember that the very things you are so entangled with today, and the world which you are trying to make better by reform and education, etc., is under the curse of God for the murder of His son; and is doomed."[32]

For classic dispensationalists, the rejection of society as a reality that could be reformed or could participate in the establishment of the kingdom of God was clear. Yet this conviction did not mean that they believed that the church should never do the work of God in society. On the contrary, they were aggressively involved in society, both in America and overseas, primarily through mission work that focused on evangelism. But they did not typically focus on projects that aimed at improving the life of people in this world.[33]

Despair of cultural reform also led to a very narrow view of the church's witness. If there was no hope for this world, then the only world worth working for was the world to come, the entrance requirement for which was belief in Jesus. Thus, the *entire work* of the church in the world was evangelism. As J. E. Conant remarked,

> It is perfectly clear, therefore, that the church is not commissioned to convert the world, nor to educate it, nor to civilize it, nor help solve its economic problems, nor to Christianize its social order, and certainly take no part in governing it. She is simply to "preach the gospel to every creature," nothing else, nothing less, that whosoever is willing to believe the "good news" may experience the power of God unto salvation and transformation.[34]

Thus we see in dispensationalism a radical millennialist movement, extreme in its transcendent perspective of the entirely future kingdom and in its subsequent loss of hope in and disengagement from society. The important point in all of this is to see that how the church understands its relationship to eschatology, to the kingdom of God, has a significant effect on how it understands its relationship to the culture in which it exists. To depart from the dialectic of the scriptures and to opt instead for a view of the kingdom as either radically present or radically future will always affect negatively the church's ability to bear witness faithfully to the kingdom. When the church works to live in the tension of the dialectic of the now and not yet, it will always be a more faithful witness.

Echoing the dialectic of Luther's two-kingdom theory,[35] Lutheran theologian Phillip Hefner contends that the church is "transparent to the kingdom" and thus intimately related to it.[36] While it can only point to the future finality of the kingdom, nevertheless the church is the community where God intends to actualize his meanings and intentions for human creation. Because the church is symbolic of God's ultimate future, it is never an end in itself. God's future has not totally arrived in the church, nor can the church completely reform the world to bring it into conformity with God's vision. The church is accountable "to embody signals of what God is about in the world." Thus, the church is responsible for representing to the world the redemptive purposes of God, ultimately manifest in the future kingdom. So this relationship to the kingdom speaks both to what the church is and to what it must become. "Its structures, its message, its liturgy and communal life, and its outreach must always be reformed toward greater conformity with the intentions of God for the world . . . The hope of the church points to the day when it will indeed not pass away but will be transfigured in God's own work of consummation."[37]

As a representative of the Reformed tradition, Donald Bloesch argues that the church is not only the anticipatory sign of the coming kingdom, but the "springboard and vanguard" of the kingdom. The kingdom is the creative and redeeming force of God's Word and Spirit creating a new humanity in the church. The kingdom's presence in the church brings moral regeneration that reorders human relationships. The church, then, is the community in which the kingly rule of God is made visible and becomes a conduit of the power of the kingdom in its preaching and ministry, both to itself and to the world. It is, then, a visible means of grace.

For Bloesch, human history is the arena in which the kingdom is manifest, but the kingdom does not arise from history, coming instead from above to create a community where the rule of Christ as Lord is manifest in the church, as it will one day be over all of creation. It does not bring about the gradual Christianization of history. The church relates to the kingdom both as church militant and church triumphant. In an earthly millennium the church militant will reclaim a world that has lost its way. In the eternal kingdom, the whole of human creation will be made up of the church triumphant, where sin, death, and the devil are finally done away with. In the present age, the victories of the church triumphant become real in the midst of the church's existence in the fallen world. Thus, the kingdom takes root in the church, not by human progress, but by Word and Spirit.[38]

So, in bearing witness to the kingdom, the church receives by grace the transforming blessings of the kingdom of God, becoming a community that lives under the kingship of Christ, who begins the work of transforming a broken and sinful people into a "holy nation" (1 Pet. 2:9–10). This pilgrim community on the road of transformation seeks both to live out the values of the kingdom in its own relationships and to call to those outside to join in experiencing the redemption and transformation offered by Christ.

### The Church Is the Instrument of the Kingdom

Finally, the church is the instrument of the kingdom of God. By this we mean simply that the church not only points to the kingdom (witness) and opens the door to the kingdom (doorway) but also brings the blessings of the kingdom, not only to its own members, but to the world as well. What we see in the Gospel narratives before the founding of the church at Pentecost is that the powers of the kingdom are essentially limited to Jesus. Those who hear the gospel hear it from Jesus. Those who experience healing are healed by Jesus. Of course, we do find limited instances (i.e., the commissioning of the twelve in Matt. 10 and of the seventy-two in Luke 10) where the disciples are given authority to extend the power and blessings of the kingdom to the world in the absence of Jesus. But these seem to be preludes to the future authority Jesus gives to the church (Matt. 16), rather than a paradigmatic role for the disciples while Jesus was still with them. After Pentecost, however, everything changes in this regard. The resurrected Jesus returns to his disciples through the personal agency of the Holy Spirit (John 14:15–21), bringing to the world not only the kingdom's good news of the forgiveness of sin, but even the kingdom's miraculous healing power. As the disciples preach, the sick are made well and demons are cast out. Moreover, what was experienced by only a few, the blessing of being in the presence of Jesus, is now experienced by the entire church, where Christ's presence is revealed in the person of the Holy Spirit. The person of Christ, previously incarnate to reveal God and his blessings only in Jesus of Nazareth, is now incarnate in the members of the church, dwelling in them through the Holy Spirit so that they might extend his presence and blessings to one another and to the world.

Of all the early material that focuses on the eschatological nature of the church, one source that relates particularly to this chapter's image of the church drawing the future into the present and becoming the instrument of the kingdom in human culture is Gregory of Nyssa's fourth homily on the Book of Ecclesiastes.[39] At a time when no one, not even in the church, was arguing against the practice of slavery, Gregory argues, on the basis of his eschatology, that the church should reject slavery entirely. Commenting on Christian eschatology in general and of Gregory in particular, David Hart argues that the kingdom of God is a future reality that

> comes suddenly, like a thief in the night, and so fulfills no immanent process . . .
> Only thus will it complete all things. At the same time, the Kingdom has already, at Easter, been made visible within history and now impends upon each moment, a work of judgment falling across all our immanent truths of power, privilege, or destiny.[40]

To make a long and complicated argument simple, God created all of humanity with an ideal in mind, which has been broken by the fall. In the incarnation, Christ takes on this broken humanity, redirecting it toward its ideal and transcendent end. But until that end becomes a reality, the church as the mystical body of Christ is the visible form of redeemed humanity. As God's vision of humanity is one where its slavery to sin and death is overcome, so slavery to political or social powers must also be overcome. Thus, the community of the redeemed becomes the community in which the social powers which divide Jew and Gentile, slave and free, man and woman, are to be rejected. And because Christ takes on himself the whole of humanity, the condemnation of slavery must be heralded not only in the church, but also by the church in the world. Here we have a powerful demonstration of the role of eschatology in shaping the identity and mission of the church and a principle that we will come back to in chapter 5.

Simply stated, the eschatological nature of the church argues for its involvement in the issues of society, calling it both to realize the values of the kingdom (human dignity, brotherhood, and freedom) in its own existence and to bring them to the world outside the church as well. God's eschatological promise of justice and peace means the church should work to establish these realities on earth now. Paul's vision of the future healing of earth and humanity in ways that go beyond spiritual regeneration (Rom. 8; 15) means that the church should work for the healing of earth and humanity now in ways that go beyond evangelism. And when the church helps to bring justice, peace, and healing to a broken world, it is a good and godly thing, a true act of the church's role as instrument of the kingdom of God, even if overt evangelism does not take place.

## Characteristics of the Eschatological Church

We have seen that the nature of the eschatological church is that it is both a community waiting for the kingdom and the presence of the kingdom of God on earth. As such, its function is to be the doorway to the kingdom, to bear witness to the kingdom, and to be the instrument of the kingdom. What, then, does this community look like? What are the characteristics of a community that lives out in the present the hopes of its future? To these questions we dedicate the rest of the chapter.

### A Community of Restored Relationships

First and foremost, the biblical story of God's relationship to humanity is a story about relationship and community. Shortly after the beginning of that story, after the rebellion of Adam and Eve, it becomes one of transformed relationship. For humanity's relationship with God has been broken, affecting all of creation. But God is undeterred, immediately committing himself to remedying the disaster, not only restoring the relationships of creation to their rightful place, but even taking them further, to a place Adam and Eve could never have imagined.

The idea of a "people of God" begins not with the promise of the formation of a nation to come from the seed of Abraham, but with the creation of the very first human beings. As we have already seen in chapter 1, the trinitarian God, existing eternally in relationship as Father, Son and Holy Spirit, created Adam and Eve as a community of persons. The thrust of the original story of creation leads the reader to wonder at the emptiness of Adam's life, devoid of the kind of communitarian experience present even for the animals. For while he is in relationship with God, he can only ponder and celebrate that relationship by himself, like a lover of Renaissance art trying to celebrate Michelangelo's David in a museum devoid of other people. The story tells us that Adam was never meant to be alone, but to be in relationship with God through being in relationship with others. This tightly woven integration of relationships between God and creation is illustrated by the fact that when Adam sins, wounding his relationship with God, his relationship with Eve is wounded also, as well as both of their relationships with the rest of creation. Thus, the experience of finding healing community as a member of the "people of God" also becomes a means of finding God. God's eschatological promise to heal the relationships broken by sin begins here in Genesis 3:15. Through the seed of Eve, he will crush Satan, rebuild human community, and restore humanity to life in union with him and in harmony with nature, finally delivering them from death. Moreover, the story of Adam and Eve's banishment from the Garden and its Tree of Life looks forward in the narrative, not to a restoration of the status quo of the Garden, but to the City of God where, once again, we find the Tree of Life and humanity face-to-face with the living God (Rev. 21–22).

In chapter 5 of Ephesians, Paul's image of the church as the bride of Christ, illustrating the union between Christ and the church, is also eschatological, imagining an ultimate healing of relationships and drawing that healing back into the present. The "already" is seen in the fact that Christ is now head of the church, having given himself for it and having made it holy through the washing away of its sin. Nevertheless, the marriage has "not yet" been fully consummated. The text looks forward to a day when Christ will present the church to himself as a fully sanctified bride. For Paul, union with Christ is never merely an individual union, but also a corporate one. As believers are one with Christ, so they are one with each other. Together they make up the one "person" of the bride. As always, with this image, Paul moves beyond abstract theological concepts to ethical ramifications. The believer's union with Christ, which also involves union with other believers, revolutionizes the relational structures of a fallen world, bringing healing to human relationships. Wives, treated as property by their husbands and shut out from most public functions in the ancient world, are to be cherished by husbands willing to give their own lives for the benefit of their wives.[41] Similarly, the structures of parent/child and master/slave as conceived of in the ancient world are also transformed. Parents are to nurture their children rather than merely to demand submission, and masters are to remember that the same Christ is Lord of both master and slave and does not follow the discriminating patterns of culture in his relationships with human beings. The crux of the eschatological focus here is that part of looking forward to the finalization of the marriage between Christ and the church is the transformation of human relationships, anticipating the ultimate reality of oneness in Christ in opposition to the relational structures of a fallen world.

Finally, scripture envisions an ultimate healing of creation, both in its own brokenness and in its broken relationship with humanity. The fall disrupted not only the God/human and human/human relationship, but also the human/creation relationship. Adam and Eve could no longer function as ideal stewards of the earth in a fallen creation (Gen. 3). The Bible's vision of ultimate salvation is not merely spiritual, but actually quite earthy. Isaiah envisions a creation of amazing productivity and harmony. Paul imagines the groan of a broken creation turning into praise at the second coming of Christ. And John sees in the new heaven and new earth a universe of pristine beauty, perfection, and peace. If then, the church is meant to draw its future back into the present, this has significant ramifications for the church's relationship with creation. The church is called to be an advocate for the healing of a broken environment in anticipation of its ultimate healing, transforming the human relationship to creation from one that is often adversarial and utilitarian to one that is supportive and protective. This is a significant ramification regarding restored community, to which we will give more attention in chapter 4.

### A Community of the Messiah

Old Testament scholar Walter Kaiser, among others, has identified the tripartite promise of the OT as "I will be their God, they will be my people, and I will dwell in their midst."[42] There is a progressive realization of this promise in part throughout the story. But there is also always the sense that the promise of a people for God's own possession and presence is still a future hope. Genesis 12 looks to the fulfillment of the promise through the formation of Israel but also recognizes that the fulfillment will not be complete until the Gentile nations are included. Chapter after chapter, as the descendents of Israel become the people of God, led by a great leader who takes them to the very edge of the fearful presence of God, we see that even the formation of this great people and its man of God is still anticipatory. For the Pentateuch concludes (Deut. 18) with the promise of another prophet, another Moses to come who will be the ultimate leader of God's nation, speaking the very words of God to them. What we have in the Pentateuch, then, is a fulfillment of God's eschatological promise to create a people for himself. Yet even their entrance into the land and their acquisition of a king does not fulfill their identity and mission. They still look forward both to a new prophet/priest/king and to the salvation of the nations. They are an eschatological people.

At its very outset, the New Testament picks up this theme of the formation of a messianic community. At the heart of Matthew's Gospel is a desire to demonstrate to his Jewish audience that Jesus is the promised eschatological leader of God's renewed and perfected people. A striking example of this is seen in his depiction of the baby Jesus returning from Egypt. The story is cast in the context of Hosea's comments about Israel coming out of slavery in Egypt to become the people of YHWH led by him into the Promised Land. Jesus here stands for the new Israel, the people of God—he is their representative. Thus, the people he will lead will not only be connected historically to the Mosaic community, anticipating entrance into the Promised Land, but also a new community, led by the new Moses toward a new Promised Land, the one envisioned by the prophets.

In the Passion narratives the messianic nature of the church is also illustrated through a messianic meal. In the last supper we have the eschatological meal of the people of God in anticipation of its final meal at the wedding of the Bride to Christ.[43] As the final meal is the wedding meal of the sacrificed and risen Lamb (Rev. 19:9), so this meal is the betrothal/covenant meal of the about-to-be-sacrificed Lamb who, in his self-sacrifice, fulfills his commitment to the Father, earning the right to take the bride for himself on a future wedding day. He eats with his disciples, representatives of the entire community of the church. It is the meal of the new covenant. It is the meal of forgiveness, a distinctive of the age to come. It is the meal that both realizes the arrival of the kingdom in Christ and anticipates the church's ultimate fellowship with him in the kingdom to come (Christ will not drink the cup of the covenant again until he drinks it with the church in his father's kingdom). And, in the theology of Paul, it becomes the meal of remembrance of Christ's death and resurrection, in celebration of his presence in the church, and in anticipation of his coming again (1 Cor. 11). The point here is that this foundational celebration of the church is an eschatological celebration, recognizing both Christ's presence now and hoping in his future coming. Thus, the future coming Christ is brought into the present life of the church through the eucharistic meal.

For Paul, the man who could not possibly be the Messiah, having been crucified by Romans, has been shown by his resurrection to be both Lord and Christ (Rom. 1–4). And the church is a community of persons who have been transferred from one kingdom to another, from the kingdom of darkness to the kingdom of his Son, Christ, the Anointed One, or Messiah (Col. 1:12–13). It is the community over which Christ now reigns as head (Col. 1:18) and in which he reveals himself through Word and Spirit, bringing the promise of messianic redemption.

The church is a messianic community. In it God has begun the promise to dwell with his people. The church is no mere community that teaches truth about God, but one which celebrates his very presence. Wherever the church gathers, it experiences the authentic presence of the Messiah, not just hearing about him, but worshipping, loving, and submitting to him personally as he dwells in their midst in anticipation of his visible, touchable presence at the end of the age.

### A Community of the Holy Spirit

In Acts 2, the eschatological promise of the Holy Spirit (Joel 2) is fulfilled as the new community created by the Holy Spirit at Pentecost begins to display some of the characteristics expected by the prophets. Wonders and signs are performed by the apostles (Acts 2:42–48), validating the kingdom nature of the church in the same way that Jesus validated his own status as the one who brought the kingdom (Matt. 4; Luke 7; etc.). In Acts 6 we see how leadership becomes fundamentally a matter of those who are filled with the Holy Spirit and wisdom, not of being a member of a priestly caste.

This eschatological promise of the Holy Spirit figures prominently in Paul's ecclesiology as well. For the promised redemption has already begun for the church as it experiences righteousness, peace, and joy in the Holy Spirit (Rom. 14:17). While the church is founded upon Jesus Christ, the power to live according to the kingdom is made possible because its life is "in the Spirit" (Rom. 8). Moreover, God's love has been poured into the hearts of believers (Rom. 5) by the Holy Spirit, turning hardened, rebellious hearts, which could not be transformed by the law, into those that desire God more than all things (cf. Ezek. 36). This community of the Spirit not only experiences this heart-transforming "justification" (Rom. 8:1ff) but, in Paul's words, has also already been glorified (Rom. 8:30). Thus, the eschatological is drawn into the present in the life of the church. Moreover, Paul's temple imagery for the church (1 Cor. 3, for example) harks back to Ezekiel's eschatological imagery of the return of the Spirit to the temple of YHWH. Here, believers filled individually with the Spirit come together to create the eschatological corporate temple of YHWH, which is the body of Christ.

Irenaeus also sees the initiation of the blessings of the eschaton as present in the church through the Spirit, contending that "where the church is, there is the Spirit of God; and where the Spirit of God is, there is the church, and every kind of grace . . . Those, therefore, who do not partake of Him, are neither nourished into life from the mother's breasts, nor do they enjoy that most limpid fountain which issues from the body of Christ."[44] Here, the eschatological promise of the Holy Spirit is realized in the church in anticipation of the full realization of the age to come.

As a mystical communion through union with Christ through the Holy Spirit, the church is a social reality that continues in heaven. Thus, the church in its present state is not merely a promise or a pledge of the heavenly church, but an anticipation of it. The eschatological gift of the Holy Spirit is already poured out on the church. The sacraments demonstrate that the kingdom is mysteriously present now in the church. They are signs that point to the future, but more than that, they indicate its presence in the church now. The Vatican II document *Lumen Gentium* expresses it this way:

> It is especially in the sacred liturgy that our union with the heavenly church is best realized; in the liturgy, through the sacramental signs, the power of the Holy Spirit acts on us, and with community rejoicing we celebrate together the praise of the divine majesty, when all those of every tribe and tongue and people and nation who have been redeemed by the blood of Christ and gather together into one church glorify, in one common song of praise, the one and triune God.[45]

Combined with this sacramental view of the presence of the Holy Spirit should be a Word-centered view. Theologian Karl Barth contends that when the Word is preached it is actually an eschatological event, because it is God himself who is being revealed in the preaching.[46] For when God reveals himself to his people, he never does it simply by communicating concepts, truths about himself. Rather, he always reveals himself relationally. He engages us with the Word, both written and incarnate, through the relational ministry of the Holy Spirit as the Spirit of truth (John 14). Further, Paul tells us that the wisdom of God expressed in his Word can only be fully embraced by those who have been transformed by the Spirit (1 Cor. 2:6–16). And only those who encounter the Holy Spirit find the freedom to recognize Christ as the fulfillment of the eschatological promise and to be gradually transformed into his image (2 Cor. 3:12–18).

The upshot of all this is that God, in the person of Christ, through the ministry of the Holy Spirit, is personally and relationally present with his people when they gather as the church. As they worship together they are filled with the Holy Spirit (Eph. 5:18–21), who begins to transform them into a community that not only submits to Christ, but even to one another out of love for Christ. Without the Holy Spirit, the church is a lost cause. For, created by a relational God, we can become the community where God is healing the brokenness of this world only if we can encounter God personally. The person of the Holy Spirit, present to the church through the now and not-yet reality of the kingdom, encounters us in the church when we gather, drawing our minds, hearts, and bodies into deeper relationship with God in anticipation of the day when we will be like him as we see him face-to-face. Then this eschatological community, empowered by the Spirit, begins to live in new ways.

### A Community of Social Righteousness

From the fall onward, the biblical narrative is concerned with restoring humanity to a place of righteousness, both personally and socially. Individual humans are crippled by unrighteousness that comes in the form of rebellion against God, a rebellion consisting of both sinful behavior and hearts at odds with God. But humanity is also unrighteous socially. Personal unrighteousness manifests itself in the animosity of persons toward each other and in the creation of barriers and prejudices based on personal and social distinctions.

Thus, the biblical theology of righteousness is, at its core, about relationship. Individually, it is about the restoration of one's broken relationship with God. It is, as theologians commonly say, a right relationship with God, provided by God. This personal righteousness, then, forms the basis of social righteousness. As individuals grow in the rightness of their relationships with God, they should also grow in the rightness of their relationships with one another. Thus, biblical eschatology envisions a future community of social righteousness. Since the theology of personal righteousness is more properly addressed by soteriology, the theology of salvation, we will here address mainly the concept of social righteousness, addressing personal righteousness primarily as a transformation that leads to social righteousness.

Nowhere in the Hebrew Scriptures is the concept of social righteousness more clearly addressed than in the Prophets. The ethos of the prophetic literature of the Bible is one that fundamentally looks both to the present and to the future. The prophets, usually speaking during a time of Israel's suffering or disobedience, look forward to a time of the coming of God both to judge his people and to save them, to the coming of a great Messiah/King who will establish the kingdom of God in righteousness and peace. This future salvation image is not depicted in terms of individuals, but of a nation, a people bound together by obedience to the king and the worship of God. Thus, for suffering and broken Israel, its own self-understanding is always at least partly a function of its hope that God will one day come and make all things right for his chosen community. Nevertheless, the prophets do not intend these images of the future simply to create a hope that things will one day be better. Indeed, they present these images as part of a call to the people of God to begin to conform now to the image of their future.

In his extended imagery of God's glorious future for Israel, Isaiah looks forward (chs. 60–66) to a restored community, the people of God inhabiting a place that is both a new creation and a renewed one. It will be a community of peace, prosperity, and righteousness, where God will be present to delight in his people. Jeremiah envisions a community of people whose hearts are transformed such that knowing God and obeying him is not a matter of the external compulsion of the law, but the ready response of a transformed mind through the new covenant (chs. 30–31). Ezekiel sees the departure of the glory of God from the temple and looks to a time when his glory will return and God's people will worship him in righteousness. Thus, the eschatological anticipates a community of worship. Moreover, in his vision of the valley of dry bones, Ezekiel imagines a people returned from exile and living in the land of God who dwells in their midst in the person of the Spirit. Malachi 3–4 looks to a day when YHWH himself will come in the person of his messenger of the covenant, both to judge and to reclaim for himself a nation that worships him in righteousness, a kingdom of healing, joy, and perfect community. But for all these prophets, painting a glorious picture of the future of the people of God also includes an admonition of drawing that future into the present. Isaiah calls for the people to seek justice and care for the poor now (cf. chs. 58–59), and to worship God in integrity and righteousness (61:10–11). Jeremiah, already having foretold the exile and future glorious restoration of Israel, calls upon those who survived the destruction of the city to remain there and live in obedience to YHWH (ch. 42), so that he could bring restoration to them in the present in anticipation of future glorious restoration.

This motif is continued in the Sermon on the Mount. Jesus the new Moses preaches the fulfillment of the law by his giving of a new law, the law of the transformed heart. This is the ethics of the kingdom, the ethics of the eschatological people of God, who will know and follow God's law from their hearts (Jer. 31). This righteousness of the kingdom is not meant only for individuals; it is to be lived out in community as well. Those who hunger and thirst for, and then are filled with, righteousness, will respond by being merciful, and by being peacemakers (Matt. 5:6–9). They will mend relationships with one another before offering sacrifices to God (5:23–24).[47] They will remain faithful in their marriages (5:27–32), true to their promises (5:33–37), say "no" to revenge (5:38–39), give sacrificially to those in need (5:40–41), and love their enemies. It is to this eschatological vision of community that Jesus calls his followers. Yet it is a community reality that the disciples seemed not to fully grasp until the arrival of the Holy Spirit to transform their hearts and, subsequently, their social barriers and prejudices.

Indeed, the church of Acts begins to break down barriers that were meant to be broken down by the eschaton. Gentiles, included in the promise to Abraham and envisioned by the prophets (Gen. 12; Isa. 49:6, 22; Hos. 1:10; Zech. 2:10–11; etc.) as part of the kingdom community, are embraced by the church. Women, upon whom Joel declares the Spirit of prophecy will fall in the last days, are included in the leadership of this new community. And the needs of the poor are met by the sacrifice of wealthier members. Thus, the people of God, heretofore embodied in a hierarchical, monoethnic, national community, begins to look like the images of its ultimate status as a community made up of people from every tongue, tribe, gender, and socioeconomic status.[48]

Paul also pictures the church as a community of social righteousness. In Galatians, this eschatological community is one that, like the Israel of the exodus, was created through God's mighty work to free people from bondage. At one time, Paul says, the whole world was a prisoner of sin. Then, as a result of legalism, the Jewish community was a prisoner of the law. Now, there is one new community of promise, where all are sons of God by faith, a transformation that Paul says makes us free (Rom. 8:21). But for Paul, this new freedom is not merely individual; it is not merely the freedom from sin and guilt experienced by the individual believer. It is a freedom created by the promised Holy Spirit that results in love of neighbor (Gal. 5:13–15). It is also a community freedom, in which social structures such as Jew/Gentile, slave/

free, and man/woman are transformed (3:28). Galatians 3:28 is a highly debated passage in which some commentators see only the idea that individual persons, no matter what segment of society they come from, are equally saved by faith in Jesus Christ. We contend that while this is certainly true, it does not take the passage far enough. Paul does not say here, "You are all individually saved through faith in Christ." Rather, he argues that "you are all one in Christ Jesus." Moreover, since it is unlikely that Paul or any of his readers would have thought that Greeks, slaves, and women could not be saved, his intention must go beyond individual salvation to social transformation.

This is a passage about how the gospel not only frees individuals from the bondage of sin and law, but also creates a new community, free from destructive social structures such as racism, slavery, and gender discrimination. It is Paul's fundamental proclamation about the eschatological nature of the structure of the church. In Christ, believers are being brought together by the Holy Spirit to become the eschatological temple of YHWH, relating to each other not as master/slave, Jew/Gentile, or even husband/wife, but as equal members of "God's household" (Gal. 2:19), siblings in the "family of believers" (Eph. 6:10). Thus, believers are called to create a community that breaks down social barriers, anticipating a future people of God where all segments of humanity have not only equal access to God, but also equal places of worship and service in his kingdom,[49] a community imagined by John's revelation in which nationalities and social distinctions are not abolished but are simply no longer a source of separation and animosity, rather of celebration and richness. Similarly, in his discussions about faith and righteousness, James admonishes the church for favoring the rich and degrading the poor, and for fostering dissension among believers (James 2:1–7; 4:5–5:6). For him, the claim of individual righteousness is dubious in the absence of community righteousness.

It is to this vision of social righteousness that the church is called today in anticipation of its final perfect community experience. Improper social barriers and prejudices based on race, class, gender, wealth, age, etc., must be recognized and rejected. Personal righteousness must lead to social righteousness. How sad it is when secular institutions, knowing nothing of the grace and mercy of God, do a better job of removing these barriers than does the church.

### A Community Where Satan Is Disarmed

Finally, in any discussion of the characteristics of the church as an eschatological community, we would be remiss if we did not discuss the disarming of Satan. From the first mention of an eschatological promise to redeem the fallen world, God looks forward to the crushing of Satan's head (Gen. 3:15). As Satan was instrumental in the derailing of God's plan for perfect relationship with his creation, so the destruction of Satan must be part of the resolution of the problem.

While the writers of the Hebrew Scriptures are aware of Satan as an adversary (the fall, the prologue to Job, David's numbering of Israel, etc.), it is not until we get to the New Testament that we begin to see God's plan to confront and finally vanquish Satan. Moreover, it is in the church and for the church that Satan will be disarmed. In Jesus's desert battle with Satan (Matt. 4), we find an interesting indication of the eschatological nature of Jesus's mission and foundation of the church. Much modern preaching and commentary on this event sees in it an example of how Christians should battle Satan. While the passage may be valuable for that subject, it is not Matthew's main interest. Irenaeus captured what is surely the more important motif.[50] This scene is a Garden of Eden redux, where Jesus represents his people, with whom he has just identified himself in baptism, defeating Satan on our behalf in anticipation of the complete defeat of Satan in the resurrection and second coming. Here, Jesus begins the fulfillment of the promise of Genesis 3:15, initiating the crushing of Satan's head, which will continue through the crucifixion, resurrection, and finally, Christ's victorious second coming. It is this eschatological leader who gives his people the keys to the kingdom of God, empowering them to follow his lead, challenging and defeating the power of Satan in the church, even through the brokenness of a fallen world, until he meets his final destiny at the hands of the victorious Christ (Rev. 19–20).

Further, one of the meanings of Jesus's casting out of demons (Matt. 12) is to demonstrate the presence of the Holy Spirit and, thus, of the kingdom of God. This power to face, reject, and cast out Satan was then given by Christ to the church through the Holy Spirit. So as the apostles cast out demons in the church, God is working through them to validate that this new community is indeed the community of the kingdom, the community against which the gates of Hades would not prevail (Matt. 16:18).

For Paul, the church is the eschatological community that witnesses to the rulers in high places regarding Christ's victory over them, assuring the demonic realities of their ultimate defeat. For Christ's eschatological disarmament of the "powers" (Col. 2:15) is demonstrated in the victorious life of the saints. As the church engages in battle against demonic forces, it employs the weapons of the eschatological community (faith, truth, righteousness, gospel, salvation—Eph. 3 and 6), through the power of the eschatological Spirit, waging war in anticipation of Christ's final victory.[51]

This sense of the disarming of Satan was retained in the early church. In his sermon to the catechumens who were being baptized, Cyril of Jerusalem (c. 315–386) comments on their act of stepping into the water, facing west, verbally rejecting Satan and all of his pomp and all of his ways, then turning east to embrace Christ as Lord. In his death, burial, and resurrection, represented by baptism, Christ had vanquished Satan. And although he still roamed the earth like a roaring lion seeking to kill, his power was broken in the church. There, he had been declawed.[52]

While Satan remains active, and while the church remains the object of his fury and a target for his destructive efforts, as it walks in the power of the Spirit, the church need not fear Satan or be captive to either his deception or his power. And at every time and place that the church gathers, it can rejoice that its future is secure despite all of Satan's attacks, for by his death, Christ has secured the destruction of him who has the power of death (Heb. 2:14).

## Conclusion

We have seen that the church is an eschatological community, fully engaged in the present through its identity as God's community of the future. How, then, does this perspective help the church better understand its identity and mission? Following are several suggestions, the first being general and the rest more specific:

(1) The church should work to understand the values and structures of its eschatological identity as revealed in the scriptures and as best understood by the church's historical traditions. These values and structures should then be drawn back into the life of the local church as its leaders construct statements on the church's purposes, values, and mission.

(2) If the church seeks to build a community in the present that resembles the community of its future, this means, in part, that the church must be a community for the whole human family, a place where people of every race, every socioeconomic status, male and female, adults and children come before God on an equal footing as servants of Jesus Christ. While there are other important images of the church's future, this community image is one the church has done little to fulfill, historically speaking. Often, secular institutions are more reflective of this biblical image than the church is.

(3) The church should live in constant hope of its future redemption at the return of Christ. As such, the church must be wary of placing ultimate value on things that are temporal. In the prosperous West, this means that the church must constantly be wary of consumerism.

(4) Because eschatological images are communal rather than individual, the church should value ministries that build community over those that cater to individual interests.

(5) Because it is the instrument of the coming kingdom, the church should work to bring the values of the kingdom to the world. This means going beyond verbal proclamation to social action. It also means going beyond bringing the values of the kingdom to individuals, expanding the work of the church to encourage kingdom values in the structures of society.

(6) The eschatological ethos of the church should also motivate the church for evangelism. The coming kingdom of God engages the world both for redemption and for judgment, calling humanity to repentance as well as to

hope. The church must do more than simply work for social justice. As it lives in the shadow of the return of Christ, it must urge the world to turn to him for salvation.

Our study of the church as an eschatological community has shown that the bride of Christ exists, metaphorically speaking, with one foot in this world and one foot in the next. The church is a community that lives in the hope of the coming kingdom of God, both to redeem it from this fallen world and to perfect it for the age to come. While the church waits for that redemption, it must strive to become, as much as possible now, the spotless bride it will be on the day Christ comes, creating in the present age a community that seeks to conform to its eschatological identity and live out the values of the eschatological kingdom in its engagement with the world.

## STUDY QUESTIONS

1. What do people usually think of when they think of eschatology?
2. What are the downsides of disconnecting eschatology from our understanding of the church?
3. In what ways is the church changed when we draw its biblical future into its present ministries?
4. What does it mean for you to think of yourself as part of God's kingdom community today?

# 4

# Eschatology, the Church, and Ecology

For many of us who grew up spending significant moments making forays into nature—perhaps camping, backpacking, or simply sitting on the beach watching the crashing of ocean waves, becoming captivated by the beauty, power, and majesty of nature—but who also grew up seeing the increasing ecological devastation of the industrial era, a theology of the environment has become an increasingly important issue. In the 1980s, many Christian theologians were alarmed at Secretary of the Interior James Watt's use of a Christian worldview in support of negligent environmental policies. Surely he did not represent God's view of the cosmos, as he purported to. But neither should the church be impressed by scenes of pantheists weeping and wailing in the forest, pleading with the trees to forgive them for cutting down their brothers. The problem is that the biblical metanarrative has been used by many, perhaps especially in the twentieth century by those in the evangelical tradition, to argue for positions that degrade the environment and foster its abuse. Tom Sine has contended, for example, that Tim LaHaye, influential coauthor of the wildly successful *Left Behind* series, argues for a worldview of cosmic escapism that leads to the rationale that it doesn't make much sense to be overly concerned for the environment when the world is just going to burn anyway.[1] Other popular evangelical authors like Frank Peretti and Larry Burkett have also cast care for the environment in a negative light, Peretti portraying environmentalists as people deceived by lying spirits, and Burkett supporting the human dominance paradigm of creation, suggesting that our concern should not be for the care of the environment, but merely for the use of it to benefit humanity.[2]

Unfortunately, these types of responses to the environment from popular Christian writers only serve to bolster the argument made by philosopher Lynn White, in his historic 1967 essay, that the main responsibility for environmental degradation lies with the Christian worldview.[3] In spite of the fact that White's grasp of historic Christianity is lacking, the overwhelmingly anthropocentric (or human-centered) theology of twentieth-century evangelicalism serves to support his stereotype. In response, we will contend that the overwhelming focus of the biblical narrative, the blessed hope of the kingdom of God, argues for a salvation that includes the entire cosmos. Accordingly, the Christian faith best understood calls upon the church, as an eschatological community, not only to care for the environment, but also to be part of healing its present brokenness, in anticipation of the glorious consummation of the kingdom.

The biblical vision of future salvation clearly contains a number of otherworldly images. But the kingdom of God is neither the hope for a future spiritual existence nor the hope for an escape from this world to an entirely heavenly creation. Rather, it is the hope for a redeemed bodily existence in the present cosmos and on the present earth, renewed by having been released from its bondage to sin and the curse that has corrupted it. Historically, Christian theology has emphasized the anthropocentric nature of the fall and, thus, of the salvation of the kingdom.[4] Adam and Eve sinned, breaking their relationship with God and leading to death, both physical and spiritual. And while theologians have often noted the cosmic nature of the fall, they have rarely concentrated on the effects of the fall beyond the resulting degradation in human relationships with God and one another. Of great importance also is the broken relationship between humanity and the environment. Not only did humans become alienated from God and other humans, but as Richard Young writes, "It is clear from Scripture that nature was affected by the fall and that the curse on the ground marks a relational skewing between humanity and the earth."[5] As a result of his sin, Adam the formerly carefree grazer would now be Adam the sweat-breaking farmer, struggling to wrest an existence for himself and his family from a land made cruel by its own suffering under the curse. But the God of grace would not leave his creation without hope. In Genesis 3:15 we see the first note of the promise of a savior, the one who would be king of the kingdom of God, whose salvation would lift the curse and, once again, make the cosmos the way it is supposed to be.

Simply stated, the kingdom of God is about the redemption of not only the church, but also of the whole creation. From the very beginning, the story of salvation is a story not merely of the restoration of relationship between God and his people, but of God dwelling in the midst of his righteous people in a glorious land. "Deliverance in this sense," writes Paul Santmire, "as tending to a fecundity experience in the land, is a central, if not *the* central motif of the Old Testament, as Walter Brueggemann has shown. 'It will no longer do to talk about Yahweh and his people,' Brueggemann states categorically, 'but we must speak about Yahweh and his people and his land.'"[6] God's salvation would not be simply about people, but about the earth.

As a prophet of God to the nation of Israel, Isaiah's vision of salvation is clearly one of national and political renewal. But more than that, it is a theology of a redeemed earth. Isaiah's vision of the future is a vision where all the elements of nature once again exist in harmony with one another, a vision expressed in Isaiah 35:1: "The desert and the parched land will be glad; the wilderness will rejoice and blossom." Isaiah gives us images not of a world destroyed and completely remade by God, but of one that is purged of sin, restored and renewed, illustrated by his nostalgic images of pre-fall creation. He writes, "The LORD will surely comfort Zion and will look with compassion on all her ruins; he will make her deserts like Eden, her wastelands like the garden of the LORD" (51:3, TNIV).

In the Gospels, while we do not find nearly as much earth-oriented language or teaching as in the Hebrew Scriptures, we do find both a dependence upon the Old Testament earthy vision and a number of references that imagine the kingdom in terms of the renewal of the present rather than an entirely new creation ex nihilo (out of nothing). If we begin at the beginning, that is, with the annunciation of the birth of Jesus, we encounter not only the otherworldly voices of an angelic choir singing to shepherds, but the very earthly voice of a mysterious star, as if to say to a group of mysterious Gentiles from far away, "Come, and I will show you the one born not only to be king of the Jews, but King of the whole earth."

The miracles of Jesus, which verify the arrival of the kingdom, also argue for a salvation that goes way beyond the spiritual, to the human body and even to nature. The one who heals human bodies, miracles often referred to by the *sozo* (salvation) group of verbs, connecting them to salvation, is also the one who stands up against an angry sea and shouts, "Be quiet!" (Matt. 8:26–27). Not merely an illustration of the authority of the God/Man over nature, this command, similar to his commands to the demons who torture the sons and daughters of men, illustrates that both the earth and humanity must experience healing to live together in harmony.

Three more scenarios illustrate a continuity between this world and the next in the Gospels' portrayal of salvation. First, Jesus's victory over Satan and temptation in the desert indicates that salvation begins in an earthly sphere. Salvation is not escape from the earth, but godliness in the midst of it. Second, the incarnation rejects any spirit/matter dualism in the doctrine of salvation. God comes to his creation not as a spirit to rescue humanity from a hopelessly cursed earth, but as part of creation itself. Recalling the visible, touchable tabernacle and temple of Israel, symbolizing the presence of God with his people, John tells us that in the incarnation, God took on flesh and dwelt among his people as a visible, touchable human being. In Christ, even under the veil of mortal flesh, humanity witnessed the glory of God. But more than merely a symbol for God's desire to save humanity, the incarnation speaks of God's original intention that his glory should be manifest through all of his creation and anticipates the day when a renewed creation will once again declare God's glory with an unfettered voice.

Third, as the paradigm for the redemption of creation, the resurrection of Jesus indicates that victory over death is not victory over the limitations of creation but anticipation of a glorified creation. For the risen Christ retains a body forever, even bearing the scars of his physical degradation, yet renewed to glorious power and beauty. Thus, the glorified body of our Lord is both a new body and a healed body, foreshadowing both our resurrection bodies and also the very nature of a redeemed creation.

For Paul, the gospel is expansive, breaking beyond barriers of gender, class, and race to become the good news to the whole world. Thus, his images of the entire cosmos as part of the salvation of the kingdom are fitting. In Romans 8, Paul makes explicit what is implicit in the Genesis story of the fall and of the hope of redemption. As a result of the curse, the whole of the creation has been subjected to frustration, crippled by decay, unable to achieve its creation purpose—the world is not the way it is supposed to be. Nevertheless, having been led into this bondage by the rebellion of humanity, the creation will also be led into freedom, becoming a beneficiary of the glory of the sons and daughters of God whose victory over the curse has been secured by the Son of Man.

Moreover, we also see Paul's theology of the kingdom of God at work here in this passage, which argues for the already completed work of justification leading to the hope of complete sanctification and glorification in the eschaton. So closely connected are humanity and the cosmos in this kingdom pattern of salvation for Paul that he can even picture the creation as a pregnant woman groaning in labor, assured of a glorious new birth, but suffering all the way until the moment she is delivered. In Colossians 1, we again find Paul connecting the salvation of the kingdom to the entire cosmos. Here too, it is the redemption of humanity, the church's transferral from the kingdom of darkness to the kingdom of the beloved Son, which leads the way for the glorified Christ. And the glorified Christ is both redeemer and creator, reconciling both humanity and the entire cosmos to God. More, this reconciliation of the cosmos is accomplished by the blood of the cross, leading Paul to exult in the fact that this cosmic salvation is the gospel that, perhaps in anticipation of St. Francis of Assisi, has been preached to "every creature under heaven." As the New Testament scholar David Garland remarks, "The cross establishes a new relationship between God and humans, which overcomes the rupture created by sin—estrangement from God, estrangement from other humans, and estrangement from created things."[7] Thus, Christ, the kingdom bringer, establishes the basis not only for a new relationship with God and other human beings, but for the church's relationship with creation as well, which becomes a partner with the church in the redemption from death to life.

Finally, the earthiness of the kingdom of God is found in the imagery of the biblical metanarrative as a whole. The story of salvation begins in a garden and concludes in a city filled with nature—even some of the very same elements of nature found in the primeval garden. Revelation 21 and 22 lead us into a New Heaven and Earth, not entirely recreated de novo, but, like its human population, redeemed. For the church, as the New Jerusalem, descends to earth as God proclaims that he is making all things new. In this radical transformation to the new, the old is not forgotten as the "kings of the earth" bring their splendor into the city. Even the imagery of the city itself is filled with building materials well known on earth, but redeemed in their ability to show forth God's glory in a way they never could before, crippled as they were in their unredeemed fallenness.[8]

So, given that the redemption of the cosmos is part of the ethos of the kingdom, and that the church is the instrument of the kingdom, we argue that the values of that redemption should be drawn back into the present—the church should care about the environment. At this point someone may protest, "Wait a minute! It's one thing to draw the future elements of God's redemption back into the church's present, because redemption has already begun for us. We experience actual realities of our redemption now in Christ through the indwelling of the Holy Spirit. But the cosmos does not experience any aspect of its future redemption now, so why should we draw the realities of the future redemption of the cosmos back into the present?" Indeed, the material redemption of the cosmos has not begun, that we know of. But neither has the redemption of human government begun. Nevertheless, Christians still work for civil laws that reflect biblical values, desiring a government that though not yet actually redeemed, can reflect now some of the characteristics of its future redemption under the perfect rule of Christ. In the same way, the theology of the kingdom of God encourages the church to engage culture and the cosmos, bringing the values of the future even to the unredeemed present, in anticipation of the full and final redemption of creation at the second coming. As the presence of the kingdom now has made the healing of salvation a present reality for human beings, so should it bring, as Francis Schaeffer has argued, "substantial healing" for the environment.[9] And as God uses the church to bring his healing grace to humans, so the church should be used by God to bring his healing grace to the earth, drawing the glories of its future back into the present.

This means that when it comes to caring for the environment, maintaining the status quo is not enough. As the church works to bring believers into increasing conformity to Christ now in anticipation of eschatological perfection, so it must work now to bring nature into greater conformity with its glorious future. Moreover, it is not merely an issue of moving creation toward its future status as glorious in its own right. For the cosmos, like humanity, is designed to declare God's glory. The psalmist proclaims that, even in the here and now, the creation declares the glory of God (Ps. 19). And Isaiah announces that the trees themselves will clap their hands at the arrival of the kingdom (Isa. 55:12). But, as Paul reminds us in Romans 8, the ability of creation to serve this function has been degraded. The earth has a voice made for the purpose of praising God; but that voice has been muffled and distorted by the curse; thus, it groans. So as the children of God experience the salvation of the kingdom of God through the firstfruits of the Holy Spirit, creation can begin to experience its own deliverance through the ministry of the church working to heal its voice of praise. As theologian Ernest Lucas notes, "There is an eschatological motivation in the concept that we are trustees of the inheritance which Christ will one day come to claim . . . It [the motivation] is . . . implied in Colossians 1:16, which says of Christ that 'all things were created through him and *for him.*'"[10]

Here then, is a very present motivation for the Church to participate in the care of the earth. For the earth, which will one day proclaim God's glory perfectly, was created in space and time and has existence now, not only *by* Christ's power, but also *for* his glory. Thus, as believers heal the earth, we free the cosmos to glorify Christ more clearly now and in concert with us. The human ability to declare God's glory increasingly conforms to God's eschatological vision as it moves beyond individuals to the church and, ultimately, to the gathering of all the nations in the New Jerusalem. So too is human praise completed when it is joined by the voice of the cosmos in exaltation of the One who, as the hymn writer proclaims, is the "joy of the whole earth."[11] Here the earth, once perfect, now broken, and one day to be glorious again, is brought together with the church in its own eschatological anticipation. The kingdom of God demands that we look not just to the Genesis history of creation, but to the eschaton in order to understand the nature and purpose of nonhuman creation and to discern our role in caring for it. Unless the church understands this radical vision for the future and makes this vision a part of its theology of creation and redemption, it will continue to languish in apathy for the environment. Or, at best, it will act as a paid tenant in God's vineyard rather than as the bride preparing the garden for her husband's return.[12]

## STUDY QUESTIONS

1. What do you make of the statement attributed to Martin Luther, "If I knew the world were to end tomorrow, I would plant a tree today?"
2. What are the dangers of the church focusing too much on the redemption of the creation?
3. In light of God's future plans for the creation, should taking care of creation in the here and now matter to you?
4. In what ways can the church be involved in caring for the creation today?

# 5

# The Church as a Worshipping Community

> The Church is first of all a worshipping community. Worship comes first, doctrine and discipline second.
>
> George Florovsky[1]

## Worship as the Church's Primary Task and Chief End

If a roomful of theologians were asked, "What is the first or greatest priority of the church?" one would not be surprised to find "worship" as the most common answer. Florovsky's affirmation reflects the sentiments of the Eastern Orthodox tradition on this question.[2] But the West also places worship at the top of the list, as illustrated by the Westminster Larger Catechism's contention that the chief end of humanity is to glorify God and enjoy him forever.[3] We likewise would contend that worship, a response of love to God for his love to us in Christ through the Spirit, is the primary task and highest end of the church. For this chapter we will consider worship as the specific activity of the church when it gathers for its weekly services. While it is often argued that all of life can be considered worship in some way, we will address only that function of the church commonly called the worship service. We will define worship as that activity of the church where it, as a community, proclaims and celebrates God's person and redemptive work through participation in his trinitarian community.

## Worship as Trinitarian

In our first chapter, we argued that the trinitarian nature of God forms the basis for the nature of the church. It is a community whose life is found in relational participation in the trinitarian community of God. If, as Irenaeus and many since him have argued, God does all things trinitarianly, this would include the things God does "passively," like receive worship.[4] As God does not save us simply as the Son or the Father, neither does he receive worship singularly. Whenever God is truly worshipped, he receives that worship as Father, Son, and Holy Spirit (Rev. 4–5).[5]

In the biblical narrative, we find all three persons of the godhead included in worship. In the Hebrew Scriptures of course, since reference to the trinitarian God is not explicit, worship is simply directed toward the one God. In the New Testament, trinitarian worship becomes more pronounced. The worship of the one God of the Hebrew Scriptures is affirmed in the Gospels through Jesus's practice and command of worshipping God as Father. In John 4, Jesus says that the Father seeks those who will worship him in spirit and in truth. And in the sermon on the mount, prayer as an act of worship is directed to "our Father in heaven" (Matt. 6:9).

Worship also has a christological focus in the New Testament. In the midst of the clear awareness in the Gospels that Jesus is fully human, there arises the conviction that he is also God. In the Olivet discourse, Jesus is the king of the kingdom of God. In John, the one who comes to us in human flesh is the eternal *logos,* creator of all that is. In Revelation, John dramatically brings into focus his theology of Christ as the incarnate God in the context of worship. In chapter 5, the Lamb receives the very same kind of worship as the Almighty YHWH does in chapter 4. For Paul, Christ is the focus of worship as well, having been exalted by the Father to the highest place so that at the mention of his name, every knee should bow in worship and every tongue proclaim that Jesus is Lord (Phil. 2:5–11).

Finally, the role of the Spirit in worship is consistent with his role both within the Trinity and in God's work with humanity. As Paul refers to the Spirit as the mediator of divine love for us (Rom. 5:5), so we believe that in the trinitarian life, it is the Spirit through whom the love of the Father for the Son and of the Son for the Father is communicated.[6] In God's work with humanity, it is the Spirit who brings God and humanity into relationship with each other. As Paul says, it is by the Spirit that we are able to call God with the relational name of "Abba/Father," and through whom we are able to proclaim "Jesus is Lord" (1 Cor. 12:13). And it is through the Spirit that even the unconscious desires of our hearts are brought before God in prayer, for the Spirit who knows intimately our human minds also knows the mind of God (Rom. 8).

As to the issue of the Spirit being worshipped directly, there is little direct discussion of this in the scriptures, presumably because of his role as facilitator and communicator of the love and work of Father and Son. However, there is evidence that the Spirit is directly affected, and even addressed, by human beings. He is affected by our behavior in that he can be grieved (Eph. 4:30). And in Acts 5:3–4 we see that in lying to God, Ananias actually lies to the Holy Spirit. If he can be grieved and lied to, and if he is God, it is reasonable to conclude that the Spirit also may be worshipped.[7]

In Ephesians 5:18–20, Paul brings the pieces together for us, showing how all three persons participate in the worship process. Believers are filled relationally with the Holy Spirit, which moves them to acts of worship, by which they give thanks to God the Father in the name of the Lord Jesus Christ. Thus, our worship is relationally motivated by the Spirit, and mediated by the person and work of Christ our High Priest, culminating in thanksgiving to the Father. This is not to say, however, that the Father is the sole, or even ultimate, target of our worship. The creed from the Council of Constantinople confesses: "We believe in the Holy Spirit, the Lord, the Giver of Life, who proceeds from the Father; who with the Father and the Son together is worshiped and glorified."[8] These sentiments are repeated in the doxology called the Gloria Patri, which dates back at least to the fourth century and proclaims "Glory be to the Father, and to the Son and to the Holy Ghost." The church is correct in proclaiming worship to any and all persons of the Triune God. And as it does, God receives that worship not as the God who is alone without us, but as the God who welcomes us into the communal life of Father, Son, and Spirit.

To ask a rather crude question about all this, what is the payoff that God's trinitarian nature brings to worship? So often, the Trinity has been taught by theologians in a way that makes it appear esoteric and irrelevant to the church. But the significance of the Trinity for worship is titanic. Trinitarian worship, says theologian James Torrance, is the gift of participating through the Spirit in the Son's communion with the Father. And as we participate in this communion, God engages us in worship that authenticates what it means to be truly human. For personhood at its best and fullest is being "in relation, in love, in communion."[9] Non-trinitarian views of God, which typically focus on Christ as example, are in danger of turning worship into a response to God's call for behavior modification in order to placate him.[10] For a non-trinitarian God, who is ontologically nonrelational, remains either distant and austere or immanent and impersonal.[11] But the Triune God is neither distant nor impersonal in worship. For through his eternal relational love, the Father sent the Son to become one of us and, through the Spirit, one with us.

To take this one step further, trinitarian worship begins with the eternal community of Father, Son, and Spirit, which calls the church into worship as participation in the divine life. This, then, results in a horizontal community of worship. Worship is not merely the church, eyes toward heaven entering into the life of God, but it is also the members of the church declaring God's worth to each other ("speaking *to* each other in psalms, hymns, and spiritual songs," Col. 3:16, italics added). Worship is an activity, indeed, the activity par excellence of true human community.

## Worship as Eschatological

If worship is the activity of the church in which it proclaims and celebrates God's person and redemptive work, then worship must be eschatological. For, in worship, especially in the liturgy of the Eucharist, God comes to us in the person of the resurrected Christ, through the Spirit, engaging us as the One who has already realized the victory promised to us in our own resurrection on the last day. In his institution of the Eucharist, Jesus designates the meal as an eschatological celebration, proclaiming, "I tell you, I will not drink of this fruit of the vine from now on until that day when I drink it anew with you in my Father's kingdom" (Matt. 26:29). Paul continues this theme for the church, explaining that whenever the church takes the bread and the cup, it proclaims Christ's death until he comes (1 Cor. 11:26). And the redemptive work that the church celebrates, having been accomplished by Christ, still looks forward to its final application for a broken humanity. So when the church worships, it celebrates its future, already fulfilled in Christ's resurrection, but not yet fully realized in his corporate body.

This eschatological aspect of worship begins, however, not in the New Testament, but in the Old. One of the great benefits of examining worship in the Hebrew Scriptures is that, in the Psalms, we have an actual manual of worship. But, more than a manual, it is also a theology of worship.[12] In it we see a progression from the early psalms dominated by lament to the later ones where praise is more prominent. One of the reasons for this is that the later psalms begin to shift their focus from the present to the eschatological, as illustrated in Book Five, Psalms 107–50. Psalm 107 introduces the final book, reflecting upon the captivity and return. It makes clear that the captivity was just—the result of Israel's rebellion (v. 11), but also that YHWH has heard the cries of his people and restored them, gathering them back from being exiled in every direction. In Psalm 110 we see Hebrew worship looking forward to the fulfillment of the Davidic covenant, yet the affirmations of this psalm go way beyond David. Verse 1 speaks of a king who is coregent with YHWH. This prophecy of one who would be both king and Lord is attributed to the Messiah by Jesus (Matt. 22:44), and to Jesus by Peter (Acts 2:34ff). Verse 4 looks forward to a king who would also be a legitimate and enduring priest, according to the order of Melchizedek, whose priesthood was seen as coming from a higher order and predating that of Aaron. Even as the Jews come back to the land, it is evident that they will need someone greater than David to make Israel preeminent again. Only the Messiah will do. The final psalms of the book (147–150) rejoice again in the restoration and rebuilding of Jerusalem, ending the Psalms with overwhelming praise for YHWH from all the earth—all creation and all people. The pain of earlier psalms has given way to rejoicing and hope. Thus, the worship of Israel in the final book of the Psalms both rejoices in God's present salvation, which has taken place in the form of the return from exile, and sings praise to God in the hope of the final deliverance of the kingdom of God.

As we come to the New Testament, we find a great deal of continuity with the Hebrew Scriptures on the themes of worship. But there are certain changes as a result of the fulfillment of realities only anticipated in Israel's worship. God has not changed, but he has brought himself to a new place of relationship with his people. In the New Testament we see the worship of the church take on an increasingly eschatological character, moving from anticipation to fulfillment, at least in part. In the Synoptics, the theme of the arrival of the messianic kingdom brings an eschatological character to all of its theology, including worship. In Luke, for example, the praise songs of Mary (1:46–55) and of Zechariah (1:67–79) are filled with Old Testament images of expectation of the messianic era, now fulfilled in the upcoming birth of Christ. Moreover, Simeon's prayer (Luke 2:28ff) and Anna's declaration at the dedication of Jesus (Luke 2:36ff) give glory to God for the fulfillment of his kingdom promises.

The Gospel of John is also filled with eschatological worship images. In John chapters 1, 2, and 4 we see a temple imagery that harks back both to temple worship in general and to the eschatological anticipation of renewed temple worship found in passages like Ezekiel 43. In his graphic visions of the temple, the prophet watches, stunned, as YHWH responds to idolatrous priests by removing his glory from the temple. Then God shows Ezekiel the future, looking forward to a day when YHWH's glory will return to the temple: not to the temple built by Solomon, or even Herod, but one described in terms that transcend bricks and mortar. This is most likely the image in John's mind as he connects Jesus to the temple. In John 1, the eternal Word of God takes on flesh and "tabernacles" (*skene*) among human beings, and as he does, the disciples become witnesses of his glory. In John 2 he is the temple who will one day raise himself up after destruction. And in chapter 4, he is the new temple to whom all true worshippers will come to worship the Father. In Christ, the glory of God returns to the temple, which is Christ himself. Thus, it is now through Christ that all true worship will come to the Father. For John, Christian worship is fulfilling the Old Testament promise of a renewed worship, but as we would expect, it does so in a here and not-here kind of way. The worship of God through Christ, the new temple, reaches its apex for John in the New Jerusalem, where there is no temple, "because the Lord God Almighty and the Lamb are its temple." And the city does not need the light of the sun, "for the glory of God gives it light, and the Lamb is its lamp" (Rev. 21:22–23).

In Revelation, one of the key theological themes from beginning to end is worship. After showing John the church on earth in various stages of brokenness, God pulls back the curtain of heaven. When John looks up he sees worship. There, innumerable persons, angels, and images representing all of creation worship God and the risen Lamb. Later (Rev. 20), we find that some of the beings in the presence of God are humans who have died for their faith. Combined with the heavenly vision of the church in Hebrews 12:22–23 and Paul's theology of the believers' immediate entrance into the presence of Christ at death (2 Cor. 5:1–10), the church is depicted here as a community that exists and worships concurrently on earth and in heaven. In Eastern Orthodoxy, this Johannine imagery has resulted in a concept of worship that brings both arenas together such that when the church on earth gathers to worship, it actually participates in the worship of the community of heaven. The idea is that whenever a local congregation worships, the universal church is present, including "the saints, the angels, the Mother of God, and Christ himself."[13] By the end of the biblical story, we find the nations and the kings of the earth coming before God/the Lamb, bringing the splendor and glory of their own kingdoms as they offer themselves to God in worship.

So then, if the church understands its worship to be eschatological, how should that affect what worship looks like? Bottom line, the worship of the church should reflect the here and not-here ethos of the kingdom of God. As such, it should create forms that recognize the presence of God in the worshipping community in the person of the risen Christ, both inviting him to be king over the church now and celebrating his presence with us in our brokenness. For example, actually getting up out of one's seat and going forward for the Eucharist can symbolize Christ's kingly presence with us as we actually go to the table to meet him. This symbol is less clear when the bread and wine are simply passed through the rows of seated worshippers. Also, worship practices that allow for the corporate confession of sin teach us that Christ is graciously present with us in our brokenness. Other forms of worship should express the church's hope in the return of Christ to finally and fully redeem our broken lives. Eschatological worship should also be ecumenical and multicultural. If the final community of worship will include the entire church in unity, the church should find ways to seek that unity now, perhaps using worship as a way of occasionally bringing together churches that may be separated by historical theological differences. In John's eschatological image of worship at the end of Revelation, we find that eschatological worship will also be multiethnic and multi-socioeconomic. People from every nation, from kings on down, will come as a community before God in worship. This is no mere vision of the future for John but has significant ramifications for the church now. If the worship of the future is to be drawn into the present, then the church today should do what it can within its particular cultural setting to bring together worshippers from various ethnic and economic backgrounds.

In heaven, white people will not worship in one building while black people worship in another a couple of blocks away. Rather, all will come together before the Lamb. There, the social diversities that, in a broken world, create animosity will be healed, bringing the richness of the whole of humanity into worship. If this is God's ultimate goal in worship, then it should be the church's goal now, as much as possible.[14]

## Worship as Encounter

In keeping with what we have said to this point, numerous theologians of the Hebrew Scriptures have agreed that there is a basic, three-part promise from God that weaves its way through the story from beginning to end, shaping every area of its theology—"I will be their God, they will be my people, and I will dwell in their midst."[15] The theology of worship that arises from the scriptures reflects the elements of this promise. From the fall onward, God's redemptive engagement calls forth from his people a response of worship. This worship, then, plays a key role in giving Israel the sense that they are not just a people, but his people.

The narrative of the Hebrew Scriptures shows that God is the initiator of worship, or to say the same thing from a different direction, worship is a response to an encounter with God. Again and again it is God's initiative through redemptive action that calls forth a response of worship. In the story of the flood (Gen. 8), Noah leaves the ark after the floodwaters have receded and builds an altar to worship the Lord. Only after the flood can he possibly conceive of the magnitude of the disaster from which God has saved him, and his response is worship—thanksgiving for so great a salvation. In Genesis 12, Abram is called by God, heretofore unknown to him, and is led away from his polytheistic homeland. As he arrives on the outskirts of Canaan, God appears to Abram and shows him the land that will one day be a home for the nation of people who will come from Abram's family. Abram's response is to build an altar of worship. As we move on through the Old Testament story, we find similar events. The voice of God calls to Moses from a burning bush, and Moses removes his shoes in response to God's holiness. And of course, the exodus becomes the paradigmatic event for the entire story. Again and again, when God is confronting his people about their response to him, he reminds them of his redemptive act of delivering them from Egypt (1 Sam. 10:18; Neh. 9:18; Jer. 2:6; 11:4; Ezek. 20:10; Mic. 6:4). As this redemptive act led to worship and obedience, so should their remembrance of his deliverance lead to worship.

Related to the power that the redemptive acts of God have to call forth worship is the power of God's intrinsic awesomeness as a person. Israel responds to him in worship, not only for what he has done, but also for who he is. The

God whose very presence brought thunder and lightning over Mt. Sinai is a fearful being. And when God pulls back the curtains for Isaiah to see him in heavenly glory, the prophet can only lament that he is surely as good as dead, for he, a sinful man, has seen the holy and almighty YHWH (Isa. 6). In his classic work *The Idea of the Holy*, Rudolph Otto speaks of the paradoxical aspects of the presence of God as *tremendum* and *fascinans*. He is the one whose awe-full manifestation reveals him as the Wholly Other who, at the same time, both attracts and repels us.[16] His self-revelation to Isaiah, for example, was not meant to destroy the prophet, but to attract him. But Isaiah's fear can only be ameliorated by a messenger from God sent to purify him from his sin. Thus, the believer's approach to God, New Testament scholar Ralph Martin says, "will be in the constant awareness of our weakness and sinfulness; and we shall draw near with becoming reverence and fear . . . One cannot be . . . flippant with the God who is an all-consuming fire!"[17] Yet we are allowed to draw near to this awesome God despite our fear because, as Otto explains, the All Holy is also the All Gracious.[18]

To put it another way, while God comes to us as the Holy God, his holiness is always subordinate to his love. Yet even his love is a holy love, calling for holiness in us as he encounters us. It was this God Luther finally discovered in his search for a gracious God, prompting him to contend that liturgy and preaching should always include both law and gospel, for, as Lutheran theologian Marva Dawn argues, we experience proper exhilaration only when we understand that God's love and grace reigns in the midst of his wrath.[19] Perhaps Søren Kierkegaard best explains how encounter with a holy God can call forth such a response of joy in worship:

> Father in Heaven! Hold not our sins up against us but hold us up against our sins so that the thought of You when it wakens in our soul, and each time it wakens, should not remind us of what we have committed but of what You did forgive, not of how we went astray but of how You did save us![20]

As in the Hebrew Scriptures, the worship of God in the New Testament retains the idea of God's initiation and the human response to encounter with him. This encounter takes place in a number of ways. God reveals himself through mighty acts, through the relational presence of the Spirit, and through the preaching of the Word. We see all three of these means in the story of the early church in Acts. In Peter's preaching, God is represented to the hearers primarily through proclamation of the gospel, a description of the mighty and gracious act of God on behalf of humanity in Jesus Christ. The message of God's work confronts its hearers with the awesome and gracious person of God, to which they respond with conversion and worship. At the end of Peter's speech in Acts 10, for example, at the house of Cornelius, the response of the hearers is conversion and praise to God.

In each of these situations of conversion and worship, God also reveals himself through the Holy Spirit. In Acts 2 to the disciples, Acts 8 to the Samaritans, and Acts 10 at the house of Cornelius, Luke writes that the Holy Spirit came upon the people, bringing them into a personal, relational encounter with God. The result was praise and worship.[21] Finally, God also revealed himself to his people through mighty acts. The worship of the community in Acts 2:42–48, for example, is partly a response to the miracles God was doing through the apostles. And in Acts 4, the community worships in response to God's miraculous release of Peter from prison.

## Location

Worship is about God's people experiencing his presence. Ironically, even though the biblical narrative consistently recognizes God's omnipresence, for God's people to experience most fully the presence of their God, they have to come together in a particular location. For the nation of Israel, that location is the tabernacle and, eventually, the temple in Jerusalem. During the wilderness wanderings, the God who makes himself visible in the cloud and the pillar of fire draws the nation into his unique presence at the tabernacle (Exod. 25). While they know of and understand God's forgiveness of their sin on every day of the year and in every tent of the community, when they gather around the tabernacle on the Day of Atonement they encounter God and his forgiveness specially, as at no other place (Lev. 16). Visually, they encounter the presence of God as they watch the sacrifices. With their hands they experience his work for them as they place their hands on the scapegoat, sensing their sins being transferred to an innocent substitute and banished to the desert. Here, in this location, God makes his presence known to his people more vividly and intensely than he does anywhere else.[22]

Not until King David conquers Jerusalem and makes it the city of his residence does this city become a fixed location for the worship of Israel. David brings the ark of the covenant to rest there in permanent residence. And eventually, Solomon fulfills David's dream of replacing the itinerant tabernacle with a permanent temple for YHWH. In his prayer of dedication, Solomon remarks that this temple is now the dwelling place of the omnipresent God. Here he will dwell with his people. He asks, "Will God really dwell on earth? The heavens, even the highest heaven, cannot contain you" (1 Kings 8:27). Yet, during this very service of dedication, God appears in the temple in a cloud, his glory being so overwhelming that the priests are unable to perform their tasks. This presence of the glory of God, resident in the temple, is so powerful to the nation, so key to its life, that the reader of the story of Israel's history is moved to grief as Ezekiel recounts his vision of the glory of God departing from the temple as a result of the detestable worship practices of Israel's temple priests (Ezek. 10). Here is the low point of worship for the nation. Most of the people cannot worship properly, because they are away from the temple, captive in Babylon. Yet even those who remain in Jerusalem cannot worship properly. For while the ruined temple remains present in the city, YHWH is no longer present in the temple. The supreme importance of the temple as the dwelling place for God and of the idea of location in worship is seen again when the top priority of the exiles in their return to Jerusalem under Ezra is to rebuild the temple (Ezra 1:1–8).

Worship in the New Testament also carries a sense of location, but in a different sense. As discussed above, temple imagery in the New Testament has been transformed from a geographic location to a relational one, such that now Jesus himself and the church are the temple, the location of true worship. As the ground upon which Moses stood was holy because of the presence of God there with him, so Paul tells us that the church becomes sacred space as God dwells in the midst of his people through the presence of Christ by the Spirit (1 Cor. 3:16).

What this discussion about worship and location says to the church is that neither the omnipresence of God nor his presence through the Holy Spirit in each individual believer (1 Cor. 6:19) eliminates the need for Christians to come together in a particular location for worship (Heb. 10:25). Moreover, while an individual can worship God while alone, such a worshipper simply cannot experience the presence of God to the fullness in which he is encountered in the gathered church. For God desires to be worshipped as he dwells in the midst of his people. Only as believers share with one another their individual union with Christ can the presence of God in Christ be experienced in its earthly fullness, which leads us to the next characteristic of worship. A communal God desires communal worship.

### Community

Worship in the Hebrew Scriptures is communal, for it is the worship of the people of God. Granted, the patriarchs, at various points in their journeys, seem to worship when they are alone. But the regular and organized images of worship in the Hebrew Scriptures are functions of the whole community. The Psalms of Ascent are to be sung by groups of people as they make their way to Jerusalem and the temple for annual national worship celebrations. And major worship events in Israel's history make one wonder if there was anyone left to watch the sheep, since the entire nation seemed to have turned out. Solomon called out "the whole assembly of Israel" for the dedication of the temple (1 Kings 8), and there is the sense that everyone has to be there for this great worship service to be right. Indeed, the text says that the priests do not take up the ark of the Lord to begin the worship event until all the elders of Israel arrive (v. 3). And while there is, perhaps, more drama at this worship service than at any other in Israel's history, it is more than theater, more than an event to be observed by the crowd. For after the king offers a prayer, which is filled with requests regarding the relationship between God and his people, the story tells us that all Israel joins the king in offering sacrifices. Further, Israel's worship is communal in both the vertical and the horizontal senses. It is a participation in one another's lives as well as in the life of God. At the end of the worship event (fourteen days in all), after being blessed by the prayers of the king, the people respond by blessing him. Moreover, Solomon's prayer is filled with pleas for redemption and reconciliation among members of God's community who have sinned against one another (1 Kings 8). Thus, the joy they sense in their hearts as they leave is surely not only because of God's great work on their behalf, but also because worship has brought them to a place of reconciliation with one another. Later, Jesus understands this horizontal aspect of community in worship, urging his followers to reconcile their own broken relationships, as far as it is possible with them, before they offer sacrifices to God, the great reconciler (Matt. 5:23–24).

As Jesus's urging indicates, the community aspect of worship found in the Hebrew Scriptures is also a key component of worship in the New Testament. In the story of the early church in Acts, the general pattern is that the Holy Spirit falls upon groups of people, who then respond in worship. And the church understands that it is to come together often as a worshipping community (Acts 2:42ff). In Paul we also find that worship is about community in Christ by the Spirit. In Ephesians 5:18ff Paul sees worship as the result of individual believers being filled by the Spirit, who then brings them together. Here we see that community worship is dialogical, in two ways. It is not simply a group of people proclaiming God's worth to him as he engages them by the Spirit, but it is also believers proclaiming God's glory to one another. It is as the believers sing God's praise to one another that they also sing to God. Worship is not meant to be a corporate collection of individuals all facing the same direction with closed eyes, as if the only persons in the room were the individual and God. No, in worship we speak to one another as well as to God. We rejoice in God by rejoicing *with* one another. Only then is worship truly a community celebration of the person and work of God.[23]

To take this further, believers in worship not only celebrate Christ *with* one another, but they also represent Christ *to* one another. Peter argues that the church is the fulfillment of God's ancient desire for his people to be a royal priesthood. From this the Reformers contended against the medieval church for the "priesthood of all believers." For modern evangelicals, this has come to mean that the pastor of the church is not a priest any more than the other members of the church—that he does not represent God to the congregation or the congregation before God, but that he leads the congregation as they represent Christ to one another and come before God as equal participants in an offering of thanksgiving. The position of the Roman Catholic and Orthodox churches is that while all believers are priests in a sense, the ordained priest has a unique role in representing the congregation to God and in dispensing God's grace to the congregation.[24]

Paul illustrates the community aspect of worship in another way in 1 Corinthians 10. Here, in anticipation of his discussion of the Lord's Supper, Paul contends that the members of the church have *koinonia,* fellowship/community, in the bread and wine. So the worship activated in the Eucharist affirms not only the believer's union with Christ but his or her union with all other believers. Further, 1 Corinthians 11 and 14 picture an ordered community worship, one that is unified in its practice and discipline, but also one that gives space for all. Women are included in worship along with men, the prophet along with the tongues speaker, and the hymn singer along with the teacher. Even the unbeliever is given a certain space as Paul urges the community to worship in a way that makes sense to the uninitiated, making worship a truly public act of the community.

### Love

Many theologians, especially those in the Reformed tradition, typically begin their definitions of worship by explaining that it is the church's corporate act of proclaiming God's glory.[25] In fact, this is an appropriate definition of worship in a sense, and an aspect of worship we will discuss below. But given the trinitarian foundation of worship articulated above, we believe it is better to characterize worship, first and foremost, as a relational encounter initiated by God. As such, it is important to discuss love before glory. For just as humans can rightly worship God only after they understand his love in the midst of his holiness, so humans can truly glorify God only in response to his love. For humans with no awareness of God's love can respond to him only in terror or fear.[26]

As a relational activity through and through, worship must be more than a corporate declaration of the greatness of God, and even of his great acts of salvation on our behalf. Such worship can be too objective, lacking the subjective, relational component that is also important for true worship. What God initiates in his encounter with humanity, before all other things, is not a decree to save, but an objective and personal act of love that saves us. As John puts it, "We love him, because he first loved us" (1 John 4:19, KJV).

And John's approach is by no means restricted to the New Testament. For the law, which one might expect to be filled with dutiful responses to God because of his holiness, is actually filled with this same principle of human love for God in response to his initiation of love. The word for "love" is used in Deuteronomy over twenty times.[27] Most of them are for human love for God. But, clearly, that human love is in response to God's initiatory love. For his covenant with Israel is a covenant of love (7:9, 12) and he promises to love his covenant people for a thousand generations (5:10; 7:9).

For Paul as well, more than a right doctrine of God is necessary for the kind of encounter with God that transforms us from rebellious sinners to worshipping sons and daughters. The Holy Spirit brings us into relational union with Christ, pouring God's love into our hearts (Rom. 5:5). The result of this encounter is that we no longer relate to God as a distant judge, but as a dear father, *Abba* (Rom. 8:15). True worshippers, says Paul, are those who worship by the Spirit (Phil. 3:3) and are filled with the Spirit when they are together (Eph. 5:18). The Spirit, engaging the gathered church with the relational love of God in Christ, elicits a response of love in return, which leads to the desire of the church to glorify God.

### Glory

At this point, it is totally appropriate to talk about worship in terms of glorifying God. It is here that we talk of worship as the act of declaring God's immeasurable worth by proclaiming the glory of his person and works. Now glorifying God takes the form of celebration and thanksgiving. We celebrate and thank him for who he is—for being the God who loves us, after which we can joyfully praise him for his holiness, and for all his other glorious attributes. We praise him for being the Creator, the one who has given us existence and who has manifested himself in his creation (Rev. 4:11; Ps. 29:3–10).

We also celebrate and thank him for what he has done and will do. The people of Israel consistently rehearsed and rejoiced in the saving acts of God on their behalf, especially the paradigmatic redemption of the exodus, prefiguring the work of the Messiah, who would redeem his people from slavery to sin. Imagine the celebrative atmosphere of the Israelites as they find themselves separated from Pharaoh's army by the Red Sea. Hundreds of years of slavery to Pharaoh are put behind them as God invites them into a new relationship as his "captive" covenant people. There, on the shores of the Red Sea, Moses and Miriam lead the people in a song of celebration and thanksgiving, both for who YHWH is and for his great act of salvation (Exod. 15:1–18). Stanley Grenz summarizes the matter this way:

> Above all . . . the people of God were to worship him for his saving acts . . . Through its corporate worship life, the community gathers to commemorate the foundational events of our spiritual existence, at the center of which is the action of God in Christ delivering humankind from the bondage of sin.[28]

### Dedication/Sacrifice

As we begin to understand the nature of the trinitarian God as the one who, from all eternity, has existed in mutual self-giving love, we have the foundation for understanding that worship finally includes dedication and sacrifice of the self to God. Having been captivated by his love, resulting in a desire to give him glory, the church can finally do no less than offer herself fully to God, her lover. After a long theological discourse focusing on the gracious act of God to save a rebellious and broken humanity, Paul ends the eleventh chapter of Romans with a poetic exclamation of God's unfathomable greatness. Then he calls the church to respond: "Therefore, I urge you, brothers, in view of God's mercy, to offer your bodies as living sacrifices, holy and pleasing to God—this is your spiritual act of worship" (Rom. 12:1–2). Indeed, this sacrifice of the self is the response God has always wanted. Throughout the prophets we find God rejecting the legally proper sacrifices of his people when they come without a heart and life dedicated to God.[29] King David, in despair and guilt over his sins of adultery and murder, cries out to God with great understanding of this fact: "You do not delight in sacrifice, or I would bring it; you do not take pleasure in burnt offerings. The sacrifices of God are a broken spirit; a broken and contrite heart, O God, you will not despise" (Ps. 51:16–17).

Numerous concepts reside in the image of dedication/self-sacrifice. Two of those are the giving of the whole self and confession of sin. Paul's image causes the reader to imagine himself crawling up on an altar of sacrifices. There is clearly a death image here, which in this situation simply speaks of a total self-giving. The sacrificed animal gives all it has—its very life. So, the church, in response to the unfathomable person and work of God in Christ, rightly offers itself, holding nothing back. It is the most reasonable response of worship. David's self-dedication in Psalm 51, also a temple sacrifice image, recognizes that what is given to God must be pure and holy. For sinful human beings, this means confession of sin, which is exactly what David is doing in Psalm 51. For the church at worship, this means that there should always be an opportunity for worshippers to deal with unconfessed sin.

## Worship as Act

So far, we have said that worship is, fundamentally, the gathered church's response to an eschatological encounter with the one God, who always encounters us trinitarianly, as Father, Son, and Holy Spirit. We have argued that true worship is relational—it is a declaration of the glory and worth of God and thanksgiving for his great work of redemption by those who have been captivated and transformed by his love in Jesus Christ, communicated to them by the Holy Spirit. From this foundation, we can then argue that the goal of the church in its worship services is to bring the people of God into a relational encounter with him, leading to a proper response of worship. So, how does the church do this, and what form does that response take? We devote the rest of this chapter to suggesting answers to these questions, outlining categories for the various means and shapes of worship.

## Drama

Human beings have long understood that there are few things as powerful as a stage play, and especially a musical, to give us the sense that we are being drawn into a living story. And when the audience knows the story and its songs, it is almost impossible to keep from singing along with the players as they pour out their hearts onstage. Even more powerful is the experience of the actors themselves. Having spent months doing character studies and rehearsing their lines, they actually become the characters they are playing in the story, sensing their pain, their joy, their frustration and excitement as they live the story themselves. Perhaps for these very reasons, drama has always been a part of worship. From the drama of Israel's feast days to the church's rehearsal of Christ's passion in the Eucharist, the people of God have engaged, not as audience, but as participants in a kind of virtual reality exercise, allowing themselves to be drawn into the story of their redemption. One of the main purposes of the church in worship should be to retell the gospel story, inviting people into the story to encounter Christ, the story's hero. Robert Webber argues that in worship, the church re-creates and thus re-presents the historical event of Christ's redemption, so that it is not merely a retelling of the story but becomes a personal encounter with God. According to this approach, pastors and worship leaders are directors, and congregants are not the audience, but the players, retelling and reenacting the drama to God and to one another.[30]

At various times in the history of the church, most of its denominational traditions have made the mistake of minimizing, sometimes even eliminating, participation from the congregation, so that it becomes little more than an observer, passively watching while the priest/choir/pastor is engaged in the action. The pre–Vatican II Roman Catholic worship service was in Latin, and the priest said mass with his back to the congregation, separating them both visually and linguistically from the story of redemption.[31] Vatican II made great strides in reengaging the whole church in the drama of worship, changing the mass from Latin to the vernacular, turning the priest toward the people, and inviting laypersons to aid the priest in the eucharistic celebration. On the other end of the spectrum of traditions, the evangelical church in America has also inhibited congregational participation. As a result of the fundamentalist/modernist controversy of the early twentieth century, millions of Christians departed from mainline churches (which were generally liturgical before the controversy), creating thousands of independent churches and new denominations. Many of these dispensed with traditional liturgical elements of worship, associating them with denominations they accused of becoming theologically liberal.[32] The result was that, for many of us who grew up in the American evangelical tradition, worship participation was limited to singing hymns. There was no kneeling, no responsive reading, no recitation of the creeds. Virtually everything was done by the pastor and his staff for the benefit of the congregation. Moreover, the fact that most evangelical Protestant churches have limited the Eucharist to a monthly, or even quarterly, event limits congregational participation. But to draw people effectively into an encounter with God, the church must move beyond passivity in worship and make participation a priority.[33]

Historically, in order to facilitate authentic worship, drawing believers into the drama of Christ's redemption, the church developed liturgy, by which we mean nothing more than the forms and arrangements of public worship. From its earliest days we see that, when the church gathers, it has regular elements involved in its worship. Acts 2:42 lists the teaching of the apostles, fellowship, the breaking of bread, and prayer.[34] Near the turn of the second century, Ignatius indicates that prayer, listening to the teaching of church leaders, and the Eucharist are part of regular church services.[35] Justin Martyr indicates that these same forms are a regular part of worship in the second century.

> And on the day called Sunday there is a meeting in one place of those who live in cities or the country, and the memoirs of the apostles or the writing of the prophets are read as long as time permits. When the reader has finished, the president in a discourse urges and invites [us] to the imitation of these noble things. Then we all stand up together and offer prayers. And, as said before, when we have finished the prayer, bread is brought, and wine and water, and the president similarly sends up prayers and thanksgivings to the best of his ability, and the congregation assents, saying the Amen, the distribution, and reception of the consecrated [elements] by each one, takes place and they are sent to the absent by the deacons.[36]

As worship forms develop during the early church period, it is clear that there is both form and freedom. Some prayers, for example, were not fixed (i.e., the president of the congregation prays "to the best of his ability"), while other forms became fixed, such as the eucharistic prayers we see in documents like *The Apostolic Tradition*.[37] After the conversion of Constantine changes the status of the church in the Roman Empire, the more rapid spread of Christianity leads to the development of new lines of worship tradition, such that worship in the East begins to take on its own character somewhat different from that of the West. Even in the West there are Gallican rites and Roman rites until the West is unified under the Roman rite in the ninth century.

The point of this foray into the history of liturgy is that the church has always had forms for public worship. Even independent Bible churches have forms of worship. And those forms have been meant to function in at least two major ways—to draw the church into an encounter with God and to proclaim the truths of his redemption. With the exception of some minor traditions, the church has used two kinds of forms—those which it believes were clearly instituted by Christ himself or are direct products of the scriptures (e.g., baptism, Eucharist, singing the Psalms), and those which the church has created on its own (e.g., recitation of creeds, singing hymns/songs, kneeling/standing at various times).[38] Liturgy, says Lutheran theologian Philip Hefner, is the church's public act of prayer, praise, and devotion. It brings the believer into fullest possible communion with the faith. It is the expression of the faith that gives life to the church, and which witnesses to the world of God's redemption in Christ. As an embodiment of God's plan of reconciliation of creation with himself, the liturgy is centered in Christ. More, it brings the believer into the presence of Christ and into relational sharing with him. It is made up of symbolic actions and words that allow people to participate, receiving together God's revelation and responding in praise.[39] In those churches which are more sensitive to the historical patterns of the church, the liturgy has a distinct order, meant to lead the worshipper through an ordered experience. Hefner explains the Lutheran liturgy this way: the first section of the service consists of readings from scripture along with singing, prayers, and preaching that relate God's work to contemporary life. This is followed by the Eucharist, celebrating the saving work of Christ, closing with a petition for the Holy Spirit to incorporate the lives and work of the believers into the work of Christ in the world. The kiss of peace, also an important part of the liturgy, reflects love and unity with fellow Christians.[40] It illustrates that the liturgy is meant to be received in the midst of the community of God's people; it is not meant to be solitary. Thus, the liturgy is both vertical and horizontal. Hefner writes:

> The reception involves intimate appropriation by the individual of Christ's benefits, but it also involves intimate horizontal love for and sharing with fellow human beings. Both the reception of grace and the expression of that grace in the life of love and service are thoroughly enfleshed, embodied, earthly.[41]

In its own theology of the drama of worship, the Roman Catholic Church is conscious of the trinitarian nature of the liturgy. Similar to the Lutheran idea, the Catechism of the Catholic Church teaches that in the liturgy the church confesses the mystery of the Trinity and God's plan to redeem creation.[42] The Father accomplishes the mystery by the giving of his Son and of the Holy Spirit for the redemption of the world. Liturgy facilitates the participation of the people of God in the work of God. Through the liturgy, Christ our high priest continues his work of redemption in, with, and through the church. This issue of participation is very important in Catholic liturgy/worship. It is a relational participation with Christ through the Holy Spirit. In the liturgy, the faithful are initiated into the mystery of Christ. Through the visible symbols/signs the believers move to the thing signified. Thus, the symbols of the liturgy actually connect people to Christ. Liturgy combines celebration, proclamation, and active charity, engaging the faithful in the life of the community of salvation and involving the participation of everyone.

The liturgy is the work of the Father, for in it:

> The Father is acknowledged and adored as the source and the end of all the blessings of creation and salvation. In the Word who became incarnate, died, and rose for us, he fills us with his blessings. Through his Word, he pours into our hearts the Gift that contains all gifts, the Holy Spirit.[43]

The church blesses the Father for his inexpressible gift of the Son and asks for the Holy Spirit to allow that the blessings of God come to life through the fruits of life that result in the praise of God.

Christ is also at work in the liturgy, for he is seated at the right hand of the Father, serving as High Priest, pouring out the Holy Spirit upon his body. He does this by acting through the sacraments of the church to make himself actually present and to make his grace efficacious. Most importantly, the Paschal mystery is made present, along with its grace, to the life of the church. Christ is present also through the Word, since it is he himself who speaks when the scriptures are read. And he is present when the church prays and sings.

The Holy Spirit's role in the liturgy includes being the church's teacher:

> The desire and work of the Spirit in the heart of the Church is that we may live from the life of the risen Christ. When the Spirit encounters in us the response of faith which he has aroused in us, he brings about genuine cooperation. Through it, the liturgy becomes the common work of the Holy Spirit and the Church . . . [The Holy Spirit] prepares the Church to encounter her Lord; he recalls and makes Christ manifest to the faith of the assembly. By his transforming power, he makes the mystery of Christ present here and now. Finally the Spirit of communion unites the Church to the life and mission of Christ.[44]

In its own very short history, the twentieth-century evangelical movement in America has tended to see itself as a nonliturgical church. To illustrate this, an examination of the indexes of three popular evangelical systematic theologies reveals only two references to the word *liturgy*.[45] Wayne Grudem's remark, while cautioning evangelicals not to despise historic forms of liturgy, is telling. "Evangelicals need to be cautious . . . that they do not too quickly dismiss unfamiliar forms of worship . . . Regarding the unison reading of a liturgy, if Christians can worship and pray by *singing* words in unison, there is nothing to prevent them from genuinely worshiping and praying by *reading* words aloud in unison!" (italics original).[46]

Of course, evangelicals do have liturgies, but they have tended to reject many of the historic forms because of their connection with churches they have considered liberal. The strength of evangelicals regarding forms of worship is their commitment to biblical models. The classic ecclesiology by Robert

Saucy is a fine example.[47] He goes to the New Testament text to cite examples of the centrality of the scriptures and of the importance of all members of the congregation having the opportunity to contribute through the vehicle of the word (each one having a word of instruction, a revelation, a tongue, an interpretation [1 Cor. 14:26]). He notes the various types of prayer included in worship—supplication, intercession, thanksgiving—and discusses biblical forms of singing. He also suggests that biblical worship includes the recitation of short creedal statements, such as those found in 1 Corinthians 15:3–5 and Romans 4:25. What he lacks that is central in the liturgical/historical traditions is the whole philosophy of worship as reenactment of the events of salvation and of participation by the believers in the blessings of those acts through the Holy Spirit. There is also little sense of order or progress in the liturgical service itself. In addition, evangelicals have generally dispensed with the liturgical year or church calendar. Such tendencies have robbed evangelicals, both of the sense of the rhythm and development of God's participation in the life of the church throughout the year and of the rich experience of each act of gathered worship as rehearsal and reenactment of the story of God's redemption in Christ. Evangelicals, while rightly remaining committed to the priority of the scriptures in all functions of the church so as to stay true to God's desires for his people, could learn much from the historic liturgical churches that would help them draw their people into a more holistic encounter with God.

Finally, the charismatic movement, especially among evangelicals, has made a major contribution to forms of public worship. While charismatic pastors and theologians do not represent a unified approach, there is no question that a fundamental principle of charismatic worship is freedom in the Spirit (2 Cor. 3:17). This means that charismatic worship entails a significant amount of spontaneity and congregational participation. When the Spirit lays a word upon the heart of a worshipper, she should speak it. If someone in the congregation says he has a new song on his heart, let him sing it. It is not that charismatic churches eschew all order, for most would recognize Paul's call to order and sanity in 1 Corinthians 14. Nevertheless, the need for order should never be allowed to quench the freedom of the Spirit.

*Symbol*

Church historians have occasionally remarked that the genesis of stained glass windows was to help the largely illiterate population of the ancient and medieval world learn the stories of the Bible without having to read them. While such a generalization overlooks the fact that peasants could not have afforded a Bible even if they could read, the point is well taken. Visual symbols can be just as effective as words in communicating the biblical story of redemption. The biblical story itself is filled with symbols from beginning to end, perhaps the apex of all of them being the moment when Jesus, in the upper room, hands a broken piece of bread to his disciples and proclaims, "This is my body."

The church has always understood that God reveals himself to humanity in ways other than words. Webber remarks, "Forms are not mere externals but signs and symbols of a spiritual reality. Even as God who is immaterial met with humans in the material form of a human person, Jesus, so Christians meet Him in worship in the context of visible and tangible forms."[48] The scriptures indicate that God communicates himself through historical events, such as the exodus. And the Psalms contend that the material creation reveals God, declaring his glory through the majesty of nature in a way that can be recognized by believers and can draw them to praise and love him. In its early battles against the Gnostics, the church affirmed material creation as the product of God and as good. At stake was the incarnation itself, which is really the key event in this theology. The Word became flesh and tabernacled among us. God's use of a human body to reveal himself shows that physical realities have a place in worship. This is not idolatry. It would have been idolatry if the disciples worshipped the flesh of Christ. But they worshipped the God revealed in the flesh. Likewise, to worship a sacrament or a picture is idolatry. To worship the God revealed through them is not.

For the church of the ancient and medieval world, the idea that God revealed himself through visual symbols was axiomatic. But the philosophical revolution of the Enlightenment elevated rational means of communication, diminishing the value of imagistic communication among some modern Christian traditions. In the contemporary culture of postmodernism, however, imagistic communication has begun to experience a renaissance. Indeed, recent movements in America such as the "emerging church," filled with young believers birthed in a culture of virtual reality, have rediscovered the value of symbols such as icons. While every era has its tools for constructing symbolic realities, no era has known the technological resources that have made the creation of virtual realities such a defining characteristic of postmodernism. As culture watchers have recognized this trend, a number of authors have noted the natural and historic relationship among symbol, simulation, and religion. In his call for the evangelical church to rediscover this relationship, Robert Webber quotes approvingly from Peter Roche de Coppens's *The Nature and Use of Ritual*, contending that "in short, symbols are the 'psychospiritual means by which we invoke a certain presence, induce a certain state of consciousness, and focus our awareness, by which we recreate, in ourselves, an image, facsimile, or presentation of that which is without or above us.'"[49]

The most obvious symbols of the church are the sacraments. Besides them are the cross, the table, the pulpit, icons, vestments, candles, kneeling, bowing, raising hands, etc. These symbols allow the whole person to be involved in worship. Symbols are not an end in themselves but represent something beyond themselves and trigger the imagination and heart response of worshippers.

Symbols are like parables whose meanings are revealed to those who have faith, and hidden from those who do not. To the believer, the symbol's spiritual meaning is accessed by faith, connecting him or her to God relationally through material things in a way similar to how a picture or personal item (a deceased father's pocketknife, a grandmother's hairpin) can enable us to sense our relationship with a loved one. Relational communication is holistic. Many of us have in our workplaces, for example, photographs of family members, pictures drawn by our children, maybe even an old love letter from our spouse, which is itself an image of relationship between a husband and wife. The point is that all these are symbols, each of which communicates relationship to us in a way different from, but no less profound than, the spoken word.

## Word

While certain segments of the church have experienced a lack of symbolic encounter in worship, others have failed to expose people properly to God through the Word, the scriptures. The Reformers were right to call for a renewal in biblical preaching, which had diminished in the Middle Ages. The Bible has a unique transforming effect on the lives of believers. King David put it this way: "I have hidden your word in my heart that I might not sin against you" (Ps. 119:11). Jesus also recognizes that the word of God has a transforming effect, praying for his disciples, "Sanctify them by the truth; your word is truth" (John 17:17). In the apostolic era, listening to the apostles' teaching of the scriptures was central to the worship life of the church (Acts 2:42). For Paul, the reading of the scriptures and the development of right doctrine is a crucial component of worship. It is through the scriptures that we encounter God authentically, because they allow us to see him truly and to be transformed by him. Paul tells pastor Timothy to make sure that the scriptures are always read and taught in the public worship service. He encourages Timothy to watch both his life and doctrine closely, presumably because right doctrine should lead to a right response of life, and vice versa (1 Tim. 4:13–16).

In the early church, the reading of the scriptures became a regular part of the weekly worship celebration. Very early testimony (ca. 150) is found in Justin Martyr (cited above). By the third and fourth centuries, the patterns of Bible reading in worship had become fixed. The worship service was divided into two sections, the first being the "Liturgy of the Word," made up of biblical readings, instructions, and prayers. In his history of the mass, Adalbert Hamman writes:

> The readings which open the celebration are three in number . . . according to John Chrysostom and the *Apostolic Constitutions*: a prophecy taken from the Old Testament, an excerpt from Acts or one of the Epistles, followed by the

Gospel. Between the readings the psalms were chanted, where the people took up the refrain linked with prayers . . . The readings are followed by a homily. This consists of a commentary on the Scripture just read whose text had been chosen with a view to the sermon. The preacher applied the text to daily life.[50]

This demonstrates the centrality of the scriptures to church worship. Not only were the scriptures read, they were also sung, explained, and applied to life. Only after the church had encountered God through his written Word, did it move to encounter him symbolically through the Eucharist.

This pattern of Word and table is one that historians universally recognize as the norm for worship from the earliest days of the church. The pattern's universality should encourage some segments of the contemporary church to rethink their philosophies of worship. Many of us who are lifelong members of the American evangelical tradition grew up without the historic balance of Word and table.[51] Among the negative effects of this lack of balance is the disconnection of the ministry of the Word from worship by its exaltation above the other elements of worship. It is typical among evangelicals to see worship as encompassing only the singing and other elements that include the participation of the congregation. A result is that worship is often understood to be a "warm-up" for the main event, which is the preaching of the scriptures. Perhaps in an ironic twist of worldviews, the rationalism of the Enlightenment, rejected by evangelicals for its liberal modernism, has left its mark anyway, such that evangelicals have typically prized the rational exposition of the Bible over the existential and symbolic as the means of encountering God. This tendency is further evidenced by the fact that most evangelicals hold a memorial view of the Lord's Supper, as opposed to any sense of real presence.[52] It is encouraging that the "emerging church," generally understood as an outgrowth of evangelicalism, has begun to revisit both the historic balance of Word and table, and to focus more on symbolic encounter as an important balance to the teaching of the scriptures as a means of encountering God in worship.[53]

### Table

In light of the fact that we will include an entire chapter on the sacramental nature of the church, the discussion here of the table, the Eucharist, will be brief. In the Eucharist, the church has its most powerful liturgical symbol of the presence of Christ. Whatever a church's view of the nature of the symbol (memorial or real presence), the bread and wine re-present Christ to his gathered church. Here, the theology of encounter is dramatically played out as believers come to the table to encounter the risen Christ. For it is his table, not the table of the priest, pastor, or elders. In the story of Jesus's encounter with the disciples on the Emmaus road, Luke powerfully illustrates that where Jesus is present with his disciples, he is the host of the table (Luke 24:30–32).[54]

In addition to facilitating an encounter with Christ, the Lord's Supper is also an element of worship, in that it gives God glory for his redeeming work in Christ. As we have noted, Paul contends that every time the church takes the bread and the cup, it proclaims Christ's death (1 Cor. 11:26). Moreover, the worship of the table is eschatological, for in it the now and not-yet nature of the kingdom of God is realized in the proclamation that the risen Christ is now present with his church but is also yet to come. The Eucharist also provides an opportunity for dedication and self-sacrifice. As the believer comes to the Lord's Table to meet him, she or he participates in a very physical imagery of humbling self before Christ and surrendering to his lordship. Further, the sacrificial ethos of the bread and wine as the body and blood of the Lamb of God calls to the participant to offer himself or herself as a living sacrifice to God for the sake of Christ (see Rom. 12:1–2).

## Music

Robert Saucy writes: "Above all, the church praised God in song. Even as God's people in the Old Testament found music a fitting instrument of praise, with many of the psalms being intended for use in congregational worship, . . . so the church expressed its joyful enthusiasm in the Spirit through singing."[55] In the Psalms, we not only have a worship manual for the nation of Israel, but also a hymnal. After the profound worship of the last supper, Jesus and the disciples leave singing a hymn (Matt. 26:30; Mark 14:26). And Paul encourages the church to sing when it worships (Col. 3:16; Eph. 5:19).

Why is singing so appropriate for worship? First, the scriptures indicate that singing the glories of God is a feature of the whole created order, not just humans. Metaphorical though it may be, when Isaiah imagines creation praising God, he imagines it by way of singing, calling on the mountains to burst out singing in praise of God (Isa. 49:13; 55:12). Moreover, the angels praise God with singing. The annunciation of the birth of Christ is made by a choir of angels (Luke 2:13–14). And as God pulls back the curtain of heaven for John, he is overwhelmed by the sight of millions of angels and other creatures singing the glories of God (Rev. 5). This suggests that music and singing are not merely products of human culture, but are part of the fabric of God's creation. Music is part of God's intention for his creation. It is part of the beauty of the creation which he declared good (Gen. 1:9ff).

But music and singing are also important means of worship because they help humans worship with all that we are. Grenz writes:

> Although its forms may vary among cultures, music seems to be a universal part of human life. Music offers people a medium through which to give expression to the broad dimension of their being. Song can incorporate the cognitive aspect of life, expressing in lyrics and in the structure of the music the composer's

conception of the world. But music also reflects the noncognitive. It captures feelings, emotion, and mood, thereby giving expression to what cannot be said through words alone.[56]

Music is a window to the soul. Through it the message, and thus the person, of Christ can touch us like no other form of expression. And with it we can respond to God from the deepest places in our hearts.

Singing also facilitates community in worship, allowing the entire congregation to actively celebrate Christ. One of the beauties of congregational singing is that even those who are not gifted singers can participate joyfully because the volume and power of the entire community in song minimizes any mistakes or sour notes by an individual singer. Indeed, there is transforming power in being part of a large community singing praise to God. No one who has experienced singing with thousands of other Christians in a stadium, for example, will forget the captivating force of that moment.

Finally, we also use music in worship because it can teach us, through its lyrics, the truth about God and it can also cement that truth in our hearts. Even young children, who cannot read a theology text or the Bible, can learn much through song about the glorious nature and wonderful redemptive work of God. Because of the power of music to teach theology, the church must take care to make sure that its music is theologically sound. Few churches would be interested in hiring a preaching pastor who did not have solid biblical and theological training. The Bible is clear about how destructive false teaching can be to the body of Christ. But given the shallow and even unbiblical theology of many songs sung in thousands of churches each week, one wonders if the church cares at all about the biblical and theological training of the people who write worship songs and those who lead the church in choosing and singing them.

### Prayer

It is interesting to note that the manual for all worship in the Anglican/ Episcopal Church is called the *Book of Common Prayer*. The manual is filled with prayers of praise, confession, and requests for every kind of occasion and need in the life of the church. From its earliest days, well before the *Book of Common Prayer* was written, the church has recognized that prayer is a crucial aspect of its community life. In the book of Acts we see the church in corporate prayer often, whether in homes (Acts 2:42) or in the temple (Acts 3:1). Worshipping Christians prayed when they needed guidance (Acts 1:14, 24), when they were persecuted (Acts 4:23–31), and when they set apart disciples for ministry (Acts 6:6; 13:3). Paul encourages the church to "pray in the Spirit on all occasions with all kinds of prayers and requests" (Eph. 6:18). He encourages Timothy to lead the church in "requests, prayers, intercession and thanksgiving" (1 Tim. 2:1). The content of the church's prayers can generally be categorized under the headings of requests, intercession, confession, and thanksgiving/praise.[57] These categories are reflected, not only in the few prayers we have in the New Testament text, but in hundreds of prayers developed by the church for its liturgy. In these the congregation regularly confessed sin, thanked God for his gracious work in Christ, asked for help to live God-honoring lives, and often included some form of doxology. Many of these prayers were shaped to apply to specific occasions in the life of the church—Eucharist, Easter, Good Friday, etc.[58] Others were shaped as intercessions for various people and times—prayer for those about to be baptized, for the sick, or for a good harvest. All these reflect the church's conviction that God desired to encounter his people in every event, issue, and time of life.[59] These categories have continued into the present day in the historic Orthodox, Catholic, and Protestant churches. The one category of prayer that has not been as widely retained, especially among American evangelical churches, is that of confession. Richard Leonard rightly remarks, "Prayers of confession are not usually found in the corporate worship of evangelical and charismatic churches; confession of sin is an act that usually accompanies individual conversion to Christ and personal counseling situations, rather than the life of the gathered assembly."[60] The early church recognized the value of these prayers, as they allowed for believers to deal with unconfessed sin, clearing up barriers between the believer and God in the process of worship.

Here is another place where the contemporary church, especially the American evangelical tradition, can benefit from studying the liturgy of the historic traditions. The value of studying the public prayers of the historic church is not necessarily in reproducing them in public worship today. But through them we can see how the church has worshipped God in public prayer, how it has included such elements of worship as glory, love, dedication, and confession. We also see how prayer has been used to create community, drawing the congregation into the process through responsive prayer, unison prayer, and in prayer for one another. If prayer is to be an act of public worship, then the best worship leaders are those who not only encourage prayers that address issues appropriate for the church at worship, but also those that draw the congregation into the worship event.

Of all the prayers that have become part of the life of the church, none has been so universally embraced as the Lord's Prayer, or the Our Father. When the disciples asked Jesus how to pray, this is the prayer he gave them. Moreover, it is a prayer that addresses the whole of the church's community life as well as its relationship to God and the world. It begins by recognizing both the vertical and horizontal relationality of corporate worship (our Father in heaven). Here the church looks up to a God who is both transcendent and immanent, the One who is in heaven above and yet condescends to be known as *Abba,* the tender address of a child to his daddy. As "our" Father, he is also the God who binds the diverse community of his church together into one body. Cyprian of Carthage writes about this phrase:

> We do not say: "My Father, who are in heaven," nor "Give me this day my bread," nor does each one ask that only his debt be forgiven him and that he be led not into temptation and that he be delivered from evil for himself alone. Our prayer is public and common, and when we pray, we pray not for one but for the whole people, because we, the whole people, are one.[61]

By the phrase, "your kingdom come, your will be done on earth as it is in heaven," the church prays eschatologically, both placing its hope in Christ's return and asking him to help it live out the values of his kingdom now, values that can be lived out only as God protects his church from the devastating effects of temptation and evil. By asking for its daily bread, the church recognizes that even its most basic needs are supplied by a gracious God. And by the church's request for forgiveness, it recognizes that as bread is the basic physical need, forgiveness is the basic spiritual need. Closing with a doxology, the Our Father becomes a prayer that spans the theology and experience of worship. In it the church, recognizing God's loving Father relationship, gathers as the community of God, inviting him to reveal his loving presence in every area of church life, and declaring his glory as the church hopes in a future fully redeemed by the consummation of his kingdom. Thus, we have the ultimate example of prayer as worship.[62]

## Conclusion

All the world worships. And worship is always relational. From the pagan cultures of Abraham's day to the present, the worship of religious idols has always been about connection with and favor from the person of power represented by those idols. And as Americans worship at the altar of consumerism, bowing down before more and more stuff, worship is still about relationships. From the college guy who saves his money for a sports car to "impress the chicks," to the woman who hopes for a bigger house in order to run in a more elite social strata, we are all willing to sacrifice ourselves for and pay homage to whatever will make us more well connected. God wants to be well connected to his people, and his people to be connected to one another, for they, together, are his beloved bride. It is in the church's worship that the communal God engages his communal bride.

## STUDY QUESTIONS

1. How might trinitarian theology shape worship?
2. How does liturgy have the capacity to enhance the relational component of worship?
3. What are the advantages of making our worship methods more "holistic," such as employing the arts?
4. If the eschatological kingdom community is diverse, how can we bring that diversity into our worship structures today?

# 6

# The Worshipping Church Engages Culture

## Worship and Culture

Those of us who are baby boomers and grew up in evangelical churches in America experienced firsthand the birth of "contemporary Christian music" and the ecclesial battles it spawned. The cultural revolution of the 1960s affected every institution, including the church. For one of us, living in southern California during the 1970s meant witnessing the culture shift brought to the church by the Jesus Movement, giving rise to Maranatha music and Christian rock bands playing every Saturday night for thousands of young people at the original Calvary Chapel in Costa Mesa. On the other hand, it also meant being lectured by ex-rock-musicians-turned-Christian, who warned Christian teenagers to stay away from rock music, even when it had Christian lyrics, because, as everyone knows, "volume plus pulsation equals manipulation."[1]

The church has experienced a number of transitions and developments in its musical forms. From the introduction of the Gregorian chant to the adaptation of pub tunes by Martin Luther, the first person thought to have asked the question, "Why should the devil have all the good music?" to the popular hymn styles of Isaac Watts, Charles Wesley, and Fanny Crosby, the church has both tracked with and influenced culture with its music and integrated the results into its worship. But perhaps none of these historic developments has been as monumental as the most recent one. For the shift in musical style precipitated by rock music has been accompanied by an even more monumental transition as culture has moved into the postmodern era. The purpose of this chapter

113

is not to examine the effects of rock music or even of postmodernism on the church and its worship. Rather, we will look briefly at the relationship between the church and popular culture, focusing specifically on what happens when worship forms are influenced by that culture, with the goal of helping worship leaders and church members ask productive questions about adopting contemporary forms for worship.

### Culture and the Spirit of God

The main question we want to address here is, How should the church think about its use of popular culture in its worship? And, if it does embrace popular culture in its worship forms, what are the benefits and risks of doing so? More fundamentally, as Stanley Grenz suggested, we can ask whether popular culture can be a "playground of the Spirit" or is only a "diabolical device" of the devil. If popular culture belongs to the devil, then obviously the church should not use its forms to worship God. On the other hand, if God is at work in it, culture may offer the church powerful forms for worship.

Before answering Grenz's question in the positive or negative, we need a definition of popular culture. Summarizing the work of Christopher Geist and Jack Nachbar, Grenz describes four dimensions of popular culture. It involves "(1) the beliefs, values, superstitions, and movements of thought shared by a large percentage of the population, which come to expression (2) in artifacts and images of people, (3) in the arts, and (4) in the rituals or events that garner a wide following."[2] The symbols of popular culture transmit the shared meanings by which a people understand themselves, identify their longings, and construct the world they inhabit. And these symbols transmit meaning by the mere fact that they are value laden. In other words, there are no truly neutral symbols, images, or rituals of popular culture.

Whether popular culture and its symbols are inherently evil or good has been a matter of much debate throughout the history of the church. The early church generally advised Christians to stay away from certain events of culture like the theater, the arena, etc., since most of the entertainment there was sexually explicit or violent. Similarly, the American fundamentalist movement and many evangelicals have generally rejected culture symbols like movies, theater, and the arts in general, contending that they are part of a fallen and reprobate culture and can only degrade a person's faith. But while there may have been some good motivation behind fundamentalism's rejection of culture, the results have been detrimental to the church's witness. For fundamentalism lost the ability to find God in culture, developing the tendency to be unable to hear God speak through the fallen and broken. Thus, the message of the kingdom of God preached by Martin Luther King and the civil rights movement, for example, is still missed by most fundamentalists (and evangelicals as well), because of King's personal infidelities.[3] One wonders how a God so gagged could speak through Caiaphas, or even a donkey. Moreover, fundamentalism lost much of the ability to hear and understand the authentic human search for God. More broadly, much of American Christianity has tended to view culture through the lens of a kind of popular Calvinism that argues that culture, as totally depraved, is incapable even of looking for God. Better the imagery of Augustine, who identifies an emptiness of which humans are aware, and which they desperately attempt to fill with many things, but which can be filled only by God.[4] Culture does search for God, if only to end up often being satisfied with a lesser god, perhaps because when human culture actually encounters the true God, he strikes us as not exactly who we were looking for.

On the other hand, liberals have sometimes acted as if any and every symbol of popular culture can be profitable in engaging the church with God. Consider the recent struggle of the Presbyterian Church U.S.A. regarding goddess images in their 1993 "ReImagining God" conference. Most Presbyterians responded by doubting that a goddess image is really going to engage people with God as he is revealed in Christ. It seems axiomatic that certain symbols simply will not properly engage the church with God. Can one possibly imagine, for example, how a swastika could be used in worship? There are certain symbols inherently laden with values so antithetic to Christian worship that using them will always be counterproductive.

But the fact is that, like it or not, as Tom Beaudoin contends, "we express our religious interests, dreams, fears, hopes, and desires through popular culture."[5] Religious expression is a cultural reality. Christian symbols were not pristinely "dropped from the sky." As the incarnation so profoundly illustrates, God reveals himself in the common. As he reveals himself through the common reality of flesh and blood, so we engage him through the common elements of bread and wine. Even more astounding, God reveals himself even through nonreligious symbols of popular culture such that when Don Henley of the Eagles, for example, proclaims in his song "Heart of the Matter" that undeserved forgiveness is the only thing that can save us from self-destruction, we can know that we are hearing the voice of God. At the end of the day, we conclude that culture is both an arena from and to which God speaks, but also one that distorts God's self-revelation. So it is not only acceptable, but also necessary, that we bring popular culture and its symbols into the church, for through them God engages us and we respond to him. But since culture's symbols can also distort both God's engagement and our response, we must also be wary.

## The Function of Worship Forms

Moving from what popular culture symbols are to what they do, Grenz writes, "Pop culture both *ref*lects and *aff*ects the values and outlooks that people construct for themselves."[6] In other words, culture reflects humanity's search for God, dictates to a large extent how we search for and engage him, and shapes what he looks like when we find him. The church has used and adapted thousands of cultural symbols for worship that reflect and shape its view of God and of the gospel of salvation. Pulpits, kneeling benches, vestments/robes, fish symbols, pictures of Jesus and the disciples, video screens, incense, movie clips, etc., all affect the church's view of God and the communication of the gospel. The result has been a consistent tension in the church between form and function. If the forms of worship are meant to communicate God and his message of salvation (the function), then as culture precipitates a change in forms, this change necessarily affects the function. The basic question the church must address is, Do changing worship forms adapted from popular culture facilitate an authentic encounter with God in Christ through the Holy Spirit as described by the scriptures and as understood by historic Christian orthodoxy? We will examine this question through the lens of several affirmations for worship framed by John Witvliet in his excellent book *Worship Seeking Understanding*.

One: All liturgical action is culturally conditioned. Witvliet writes, "Liturgical enculturation best begins with an accurate description of existing cultural influences on liturgical celebration."[7] Simply stated, since worship will necessarily involve elements of popular culture, the church must examine its worship forms, asking how contemporary culture has influenced its worship.

Two: The relationship between liturgy and culture is theologically framed by the biblical-theological categories of creation and incarnation. If creation is highly valued and understood as providing the basis for human cultural activity, then Christian cultural engagement will likewise be highly valued and seen as containing great potential for good. Moreover, the incarnation provides the model for the church's involvement with culture. The church in the world mirrors the christological pattern. Thus, if in the incarnation, God taking on the form and identity of a creation/culture reality in Jesus facilitates the clearest image of who God is, then the church must recognize that popular culture symbols have the potential for a powerful and positive place in worship.

Three: Liturgical enculturation requires theologically informed cultural criticism of one's own cultural context. "The goal for all thoughtful liturgists is not simply to arrive at an apt description of culture but rather to discern how particular cultural traits both enhance and obscure the nature and purpose of liturgy, and how liturgical reform can capitalize on the unrealized potential of contemporary cultural traits."[8] Here is perhaps the key element in the whole issue of culturally shaped worship—that of culture critique. Worship leaders need to critique the culturally generated worship forms they use, asking whether each form enhances or degrades authentic worship. Contemporary forms must be examined to see if they not only engage the church through commonly understandable symbols, but also if they are able to represent God and the gospel with integrity. Few people, perhaps, would question the argument that popular cultural worship forms have the ability to engage a broad spectrum of people in worship with instant recognizability, understanding, and commonality. People who already identify intellectually and emotionally with contemporary music and computer graphics will find that they are easily drawn into the worship experience when such forms are used. This is the positive side.

But thoughtful worship leaders and theologians have recognized that there can be a downside as well. Donald Bloesch argues that the search for more contemporary and comfortable worship forms can lead to a focus on the self and one's own comfort rather than on God, given the rampant consumerist impulses of our culture. He writes:

> Worship is now a means to tap into the creative powers within us rather than an occasion to bring before God our sacrifices of praise and thanksgiving. Hymns that retell the story of salvation as delineated in the Bible are being supplanted by praise choruses that are designed to transport the soul into a higher dimension of reality.[9]

Worship is not about a search for meaning or experience, but an acknowledgment that meaning and salvation are found in God's incomparable act of redemption in Christ. Methodist pastor Craig Rice agrees: "As long as the church continues to confuse the hunger for God, extant in every human heart, with the same yearnings that drive a market culture, and a consumerist society, its worship will remain irrelevant at best, and an outright impediment at worst."[10] There is no question about the fact that authentic worship will meet people's needs. The problem occurs when worship forms are focused on meeting people's "felt needs." Each week, the church is filled with people whose felt needs have been defined for them by a consumer culture that generally urges them to focus on self-fulfillment. As good as it is may be to be aware of felt needs, the role of the church in worship is not to meet felt needs, but to show people that their real needs go deeper. Can contemporary worship forms address people's real needs? Certainly. But in choosing only forms that are comfortable and familiar, there is always the tendency to cater to what people want to hear and feel, rather than confronting them with God, whose presence is not always so comfortable. And a God made comfortable by market-driven worship is unlikely to confront sinners with their need for repentance or a gospel that is fundamentally about self-denial rather than self-fulfillment. Quoting Martin Marty, Marva Dawn remarks, when worship is driven by the market, it "draws crowds, but it is so fully adapted to the not-yet-born-again 'that worship becomes measured by the aesthetics and experience of those who don't yet know why we should shudder.'"[11]

Four: The extremes of either complete identification with or rejection of a given culture are to be avoided at all costs. Here, Witvliet rightly calls for a dialectical approach to culture and worship forms. "In sum, the twin dangers that cultural engagement seeks to avoid are 'cultural capitulation,' on the one hand, and 'cultural irrelevancy,' on the other. In every instance of cultural engagement, there must be a yes and a no, a being in but not of, a continuity and a discontinuity with accepted cultural practices."[12] Marva Dawn agrees, suggesting that

> the Christian faith has always been odd, and we must emphasize the importance of that dialectical pole. However, when churches take this pole to the extreme— becoming completely alien to the culture in sticking to traditions or celebrating them in ways irrelevant to normal life—then Christians separate themselves from the world in a sectarianism, provincialism, or esoteric gnosticism that prevents ministry to the culture from which they remove themselves.[13]

Simply put, the best array of worship forms will illustrate that the church is both embedded in culture, speaking through its constantly changing forms in a way that reflects the God who became part of human culture, and also a countercultural community, one that represents transcendent values and truths that confront culture's fallenness.

Five: Liturgical action must reflect common elements in the Christian tradition through the unique expressions of a particular cultural context. There must be a judicious balance of particularization and universality. Geoffrey Wainwright remarks, "While indigenization is necessary on account of the relevance of the Christian gospel to *every* culture, a concomitant danger is that this particularization may be understood in such a way as to threaten the universal relevance of the gospel to *all* cultures."[14] The point is that if we adapt the church's worship forms too fully to the unique forms of a particular culture or subculture, those outside of that culture who come to the church may have no idea of the transcendent meaning of the form and will not be able to connect it to God or the gospel. Moreover, the unchecked use of cultural forms for worship runs the risk of producing a national Christianity, or worse, a national (American) Jesus, or a Gen-X, baby-boomer, or postmodern Jesus, with the result that the church begins to bear witness to a God made in culture's own image.[15]

A contemporary situation addressed by this struggle of particularization in the midst of a common faith is the practice of many large churches to try to solve worship style frustrations by opting for both a "traditional" service and a "contemporary" service. While this may seem like an obvious solution, we believe it is fraught with problems. To do this is necessarily to divide a local congregation into two congregations based on the age of the worshippers— the older worshippers attending the traditional service, and the younger attending the contemporary one. Given that most American churches already divide the other smaller church gatherings, (e.g., adult Bible classes, youth groups, etc.) on the basis of age, where then does the church come together as a multigenerational community to worship its Lord? Where do young people rub shoulders with grandparent types who can share with them the wisdom gained from decades of following Jesus in a broken world? Where do older adults engage young people, finding their own long-held faith challenged by the energy, hopes, and piercing questions of youth? Where do young people learn the riches of "ancient" worship symbols, and where do old Christians learn to worship the same God in new ways, helping them to continue engaging an ever-changing culture? Unless it comes up with other creative and effective ways to bring the generations together, the church that chooses this silver bullet to end the "worship wars" will do so at a significant cost.[16]

Six: The constituent liturgical actions of the Christian church—including proclamation of the Word, common prayer, baptism, and Eucharist—are among the "universal" or common factors in the Christian tradition. And these kinds of symbols should remain universal for at least two reasons. First, the church is not only a multicultural community, but also a historical community, one that always finds its identity in the same God revealed in Jesus Christ. Thus, as there are theological and relational realities that unify the church through the ages, this unity should be reflected in a consistency of symbols. Moreover, the use of historic forms of Christian worship allows a congregation to understand experientially that it is not merely a present community, in danger of passing away along with other fads of modernity, but is a community in living union with believers of all time, coming to the same table to meet the same Jesus encountered by the disciples at the last supper two thousand years ago. The church that is obsessed with constantly reinterpreting itself through ever-newer symbols is in danger of forgetting who it is and why it exists. Walter Brueggemann laments,

> In a stupor of amnesia, a community may think there is only "now," and there is only "us." . . . People with amnesia are enormously open to suggestion, blind obedience, and easy administration. These memories . . . [embedded in the church's historical forms] make one angular, odd, and incapable of assimilation. It is clear that consumerism depends upon amnesia, in which "products" are substituted for social reference points, and in time, such "consumer values" lead to a shameless kind of brutality.[17]

The worldwide Jewish community, throughout centuries of exile and oppression, has learned that to forget a community's past is to lose the ability to understand who it must be in the present and future. Thus, their insistent motto regarding the Holocaust—"Never forget!"

But some might object, "Why do we have to retain ancient forms and symbols to remember who we are and who God is? Can't we represent enduring realities best in the language of contemporary culture?" In regard to certain symbols, the answer is definitely no, which leads us to the second reason to keep certain worship forms consistent despite a changing culture—scripture sometimes ordains not only the function, but also the form. An obvious example is the Lord's Supper. To a certain extent, the form *is* the function here. During the early church era, the form of Eucharist was offensive to pagans, who thought it was a kind of cannibalism. But the church was unwilling to change the form because it was so closely connected to the message it represented. Some have suggested that since symbols like bread and wine do not have the same meaning in all cultures as they did in the ancient Middle Eastern culture, the church should use "cultural equivalents," that is, symbols from each culture that have the same meaning. The problem is that cultural equivalents are never exact, and usually not even that close in their meaning. For example, some have suggested using rice instead of bread in Asian cultures for the Eucharist, since rice, like bread, is the basic food source of daily life. The problem is that bread represents much more than this in the biblical narrative. It represents the presence of God, as illustrated by the showbread in the Temple. Also, unlike rice, the ability of bread to be broken is of supreme importance to the image of the broken body of Christ. Similarly, one is unlikely to find a cultural equivalent for wine, which represents not only a basic meal drink in the biblical text, but also life, blood, and judgment.[18] Better simply to teach people the significance of the ancient signs and preserve them intact.[19]

## Conclusion

So then, what is the solution to the "worship wars," to the battle over contemporary versus traditional worship forms? As intimated above, the answer must lie in a dialectical approach, a yes-and-no approach to changing worship forms along with culture. When contemporary forms draw a broad community of worshippers more effectively into authentic engagement with the trinitarian God, yes. When they accurately represent the biblical gospel, yes. When they present an image of God or the gospel that lacks the fullness of or distorts the image given by historic Christian tradition and the biblical narrative, no. When they create unmitigated separations in the local church, no. If the biblical image of the church is multiethnic, multigenerational, and multicultural, then the church should prize such diversities even in the midst of their difficulties, seeking always to bring the diverse elements of its community into unity through worship. When it comes to the challenging dialectics of worship and cultural engagement, Marva Dawn has said it well: "The primary key for holding the two poles of this dialectic together is education—teaching the gifts of the faith tradition to those who do not yet know and understand them and teaching those who love the heritage some new forms in which it can be presented to others."[20]

## STUDY QUESTIONS

1. How do you know when adapting worship to cultural forms has gone too far?
2. What would be the criteria for making worship more culturally relevant without compromising scripture?

# 7

# The Church as a Sacramental Community

## Sacrilege and the Sacraments

In the movie *The Godfather*, Michael Corleone serves as the godfather for his sister's baby at its baptism into the family—God's family of the church. During the baptism in cold water, Michael renounces evil on behalf of the child; the scene shifts and the viewer witnesses Michael's men simultaneously "renouncing evil" by gunning down rival Mafia families in cold-blooded murder.

In a bizarre yet memorable way, this clip illustrates two points of central importance to our discussion of the church as a sacramental community. First, the sacraments (or ordinances) are community events whereby we participate in God's story and God's family's life. Second, the sacraments are theo-political events whereby we renounce evil and combat the forces of darkness and bear witness to God's victory in the crucified and risen Christ.[1]

The communal and theo-political nature of the sacraments reflects the trinitarian and kingdom reality, which governs this volume and which must also come to govern the daily life of the American church. Unfortunately, all too often our ultimate family and political allegiances lie elsewhere, as in the case of the *Godfather* tale above; when this happens, we reduce the sacraments' significance to sacrilegious though pious symbols for rites of passage and private parties for niche, tribal, and nationalistic factions.

In place of this reductionistic account of the sacraments, baptism and the Lord's Supper are communal and theo-political events that institute and constitute the church as the Triune God's family and theo-political community.

The church is a sacramental community; along with the Word, the sacraments shape the church's life and practices so that the church might experience more fully trinitarian kingdom life, given its participation in God's story.

At the heart of the church's worship is the rehearsal of the Triune God's story of redeeming love in anticipation of the reconciliation of all things in Christ. As briefly noted in chapter 5, through the sacraments the church not only retells the story, but also reencounters God himself through the presence of Jesus Christ by the Holy Spirit. Baptism, Eucharist, and other sacred symbols serve as "virtual realities" through which the sacred community is drawn into the story of redemption, and thus into Christ's presence. Sacramental worship, then, becomes a kind of community theater in which the church experiences the grace of God through reenacting the gospel drama. A biblical, historical, and communal theology of the sacraments gets beyond arguments about real presence and institutional grace, moving Christians from all traditions to an understanding that the Triune God's fullest expression of his presence and grace can be known only in his eschatological community—the church.

In what follows, we attempt to recount the biblical drama, highlighting the central significance of the sacraments in that epic story. Attention is given to understanding the significance of the sacraments in terms of the Christian community's identity, purpose, and activity. Moreover, we consider how the various traditions view Christ's presence in relation to the sacraments, and how the biblical drama can make sense of these diverse perspectives. Along the way, we will address the sacraments' significance for the church's existence as a communal reality and theo-political force.[2]

### Baptism and the Supper: Rehearsing the Biblical Drama

Baptism and the Lord's Supper rehearse the biblical drama, just as Paul rehearses the biblical drama through recourse to baptism and the Lord's Supper in 1 Corinthians 10 through 12. The Corinthians had forgotten where their true allegiance lay and what their family of divine origin was, so Paul sets out to remind them. Given over to warring factions and class divisions (see 1 Cor. 1:10–17 and 11:17–22), as well as idolatry and immorality (1 Cor. 6:12–20 and 10:6–22), Paul recounts Israel's story as a warning to the carnal Corinthians. The Corinthians had made a sacrilege of the sacraments. And so, like many among Israel's multitudes who ate and drank of Christ, their own bodies were being scattered over the desert wasteland of their rebellion (see 1 Cor. 10:3–6; 11:28–32).

As in the case of the church, Israel was both God's family and army (though the church's battle is not with flesh and blood, as Eph. 6:12–17 makes clear). The exodus narrative tells us that "the Israelites [the children of Israel, the patriarch] went up out of Egypt armed for battle" (Exod. 13:18). Their baptism into Moses at the Red Sea (1 Cor. 10:2) as well as the Passover celebration served as signs of God's judgment on all of Egypt's gods (Exod. 12:12) and Pharaoh and his forces (Exod. 14:13–14). As the church recounts Israel's story of baptism and Passover at the exodus during its own baptisms and Paschal celebrations, it also looks forward to its ultimate deliverance before God from the world, the flesh, and the devil at the fall of Babylon's whore and the dawning of the Lamb's marriage supper (see Rev. 18 and 19). These acts of recollection and anticipation at baptism and the Supper are themselves virtual and vital means of storied participation. Later we will explain what we mean by "virtual and vital means of storied participation"; for now, we simply want to say that baptism and the Lord's Supper are familial and theopolitical events whereby the church recollects, participates in, and anticipates its family's history and destiny under God's reign.

After Israel witnessed God's consuming of Pharaoh in the same waters in which they had been baptized, Israel journeyed across land, eating manna (see Exod. 16:1–22) and drinking water from the rock (see Exod. 17:1–7). Jesus declares that the giving of the manna foreshadows him and his work as the one who gives himself as the bread of life (John 6:30–59), and Paul claims that the rock from which Israel drank was Christ (1 Cor. 10:4). It is quite possible that the Lord has both images—bread from heaven and water from the rock—in mind when he proclaims, "I am the bread of life. He who comes to me will never go hungry, and he who believes in me will never be thirsty" (John 6:35). Even so, his person is ever and only the true bread and water of life because he is the Paschal Lamb slaughtered to bring life:

> I tell you the truth, unless you eat the flesh of the Son of Man and drink his blood, you have no life in you. Whoever eats my flesh and drinks my blood has eternal life, and I will raise him up at the last day. For my flesh is real food and my blood is real drink. Whoever eats my flesh and drinks my blood remains in me, and I in him. Just as the living Father sent me and I live because of the Father, so the one who feeds on me will live because of me. This is the bread that came down from heaven. Your forefathers ate manna and died, but he who feeds on this bread will live forever. (John 6:53–58)

God commanded Israel to celebrate the Passover and Feast of Unleavened Bread as a lasting remembrance of God's deliverance of Israel from Egypt. Only those who obeyed the Lord by sacrificing and eating a perfect lamb and sprinkling its blood on the doorframes of the house would be spared the destruction of the firstborn, and only those who ate unleavened bread would remain a part of the community of Israel (see Exod. 12). So too, only those who eat and drink of Christ will live forever (see John 6:53–58 above).[3]

God set apart his firstborn son as the spotless lamb of sacrifice while sparing Isaac as well as the firstborn males of Israel on the night the Angel of Death passed through Egypt (see Gen. 22 and Exod. 12, 13). God commanded Israel to remember the Passover event annually, teaching the young, "It is the Passover sacrifice to the LORD, who passed over the houses of the Israelites in Egypt and spared our homes when he struck down the Egyptians" (Exod. 12:27). Out of Egypt, God called his son—his national son, Israel, and his personal Son, Jesus (see Hos. 11:1; Matt. 2:15), and on the mountain of the Lord, God provided the ram—a foresign of his one and only Son—in the thicket for the sacrifice in place of Abraham's one and only son (Gen. 22:13–14; John 3:16; 8:56; Heb. 12:22–24). On the mountain of the LORD, it has been provided.

John 6 foreshadows the ultimate Passover celebration; many of Jesus's disciples stumble and turn away because of his words (John 6:60–61, 66), for his words convey that he will become a bloody, dead Messiah—the bread of life and Lamb of God who takes away the sins of the world. While Peter comprehends that Jesus alone has the words of eternal life, and so does not turn away (John 6:68–69), he cannot fathom how these things could happen to God's Anointed One. Only on the night of the "final" Passover celebration itself does the horror of it all begin to dawn.

Interestingly enough, John's Gospel does not give an account of the institution of the Lord's Supper, only references to the dinner as well as a discussion of Jesus washing the disciples' feet. We find the institution of the Lord's Supper in Luke's Gospel. As Rabbi and head of his family made up of his disciples, Jesus recounts Israel's history that evening, in accordance with the custom instituted by God in Exodus. When he comes to the breaking of unleavened bread and discussion of the Passover lamb, the Lord startles his disciples by interjecting lines not in the official script (but certainly between the lines of the Old Testament text). Here are those lines: "And he took bread, gave thanks and broke it, and gave it to them, saying, 'This is my body given for you: do this in remembrance of me.' In the same way, after the supper he took the cup, saying, 'This cup is the new covenant in my blood, which is poured out for you'" (Luke 22:19–20).

A few verses earlier the Lord tells his disciples: "I have eagerly desired to eat this Passover with you before I suffer. For I tell you, I will not eat it again until it finds fulfillment in the kingdom of God" (Luke 22:15–16). Here the Lord is referring to his return and the marriage supper of the Lamb at the close of this age and the dawning of the next. The Lord himself eagerly awaits that day, just as Paul longed for that day's appearance. And whenever the church celebrates the Lord's Supper, God's people proclaim the Lord's death until he comes, as Paul instructs the Corinthians (1 Cor. 11:26).

Until Christ returns and raises us to new life, we participate in his sufferings and death here on earth. While passing through the baptismal waters and drinking from the cup of life, we also experience the sufferings and death of our Lord. For these are all parts of the same story. Thus, we are baptized with his baptism and drink from his cup (Mark 10:38–39). While we do not die for our sins—Christ's work alone accomplishes atonement—we die because of our sins and the sins of the world. We must die to ourselves and to the world and its passions, which wage war against the Spirit, if we are to enter into the fullness of life.

Between Pentecost and the marriage supper, the church endures tribulation at the hands of Egypt-Babylon-Rome. While the church will be spared from God's outpouring of wrath on the fallen principalities and powers at the height of the apocalypse at the end of the age (God's mark will be on our foreheads just as the blood was on Israel's doorposts), the church will experience oppression at the hands of those powers as those powers themselves endure the "plagues of Egypt." The same Lord who baptizes with the Holy Spirit also baptizes with fire (Luke 3:16–17).

John the Baptist learned firsthand what it meant to identify with Jesus in his baptism and by proclaiming the baptism with fire. Upon telling the people, "He will baptize you with the Holy Spirit and with fire. His winnowing fork is in his hand to clear his threshing floor and to gather the wheat into his barn, but he will burn up the chaff with unquenchable fire," the text tells us that Herod put John in prison (and later at the plotting of his wife had him executed) for rebuking him for all the evil he had done (Luke 3:16–20).

Just as John identified with Jesus, Jesus identifies with us by undergoing the baptism of John (Luke 3:21). John's baptism was one of repentance, and Jesus underwent it (over against the protests of John [Matt. 3:14]) to fulfill all righteousness (Matt. 3:15) and so begin the process of recapitulating all things. Matthew, Mark, and Luke offer accounts of Jesus's baptism (Matt. 3:13–17; Mark 1:9–11; Luke 3:21–22), and John's Gospel alludes to it (see John 1:26–34).

After Jesus's baptism (at which time the Spirit descends upon him), Jesus is led into the wilderness to be tempted by the devil (see Matt. 4:1–11; Mark 1:12–13; and Luke 4:1–13). It is striking that—once again—all three Synoptic Gospels include accounts of Christ's temptation. And just as all three bear witness to the Spirit having descended on Christ at his baptism, all three indicate that the Spirit led Jesus into the wilderness to be tempted. Luke tells us that after the temptation Jesus began his public ministry in the power of the Spirit, at which time he proclaimed the coming of the messianic age (which would appear with the Spirit's anointing of the Messiah; see Luke 4:16–21). As we are baptized into Christ through the Spirit, we participate in the messianic age and wage war with those forces that belong to the age that is passing away (regarding the passing away of this world, see 1 John 2:15–17).

Fourth-century theologian Cyril of Jerusalem rehearses the biblical drama in his *Lectures on the Christian Sacraments*. Here is what Cyril says of the Old Testament typology pertaining to baptism:

> Now turn from the ancient to the recent, from the figure to the reality. There we have Moses sent from God to Egypt; here, Christ, sent by His Father into the

world: there, that Moses might lead forth an oppressed people out of Egypt; here, that Christ might rescue mankind who are whelmed under sins: there, the blood of a lamb was the spell against the destroyer; here, the blood of the unblemished Lamb Jesus Christ is made the charm to scare evil spirits: there, the tyrant pursued even to the sea that ancient people; and in like manner this daring and shameless spirit, the author of evil, followed thee, even to the very streams of salvation. The tyrant of old was drowned in the sea; and this present one disappears in the salutary water.[4]

Those preparing for baptism (catechumens) were to renounce the tyrant Satan, his works, pomp, and service, before entering the baptismal waters.[5] Upon entering the waters, the garments of their old humanity were put off, and they were not permitted to put these garments—the lustful desires of the flesh—on again; for the powers of the enemy had made their abode in fallen flesh. These new believers were to triumph over the powers of the enemy by renouncing their fallen passions, just as Christ exposed and conquered the fallen principalities and powers through his nakedness and shameful suffering on the cross.[6] Early catechumens shed old clothing into nakedness and, rising from the baptismal waters, were clothed in the new garments of Christ. Regarding the "old man," Cyril writes,

> May no soul which has once put him off, again put him on, but say with the Spouse of Christ in the Song of Songs, *I have put off my coat, how shall I put it on? O wondrous thing!* Ye were naked in the sight of all, and were not ashamed; for truly ye bore the likeness of the first-formed Adam, who was naked in the garden, and was not ashamed.[7]

For Cyril, baptism conveys remission of sins and adoption into God's family. It also signifies participation in Christ's suffering. Cyril believed baptism to be salvific.[8] The sole alternative for Cyril was the baptism of blood martyrdom.[9]

Cyril no doubt saw a connection between renouncing Satan's works and pomp and the Roman system, for the orthodox church that he served experienced periodic repression; it had been a long time since the church was recognized as having official religious status in the Roman system (albeit through Judaism). In the book of Revelation, written near the end of the first century, John was only twenty years removed from the sacking of Jerusalem; the belief that Christ would return soon was still a pressing conviction for many. By the time of Cyril, however, the church's theo-political concerns had become spiritualized; there was no real possibility of the church being viewed as a theo-political force demanding serious attention. Today, however, the American evangelical church wields great power and must recall that God's power is displayed ultimately through the weakness of the cross and ensuing resurrection, not by lobbying Washington and forming allegiances with those from reigning political parties.

John's Apocalypse is a very political book, but one in which the church of Christ's kingdom triumphs through weakness—not by trying to take matters into its own hands by a show of force, but by looking to God to redeem his people. When the church abandons a strategy of power through the weakness of the cross for power over weakness, it inadvertently sets itself up as a pseudo-state and rival to Christ's kingdom. Alternatively, when the church sees Christ's kingdom as otherworldly and/or completely future, it inadvertently creates a vacuum whereby "rival" kingdoms can flourish, competing for the church's ultimate allegiance; a church that takes matters into its own hands and a church that remains silent both fail to bear witness to Christ's eternal kingdom in the here and now.

While Christ's kingdom is not of this world, it does put a check on this world's powers. The throne-room scene in which the Lion who is a Lamb triumphs (Rev. 5), the martyrs under the altar who dwell in the shadow of the Almighty (Rev. 6), and the destruction of Babylon's whore and the marriage supper of the Lamb (Rev. 18 and 19) all bear witness to the fact that Rome's rule by retribution will not endure.

Like the book of Revelation, baptism and the Lord's Supper are theo-political in nature. As already suggested, they are also communal events. John calls on his churches (not simply on individuals) in Asia Minor to overcome the fallen powers in the present in view of the kingdom that will one day come in its fullness with the dawning of the new heavens and earth. John's people can rejoice in the fact that, as they bear the mark of the Lamb (Rev. 7:3; 14:1)—just as Jewish homes in Egypt bore the mark of spotless lambs on their doorposts—God will spare them from the wrathful plagues that will consume their enemies, and will lead his people forward to feast at his table in the Promised Land (Rev. 19). The God who will dwell in their midst, tabernacling among his people (Rev. 21:2–3), gives them the strength to persevere and to overcome as they recollect what God in Christ has done for them, as they participate in God in Christ through the Spirit, and as they anticipate Christ's return, led forward by the Spirit (Rev. 22:17)—until that day when faith becomes sight. The scriptures and the sacraments' theo-political and communal significance is bound up with the reconfiguration and transformation of our time and space as God's people come together to recollect, participate in, and anticipate the one who was and is and is to come. This all-encompassing sacred story and its symbols confirm the church in its identity, purpose, and activity.

## The Sacred Story and Symbols' Significance for Identity, Purpose, and Activity

Through the ages, the sacred story and its symbols have served to confirm God's kingdom community in its shared sense of identity, purpose, and activity. It is little wonder that Word and sacrament always go together. Such confirmation of identity, purpose, and activity is bound up with the reconfiguration of the spatial-temporal sphere, whereby God reconstitutes our lives so that they become part of God's overarching story of salvation history through Word and sacrament. The sacred story reshapes our sense of time, and the sacred symbols reshape our sense of space. No longer should we look at going to church as making space and time for God, but as God making space and time for us. The church is God's communal meeting place whereby we reenact the particular history of Israel's Christ—the story for all times—through Word and sacrament. When God's kingdom community fails to rehearse the sacred story with its symbols, God's people lose sight of who they are and what they are called to be and to do.

Israel was a community that lived between exodus, exile, and return, whose sense of identity, purpose, and activity was bound up with rehearsing its story while practicing the sacred rites. The church is a community that lives between exodus, exile, and return—deliverance and captivity, and whose own identity, purpose, and activity are bound up with rehearsing its story while practicing the sacred rites. Without this awareness and conviction, the church is easily reduced to being a voluntary association of religious, pious individuals whose true allegiance lies elsewhere—namely, with such fallen principalities as the state or the market.

The rehearsing of the biblical story and the remembrance of Christ in the Lord's Supper and baptism bear witness to Christ's victory over the fallen principalities and powers, which make it their ambition to separate people from God and people groups from one another. These fallen powers operate based on the age-old strategy of "divide and conquer." They trick the church into living a divided life—keeping it impotent. The movie *Romero* reveals that the late Archbishop Oscar Romero of El Salvador determined to baptize the infants of the aristocracy, often of Spanish descent, with the infants of the indigenous peasants, incensing the former.

William Cavanaugh claims that Romero also determined to bring the rich and poor together to celebrate the mass. Again, the former group was incensed. Cavanaugh claims that in spite of their protest, Romero drew sustenance and strength from the Eucharist and resolved "to collapse the spatial barriers separating the rich and the poor." Romero did this "not by surveying the expanse of the Church and declaring it universal and united, but by gathering the faithful in one particular location around the altar, and realizing the heavenly *Catholica* in one place, at one moment, on earth."[10] Romero understood well that the sacrament serves to reconfigure our sense of space. Together with Romero's protest of the fallen powers for oppressing the masses and taking their property and killing them, and his efforts in creating solidarity among the masses by celebrating the Eucharist, it is little wonder that the fallen powers had him shot to death while he performed the mass.

Christ is present to his community in a special way in the celebration of the sacraments. Without a vital sense of his vital presence through faith in the Word of promise and sacramental participation, the church would not endure assaults on its identity, purpose, and activity. Christ's church would become faint of heart and lose the courage and strength to confront those societal forces that weigh against the church—seeking to reduce Christ's kingdom community to a voluntary association of religious individuals whose true identity lies elsewhere.

The real presence of Christ in the sacraments strengthened Romero and his little flock in El Salvador. The real presence of Christ in the sacraments will also strengthen Christ's little flock in our midst today in North America in the face of the empire that will surely strike back for not knowing our proper place as a ghettoized community of privatized and individualized affections.

Colonizing governmental and market forces have no trouble with Christian communities coming together; but they would be greatly troubled if such communities were to conceive of their religious symbols as conveying more than pious sentiment, having theo-political, communal significance that calls into question the liberalizing and individualizing forces of the state. For strength is found in numbers, not in isolation. With this in mind, the scriptures and the sacraments' strategic role and placement in the sanctuary and worship celebration serve as effective symbols of protest to what Stanley Hauerwas calls the modern devaluation of religious communities to "arbitrary institutions sustained by the private desires of individuals."[11]

Romero's baptismal and eucharistic assembly counters this modern trend, signifying that the church is by no means an arbitrary institution, but a critical kingdom witness sustained by God's very public desires concretized in communal practices centered in Christian scripture and the sacraments. Over against those liberalizing and individualizing forces that would keep the church from realizing how potent and profound its sacred text and symbols are, scripture urges God's people not to stop meeting together as some are in the habit of doing, but to encourage one another as they see that day approaching when they will enter into the Promised Land with all God's people throughout the ages (Heb. 10:24–25; 11:39–40). Through Christ the sacrificial lamb and great high priest, God's people have been called to ascend—even now—Mount Zion, which is in the Promised Land (Heb. 12:22–24). The result of such remembrance and rehearsal will no doubt bring about the shedding of their own blood in some instances and the confiscation of property and imprisonment in other instances but will also give way to eternal life in all instances (see Heb. 10:32–39). Such hope sustains and transforms the community, as God's people live now in light of what will be.

Churches fall prey to liberalism's devaluing and reducing of Christ's church to "arbitrary institutions sustained by the private desires of individuals" when they fail to rehearse the gospel story and/or reconfigure sacred space around the sacraments. One instance of this failure resulted from the eclipse of biblical narrative beginning in the modern period. Hans Frei's *The Eclipse of Biblical Narrative* chronicles this.[12] Modern attempts to justify scripture's legitimacy as fundamentally a textbook for gleaning doctrinal truths (fundamentalist-evangelicalism), exemplifying moral and philosophical ideals (liberalism), and demonstrating relevance for practical living (seeker-sensitive Christianity) fail to register that the Bible is the paradigmatic story and that it envelops ours. The ancient and medieval perspective that God's story is all-encompassing is profound and life-giving; once we make the shift in our thinking from trying to find a place for God in our lives—carving out a place for his story in our faith journey—we find that God has actually made us participants in *the* story, which constitutes reality and makes our lives relevant and worth living.

Another instance of the failure to rehearse the gospel story and/or reconfigure sacred space around the sacraments resulted from the neutralizing of sacred space in the 1980s for the purpose of making seekers feel more comfortable. The neutralizing of sacred space involved the removal of crosses and other specifically Christian symbols from places of prominence in church sanctuaries and centers of worship. Now some will argue that while such neutralizing of sacred space was appropriate at the time, given seekers' wariness of sacred symbolism in the modern world, the reemergence of sacred symbolism among postmodern seekers today makes it necessary to bring back sacred space.[13] In contrast, we would argue that such a pragmatic perspective (one that suggests that it is all right for churches to neutralize or revitalize sacred space based on the type of seeker it targets) fails to comprehend that religious symbols are not ornamental window dressings but constitutive signs of the eschatological kingdom's presence in our midst. If indeed "the medium is the message," the theo-political kingdom community's message has been lost with the neutralizing of the sacred medium and is by no means rediscovered if "postmodern" churches revitalize space as sacred simply to infuse their worship services with a certain mystical ambiance.

God's eschatological kingdom community—when faithful to God's calling—seeks to break down divisions between rival groups, including Jews and Gentiles, males and females, slaves and free, through reenactment of the scriptures through such practices as table fellowship. The Lord's Supper summons people from various demographics to sit down together, calling for the eradication of barriers of hostility between various groups within the church.

How unfortunate when coffee bars overshadow or displace the Lord's Supper in churches today. Those who gather together for a coffee at Starbucks are most often friends or "affinity groups," who together often represent a narrowly defined demographic. Moreover, a coffee at Starbucks often conveys leisure and expendable income on the one hand and the not-so-leisurely competitive nature of the free market trade enterprise on the local, regional, national, and global levels. The presence of a Starbucks-like coffee bar in a church certainly sends mixed signals, for its niche, leisurely, and competitive free market ambiance and impulses influence and neutralize the church's own communal and theo-political identity, purpose, and activity. The medium is the message, or at least inseparably related to it.

While people go to Starbucks to drink coffee and hang out with their friends, God's people often fail to recognize the corporate significance of baptism and the Lord's Supper. Instead, they conceive these sacred practices in very personal and individualistic terms, looking to the sacraments to sustain them in their cultivation of their individual, personal relationship with Jesus. American evangelicals have tended to make the communion event "a me and Jesus moment" where we take *communion* in *isolation* in the privacy of our pews or chairs with eyes closed. One of us grew up Lutheran, and looks back with profound appreciation for having had to go up with others to the communion rail, kneeling with outstretched arm and hand before the table to take *communion with others,* including the sick, the elderly, and the rich and poor alike.

How is it that we have turned the event of communion into a form of isolation? If we were to take seriously its theological import, we would realize that communion can never be taken in isolation. While one could choose to drink a latte in isolation, one can never do so in the case of the Lord's Supper. Even the elderly person confined to a bed at home does not take communion in isolation. One of our students is a lay leader in a Lutheran church; whenever the pastor goes to the home of a bedridden person to administer the sacrament, the pastor offers bread from the same loaf and wine from the same cup from which the congregation has eaten and has drunk. Even the bedridden person partakes of the whole Christ with the whole community. In eating from the one loaf and drinking from the one cup, the community partakes of Christ, and through Christ God's people commune with one another in the Spirit.

Over against the neutralizing tendencies noted above, we need to return to a premodern conception of sacred space, where we actually see ourselves as participating in the signs and symbols themselves, and where the church is viewed as a microcosm of the entire universe. To enter into the church is to enter into God's universe. The Eastern church father Maximus the Confessor speaks of the church as an image of the visible and invisible universe, a microcosm, which is "not divided in kind by the differentiation of its parts." Distinct spaces that make up the interior of the church building, such as the nave and sanctuary, function as sections of the entire church.[14] In like manner, the immaterial and material dimensions of reality are distinct though inseparably related, as Maximus reflects:

> The wise thus glimpse the universe of things brought into existence by God's creation, divided between the spiritual world, containing incorporeal intelligent substances, and this corporeal world, the object of sense (so marvelously woven together from many natures and kinds of things) as if they were all another

Church, not built by hands, but suggested by the ones we build; its sanctuary is the world above, allotted to the powers above, its nave the world below, assigned to those whose lot it is to live in the senses.[15]

Martin Luther King Jr. also views the church as a microcosm. Its structure reflects God's universal restructuring of creaturely reality and redemptive purposes. In King's "Afro-Baptist sacred cosmos," one perceives the divinely determined hierarchy that "acts as a critique of every human law and institution."[16] In King's historic Ebenezer Baptist Church in Atlanta, God's power is centered in the imposing pulpit and Bible. A humble communion table stands before the pulpit, and saint and sinner are seated in front of the table. One's seat in the church reflects one's status in the congregation. The pulpit looms over the congregation, with the pastor's throne just behind it. The choir sits behind the pulpit and throne, with the choir representing the angelic host, scaling upward toward the heavens. A cross hangs above and behind the choir, and a portrayal of Jesus on "colored glass" rises above the cross.[17]

The preacher occupies a place in the hierarchy of the divine cosmos as the one who is authorized to proclaim God's lordship over other powers. Because the preacher has been called directly by God, he also has a privileged perch outside the hierarchy as the one who can "see" how God's purposes are unfolding in the whole world.[18]

King would later view the church—this "Afro-Baptist sacred cosmos"—as the ark of the covenant, which he would take with him in his civil rights campaigns.[19] "Ebenezer's worship (and worship space) not only built a world for Negro survival but institutionalized a permanent critique of a world in which survival is all one can hope for."[20] Sacred space can serve as a prophetic witness against the fallen principalities and powers as a visible sign of God's eschatological kingdom.

Cyril of Jerusalem certainly viewed sacred space as just such a prophetic witness and visible sign. In his discussion of baptism, he writes:

First, ye entered into the outer hall of the Baptistery, and there facing towards the West, ye heard the command to stretch forth your hand, and as in the presence of Satan ye renounced him. Now ye must know that this figure is found in ancient history. For when Pharaoh, that most cruel and ruthless tyrant, oppressed the free and high-born people of the Hebrews, God sent Moses to bring them out of the evil thraldom of the Egyptians. Then the door-posts were anointed with the blood of the lamb, that the destroyer might flee from the houses which had the sign of the blood; and the Hebrew people was marvelously delivered. The enemy, however, after their rescue, pursued them, and saw the sea wondrously parted for them; nevertheless he went on, following in their footsteps, and was all at once overwhelmed and engulfed in the Red Sea.[21]

Cyril later explains that the reason the catechumen, during the baptismal rite, faces west to renounce Satan is that "the West is the region of sensible darkness, and he being darkness, has his dominion also in darkness." And so, "ye, therefore, looking with a symbolical meaning towards the West, renounce that dark and gloomy potentate."[22]

Upon renouncing Satan while facing west in the outer chamber, "there is opened to thee the paradise of God, which He planted towards the east, whence for his transgression our first father was exiled; and symbolical of this was thy turning from the west to the east, the place of light."[23] While Satan is associated with the west and darkness, Christ—the morning star—is associated with the east and light. Entering into the inner chamber, the initiate undresses, is anointed with exorcized oil, and is "led to the holy pool of Divine Baptism, as Christ was carried from the Cross to the Sepulchre." Upon confessing faith in the Father, Son, and Holy Spirit, the initiate descends into the water and ascends from the water three times, "covertly pointing by a figure as the three-days burial of Christ."[24]

Cyril claims that while the new believer does not literally die, is not literally buried, does not literally rise again—"the imitation" being a figure—the "salvation is in reality."[25] "Imitation" here should not be taken to mean "unreal." Given the ancient emphasis on symbol, the believer enters through the virtuality of the symbol of baptism into the actual experience of Christ's passion, death, and resurrection life. As stated at the outset of this chapter, baptism, the Eucharist, and other sacred symbols serve as "virtual realities" through which the sacred community is drawn into the story of redemption and thus into Christ's presence. As we have indicated, sacramental worship becomes a kind of community theater in which the church experiences the grace of God through reenacting the gospel drama in space and time. Such reenactment reconfigures our sense of identity, purpose, and activity. In this drama we die to the unreality of sin—the world, flesh, and devil—and live to God's reality of righteousness made possible through Christ's atoning work in the power of the Spirit.

Discussion of "imitation," "virtual reality," and "Christ's presence" require further exploration. These and similar terms go to the heart of the historic debate over "real presence" in the sacraments—one that arose with Luther's attack on the Roman Catholic Church's view of the sacraments in *The Babylonian Captivity of the Church*. For the sake of ecumenical dialogue as well as Christian experience, it is important to understand the basic categories and terms of this debate in order to get past the age-old divide in search of more profound communion.

### "The Babylonian Captivity" Revisited: The Real Problem of Real Presence

Martin Luther's historic treatise, *The Babylonian Captivity of the Church*, was an attack on the Roman Catholic Church's doctrine of the sacraments.

The most significant and far-reaching aspect of his critique was his discussion of the Eucharist. Outraged over what he saw as the Roman Catholic Church hierarchy's apparent belittling of God's sovereign purposes, and holding people captive, keeping them from experiencing Christ, Luther claimed that the priest has no power to make the Eucharist effectual to the recipient. Thus, the sacrament does not operate by a power from within itself (*ex opere operato*). Rather, it is effectual only by faith, which is itself the gift of God. As Luther says, "Nothing else is needed for a worthy holding of mass than a faith that relies confidently on this promise, believes Christ to be true in these words of his [Christ's words of institution at the Last Supper], and does not doubt that these infinite blessings have been bestowed upon it."[26]

Luther also challenged the teaching that Christ is sacrificed at the celebration of the mass. It is important to pause and note that contrary to popular Protestant opinion, official Roman Catholic teaching denies that Christ is, in the mass, sacrificed time and time again. According to *The Catechism of the Catholic Church*, "The Eucharist is thus a sacrifice because it *re-presents* (makes present) the sacrifice of the cross, because it is its *memorial* and because it *applies* its fruit."[27] This making present of the once-for-all sacrifice is called *anamnesis*.[28] The Roman Catholic Church also claims that "the sacrifice of Christ and the sacrifice of the Eucharist are *one single sacrifice*."[29] Even though Protestants often misunderstand official Catholic teaching, there was no misunderstanding the import of Luther's challenge to the Catholic doctrine of the mass as sacrifice; Luther called into question the indispensability (and thus the societal power) of the Catholic institution as a medium of grace.[30]

Luther rejected the Catholic doctrine of transubstantiation,[31] which the Council of Trent summarizes as follows: "By the consecration of the bread and wine there takes place a change of the whole substance of the bread into the substance of the body of Christ our Lord and of the whole substance of the wine into the substance of his blood. This change the holy Catholic Church has fittingly and properly called transubstantiation."[32] Luther's own view is often mistakenly termed consubstantiation (a medieval teaching that claimed that Christ is locally present to the elements).[33] Rather, Luther has been quoted as saying that the body and blood of Christ is truly present "in, with, and under" the elements of bread and wine in a mysterious and nonlocal manner. As stated at the Marburg Colloquy in conversation with the Swiss, "Christ is truly present, that is substantively, essentially, though not quantitatively, qualitatively, or locally."[34]

The Marburg Colloquy (1529) brought together various Protestant leaders, including Luther, Melanchthon, Zwingli, Bucer, and Oekolampadius. While Zwingli is often thought to claim that the Lord's Supper is merely a memorial, here he advanced the view that Christ is spiritually present. For his own part, Luther maintained that however Christ is physically present, his presence is of no benefit apart from faith. Perhaps the chief difference between the two

Reformers was that Luther claimed that Christ is physically present, and Zwingli held that Christ is only spiritually present.

Beyond Marburg, the debate between followers of Luther and Calvin over the real presence of Christ relates to the communion of natures in Christ's person. Whereas the Lutheran tradition maintains that Christ's human nature relates directly to the divine nature in Christ's person—and so participates in the divine attributes such as omnipresence, the Calvinists maintain that Christ's human nature relates indirectly to the divine nature through Christ's person. Given this claim, the Reformed argue that the human nature does not participate in the divine nature and its attributes, such as omnipresence. Thus, whereas the Lutherans maintain that Christ's human nature is present everywhere (though not locally) that he chooses to make himself known, the Reformed maintain that Christ's human nature is located in heaven, where Christ is seated at the right hand of God.[35] While those following Calvin emphasize that Christ is truly present to the believer in the sacrament, it is the Spirit who makes Christ in his humanity present by lifting our hearts to heaven (*sursum corda*) to the place where the God-Man is seated at the right hand of God.[36]

While all Protestant traditions maintain that faith must be present for the sacrament to be efficacious, the Baptist heritage does not share Luther's, Zwingli's, and Calvin's conviction that Christ is really present at the sacrament. Rather, the Lord's Supper is an ordinance and a memorial. That is, the Lord's Supper is not a sacrament whereby the grace of Christ's presence is mediated to the believer at the table; moreover, from the Baptist perspective, the Supper functions exclusively as a memorial—a time to recall what Christ has done for us.[37]

We certainly share our Baptist brothers and sisters' view that we do indeed recall what Christ has done for us in his atoning work when we gather at the table. This notion is profoundly biblical and existentially significant. The Lord himself said that whenever we celebrate the Lord's Supper, we are to celebrate in remembrance of him (1 Cor. 11:24–25). However, scripture also teaches that we participate in Christ at the table (1 Cor. 10:14–22), as well as anticipate his coming when we gather there (Luke 22:14–18).[38] Thus, the church is called to approach the table from a heart and mind-set of recollection, participation, and anticipation on account of the Lord Jesus, who was, and is, and is to come.

As we recollect Christ's work at the table, the ascended Christ presents himself to us in the power of the Spirit and quickens within us a sense of anticipation as the day draws near for his return. While the elements of bread and wine have no sacramental significance in and of themselves, their proximity to Christ at the table celebration makes them significant. In his rebuke of the Corinthian church for taking part in pagan feasts, Paul says that the food offered to idols and the idols themselves are nothing; nonetheless, the food and idols participate in the presence of the demons to which they are offered and which they signify. Paul warns the Corinthians against participating with demons at these feasts, especially as these same Corinthians participate with Christ at his feast as his followers. One cannot participate in both celebrations without arousing the Lord's jealousy and judgment (see 1 Cor. 10:18–22). As Paul will say in the next chapter, many of them have become sick and have fallen asleep for eating and drinking at the table in an unworthy manner (1 Cor. 11:27–32). The Lord is present at the table to bless and to judge those who participate in his presence.

The conviction that we participate in Christ's presence at the table is a radical notion; we dare not take access to the table lightly. While the classic Protestant critique of the Roman Catholic Church's theology and practices concerning the Eucharist was radical in its historic context, the claim that Christ is present at each celebration of the table never ceases to be radical: the Lord himself is present at the table, *ever near*. Thus, in place of the typical evangelical mantra that we should not celebrate the Lord's Supper often, so that it does not become rote (often bound up with a memorialist perspective), we would argue that Christ presenting himself time and time again—not as a corpse but as the one who was dead but who is alive forevermore—can never get old. It is *ever new*. The problem with Christian worship—including the proclamation of scripture, prayer, and celebration of the Supper—becoming rote stems not from the sacred and radical practices of rehearsing the biblical drama through Word and sacrament themselves, but from God's people's calloused hearts and dull minds.[39]

Equally radical is the Radical Reformation's emphasis on community life. While we disagree with our Anabaptist friends, who often do not place the same amount of importance on celebrating the Lord's Supper as other traditions do, we admire their commitment to community life. There is something to be said for their view that each and every daily meal should be a profoundly spiritual experience. Moreover, those belonging to the Quaker tradition claim that every meal is a Lord's Supper. They also believe that all of life is sacramental, and that membership in Christ's body requires an inner transformation of the whole of one's life, not observance of an external rite such as baptism or the Eucharistic celebration.[40]

Quakers aspire to a very integrative spirituality. We share their aspiration for an integrative spirituality. Thus, while we believe that there is a qualitative distinction between celebration of the Lord's Table and all other occasions for table fellowship—for the Lord's Supper was celebrated as the fulfillment of the Passover celebration—this ultimate meal should shape our Christian existence and community life profoundly, including other forms of table fellowship. Many within the Radical Reformation and Quaker traditions often have a more profound sense of community life than those from other traditions; perhaps this is because they see the church as a remnant community and thus are more attentive than most to attempts to reduce the church to a voluntary association of pious individuals whose true allegiance belongs to promoting the state and/or market's well-being—a modern form of Babylonian captivity.

All too often, Christians celebrate the Lord's Supper in a private and individualistic manner, reflecting only upon their relations with God, failing to account for one another as members of Christ's countercultural kingdom community of the new humanity. Adapting Anabaptist theologian John Howard Yoder's claim that Jesus is the head of the church, which is "a community of consumption,"[41] the church's practices such as table fellowship bear witness to the identity, purpose, and activity of the new humanity, where race, class, and gender divisions are consumed. Again, to commandeer Yoder's words:

> The very existence of the church is [the church's] primary task. It is in itself a proclamation of the lordship of Christ to the powers from whose dominion the church has begun to be liberated . . . The Church must be a sample of the kind of humanity within which . . . economic and racial differences are surmounted.[42]

The church—and communion within it—is a foretaste of the eschatological kingdom's transformation of creaturely life. Such a view of the church is radical and reflects a radical conception of its practices, including the Lord's Supper and table fellowship generally. The significance appointed to Christian table fellowship also reflects a priestly conception of the entire Christian community—all believers are priests. Here they are taking forward one of the most profound claims of the Protestant Reformation—the priesthood of all believers.

In light of the preceding point, it is worth returning to Luther's debate with the Catholics over the Eucharist. Luther rejected the practice that only the ordained priest—and none of the laity—could drink from the cup.[43] While the Catholic Church maintained that Christ addressed his words, "Drink you all of it," to his apostles, Luther retorted that all believers are priests.[44] Luther's call for taking back the captive cup from the trophy case in Babylonian Rome was ultimately a call for freeing the captive Christian from a Christian caste or class system where those of the cloth belong to a higher Christian class. This claim was considered radical in Luther's day, not unlike his view of translating the Bible into the language of the common people. Such radicalism had led to the disinterring and burning of pre-Reformation figure John Wycliffe's body and the burning of John Huss.

While Luther's views of the Eucharist were radical in his day, his views concerning baptism were conservative. While his doctrine of the Eucharist led him in the direction of congregationalism (the church is made up of believers only), his doctrine of baptism led him in the direction of the state church (the church is in an alliance with the state; thus, all citizens are baptized into the church). For this reason, Roland Bainton terms it "the sociological sacrament."[45] Luther's doctrine of the sacraments shaped his doctrine of the church, and the church's relation to society at large,[46] just as his doctrine of justification by faith shaped his view of the sacraments.[47]

As Protestant evangelicals following the basic lines of Luther's thought, we wish to stress the personal nature of salvation. Salvation comes by faith. Yet given our ecumenical conviction that God is at work in the various Christian traditions, we wish to highlight the significance of faith without wishing to undermine the manifold ways in which the various traditions understand the mode of salvation by faith's reception. Thus, while we do not believe that people are saved by water baptism, we do believe that people who think their water baptism is instrumental to their salvation are saved in the same way that others are—by trusting in God's promise to save them through Christ. Faith itself, on our view, is the gift of God's grace granted to us in Christ by the Holy Spirit.

Moreover, while we do not believe that water baptism as such saves, we do believe that God uses creaturely means for bearing witness to himself, and to serve as symbols that participate in the salvation event. God himself became human to save us. We do not worship Christ's humanity, but the God who became human; the God who became human saves us, not Christ's humanity as such. While water from the spring, bread from wheat, and wine from the vine do not save us, they function as participatory signs of God's recapitulating work whereby God heals the creation and uses the creation to serve as a healing balm for humanity.

Advocates of water-baptismal regeneration will no doubt draw attention to Acts 2:38 in response, where Peter talks of the need to repent and be baptized to receive forgiveness for sin and to receive the gift of the Holy Spirit. However, in Acts 4:4, there is no mention of baptism when it speaks of people believing and being added to the church. In Acts 10, Cornelius and his household receive the Holy Spirit before being baptized with water (Acts 10:44–48). While we cannot say that water baptism is regenerative, we must say that it is critical for people to be baptized with water. For one, it plays a symbolically significant role in bearing witness to the biblical drama of salvation beginning with the exodus. Moreover, it is a visible sign of an inner reality—baptism of the Holy Spirit. The Bible always closely correlates spiritual and creaturely dynamics (note the use of water-like imagery to describe the new birth in Titus 3:5), even while at times distinguishing them (Jesus draws from the new covenant language of Ezekiel 36 when explaining the new birth by water and the Spirit to Nicodemus in John 3, while also remarking that flesh gives birth to flesh and the Spirit to spirit). Lastly, water baptism is critical to one's corporate identification with the visible church, as can be seen in passages already mentioned (Acts 2:41; 10:45–48). This all harkens back to the exodus event where the people of Israel passed through the Red Sea, emerging out of it as the people of God. Similarly, as the people of God passed through the Jordan River, they became the people of God in God's Promised Land. So, passing through water is always an illustration of entering into God's community in God's sacred space. Against this backdrop, water baptism signifies the *conception* of Christian communal life. Similarly, the Lord's Supper pertains to the *cultivation* of that life, just as was true of the Passover celebration in the Hebrew Scriptures.

There are various views of the significance of water baptism. Catholics and Lutherans see water baptism as regenerative (as in the case of an infant who is baptized). The Reformed tradition views water baptism as signifying entrance into God's covenantal community, though without it serving as regenerative (thus, a baptized infant is viewed as a participant in God's covenantal community; as the child grows and becomes cognizant of the gospel, the individual in question is urged to believe, participating fully in the covenant community). Baptists hold that water baptism is a public testimony to an internal reality that has already happened (in this case, only believing individuals are baptized).

On our view, water baptism does not regenerate anyone. However, baptism by water serves as a participatory sign in salvation history, functioning as a creaturely pointer to God's saving actions in our lives. We also maintain that believer baptism makes best sense of scripture's teaching on baptism (although the New Testament teaches that whole households such as that of Lydia as well as the jailer in Philippi were baptized [see Acts. 16], it is at best an inference to state that infants were included in their numbers). While the practice of infant dedication is nowhere mentioned in the New Testament as a practice of the first-century church, the same holds true for infant baptism—nowhere is it specifically mentioned. However, there are numerous texts that talk of believers being baptized. While we think that believer baptism makes better sense of the New Testament material on baptism, we also believe the church has demonstrated little sense in turning baptismal waters into a divisive subject; baptism is intended to unite people, not divide them. With this historical and contemporary context in mind, along with the New Testament's very clear emphasis on unity, we suggest that a theology of unity supersede a particular theology of infant or believer baptism; thus, we honor the baptism of infants and do not feel it is necessary for those baptized as infants to be rebaptized unless it is a matter of their conscience.[48]

As important as particular views of baptism and the Lord's Supper are, a theology of unity as well as of the Triune God's sovereign presence and working in these sacramental events must take center stage. On our view, the church is not a dispenser of God's grace. Christ and the Spirit are God's sacramental presence in baptism and the Lord's Supper. While baptismal and table events are human events, they become divine events when they are practiced in faith in the faithful Christ through the Spirit. Just as the bread and wine participate in God's sacramental presence—the Son and Spirit—through the miracle of grace, faith is itself the miraculous creation of the Triune God. So the sacraments in and of themselves do not save us, but they are indissolubly joined to the saving presence of God in Christ through the Spirit. For God always works in our midst through creaturely means.

Christ in the Spirit is the sacramental presence of God; while the visible signs or symbols of baptism and the Lord's Supper participate in Christ's sacramental reality through the Spirit every time God's people gather to celebrate them, they do not constitute that sacramental, christological (and pneumatological) reality. Christ alone gives himself to us through the Spirit in these creaturely acts; and so, he alone constitutes God's sacramental grace through the Spirit in our midst. Christ mediates himself to his people in the Spirit through Word and Sacrament. The church does not add to Christ's finished work but lives in view of it, bearing witness to Christ's saving work through these participatory symbols. We participate in these symbols that Christ constitutes, even as we participate in Christ himself, who was and is and is to come.

Emphasis on the Triune God's presence and constitution of the sacramental community along with God's creation of faith in the believer safeguards against institutionalism in any form. Revisiting the biblical story and revitalizing sacred space around the sacraments do not automatically convey faithful witness. Neither the sacraments nor those who administer them have power in themselves to make the sacraments effectual (*ex opere operato*). However, rediscovery of the biblical story and sacred symbols goes hand in hand with revival of God's people's hearts and lives. Sacraments and personal faith mutually reinforce each other. Through God's divinely appointed means of scripture and the sacraments, God draws us into the sacred drama as active participants.

While revisiting the biblical story and revitalizing sacred space around the sacraments can enhance but do not automatically convey faithful witness to Christ, failure to move forward in Christian discipleship has little or nothing to do with promoting a particular mode or form of baptism. The problem lies elsewhere—in the individual's heart and in the church's preaching and teaching. As Geoffrey Bromiley writes,

> Where infant baptism, or paedobaptism, as it is sometimes called, is practiced, it is right and necessary that those who grow to maturity should make their own confession of faith. But they do so with the clear witness that it is not this which saves them, but the work of God already done for them before they believed. The possibility arises, of course, that they will not make this confession, or do so formally. But this cannot be avoided by a different mode of administration. It is a problem of preaching and teaching. And even if they do not believe, or do so nominally, their prior baptism as a sign of the work of God is a constant witness to call or finally to condemn them.[49]

All major traditions rightly reject cheap grace in the face of God's costly grace revealed in Christ, exhorting and inviting Christ's followers to follow in his footsteps. This christologically-driven emphasis on discipleship should serve as a common thread that would bind together the various baptismal traditions, even for those otherwise divided by the waters that were intended to consume divisions. We should not be fighting among ourselves, but fighting together against our mutual enemy of the world, the flesh, and the devil in our daily lives.

The preceding discussion on the call to discipleship leads us to say that we must encourage people to guard against depending upon the faith of their parents or their own past merits and rituals to carry them spiritually; instead they must be encouraged and challenged to respond personally and repeatedly to Christ's call on their lives. The Christian life is a process, not a static event relegated to one's past. Thus, we must be very careful to caution people against thinking, "I'm saved because I've been baptized; and so I can live however I please" or its counterpart, "I prayed a prayer at a crusade and got saved, and so now I can just sit back and coast."

We must teach Christ followers to grow up to maturity in view of the ascended Christ who was perfected through suffering and who represents us as our perfect High Priest before the Father's throne. This same Jesus who has begun a good work in us will carry it on to completion at the day of his appearance (Phil. 1:6). This very same Jesus who rose from the dead and who has ascended to heaven saves us and inspires and equips us for every good work and service in the power of the Spirit for the glory of God. This same Jesus frees us from modern-day versions of the Babylonian captivity—whatever they may be—as we reenact the biblical story and participate in Christ's kingdom work through his sacramental presence in and through baptism and the Eucharist in the power of the Spirit.

## The Babylonian Captivity and the American Church

One way in which the American church experiences its own form of Babylonian Captivity is by falling prey to the propaganda machine that claims that America was founded as a Christian nation, that God wishes to reclaim America for himself as a Christian nation, and that our ultimate allegiance to Christ's kingdom comes through allegiance to America.[50]

When this perspective dominates our thinking, it is very hard for us to grasp the pastor's words at the presentation of the newly baptized—whether they are infants, teenagers, adults, or seniors—as our true brothers and sisters during a worship service. Instead of seeing these believers as vitally connected to the body, we see them as belonging primarily to their nuclear families, family stock portfolios, and the state. For unlike inclusion in these other institutions, the ecclesial family is made up of an apparently random assortment of consumers joined together by warmhearted, religious sentiment. On this view, spiritual union is based on a voluntary and possibly even momentary or short-term contractual commitment one to another. We need to get beyond this way of thinking and view the church community as bound together even more profoundly than those communities based on biological, economic, and legal ties.

In the end, it is very difficult for us to see ourselves as a sacramental community made up of those who have died to their old way of life and have embarked on a new journey that will never grow old and never end. As we write these words, Fourth of July festivities are taking place. The church must recognize how America divinizes national holidays such as today, secularizes Christian ones, as in the case of Christmas and Easter, and gives priority of place to national symbols—even over Christian ones. So much for it being one nation under God—it often seems like America is one nation over God![51]

This calls to mind the story one pastor lived to share. During one Sunday worship service, he decided to challenge people's allegiance to Christ by draping the American flag over the communion table. He then proceeded to administer communion. When it came time to lead people to drink from the cup, he purposively poured the grape juice on the flag. People were horrified. One of the elders later told this pastor that at first he was outraged, but that later, after pondering it awhile, he realized that the pastor was trying to help God's people see where their true loyalty lay. After all the people left church to go home, a man burst into the pastor's study—without knocking. He came right up to the pastor, violently thrust his finger into the pastor's chest several times, and said, "Don't you ever, ever do that to the American flag again!"

The Babylonian captivity in Luther's day stemmed in part from the clergy's fear that the laity would spill the wine—Christ's precious blood—that had been consecrated and administered during the service to purchase their salvation. The Babylonian captivity today manifests itself in the fear on the part of the laity that the clergy will spill the grape juice on such things as the American flag, which was purchased by the precious blood of countless Americans.

Without intending to disparage patriotism and America's national symbols, the church must come to see that its ultimate loyalty belongs to Christ's kingdom, to which we pay tribute at each celebration of the Eucharist. By no means simply a memorial to the war dead, the eucharistic celebration is just that—a celebration of the one who died and rose and lives forever, who reigns with God and will return, and whose kingdom knows no end.

The American church does not presently experience the red martyrdom so prevalent in Cyril of Jerusalem's day. Nor does it promote the notion that baptism in blood alone suffices as an alternative to water baptism for salvation. Nor does the American church promote the white martyrdom (monasticism) so prevalent in Luther's day, which exemplified the religious caste system of the medieval Christian community. At that time, only the clergy and people of the cloth could drink from the cup. While not calling for red or white martyrdom today, we must call on the church to cherish its sacred symbols that bear witness to the fact that we the church belong to Christ and his kingdom. The church is by no means a voluntary association of religious individuals. The Christian's ultimate allegiance lies with Christ's church, not with the state or market or nuclear family. The church's sacred symbols cannot be reduced to sources for cultivating pious emotion in the individual believer. Rather, baptism and the Eucharist signify that we the church are citizens of God's kingdom, stakeholders in God's economy, and members of God's family. As the saying goes, we drink to remember, while others drink to forget. As we eat the bread and drink the cup, let us remember who Christ is and what he has done for us. May we also remember who we are as those whose old master (Pharaoh—Exod. 14) and marriage partner (the law of the old economy—Rom. 6–7) have been buried in baptism as we have been raised to experience captivating though liberating loving marital union with Christ our Lord.

## Study Questions

1. How would you respond to those who argue that celebrating the Lord's Supper weekly robs it of its freshness?
2. How do we guard against the sacraments becoming simply institutional mechanisms for salvation?
3. In what ways is Christ uniquely present when the church celebrates the Lord's Supper?
4. How could the church make the celebration of baptism and the Lord's Supper more communal?

# 8

# Sacraments and the Search for the Holy Grail

It seems like everyone is searching for the Holy Grail—Monty Python, Indiana Jones, Dan Brown, and Joe Christian, who's in search of more authentic communion. And that's just it. The Holy Grail is not ultimately some cup or Mary Magdalene's bones, but authentic communion centered round Jesus of Nazareth at the table.

One of us grew up in a church that practiced closed communion—only those who viewed the Eucharist or Lord's Supper in the same way that the church did could take communion there. This was very unsettling. "Closed communion" seemed to suggest that a relationship with Christ is not sufficient to gain access to the table. "You have to think the same way we do" about what goes on in the bread and wine at the table to gain access.

While we deeply appreciate the theological significance of the various traditions' views of the presence of Christ to the sacraments, we appreciate even more the theological significance of visible unity in the body of Christ—the church. In a day when more and more people go to Dan Brown to get their dose of religion, and to the local pub to find true community, it is more and more important that the church delve deeply into the divine mystery of communion between Christ and his people that occurs at the table. As vital as our various views of Christ's presence to the elements at the table are, even more fundamental is the conviction that Christ is present to his people at the table,

and the difference that this conviction should make in our communion with
one another and in our witness to the surrounding world.

How wonderful it would be if Catholics, Anglicans, Lutherans, Orthodox,
Reformed, Baptists, and others could come together and partake of the table
together. How sad it is that the table that is intended to build communion is
often at the center of theological debates and church factions. For those of
us in the Protestant tradition, the rift occurred as early as Luther's famous
debate with Zwingli during the Marburg Colloquy (1529). Though church
history is a very complicated affair, and factions emerged over other matters,
it is a tragedy and tragic irony (from which the Protestant church has never
really recovered) that Luther and Zwingli broke off ecclesial fellowship over
their respective views of communion.

Communion should not ultimately be about coming together with those
who think or act or look like me. Neither should it simply be about God and
me. It is about God and his people coming together to wine and dine as participants in Christ through the Spirit in recollection of Christ's finished work
and in anticipation of his return.

Arnold T. Olson of the Evangelical Free Church once said that communion
should be for believers only—but *all* believers.[1] We agree with this claim. Now,
no doubt, someone will say that we are putting limits on access to the table,
just like those we are critiquing. Yes and no. The only limit is faith in Christ,
but that is because the Lord's Supper from its inception was intended to be
Christ's own family's meal. Having said that, there is always a standing invitation to this family celebration—the invitation always stands open to *anyone*
who would believe on the Lord Jesus, irrespective of his or her theological
distinctives, ethnicity, economic level, and maturity. Of course, believers need
to examine themselves before they come to the table, as Paul exhorts (1 Cor.
11:28)—not that they measure up to one another's expectations, but that they
come to receive of Christ's measureless overflow; not that they believe everything rightly or exactly in the same way, but that they look to the One in whom
they believe; not that they have their acts together before they come, but that
they make sure not to hinder others from coming through their actions, and
that they realize that communion is just as much about our relationship with
one another in the body as it is about our relationship with our living head.

The church mentioned earlier now claims to practice open communion.
However, while one no longer needs to be a confirmed member of that particular church and its denomination, one must believe the same way about the
presence of Christ to the elements as that church and denomination. Their
communion service materials add to this stipulation Paul's warning that those
who eat and drink of the Supper without discerning the body of Christ eat
and drink judgment on themselves (1 Cor. 11:29).

Our own interpretation of Paul's warning goes further and is based upon his
rebuke of the Corinthians earlier in this passage. The rich Christians were not

sharing with their poor brothers and sisters in Christ the abundance of their provisions at the meal. In fact, while the rich Christians wined and dined together in the dining room of the house church there in Corinth, the less-privileged believers stood outside in the courtyard looking in. These rich Christians had failed to discern the body of Christ—the *whole* church at Corinth. As a result, they had eaten and had drunk judgment on themselves (1 Cor. 11:29).

Gordon Fee claims that the sociological divisions in the church at Corinth between the "haves" and "have-nots" manifested themselves in the celebration of the Lord's Supper, which was probably part of a common meal. Fee says that in Corinth it was "sociologically natural for the host to invite those of his/her own class to eat" in the dining room while others ate in the courtyard.[2] Fee later writes, "For those who think of themselves as 'keeping the traditions' the actions noted here probably did not register as of particular consequence. They had always acted thus. Birth and circumstances had cast their lots; society had dictated their mores." For Paul, in contrast, "Those mores at the Lord's Supper were a destruction of the meaning of the Supper itself because it destroyed the very unity which that meal proclaimed."[3]

Based on this understanding of the background context to Paul's words, we maintain that for Paul "discerning the body of Christ" entails that we should no longer eat according to the customs of our culture, but according to the social mores of Christ's kingdom, for this is not some common meal, but the uncommon meal of Christ. To discern rightly here includes acting rightly toward others (while also discerning the significance of Christ's presence at the meal), which entails making sure that we do not hinder others from coming to the table. All are welcome, regardless of economic standing and the like.

To say "regardless of economic standing" is not to say that the table has no regard for economics. The table signifies or symbolizes the economics and politics of Christ's kingdom. If only churches—regardless of their views along other lines—valued economic redistribution and fought against consumerism and its commodification of human identity.

Consumerism entails getting what we want, even things we did not originally want—or need—and as much as we can possibly get. "Stuff" wins out over people, and those with the most stuff win, or in more biblical-sounding terms, people were made for stuff, not stuff for people.

Instead of giving ourselves to consuming stuff, we the church should give ourselves to consuming and being consumed by Christ himself. For as John Howard Yoder once said, Jesus is the head of "a community of consumption."[4] In place of consuming humans (*homo consumens*), Christians become increasingly consumed people (*homo consumendus*). Such consumption occurs not through buying and selling, but as the result of being bought at a steep price with the blood of Christ to the end of interpersonal communion with God through Christ by the Spirit. And all of this is exactly what we celebrate at the Lord's family feast.

Such good news should liberate us from being enslaved to consumerist impulses. But the fear of scarcity often dominates our thinking. Walter Brueggemann puts it this way:

> Though many of us are well intentioned, we have invested our lives in consumerism. We have a love affair with "more"—and we will never have enough. Consumerism is not simply a marketing strategy. It has become a demonic spiritual force among us, and the theological question facing us is whether the gospel has the power to help us withstand it.[5]

As important as the issues so often debated about the real presence of Christ in the Supper are, even more important is the issue before us now. The story of God's abundance inspires communion, whereas the headline news of scarcity bound up with consumerism destroys it. Which storyline will win out? If only Catholics, Orthodox, and Protestants could come together to get the word out through shared practices at the table and beyond that God's abundance is truly abundant. This is the real question now facing us as the church.[6] As Brueggemann says wistfully in a different context,

> Wouldn't it be wonderful if liberal and conservative church people, who love to quarrel with each other, came to a common realization that the real issue confronting us is whether the news of God's abundance can be trusted in the face of the story of scarcity? . . . The great question now facing the church is whether our faith allows us to live in a new way.[7]

Brueggemann goes on to speak of Jesus's sacramental orientation that proclaims the good news that the world is saturated with God's abundant generosity. The sacramental orientation of Jesus demonstrates that "the world is filled with abundance and freighted with generosity. If bread is broken and shared, there is enough for all. Jesus is engaged in the sacramental, subversive reordering of public reality."[8] "The profane," on the other hand, "is the opposite of the sacramental." It signifies "flat, empty, one-dimensional, exhausted. The market ideology wants us to believe that the world is profane—life consists of buying and selling, weighing, measuring and trading, and then finally sinking into death and nothingness."[9] Jesus's view of economy is quite different and "transforms the economy by blessing and breaking it beyond self-interest. From broken Friday bread comes Sunday abundance."[10]

One of the best examples of living in view of God's generosity rather than out of the fear of scarcity comes not from the rich Christians in Corinth, but from a few poor Christians in Chicago. In his book *The Case for Christmas*, Lee Strobel recounts the story he wrote when he worked as a journalist for the *Chicago Tribune*.

It was Christmas time, and Strobel was given the assignment to write a story about a poor, inner-city family. At the time, Strobel was an ardent atheist, and he recounts how he was a bit stunned by the Delgado family's attitude, despite their difficulties. The sixty-year-old Perfecta—wracked with pain from the debilitating arthritis that kept her from working—along with her two granddaughters, Lydia and Jenny, now lived in a very small and very empty two-room apartment, having been burned out of a roach-infested tenement. With only one small table in the kitchen and a handful of rice, and without furniture, rugs, and wall hangings, they hung their hopes on Christ. The two girls possessed no clothing, save one short-sleeved dress for each, and they shared a worn and thread-bare sweater. Strobel recounts how the girls would have to walk a half-mile to school each day, braving the bitter Chicago winter, taking turns wearing the sweater when the biting temperatures became too much for the one without. Despite these circumstances, the family never became bitter. Perfecta spoke with great confidence about Jesus's presence and faithfulness to them. Strobel writes, "I never sensed despair or self-pity in her home; instead, there was a gentle feeling of hope and peace."

After Strobel finished the article, he was given more high-profile assignments. But the story wasn't over. On Christmas Eve, he found his thoughts wandering back to the Delgados and their confidence in Christ's care for them. Strobel recounts: "I continued to wrestle with the irony of the situation. Here was a family that had nothing but faith, and yet seemed happy, while I had everything I needed materially, but lacked faith—and inside I felt as empty and barren as their apartment." There wasn't much meaningful news to write about on Christmas Eve, and so Strobel made a visit to the Delgado home.

He couldn't believe what he saw and heard when he arrived. The outpouring of compassion from his readership was overwhelming. New appliances, rugs, and furniture filled the little apartment, along with a host of Christmas-wrapped presents, a big Christmas tree, bags filled with food, lots of cash, and all kinds of winter clothing. As overwhelming as the overflow of compassion was, the atheist Strobel chalked it off to Christmas goodwill. What truly overwhelmed Strobel was the Delgados' response:

> But as surprised as I was by this outpouring, I was even more astonished by what my visit was interrupting: Perfecta and her granddaughters were getting ready to give away much of their newfound wealth. When I asked Perfecta why, she replied in halting English: "Our neighbors are still in need. We cannot have plenty while they have nothing. This is what Jesus would want us to do."
>
> That blew me away! If I had been in their position at that time in my life, I would have been hoarding everything. I asked Perfecta what she thought about the generosity of the people who had sent all of these goodies, and again her response amazed me.
>
> "This is wonderful; this is very good," she said, gesturing toward the largess. "We did nothing to deserve this—it's a gift from God. But," she added, "it is not his greatest gift. No, we celebrate that tomorrow. That is Jesus."

To her, this child in the manger was the undeserved gift that meant every-thing—more than material possessions, more than comfort, more than security. And at that moment, something inside of me wanted desperately to know this Jesus—because, in a sense, I saw him in Perfecta and her granddaughters.

They had peace despite poverty, while I had anxiety despite plenty; they knew the joy of generosity, while I only knew the loneliness of ambition; they looked heavenward for hope, while I only looked out for myself; they experi-enced the wonder of the spiritual, while I was shackled to the shallowness of the material—and something made me long for what they had.

Or, more accurately, for the One they knew.[11]

The Delgados embodied the sacramental orientation of which Bruegge-mann speaks. Their case for Christmas is also the case for Good Friday, Easter, and the recapitulation or transformation of all life, which the Lord's Supper anticipates. In fact, it is fair to say that the Delgados in some mysterious way were the body and blood of Christ to Strobel—so much so, that he wanted to know this One in whom they believed.

Their case for Christmas made a case for the authenticity of the story of God's abundance and typified the sacramental reality of the church in its union with Christ. The Corinthians, on the other hand, made a case for the myth of scarcity and the profane. Whereas the atheist Strobel discerned the body of the overwhelmingly generous Christ in the poverty-stricken Delgados, spurring him on toward faith, the rich though spiritually bankrupt Christians in Corinth denied Christ by failing to discern his presence in their poorer brothers and sisters.

Just as Jesus fed the five thousand and there were still some basketfuls of fish and bread remaining, and just as Jesus fed the Delgados and they gave away out of their abundant hearts at Christmas time, so Jesus will feed us too throughout the year—so that we can share with others. There is always room for more at his table—and so, there's no need for closing the door.

Prison Fellowship's Angel Tree ministry at Christmas time is one way our churches can share the bounty of the Lord with others, in this case the fami-lies of those closed off from society, behind closed doors in prison. Another way is for churches to get involved with the Advent Conspiracy, which several emergent-church pastors across the land have created. The "conspirators" of this initiative have determined to encourage their congregations to resist "Herod's empire" of greed during the Christmas season by giving of them-selves relationally, by taking a percentage of the money they would have spent on themselves for presents, and putting that money toward building wells for clean drinking water in impoverished places around the world.

Closer to home in terms of the Lord's Supper, our churches can follow the lead of those congregations that take an offering for the poor of the church after the celebration of the Lord's Supper, following the tradition of the early church. Also following the tradition of the early church, churches today could take the opportunity to celebrate the agape feast those weeks they celebrate the Lord's Table, hosting potlucks where everyone who is able brings a dish and everyone has a place at the table to eat—though not alongside their niche-group friends. Churches in the same region can even share their resources with one another: those more affluent churches can share their financial resources with their counterparts for much-needed facilities and supplies, and their counterparts can share the abundance of their hope in Christ in the midst of their difficult circumstances, so that those more affluent churches become immune to "affluenza." When we truly take seriously the gospel of God's abundance and the economics of the table, we will surely defeat the myth of scarcity and find the Holy Grail. However, when we close our minds and hearts to the gospel of the kingdom and the economics of the table, we close ourselves off from true and lasting communion and effective witness.[12]

Communion should not be closed off to those who view the presence of Christ to the elements differently from me, but to a way of being that is closed off to God's generosity and marked by the fear of scarcity. The most important issue is not the presence of Christ to the elements, but the presence of Christ to you and me as we gather at the table to share in God's abundance with one another, and as we go forward from the table refreshed and renewed.

Let's ask ourselves these two questions: Are we the church being transformed into the body and blood of Christ time and time again through the celebration of the Eucharist? And is Jesus living in, with, and under us as we relate to one another? If we can say "yes" to both questions, then we have discerned rightly the body of Christ.

In *Indiana Jones and the Last Crusade*, Jones goes in search of the Holy Grail. Finally, he locates its resting place. So too does a Nazi. A knight stands guard over a vast array of chalices, including the Holy Grail. The knight is the least of their worries, though. Neither Jones nor the Nazi know what the Grail looks like, and each of them gets only one chance at choosing correctly. They must drink the contents of whatever chalice they choose, and the liquid in every cup other than the Grail is lethal. The Nazi goes first and chooses the most ornate and expensive-looking chalice. After drinking from the cup, he shrivels up and dies, upon which the knight says, "He chose poorly." Jones is next. He recalls that Jesus was a Jewish carpenter, and so he chooses the most common of all the remaining cups. He drinks from its contents and lives. He has chosen wisely.

As stated near the outset of this chapter, we live at a time when more and more people go to Dan Brown to get their dose of religion, and to the local pub to find true community. Given this situation, it is more and more important that the church delve deeply into the divine mystery of communion between Christ and his people that occurs at the table. How will the world discern rightly that we—the church—are the body of Christ if we ourselves do not discern rightly what really matters? While we continue to wrestle with questions concerning

Christ's presence to the elements at the table, let's wrestle even more with ways of how to welcome all believers to the table, and to redistribute the bounty of the Lord's abundant harvest inside and outside the church, keeping in mind the difference this conviction will make in our communion with one another and in our witness to the surrounding world.

## STUDY QUESTIONS

1. How should our understanding of the Lord's Supper as communion help us get beyond divisions in churches and divisions between various church traditions?
2. In the biblical culture, eating a communal meal was often about welcoming the alien and the stranger. How could our practice of the Lord's Supper more fully reflect this idea?
3. How should the event of communion inspire us to move beyond race and class barriers?

# 9

# The Church as a Serving Community

The first task of every Christian is the edification of the community of believers.

Howard Snyder[1]

The life of the church in the world is always meant to be incarnational. As such, the church is to represent in its service to humanity the incarnation of Christ, who came not to be served, but to serve. This is a chapter about the church as a serving community. As such, it is not a chapter on the church as a community that serves the world. That subject is taken up in the chapter on the church as a missional community. Here we look at the church as a community where believers love and serve one another. For although the church is commanded to serve all persons, it is especially called to serve other believers, following Paul's admonition in Galatians to "do good to all people, especially to those who belong to the family of believers" (6:10). It is perhaps here that the word *community*, which is included in several of the chapters of this book, finds its fullest expression. For while worship, the sacraments, and mission are all activities that should be done in community and themselves engender community, it is in the act of loving service to its own that the church builds community in its fullest sense. It is also important to note that when we talk about service in this chapter, we mean it in a broad sense. Service is not just about helping people with their physical needs, but is holistic, including such services as teaching, using spiritual gifts, praying, sharing goods with others, and even church discipline.

## Foundations of the Church's Service

### Trinity

In his consideration of the role of the trinitarian God in the function of the church as a community of service, Dietrich Bonhoeffer writes,

> When God's Son took on flesh, he truly and bodily, out of pure grace, took on our being, our nature, ourselves. This was the eternal decree of the triune God. Now we are in him. Wherever he is, he bears our flesh, he bears us. And where he is, there we are too . . . Christian community means community through and in Jesus Christ. Everything the Scriptures provide in the way of directions and rules for Christians' life together rests on this presupposition.[2]

The service of the church flows out of the self-giving love of the trinitarian God who gives himself as a servant to humanity. Orthodox theologians, with their social doctrine of the Trinity, contend that self-giving and self-sacrifice is not merely a function of the Son, but of all three members of the Trinity. Thus God, by nature, is a self-sacrificing God. In the eternal "I–Thou" relations of the Trinity, he is a loving and serving God.[3] This has practical ramifications for the church as a serving community. Bishop Kallistos Ware writes,

> Our social programme, said the Russian thinker Feodorov, is the dogma of the Trinity . . . The human person, so the Bible teaches, is made in the image of God, and to Christians God means the Trinity: thus it is only in the light of the dogma of the Trinity that we can understand who we are and what God intends us to be. Our private lives, our personal relations, and all our plans of forming a Christian society depend upon a right theology of the Trinity.[4]

To be human in the image of the trinitarian God means to love others with a love that is costly and self-sacrificing. If the Father loved us enough to give his only Son for us, we also should lay down our lives for one another.[5] This pattern is played out across the spectrum of New Testament writings.

In the Synoptics, the Son of Man comes to give himself as a ransom for a captive and broken humanity (Matt. 20:28). In John, the Father sends the Son into the world to give his life for his sheep, an act that is an outpouring of the trinitarian Father/Son relationship, where the shared glory of Father and Son is manifest in the Son's self-sacrifice for humanity. Then the Son, speaking to his disciples as master, having just washed their feet, tells them that if the one who is God in the flesh serves them in this way, so should they serve one another (John 13:12–17). Further in John's thinking, out of the overflow of the love between Father and Son, the Holy Spirit is sent to serve the disciples by being the comforting presence of Jesus and the loving presence of the Father in their midst (John 14:15–21). In Paul, the Father exalts the Son on account of his humble decision to take on the form of a servant, giving his life for the church. Here the trinitarian equality between Father and Son does not preclude the Son's self-humiliation and service, but births it. This self-giving then becomes the example of the attitude that the church should have in its own service—"Your attitude should be the same as that of Christ Jesus" (Phil. 2:5–11).

Further, this trinitarian mutuality of love that flows out from God in service to the church serves not only as the church's example, but also as its empowerment for service. For the God who gives gifts to the church gives them as "the same Spirit," "the same Lord," and "the same God" (1 Cor. 12:4–6). Out of the loving relationality between the persons of the Trinity, the church is given gifts that foster loving service. Miroslav Volf writes: "The reciprocity among Trinitarian persons finds its correspondence in an image of the church in which *all* members serve one another with their specific gifts of the Spirit, imitating the Lord through the power of the Father. Like the divine persons, they all stand in a position of mutual giving and receiving."[6]

### Eschatology

The service of the church is also a foretaste of its eschatological hope. In the Hebrew Scriptures the eschatological hope of the people of God includes the hope for a Messiah who comes as a servant (Isa. 53). And Amos argues that one of the reasons God will crush Israel is that the rich and powerful oppress the poor among the people of God (Amos 2; 5). Only an Israel that changes its ways and cares for the needy will be restored in the eschaton. The ideal image of the people of God is of a community of those who care for and serve one another.

The New Testament carries on and expands this eschatological hope through its theology of the kingdom of God. Jesus tells his disciples that the one who is greatest in the kingdom is the one who will be a servant (Matt. 23:11). Further, the servant who will be honored at the coming of Christ will be one who has been faithful in his master's absence to take care not just of the master's financial resources, but also of other servants in the household of God (Matt. 24:45). And, perhaps most striking, those who will enter the kingdom are the "righteous," who in serving other disciples have actually ministered to Christ himself (Matt. 25:34–46). Resoundingly, the kingdom of God is depicted as a community of servants.

In Paul the kingdom of God is a realm of other-centered loving service. In Romans 14, the kingdom of God is not about self-centeredness in matters of food and drink, but about humbly caring for others in the church, doing what leads to peace and edification. In 1 Corinthians 13, the highest value in anticipation of the eschaton (the perfect) is love for others. Further, the return of Christ becomes a motivation for service to his church now. Recognizing the difficulty of other-centered service, Paul speaks especially to areas where such service is toughest, addressing those relationships that often create the deepest animosities—husband/wife, parent/child, master/slave. He calls for humble service to one another motivated by a love for God and in the knowledge that Christ will one day come again and judge believers on the basis of how they have served and cared for one another (Eph. 5:25–6:9).

### Priesthood of the Believers

In addition to our two theological foundations for the whole theology of the church (Trinity and eschatology), the priesthood of believers is an important foundation for the church's ministry of service. In the Hebrew Scriptures, priests were first and foremost servants of the people, doing their work in order to connect the community to God, and God to the community. In the New Testament, we find that the direct relationship of each believer to Christ, the ultimate high priest, makes the whole church into a holy priesthood, which not only gives each believer direct access to God through Christ, but also the ability to connect others to God by loving service (Heb. 4; 1 Pet. 2). As priests, believers when they serve one another represent God to one another through the person of Jesus Christ and the power of the Spirit.

Despite the fact that the theology of the priesthood of the believer has been emphasized most among Protestants, it is an aspect of other traditions as well. Vatican II's *Dogmatic Constitution on the Church* clearly recognizes that nonclergy have significant priestly functions.

> Though they differ essentially and not only in degree, the common priesthood of the faithful and the ministerial or hierarchical priesthood are nonetheless ordered one to another; each in its own proper way shares in the one priest-hood of Christ . . . The faithful indeed, by virtue of their royal priesthood, participate in the offering of the Eucharist. They exercise that priesthood too by the reception of the sacraments, prayer and thanksgiving, the witness of a holy life, abnegation, and active charity.[7]

In the Orthodox tradition, this priestly ministry of the laity is often referred to as "the liturgy after the liturgy." Believers continue to carry out the priestly function of the church as they minister to one another beyond the official liturgical services of the church.

## The Goal of Service: A Redemptive Community, Reflecting the Values of the Kingdom

As we noted in our discussion of the church as an eschatological community, the church is birthed by the kingdom of God and is meant both to bear witness to the kingdom and to reflect its values. As believers serve one another, representing Christ to one another, broken but redeemed persons engage other broken persons with the redemptive love of Christ to bring personal and communal transformation. The New Testament discusses many values of the kingdom that are designed to be reflected in the redeemed community of the church. Without repeating our discussion of the kingdom from chapter 3, the following represent some of the values reflected in the various New Testament writers.

In the Synoptics several values stand out. First, the kingdom has come to create a community where people are freed from captivity to Satan, a value demonstrated by Jesus's many exorcisms. In Matthew 12, Jesus explains that he casts out demons by the promised power of the Holy Spirit. He then illustrates the significance by portraying himself as the one who enters the strong man's (Satan's) house and steals his possessions (human beings held captive). The issue here is not fundamentally being freed from demonic oppression, for surely very few persons were in such a state. Rather, it illustrates that the world is held captive by structures that keep people from seeing God and being attracted to him for who he is. Thus, Jesus tells the Pharisees that their true father is not Abraham, but the devil. When Jesus releases people from such captivity, they see him for who he is and become captivated by him instead. In the church we perform this service when we introduce people to Jesus Christ and help them build a relationship with him that frees them from captivity to sin and self.

Connected to this, we also see in the Synoptics that the kingdom looks to build a community where sinners are met with grace and forgiveness. Jesus demonstrates this value often by embracing "sinners" and pronouncing their forgiveness. Perhaps the most powerful illustration is found in his parable of the prodigal son. Here, the most shameful of sinners is welcomed back by a forgiving father, and not just to be forgiven by him personally, but also to be received by grace back into membership in the community. Thus, the father in his service to his lost son is the head of a community of servants that functions by grace.

Third, the portrayal of the kingdom in the Synoptics anticipates a community where those captive to physical brokenness and social barriers are freed. Of course, Jesus's miracles of healing illustrate this kind of service. For while Jesus sometimes connects physical healing with forgiveness of sin, sometimes he just heals people without addressing sin. Moreover, in his healing of the ten lepers, his main concern beyond the physical healing is that the healing will allow them to reenter the community—thus, he tells them to go show themselves to the priests in order to be declared clean. The community envisioned by the kingdom is also one where the social barriers of gender and race are broken down. Women and Samaritans are embraced by Jesus in a way that shatters the status quo cultural and religious restrictions of his day.

In the theology of John, service is centered on the giving of oneself for others and, in so doing, becoming like God in Christ. God so loved that he gave

(John 3). The good shepherd lays down his life for the sheep (John 10). The greatest love is to lay down one's life for a friend (John 15). Here, everything Jesus does is redemptive, from giving his own life for the redemption of his followers to washing his disciples' feet (John 13), symbolically redeeming them from the "grime" of the world and then instructing them that they should perform the same kind of redemptive service for one another.

In Paul we find a number of themes pertaining to Christians serving other Christians and building a redemptive community. All of his letters refer in some sense to his hope that the believers will become mature in the faith. We see this goal of maturity clearly connected to service in Ephesians 4. In verses 1 through 6, he talks about the loving service that should be characteristic of the church because of its foundational oneness in the trinitarian God. Then he shows how this service is exemplified through the spiritual gifts of individual believers, the goal being that the entire body is built up, moving toward maturity in Christ, which includes doctrinal fidelity and character formation, all of which develops as each member serves for the benefit of the whole body. In chapter 5, Paul engages the bride image to illustrate the humble, loving, and submissive service that should characterize the church. Then he addresses marriage, parenting, and slavery directly, calling on the church to become a community where these relational structures will be revolutionized, rising above the brokenness and immaturity of a fallen culture. Further, in Philemon, through his request for the master to receive back his runaway slave Onesimus, Paul illustrates that in the church, culture's hierarchies of service are to be reoriented such that now a master and his slave serve each other as brothers in Christ.

Finally, James talks about works, which for him focus primarily on relationships between church members and are the fruit of authentic faith in Christ. His goal is to give us a picture of a community freed of personal animosities and social prejudices. Wisdom, lived out though other-centered and nonprejudicial love, creates a community that experiences healing.

### The Means to Redemptive Community

The goal of building a redemptive community that reflects the values of the kingdom of God is unquestionably a daunting one. It is one thing to describe the biblical goal of a loving, serving church. It is quite another thing to get there. The following are several of the means the writers of the New Testament consider necessary for the church to move in the direction of its ideal.

#### Love

At the heart of the church's success in creating a serving community is love. The biblical idea of loving others is always fundamentally an outgrowth of love for God—and before that, of God's love for us. We love God, John says, because he first loved us (1 John 4:19). Similarly, authentic loving service to others is a product of and a response to God's love for us. As the church receives the love of God in Christ, so its members are transformed to respond in loving service to one another. In his treatise "The Freedom of the Christian," Luther argues that a Christian is "a perfectly free lord of all, subject to none. A Christian is a perfectly dutiful servant of all, subject to all."[8] Luther understood that law cannot motivate truly loving service; only the gracious love of God, which creates faith, can do that. The person of authentic faith, Luther says, thinks this way:

> Although I am an unworthy and condemned man, my God has given me in Christ all the riches of righteousness and salvation without any merit on my part, out of pure free mercy, so that from now on I need nothing except faith which believes that this is true. Why should I not therefore freely, joyfully, with all my heart, and with an eager will do all things which I know are pleasing and acceptable to such a Father who has overwhelmed me with his inestimable riches? I will therefore give myself as a Christ to my neighbor, just as Christ offered himself to me.[9]

Here, Luther reflects not just the teaching of the New Testament, but of the entire scriptures, as illustrated by Jesus's summation of the law as love for God followed by love for neighbor. The sequence is irreversible. One cannot truly love his neighbor until he is captivated by and responds to the love of God. Thus, for John's Jesus, the community that comes to be known by its members' love for one another is the community that has come to understand the sacrificial love of its Lord, who laid down his life for his friends. This love is the primary means by which the church becomes a serving community.

### Grace

Thomas à Kempis writes, "The purpose of righteous men depends on the grace of God more than on themselves and on their own wisdom. Man purposes, but God disposes. The way that a man shall walk in the world is found not in himself, but in the grace of God."[10] The particular insight of grace as a means of creating serving community is that, unlike love, which may act in response to a deserving object, grace immediately recognizes that its object is undeserving. The presupposition here is that church members serve one another as sinners serving sinners. But if service in the church is from sinners to sinners, the grace that empowers this service must come from beyond the church. Paul gets at this by arguing that as the community encounters the grace of God in Christ, it becomes a community that lives in and by that grace, its members manifesting grace to one another. Grace is given to the church in order to, in turn, be expressed by the church. In Ephesians 4, just preceding his discussion of service through the means of spiritual gifts, Paul tells us that the foundation for these gifts is grace (Eph. 4:7; cf. Rom. 12:4–6). And this grace does not come to us as a quantity or substance or as an ability, but as a person. The grace Paul speaks of is relational. For it comes to the church as the God who is over all and in all through the person of Jesus Christ by the Holy Spirit (Eph. 4:4–6). This relational encounter of grace is then, for Paul, the means by which believers come to be "humble and gentle, bearing with each other in love" (4:2).

### Gifts

Hans Küng writes,

> All charisms are expressions of God's grace and power, in the Spirit. They all point to the one great charism of God, the new life which has been given to us in Christ Jesus; . . . In the fullness of Christ's grace the riches of spiritual gifts are revealed to us . . . Whether a man is an apostle, a prophet, teacher, evangelist, a bishop or a deacon, whether he consoles, exhorts, forgives, loves—all these things are gifts in Jesus Christ and point to him who is and does all these things in his own person. Charisms are the revelations, in concrete and individual form, of the charis, the power of God's grace.[11]

In the theology of Paul, the gifts (*charismata*) flow naturally from grace (*charis*) as a means of service. Gifts are not primarily tools to get the work of the church done. Rather, to use spiritual gifts is to be an instrument of God's grace to others.[12] And because grace is relational and comes to us through Christ, through the gifts we not only encounter God's grace in each other, but we actually encounter in each other Christ, the grace giver. This function is carried out through the church's existence as the body of Christ. As the head, he and his grace flow to the rest of the church through the parts. Peter confirms this fact, declaring that when believers use their gifts they administer God's grace in its various forms, suggesting that those who teach speak the very words of God to the church (1 Pet. 4:10–11).

The effects of this theology for service are profound. Instead of merely thinking of their service as getting a job done in the church, believers can envision themselves as being a channel of Christ's grace, and even of Christ himself to their brothers and sisters. This may be easier to see with the most high-profile gifts, such as teaching, which more naturally lend themselves to the idea of God communicating to his people. So this theology of gracious service may be particularly encouraging to those with low-profile gifts and places of service. Consider, for instance, the woman helping an active toddler to color pictures of a Bible story, allowing the child's mother and father a few minutes of freedom to worship, pray, and hear God's word without interruption. What thoughtful parents would fail to recognize that in this gift they are receiving the grace of God himself?

The purpose of spiritual gifts as they facilitate an encounter with Christ and his grace, says Paul, is to build up the church for service. Vatican II's *Dogmatic Constitution on the Church* says,

> It is not only through the sacraments and the ministrations of the Church that the Holy Spirit makes holy the People, leads them and enriches them with his virtues. Allotting his gifts according as he wills . . . he also distributes special graces among the faithful of every rank. By these gifts he makes them fit and ready to undertake various tasks and offices for the renewal and building up of the Church.[13]

While the purpose of the gifts is not simply to accomplish the work of the church but to relate Christ and his grace to others, this relational grace transforms believers into persons who desire to help accomplish the goals of the church. These transformed persons then serve the church through their own God-given gifts.

For the church to function well, then, individual believers need to be aware of their particular spiritual gifts. They can serve others in the way that most effectively ministers the grace of Christ. Paul says that God sovereignly distributes gifts to believers, which means that God, not the church member, determines how he will minister his grace through each person (1 Cor. 12:7). In the evangelical church in America, the awareness of spiritual gifts has led to what may be a typically American approach to discovering one's gift(s). Many of us, at some point in our church experience, were given something akin to a "spiritual gift test" designed to determine where we were gifted. Some churches have even required that parishioners take these tests in order to determine the area of service in which they should participate. Pastoral experience, however, has demonstrated the less-than-satisfactory value of such tests. What they tend to show is what respondents like doing or what they wish they could do. They do not necessarily indicate whether a person is actually gifted for such tasks.

Given that spiritual gifts are bestowed through relationship and, first and foremost, perform a relational function, it would seem that discovering one's spiritual gift(s) is something that should take place relationally. Since the gifts are designed to build up the church, it makes sense for a person's gift to be confirmed not only by her or his desire to perform a ministry for which that gift is required, but also by the recognition of others in the church that, indeed, this person is gifted for this area of service. There should be some sense of the church saying, "When you do this, we are blessed and sense the ministry of Christ." In this scenario, perhaps the most effective way for parishioners to

discover their spiritual gifts is simply to serve in a variety of different ministries and let the church tell them where they are gifted. Confirmation of gifts
meant to edify the community, then, are discovered in community rather than
in the isolation of the self.[14]

### Teaching

The church is a Word-centered community. In our chapter on worship we
talked about the Word as an element of worship. In this chapter we understand
the teaching of biblical truth as a crucial element of service. Teaching the
truth about God and humanity in Christ serves the church in several ways. It
meets the church's constant need for the message of grace. It helps to protect
the church from humanity's tendency to conform its ideas about God to the
prevailing whims of culture. Also, the prophetic aspect of the Word shows the
church what a redemptive, Christ-honoring community looks like and urges
it to pursue that kind of community life. The biblical emphasis on teaching
and learning the scriptures is so strong that one could rightly conclude that,
at least in a nonprofessional sense, the church should be filled with biblical
theologians.

This commitment to the service of teaching God's word to God's people runs
throughout the biblical metanarrative. Concluding the Torah with a second
giving of the law in Deuteronomy, Moses creates the Shema (Deut. 6:4–5),
encouraging Israel that a crucial way for them to love the one God is to learn
his commands, to memorize them, and to teach them to their children so that
they can know the character of the God who has drawn them into his story of
redemption. For the priests and rabbis to teach the law to the people of God
was a great service to them, for its statutes became a lamp (Ps. 119:11) to guide
them in the way of righteousness and wisdom. After the return from captivity,
when the teaching of the scriptures had been greatly diminished, Ezra gathered
all the priests together to teach Torah to the returnees, making sure they not
only heard it but also understood its significance for life (Neh. 8:12).

The early church also recognized the importance of the teaching of God's
Word in the church. The book of Acts shows that the people dedicated themselves to the teaching of the apostles as diligently as to prayer and the Eucharist.
And the apostles recognized that, while the church had many needs, the most
important aspects of service they could provide would be to pray and teach
the word (Acts 2:42; 6:2).

For Paul, teaching the Word was a major area of service for those who could
do it well. Living in a world a lot like ours, with a different religion on every
corner, Paul charged his young pastor friend Timothy with these words:

> Preach the Word; be prepared in season and out of season; correct, rebuke
> and encourage—with great patience and careful instruction. For the time will

come when men will not put up with sound doctrine. Instead, to suit their own desires, they will gather around them a great number of teachers to say what their itching ears want to hear. They will turn their ears away from the truth and turn aside to myths. (2 Tim. 4:2–4)

Timothy was to serve the church by preaching the Word, the message of truth entrusted to believers. It was what Paul called "well-grounded teaching," which is the literal translation of the phrase "sound doctrine." But Paul also told Timothy that lots of people would not want teaching to be well grounded. They would prefer a kind of truth that was flexible to meet their individual needs. Timothy was to serve the church by reading the scriptures and teaching them faithfully, being careful not only about how he lived his life, but also about how he taught the scriptures. Here we see an element of Paul's teaching consistent with all his letters—faithful teaching of the scriptures is connected to a faithful life (1 Tim. 4:13–16). As he argues in Colossians, teaching the truth about God serves the church as a means of moving everyone toward maturity in Christ. This apostolic emphasis on the importance of teaching as a service to the church was carried on in the sub-apostolic era as well. For example, *The Didache* (ca. 120) admonishes the church to take proper care of those who teach and serve the church as leaders, making sure that they are paid generously from "the firstfruits" of the "wine-vat" and the "threshing-floor," for they are your "chief-priests."

Not all Christian traditions over the last century, however, have been equally committed to teaching the scriptures. In America, we in the evangelical tradition have taken pride in the place we have given biblical teaching in the church. But as evangelicals, we the authors are concerned that our tradition has begun to lose its historical commitment to teaching theological truths rooted in the Bible.

David Wells, professor at Gordon-Conwell Seminary, writes,

I have watched with growing disbelief as the evangelical Church has cheerfully plunged into astounding theological illiteracy . . . The effects of this great change in the evangelical soul are evident in every incoming class in the seminaries, in most publications, in the great majority of churches, and in most of their pastors.[15]

This does not mean that evangelicals have stopped receiving religious input. Indeed, the airwaves and Christian bookstores are crammed with religious material being consumed in ever-greater quantities. But the focus and content of much of this material are troubling. Through a subtle means, the church is being stripped naked of its protective theological clothing.

First, in line with culture's postmodern shift, there has been a move over the past couple of decades from what is true to what works. A perusal of the bookshelves of Christian bookstores would lead one to believe that if one wants to make a lot of money today in the Christian book market, writing a book on theology may not be the best way to go.[16] But write about how Christians can make their lives better, and you just might have a best seller. American evangelical Christianity is being turned into a "how to" religion. And, unfortunately, most of the "how tos" reveal an unbiblical focus upon self. Nowhere is this focus more obvious than in Christian marketing and advertising. One would think that what Christians want to know most is how to be happy, how to be financially prosperous, and how to lose weight while being filled with the Holy Spirit. Christian bookstores are filled with titles like *God's Key to Health and Happiness*, *I Kissed Dating Goodbye*, *The Weigh Down Diet*, *Feeling Good about Feeling Bad*, and *How to Become Your Own Best Self*. Certainly, the church must work to show how a biblical faith is made real in everyday life. But we are concerned that, too often, personal growth and satisfaction take precedence over truth. Accordingly, another thing that concerns us is the growing trend in many evangelical churches to focus adult education on topics that help people have a better life but do not contain much biblical content. Many church schedules are filled with classes on how to improve marriage, how to manage your money, how to be better parents, and how to build a relationship that leads to marriage without ever dating. Surely, these are important subjects, and the church should be addressing them. But one wonders, where are the classes on the theology of Christ, of sin, of salvation, of the scriptures, and of the trinitarian nature of God? These fundamentals of theological education often seem nowhere to be found and have often been replaced by classes on methods for solving our personal issues.

The ultimate consequence of Christianity centered on personal issues and self-improvement is that theology becomes therapy, the search for righteousness is replaced by the search for happiness, holiness by wholeness, and truth by feeling, and God's sovereignty is diminished to whatever it takes to have a good day.[17] Christians become consumers who shop the church like they do a shopping mall, delighted to find something to meet every felt need. But with Christianity as consumerism comes a strange emptiness and the discovery that their genuine need for meaning cannot be met by consumerism. That meaning can instead be provided only by the biblical truth about God and his self-sacrificing redemption of the world in Christ.

This need of the church for an increase in biblical teaching and literacy is not limited to the evangelical Protestant church, of course. Several years ago a noted Roman Catholic scholar and author of many books remarked, "The title of my next book is going to be *Sermons Should Be Longer*. One simply cannot mine the treasures of the word of God in fifteen minutes."[18] Nor does this critique mean that the answer for this generation is a return to a form of public service in the church common among evangelical churches for many decades, one where all other elements of the service are merely a "warm-up" for the teaching of scripture.

## Prayer

One of the great acts of the church in loving service to its members is to pray for them. In the New Testament narrative, community prayer plays a major role in the life of the church. Before the foundation of the church at Pentecost, Jesus demonstrates the value of prayer for the community of God by placing his hands on children and praying for them (Matt. 19; Mark 10). He urges his disciples to pray corporately, teaching them to pray, "Our Father, who art in heaven . . ." After the church is established, community prayer is an important feature in the life of the church. Immediately after the ascension narrative, Luke shows the disciples as a group of men and women who were "constantly in prayer" (Acts 1:14). In Acts 2, we see that prayer is at the center of community life for the church. Teaching, fellowship, the Eucharist, and prayer created a community where believers cared for one another, shared their goods for the benefit of all, and saw miraculous signs in their midst. It was a community that engaged its culture positively, drawing many people to confess faith in Christ and to become members of the church.

In Paul, prayer is also a critical component in church life. More than telling the churches what they should pray for, Paul serves as an example by telling the churches what his prayers are for them. The overwhelming motif of Paul's prayer for other believers concerns their spiritual maturity. He prays that the church will, by the Spirit, come to know Christ more fully and the great power of his resurrection for a changed life in a world captive to Satanic influence (Eph. 1:18ff) and that they would know and be transformed by the great love of God through the indwelling of Christ in their hearts (Eph. 3:16ff). He prays with confidence that God will keep moving the church on to maturity in Christ (Phil. 1:4–6), and for spiritual wisdom to live a life that honors Christ and bears fruit through good works (Col. 1:10). As the gifts of the spirit facilitate an encounter with Christ and his grace, so prayer for other believers results in God engaging them with himself, his love causing personal transformation leading to changed lives that reflect Christ. Thus, prayer for others in the church, even when done while apart from them, serves the church relationally.

In addition to modeling prayer, Paul does give the church instructions for community prayer. But these instructions are quite general. He encourages the church at Ephesus to pray "on all occasions with all kinds of prayers and requests" (Eph. 6:18). And he urges the Philippian church simply to make its requests known to God (Phil. 4:6). The assumption in all of this is that God will answer prayer for the church, that believers will see him do powerful things. But for Paul, at the heart of all this prayer is still relationship. He tells the Ephesians to pray "in the Spirit" and assures the Philippians that if they present their requests to God with the expectancy of thanksgiving, the peace that comes from God will guard their hearts and minds in Christ Jesus.

This relational effect of community prayer is at least as important in Paul's thinking as are answers to particular prayers. What God gives in response to prayer is not only answers, but himself. The value of this fact for the church is not to cause the people of God to diminish their expectancy that God will "move mountains" through prayer, but to increase their awareness that what the church needs more than anything else is Christ himself. Thus, when church members pray for one another, they minister God's grace to one another by deepening their relationships with Christ and through Christ, with one another. As a final note on how prayer serves the church, its relational value is also at the heart of why verbal prayer is so important. If one member prays for another member silently, is there no benefit, since God hears and answers? Certainly, but there is not nearly as much immediate benefit as there is when a person in need actually hears a brother or sister in Christ interceding for him or her. Further, touching someone while praying for them enhances this relational benefit even more. Thus, the practice of the early church was to lay hands on those for whom they were praying (i.e., Acts 6:6; 8:17; 28:8; 1 Tim. 4:14; 2 Tim. 1:6).

### Healing

Another important image of the church as a serving community is that of healing. In John's eschatological picture of the New Jerusalem, which is his symbol for the church in its final state as Christ's perfect bride (Rev. 21:9ff), he envisions the Tree of Life straddling the River of Life. Its fruit is produced every month, and its leaves, John tells us, are for the healing of the nations (Rev. 22:1–2). Here, the people of God are reunited to the source of health and life from which they were banned after the fall, and in a profound fulfillment of prophetic vision, the nations come to Jerusalem to be healed, an image that leads the reader to ponder not only their salvation, but also their reconciliation with Israel. Later in the same chapter (vv. 12–14), Jesus's words suggest that the church ought to be living now in light of this eschatological picture of the perfectly healed church.

Much has been made of healing as a ministry of the church. From the time of the apostles to the present, the church has been seen as a place where people receive healing, sometimes even in a miraculous way. In the power of Jesus and following his lead, the apostles healed many people of incurable maladies simply by praying for them, touching them, or proclaiming healing in the name of Christ. Unfortunately, when people in America today think about healing in connection with the church, the default image is most likely of dramatic healing services on Christian television, where flamboyant televangelists "heal" sick and crippled people. These images are met with a general cynicism born not only out of numerous movies about fraudulent healers, from *Elmer Gantry* to *Leap of Faith*, but also from many reports of public "healings" that turned out to be little more than magic tricks or momentary psychosomatic relief.

The biggest disaster in all this is not the fake healings, but the development of an image of healing in the church as primarily a ministry to individuals to relieve them of their physical illnesses or, of perhaps equal value in American popular Christianity, their credit card debt.[19] Surely, there are many miraculous physical healings in the biblical narrative. And the history of the church is filled with ministries devoted to the healing of the body. Early medieval Benedictine houses (from the sixth through the ninth centuries) pioneered hospitalization and hospice care, and numerous current Catholic orders are dedicated to caring for the sick. A hallmark of Protestant missions in the nineteenth and twentieth centuries has been the building of hospitals and the training of medical personnel to care for the sick and the dying. But in the biblical narrative, such healing is never meant to be seen as the primary goal of the ministry of healing. It is more often a pointer to a much deeper and more enduring healing. At the heart of the church's ministry of healing is the healing of relationships.[20] Of course, as the greatest commandment is to love God, so the primary relationship to be healed in the church is the one between humans and God. The second relationships to be healed, and by no means a distant second ("and your neighbor as yourself"), are those between the members of the church themselves.

In his famous play *No Exit*, existentialist philosopher Jean-Paul Sartre concludes that "hell is other people."[21] If one of the fundamental characteristics of sin is self-centeredness, Sartre is on target. Fallen human beings, who at their core are motivated to fill their own emptiness and satisfy their own desires, are ever inclined to see others as tools to accomplish these ends rather than as valued creations of God to be cherished even above themselves. Thus, the New Testament is filled with hopes that when people enter into relationship with Christ, their relationships to others will be transformed. Disciples transformed by Christ, their Master, are to wash their fellow disciples' feet. Those who are constantly sinned against by their brothers are to forgive them seventy times seven. And in the church, says Paul, believers are to consider other believers more important than themselves, serving them as a means of creating relational harmony and healing natural animosities. He comes even to the point of naming names, calling on Euodia and Syntyche to be at peace with each other. They have both helped Paul in proclaiming the gospel. But if the good news of Jesus cannot bring peace between fellow church members, how can it speak of peace to a relationally torn world?

This theology of the church as a place of healing is expressed most clearly in the book of James. Illustrating his cynicism regarding the possibility of true faith without works, James suggests that if a person who professes faith sees a brother or sister without food and clothing and does nothing to bring healing to his or her brokenness, his faith is false. It is important to recognize James's notation that the broken person is a brother or sister. He is talking about the church here, and his whole theology of healing is focused on this community. Moreover, James's theology of healing, while it includes physical and even economic aspects, is primarily relational. In chapter 2:1–7 he addresses the deep relational separation between rich and poor, which is part and parcel of the world's system. James argues that if the church shows favoritism to the rich, it only perpetuates the separation between socioeconomic classes. Further, the church perpetuates the brokenness of the poor when it affirms the rich, giving them special treatment in the church even as they continue to oppress the poor, even the poor in the church. Even further, perpetuating this social sickness perpetuates the brokenness of the rich by allowing them to go on thinking that their wealth and power gives them complete control over their lives (4:13–16), ignoring the sovereignty of God from whom all good things come (1:17).

In chapters 3 and 4, James talks about the power of the tongue to degrade people made in the image of God. Driven by insecurities and corrupt desires, the tongue creates a fire of warfare and animosity in the church, leading those who should be loving each other to slander each other instead. This, says James, is not the peacemaking wisdom that comes from above, but is satanic. The church that looks to the world to satisfy it will self-destruct instead, for the world and its goods can lead only to self-consumption. But when believers look with patience for the coming of Christ, they learn to be patient with one another (5:7–9). Instead of attacking one another out of their brokenness, they learn to bring healing. James closes his book (5:13–19) with an image of the church as a community of people broken by circumstances (trouble), sickness, sin, and rebellion (wandering from the truth). Into this community comes healing brought by prayer, confession and forgiveness of sin, accountability, and perhaps even medicine (oil).

We note again: in James's healing ecclesiology, healing takes place in the community of the church. Believers are not told to get healed outside the church so they can be well enough to join the community. The fact is that everyone in the community is sick and broken. But too often, persons with certain kinds of brokenness have not been allowed to be honest about their struggles and find help in the church. For those of us who grew up in the fundamentalist-evangelical church in America, alcoholism used to be an example of one of these "untouchable" kinds of sicknesses. Often, Christians struggling with alcohol were told either to keep quite about it or to get themselves together before coming to the church. Perhaps the idea was that a church full of struggling alcoholics would damage its image. Unfortunately, it is actually this rejection of the broken sinner, the result of a view of discipleship based on behavior modification through law rather than heart transformation though grace, that damages the image of the church. The church is not meant to be a community of people who have finally become whole, but a hospital for sinners looking for wholeness in the community where Christ is Lord.

Thankfully, many churches in the evangelical tradition today have become places of healing for those struggling with alcohol and drug abuse. The same cannot be said though, for those struggling with homosexuality, who are generally told that they still need to stay in the closet. So today, the believer struggling with same-sex attraction is often relegated either to keeping quiet and struggling alone or to abandoning the biblical faith altogether, rejecting his Christianity or joining a church that affirms the unbiblical idea that homosexuality is a gift from God. Indeed, the church will take another giant step toward being a place of true biblical healing when pastors can walk to the front of the church with another man and say, "Hi. This is my friend Bob. He struggles with homosexuality. He's looking for healing and hope so he can walk in obedience to Christ. He needs us to walk with him."

Perhaps every image of the church can be overdone. The church is clearly to be a place of healing, and believers are meant to serve one another by helping one another to heal. But some theologians have pointed out that the church must be careful not to become simply a therapy center where Christianity is presented as one more self-help strategy to help people feel better about themselves.[22] True enough. For the church, the ultimate goal can never be to make people feel better, but to exalt Christ in the community of the church, knowing that he alone is the answer to all human brokenness. Augustine spoke well in saying that all human hearts are restless until they find healing by resting in Christ.[23] In the church created by the Triune God, believers serve by helping one another find rest in Christ, bringing healing in a here-and-not-here, now-and-not-yet way to all manner of maladies—physical, social, racial, emotional, and spiritual.

### Sharing

Calling for authentic Christian community is his book *The Church at the End of the 20th Century*, Francis Schaeffer writes:

> Here is something striking: the Greeks are sending money to the Jews. As the church at Antioch cut across the whole social spectrum, from Herod's foster brother down to the slave, the church and its community also cut across the difference between Jew and Gentile—not only in theory but in practice . . .
> Let me say it very strongly again: there is no use talking about love if it does not relate to the stuff of life in the area of material possessions and needs. If it does not mean sharing of our material things for our brothers in Christ close at home and abroad, it means little or nothing.[24]

From its earliest days and throughout its history, the church has recognized the biblical mandate to serve the community of God's people by sharing material goods with those in need. Justin Martyr in his *First Apology* (ca. 150) speaks of the regular practice of taking collections in the context of Christian worship for aid to widows, orphans, and the sick in the church. The writer of the *Shepherd of Hermas* (ca. 150) stresses the importance of the church ministering to widows, orphans, and the needy in a spirit of Christian hospitality. Ambrose (ca. 339–397), in his first act as Bishop of Milan, distributed his great wealth to the Christian poor. The Beguines were members of sisterhoods founded in the Netherlands in the twelfth century and called extra-regulars, as they were neither lay nor monastic. They served the sick and indigent as Christian charities. John Calvin in his *Ecclesiastical Ordinances* (1542) outlines the role of the deacons to provide for the administration of the work of charity in the church. Seventeenth-century popular Catholic spirituality is famous for its emphasis on independent lay confraternities with emphasis on ministering to the material needs of believers. The devotion of the Sacred Heart, Holy Family, and St. Joseph, being some of the most popular new lay associations that operated under close clerical supervision, and reformers like John Etudes and Jean-Jacques Olivier were all well known for their Christ-centered encouragement to ecclesiastical charity.

One of the most striking scenes in the biblical story of the church meets us in Acts 2.

> They devoted themselves to the apostles' teaching and to the fellowship, to the breaking of bread and to prayer. Everyone was filled with awe, and many wonders and miraculous signs were done by the apostles. All the believers were together and had everything in common. Selling their possessions and goods, they gave to anyone as he had need. Every day they continued to meet together in the temple courts. They broke bread in their homes and ate together with glad and sincere hearts, praising God and enjoying the favor of all the people. And the Lord added to their number daily those who were being saved. (Acts 2:42–47)

Regarding the material charity of the church in the New Testament era, Carmel Pilcher writes,

> In the early Church every Christian came to Sunday Eucharist with something to share: bread or wine, oil or clothes. Everyone, that is, except the widows and orphans or an itinerant or stranger who had nothing to give. These poor became the beneficiaries of the gifts—gifts that were brought to the table along with the bread and wine that would be blessed, broken and shared in Eucharistic communion. At the end of Eucharist the gifts not consumed were given to those in the community who needed them in the coming week.[25]

Throughout the New Testament, the practice of sharing material goods with those in need characterized the church and the teaching of its leaders. In dramatic contrast to the young men Jesus condemned for pledging money to the temple that should have been spent caring for their parents, the members of the early church considered as family persons who had no blood relation to them, sharing their own possessions or even selling them to provide money for those in need. This, along with the teaching of the apostles and miraculous signs, served to attract many people to Christ. For believers who sacrificed of their own wealth to meet the needs of the poor reflected the very character of the trinitarian God who sacrificed the riches of his own Son to meet humanity in its poverty. As Paul says it, "For your sakes he became poor so that you through his poverty might become rich" (2 Cor. 8:9). And, echoing Jesus's contention that true religion takes shape in love of neighbor, James argues that true religion consists in coming to the aid of orphans and widows in their distress (James 1:27).

In a nation where success is often described in terms of material possessions, where "he who dies with the most toys wins," and where advertisers spend millions to convince people that they deserve the benefits of their product, no matter how much they have to increase their credit card debt to get it, encouraging the church to share its wealth with others can be a tough sell. In fact, if one were to come to know the church simply by watching the most popular television preachers and visiting their websites, one might come to think that the purpose of the church is to get more money and possessions, rather than to share them. And statistics also have a story to tell. Among church members of eleven primary Protestant denominations (or their historical antecedents) in the United States and Canada, per-member giving as a percentage of income was lower in 2000 than in either 1921 or 1933. In 1921, per-member giving as a percentage of income was 2.9 percent. In 1933, at the depth of the Great Depression, per-member giving grew to 3.3 percent. By 2000, after a half-century of unprecedented prosperity, giving had fallen to 2.6 percent.[26] Research by the Barna Group suggests that one factor in this decline in giving among Christians is the growth in credit card debt in America, including among church members.[27]

The point of this section is neither to analyze giving trends among Christians nor to provide fodder for pastors to scold the church for its lack of giving. Rather, it is to remind the church of the beauty of sharing with others out of love for Christ. In the Olivet Discourse, Jesus teaches his disciples that when they give to other followers of Jesus who are in need, it is as if they are giving to Jesus himself. And the rewards for such sharing would be blessing from the Father and great enjoyment of the eschatological kingdom. In his farewell address to the Ephesian elders, Paul urged them to help the weak because Jesus had taught them that it is more blessed to give than to receive. In a world that exalts material possessions, those possessions tend to be protected to the point that they eventually possess the persons who own them. But the early church learned to see God as the ultimate owner of their goods, freeing them from possession by their material wealth and leading to a much greater wealth—that of being used by Christ to bring redemption to his disciples in need (Acts 4:32–35).

A healthy church is a place of sharing, a place where people hold on to their material possessions lightly, recognizing that there is no ultimate joy, no final satisfaction in wealth or possessions. Indeed, even though God has created all things for us to enjoy, the relational trinitarian God has made us such that only when material things are shared with others in love and self-sacrifice are they most satisfying. For it is only when we share our wealth with others that wealth has the ability to allow us to encounter Christ. It is ultimately to him that we give. As an eschatological community, the church gives of its wealth now in light of what will be—not because material goods will have no meaning in the eschaton, but because in that day it will be our joy to give all that we have to God (Rev. 21:23–24). And to give to others now is to give to him (Matt. 25:34–40).

## Conclusion

The church is getting ready for a wedding, one that celebrates her own marriage to Christ. Like any bride, the church wants to look her best for the occasion. And her expectant groom not only anticipates a bride who will arrive without spot or wrinkle, but is even by her side long before the wedding, serving her, helping her to become what she is meant to be. For the groom-to-be incarnates himself in the lives of his people, expressing his transforming grace to them through their loving service to one another. Thus, for the church, wedding preparation is not about clothing, hair, and makeup, but about believers serving one another. The members of the church serve one another as instruments of Christ's loving kindness and grace, which transform the human heart, resulting in the growth of godly character, Christlikeness, and unity. All of this, in anticipation of the day when the church will be made perfect through ultimate union with her groom.

### STUDY QUESTIONS

1. What areas of brokenness and sin most need to find healing in the church today?
2. How can the church be a healing community to these people?
3. How does the church display grace that is nonjudgmental on the one hand, while calling for change on the other?

# 10

# Church Discipline—The Lost
# Element of Service

Ask a room full of pastors what they dislike most about pastoral ministry, and you are likely to hear the words "church discipline" again and again. Few church leaders, especially those most aware of their own brokenness, enjoy confronting church members regarding sinful behavior. Moreover, in situations where a pastor or elders are called in, it is usually an occasion of grievous sin, often one that has been going on for some time and comes with serious collateral damage.

We have chosen to discuss church discipline as a form of cultural engagement for the church as a serving community for two reasons. First, church discipline needs to be highlighted because it is both rarely practiced well and not often discussed in ecclesiology texts. Second, church discipline engages culture in a strange way in that when a church member is unrepentant of serious sin, the scriptures call upon the church to treat him as if he is no longer a member of the community, sending him, as it were, back to the culture of the world, from which he came. This chapter will not offer a comprehensive theology or strategy for church discipline.[1] We will offer some biblical principles, survey some of the struggles of the historic church, and finally, recount a real story of church discipline. For only when we see church discipline in the light of redemptive story will we be encouraged to press on in practicing something so difficult.

The biblical narrative is clear about the need to address sin in the community with disciplinary action. The Mosaic law provides many specific means of discipline for specific offenses. But the New Testament, while it is clear that disciplinary action for serious sin must characterize the church, is far less specific about the methods and standards for such discipline. The foundational New Testament passage on church discipline is Matthew 18:15–20. Here, Jesus tells the disciples that the sinning person must be confronted, by more than one person if necessary. Ideally, all church discipline would stop here, with the sinning person recognizing his sin, repenting, and asking forgiveness. But Jesus goes on to address the situation where the sinning person does not respond to confrontation, in which case the elders are to approach him. And if this does not bring about repentance, he is to be reported to the entire church. If he still refuses to listen, he is to be treated as a Gentile and a tax collector, as an outcast from the community. Along with this comes Jesus's affirmation that whatever is bound by the church and its leaders on earth is bound in heaven. Thus, the church has clear authority over the life of the sinning believer. In John 20, Jesus tells the disciples that if they declare a person's sins to be forgiven, then they are forgiven, and if not, then they are not. In the midst of various interpretations, most agree that the church is given authority in issues of community sin.

Paul is also clear about the necessity for confronting sin in the church. In 1 Timothy 5:1–2, he encourages Timothy to appeal to members of the church individually about their sin. In 2 Timothy 4:2 and Titus 1:13, he urges sharp rebuke for those who reject sound doctrine. In 1 Corinthians 5, Paul admonishes the church to confront a member who is having a sexual relationship with his stepmother, calling upon them not even to eat with him, which in the very least means removing him from participation in the Eucharist. John also addresses discipline for sin, telling the church that they should intervene with God on behalf of a brother or sister who is caught in sinful behavior (1 John 5:16–17).

In the midst of the scripture's clear call for the church to discipline sinners, it is crucial to understand that the ultimate purpose of church discipline must always be redemption, not judgment. Marlin Jeschke writes,

> Too often in the history of the church the meaning of the gospel, though recognized in missionary proclamation, has been forgotten when it comes to discipline. Then the church has taken another track: charges, courts, trials, condemnation, punishment—in short, legalism and casuistry. We forget that what meets people initially as good news always remains the good news of the power of God's grace. It frees them from sin in order that they might live in conformity with God's gracious intention for humankind.[2]

While Christ's grace is a fierce grace, demanding repentance and life change, it is grace nevertheless. As the gospel of God's grace in Christ is no shallow system of behavior modification, neither is church discipline. Grounded in the gospel, it is always a call to respond to the unconditional holy love of God. Only when church discipline arises out of this foundation can it be redemptive.

The redemptive purposes of church discipline involve both the sinning individual and the community. The hope for the individual is that he or she will repent of sin and be restored to a place of healthy fellowship in the community (Gal. 6:1–2). The discipline of the church, like that of a loving parent, is never meant to disable, but to heal (Heb. 12:7–13). In the case of those involved in false teaching, discipline is meant to restore them to a place of being "sound in the faith" (Titus 1:13).[3] As wholeness is restored to individuals, so it is restored to the community. Christ's vision of his church is as a bride without spot or wrinkle. Only when the church is willing to address the sin of community members can she keep moving toward her ultimate status as Christ's pure bride. And only when the church deals with sin redemptively can it exhibit the kind of gracious healing that appeals to the needs of a broken world.

The postapostolic church recognized this biblical mandate for disciplinary and restorative measures regarding sin in the lives of members of the community. But the lack of a clear biblical system for addressing sin in the church left the church in a situation where there was struggle and disagreement about methodology. H. B. Swete writes,

> To those who believed the message and repented of the sins of their past lives Baptism was an absolution in full. Upon this point there is a remarkable *consensus* of Apostolic and other early testimony. The case of post-baptismal sin was less simple, and it does not seem to have been dealt with at first in a comprehensive way.[4]

The earliest postbiblical witnesses show that while church leaders recognized the need for repentance in the case of major sin, there was no system of penance. Ignatius, for example, seems to use *metanoia* (to turn around) only in reference to conversion of non-Christians.[5] And Polycarp speaks of a scandal that occurred among church elders but is content to show his grief and pray that the offender may come to repentance.[6] By the end of the second century, different approaches to postbaptismal sin were developing that were strongly opposed to each other. Bishop Callistus of Rome, for example, seemed willing to forgive those guilty of sexual sin and, after penance, to readmit them to communion. Others preferred the position of Tertullian, who argued that all previous sin was forgiven at baptism, but that Christians should not return to their sinful ways. If they did, there was only one more opportunity for repentance, after which repentance could not be repeated.[7] Ultimately, the church rejected the extreme approach of Tertullian, opting instead for the development of a penitential system. In this system, the main penalty for major sin was removal of the offender from the Eucharist, sometimes for a long period of time, depending on the seriousness of the sin. As the importance of the

Eucharist began to rise as an insurance of one's ability to remain in a state of grace, in other words, to stay saved, removal from it became monumental.

By the Middle Ages, the system of penance for sin had become immense and complicated, its penalties often decided by precedent. The one sure thing was that the church was completely authoritative regarding excommunication, penance, and readmittance to the Eucharist. With the arrival of the Protestant Reformation, this penitential system was eliminated for a large section of the church. This does not mean that the church no longer practiced discipline—just that the Roman Catholic system no longer applied. Further, with the splintering of the Reformation came the end to any unified approach to church discipline.

In the American church, with its historic diversity of Christian traditions and denominations, this lack of unity has only become exacerbated. Even evangelicals with their commitment to the infallibility of the scriptures have had little success in bringing any consistency to the practice of church discipline. Often, when a member of an evangelical church has been excommunicated on the grounds of major sin and an attitude of unrepentance, he simply goes down the street to the next evangelical church from another denomination and is received without question. In the Middle Ages, the power of excommunication was found in the fact that all the doors of the church would be closed to the unrepentant sinner. Today, a fractured church is unable to present such a united front, and church discipline often is of little or no effect. Here is another reason for more ecumenical partnerships.

Nevertheless, this unfortunately weakened and faded status of the practice of church discipline should not be taken as a reason for abandoning it. Just as a good parent does not give up the discipline of his or her children even when they don't seem to respond, so the church must continue to practice healthy discipline among its members, not only because it is biblical, but because when it does work, the results can be profoundly redemptive.

There are many stories of the redemptive power of church discipline, even when the sin is serious and the effects devastating. The rest of this chapter will be dedicated to one of these stories, as told by the pastor who guided the discipline process.[8]

> We have had a situation here in St. Louis that I want to tell you about. Some of you know the story, but most of you do not. I do not relate it to you for any sensational effect and certainly not to bring notoriety to the individuals involved, for that is the last thing they want. But I do it because I believe there is an illustration here of God's grace that can have a powerful effect on our church. About nineteen months ago a family came to our church to visit. They liked it right away and decided that they wanted to make this their home church. They hadn't been here but a few weeks, however, when the husband and wife both came to me individually to share their story, basically saying, "Before we try to put down any roots, we want you to know who we are and what we have done so that if we aren't welcome, we'll know it right away."

Theirs was as troubling a story as I've ever heard. He had been the pastor of an evangelical church in St. Louis County, and she had been his secretary. They got involved in an immoral relationship with one another, and when it was discovered, they separated from their spouses, eventually divorcing their spouses and marrying each other. That is a very brief description of a very complicated and drawn-out process, but I think I've said enough to establish that they were guilty of sin that was very heinous in God's sight, as well as very destructive to the body of Christ. As was most appropriate, both the local church and the denomination, the Presbyterian Church in America, carried out discipline against this couple.

In His great grace God refused to turn His back on them, and through the conviction of the Holy Spirit they began to desire to be restored to fellowship with God and with God's people. They started attending a church in the area which welcomed them and gave him an adult Sunday School class to teach. It wasn't long, however, before they realized that the doctrinal integrity of that church was suspect. After all, if they were so readily accepted without any concern for their recent past actions, it was not surprising that serious heresy was being tolerated in other areas in that church.

So they left and showed up at our church in the early summer of 1985. When I heard this story I said to myself, "Lord, why us? We're a new church in a denomination that is new to St. Louis. We're trying hard to build relationships with the P.C.A. What we don't need is an issue like this to divide us." But then I realized something I have known all along intellectually, but perhaps never before accepted so practically, and that is that the Church is a hospital, and if the hospital shuts the doors of its emergency room, where are the desperately needy to go?

So what began that day was a process of confrontation, confession, forgiveness, and healing that has taught me something new about the marvelous grace of our loving Lord. I am not going to go through the whole story, but I do want you to know that our elders decided right from the beginning that while we would welcome this family into our church, we would not ignore the discipline of another evangelical church. We told them that if they wanted to join our church, they would have to take steps to seek forgiveness and restoration from their former church and denomination, which would also require confession and perhaps even restitution to their former spouses.

When I first suggested this to them I remember getting looks of unbelief and protests like "You're asking the impossible! We could never go back to those people after the way they rubbed our faces in the dirt." But God specializes in things thought impossible, and slowly changes of attitude began to take place. It started with letters to the former spouses, expressing repentance and seeking forgiveness. Not surprisingly, those letters were received with considerable skepticism, but we refused to let that stop us.

Later, meetings were scheduled with the elders of the former church, and more meetings with the presbytery, where public confession was made and where spiritual leaders from our church also bore witness that there had been true repentance in this couple's lives. Forgiveness and restoration did not come easy for the former church or denomination, and that's understandable, for the consequences of this sin had been devastating for them. But though they moved slowly, they did move deliberately. They appointed a committee to consider the issue of restitution to the former spouses, and they worked with us to resolve a number of difficult issues.

Recently, the elders of that church voted unanimously to rescind the excommunication and to commend this family to the care of our church. Two days later, the local presbytery of the P.C.A. also voted to remove the censure and to commend them to our care. Yesterday our Elder Board voted unanimously to receive Norm and Paula Smith into the membership of our church.

It is, admittedly, highly unusual to discuss such a matter with an entire church, especially in a worship service. But the public nature of the sin and the widespread publicity it received demanded, we felt, a public restoration. We didn't want anyone to hear of this matter by gossip or grapevine and wonder whether the elders knew of it or wonder whether the Smiths had ever repented. We were also concerned that other evangelical churches and denominations know that we do not consider ourselves an independent group doing our own thing. Instead we view our church as part of the body of Christ, working with the rest of the body of Christ to present a united front for the gospel in the city of St. Louis.

I have shared these things only with the permission and agreement of our entire Elder Board and with Norm and Paula's permission. And now I'm going to ask them to come forward as I extend to them the right hand of Christian fellowship. I want you to know that they are being accepted as full-fledged members, and they are not under any kind of probation. The elders would not have accepted them into membership if they were not convinced that their repentance was real. As repentant and restored Christians, we will treat them as eligible for service in the body as we do all other members.

Not all stories of church discipline turn out this well. But when they do, it is a beautiful picture of the gospel, one that shows how the good news goes beyond the event when an individual hears the story of God's grace in Christ to live on within the community of Christ's church where his fierce grace, dispensed through his obedient people, brings healing not just to individual sinners but also to the whole community of God's people. Thus, the practice of church discipline is a crucial component in the creation of the church as a serving community. When it is practiced well, erring members of the church are saved from the brokenness of unrepentant sin, and the community is saved from the loss of beloved servants. Pastor Andrus has said recently that in all his years of ministry he has never known another couple more committed to faithful service in the church than this couple, healed by the painful process of church discipline. May the pain of the process never dissuade the church from the potential joy of the outcome.[9]

## STUDY QUESTIONS

1. How have you seen church discipline done poorly in the church?
2. How have you seen church discipline become redemptive in the church?

# 11

# The Church as an Ordered Community

If one thing is certain in this world, it is that, for us, the Church precedes the Gospel.

Henri de Lubac[1]

For myself, I believe that any period of Christian history for which ecclesiology and polity are the driving issues is decadent by definition.

Paul F. M. Zahl[2]

As the community built upon Jesus Christ, the church is an ordered community. As her head, Christ rules his body and is the source of all its true authority. In the New Testament we see a number of regular and ordered patterns for church life. Among other things, the church meets regularly (Heb. 10:25), celebrates the Eucharist (1 Cor. 10–11), gives to the poor (Rom. 15:26; Gal. 2:10), develops a liturgy, and practices church discipline (1 Cor. 5). We also see that in order for the church to manage these regular functions and remain true to the purpose and mission of Christ, he has given the church gifted persons who function in specific offices to lead and guide it under his authority. Throughout its history the church has established organizational and governing structures to preserve its identity and accomplish its mission.

In this chapter we engage the issue of church polity, considering how the church has structured and governed itself for leadership and service. We will survey the three major historical forms of church polity (the episcopal, the

183

presbyterian, and the congregational), examining the biblical and theological rationales for each and suggesting positives and negatives for each one as structures managing the church as the people of God. The central issue will be to understand how each form of church government mediates the authority of Christ, as head, to the rest of the body. But first, in order to understand authority before looking at authority structures, we will offer some general principles for leadership in the church suggested by other chapters in this text.

### The Trinity and Authority in the Church

If church leadership is to reflect the nature and character of God, then it must reflect his trinitarian existence. Church leadership structure, then, must function on the basis of community and interdependence. As each person of the trinitarian God always acts in concert with the other members, so church leadership is most authentic when it moves forward with consensus. Such community and interdependence is illustrated at the Jerusalem council in Acts 15, when the apostles and others agree on an appropriate action for the church. Of course, how the church reflects the Trinity in its leadership structures depends on whether its view of the Trinity is fundamentally hierarchical or egalitarian.[3] In any case, no church structure that creates a functional dictatorship of one person—be it an episcopal church or an independent church that is congregational in name but, for all intents and purposes, is ruled by the senior pastor—reflects a trinitarian model of leadership. For in the trinitarian structure, the Son and the Spirit do not serve merely as objects to carry out the Father's will, but as subjects with the Father in every act of God. Thus, God always acts trinitarianly.

Here the metaphor of the church as the bride is crucial. For the apostle John, who sees the church as Christ's bride (Rev. 21–22), the church is invited into the community of love and unity created by the Father and Son in the Spirit (John 17; Rev. 3:20). In Ephesians 5, Paul speaks of the very nature of the church in terms of the relationship between husband and wife. In so doing, he makes it clear that Christ, the husband, is head over the church, his wife. Yet as head, Christ also gives himself sacrificially for the church, for his primary purpose is not self-aggrandizement, nor simply the exercise of his power. His glory and the exercise of his power takes place in his own self-giving for the benefit of the church. It is the father/son, husband/wife love, unity, and service, empowered by the Spirit, that is meant to permeate the church so that the world may know that the church belongs to Jesus (John 13; 17). Thus, church government, in order to be legitimate, must be able to express authority as well as self-sacrifice, and must be able to create authentic unity.

## Eschatology and Authority in the Church

In chapter 3 we saw that the church is an eschatological community and suggested that this means the church should always be looking forward to its ultimate existence and character, drawing these future realities back into the present as much as possible. This methodology has a key role to play as the church works out its theology of government and leadership.[4] One of the key images of the eschatological church is that of a unified community, the bride, under Christ as husband and Lord. The now and not-yet eschatology of the New Testament draws the future kingship of Christ into the present through his living lordship over the church. For it is not simply the principles of Christ that guide the church; it is the very presence of the risen Christ who rules the church, in person and in anticipation of his future, personal rule over all creation.

Regarding the lordship of Christ in the church, the various models of church polity would each argue that their structure most clearly represents such lordship to the church.[5] Episcopal structures would argue that Christ's lordship is personally represented in the bishop. Congregationalists might argue that his lordship is expressed in the scriptures through the Reformation principle of *sola scriptura*. But perhaps the issue here is not structure as much as it is the environment created by the church. To conform to the eschatological image of Christ's lordship, the leadership of the church must create an environment that communicates to the people that Jesus Christ is the ultimate authority over the church in all areas of faith and practice. In a world forever changed by the effects of postmodern thought, this does not mean that every church in every era and in every location will understand in the same way how the lordship of Jesus Christ is to be lived out, nor will they come to the same conclusions on theological issues. What it does mean is that the church understands that Jesus speaks with total authority on theology, morals, and on the very life of the church, and that when culture contradicts the revelation of God in Jesus Christ, Jesus is given priority.

Here the lordship of Jesus Christ means that his church, while not anticultural, is always countercultural. For the church, culture is to be understood through the lordship of Jesus and not vice versa. Church leaders will exemplify this reality in the healthiest way when they communicate to the congregation through a variety of means that their leadership is always in submission to Christ himself through submission to the Word of God and to the teachings of historic Christian orthodoxy. In the episcopal system this may take the form of leaders submitting themselves to the historic teaching tradition of the church as a product of the scriptures. In the congregational church it may take the form of a more direct submission to the scriptures themselves. In the episcopal tradition, a weakness at times has been to allow teaching tradition and the teaching office of the church to be authoritative in spite of the lack of solid biblical evidence. On the congregational side, the tendency has at times been to tout the authority of the scriptures on their interpretation of an issue, while ignoring the fact that two thousand years of biblically based historic orthodoxy would beg to differ.[6] The issue here concerns how exactly the church accesses the lordship of Jesus Christ and reflects it in its faith and practice.

The ultimate lordship of Jesus Christ will be manifest at the parousia as he returns to earth to rule directly as Lord. In the absence of this direct rule, Christ has left his church with the need to function through mediated authority. In the American evangelical tradition, which is largely congregational, the general philosophy of authority has been that the scriptures are the supreme intermediary authority in the church and that any believer may question or even reject any other authority simply by turning to the scriptures. Depending on the Reformation principles of *sola scriptura*, the priesthood of the believer, and the perspicuity of the scriptures, congregational polity suggests that each believer is allowed to judge the authority and/or doctrinal accuracy of any official church teacher or teaching simply through his own study of the Bible.[7] In practice, however, the senior/preaching pastor of the church actually becomes the main authority in the church, interpreting the scriptures for the congregation. In noncongregational systems, the contention is that God has ordained certain officers and teachers of the church both to explain the truths of scripture and to determine how those truths are to be lived out in the life of the church.

So, which system of church government is best suited to draw the eschatological lordship of Jesus Christ back into the experience of the church today? We would argue that each church polity has strengths and weaknesses in this regard. The congregational system is most likely to recognize the scriptures alone as completely authoritative in the church. As such, the scriptures are the most powerful means for Christ's lordship to be mediated. In church government systems that emphasize an authoritative tradition or teaching office, there is always the danger of these sources taking precedence over the Word of God. The downside of the congregational system can be that the scriptures, which always must be explained and interpreted in order for Christ's lordship to be applicable, may be left without any authoritative interpretation, opening the door to understandings of the scriptures, and thus of the lordship of Christ, that depart from the faith of historic orthodoxy. Often, the strength of church polities that emphasize teaching tradition and historic teaching authority is that they protect the church from unorthodox interpretations of the scriptures and, thus, improper understandings and applications of Christ's lordship.[8]

So if, as we have suggested, there is no clearly ordained, biblical form of church government, how must the various forms of church government emphasize their strengths and guard against their weaknesses in helping the church experience the eschatological lordship of Jesus Christ? Bottom line, the leadership of every church, regardless of its polity, must look beyond itself, consistently bearing witness to Jesus Christ as Lord. In congregational churches the leadership needs to help the congregation understand that submission to Christ as Lord goes beyond the freedom of each individual or even the local church as a whole to interpret that lordship on its own. Aware of the tendency of the individual and even of a local church to interpret the lordship of Christ for its own purposes and its own comfort, influenced by its own cultural context, the healthy congregational church will look beyond itself. It will seek to understand the lordship of Christ through both the mainstreams of historic orthodoxy and the multifaceted lenses of the contemporary church in its various cultural, ethnic, and denominational representations. In this way the church protects itself from provincial and convenient misunderstandings of Christ's lordship. In churches where the congregation is not structurally connected to church authority, it is the leadership that must be most vigilant to look beyond itself. In light of the tendency of power to create a greater hunger for even more power, leadership must look to the self-giving nature of Christ's authority. Moreover, it must look to the future image of the church as Christ's perfect and loving bride so as to seek a unity that is not coerced, but is the result of a congregation captivated by the love of Christ, exemplified in its leaders.

## Spiritual Gifts, Office, and Authority in the Church

One of the key issues that must be addressed to develop a proper theology of church order is the relationship between official leadership and spiritual gifts. The question can be framed simply: is authority in the church primarily gift-based or office-based? Like most questions of this type, the answer is likely to be both. If the biblical text and its portrayal of the life of the early church is to be the primary source of instruction on this issue, the evidence is a bit ambiguous. For leadership in the early church is viewed through the lenses of gifts, office, and even character without there being a clear means of connecting any of these to authority in the church. One of the important aspects of the promise of the kingdom of God in the Hebrew Scriptures is that there will come a time when God will no longer speak exclusively through the official authority figures of the nation of Israel, but will one day pour out his Spirit upon all people (Joel 2), with the result that many who are outside of official authority structures will become mouthpieces of God to the people of God.

The initial event of this Spirit-gifted empowerment to speak for God occurs on the day of Pentecost. And while this first manifestation of the Spirit falls upon the twelve, who were given unique leadership roles by Christ, both in the early church and for the eschaton (Matt. 16:17–19; 18:18; 19:28), the manifestation subsequently spreads throughout the church, with the result that Paul not only encourages the members of the church at Corinth to desire the gift of prophecy (1 Cor. 14:1, 39), but also tells them that anyone in the church who has a prophetic word from God is eligible to share it with the whole church (1 Cor. 14:29–31). This does not mean that there is no longer a need for official leadership structure in the church, or that all church members are empowered by the Spirit to have an equal voice in leading the congregation. For it is also clear that the early church had official leaders. Paul appointed elders in the churches he planted and, as an apostle with a unique authority from Christ, gave them authority to rule the church (1 Tim. 5:17; Titus 1:5). Peter also urged the elders to rule well (1 Pet. 5:1–4).

So what we see in the early church is an interplay between Spirit-giftedness and official leadership. In this interplay the church recognizes the authority vested in the leadership office, yet also understands that God may speak and work through those gifted by the Spirit who are not official leaders. Paul argues both in 1 Corinthians and in 1 Thessalonians that prophecies must be tested, presumably to confirm that they are truly words from God. But the other assumption is that if their source is God through the Spirit, they are proclamations to be regarded with respect and obedience by the church (1 Thess. 5:20–21). Regarding this authority of Spirit-empowered persons who may not be official leaders, Bengt Holmberg writes: "The most important basis for the legitimate exercise of power or, in other words, for the exercise of authority in the Primitive Church is proximity to the sacred (Christ and His Spirit)."[9] Arguing for the priority of giftedness in leadership in the NT church, Gordon Fee writes that "those who have been recognized by the community as a whole to be gifted for ministry and leadership should receive the 'laying on of hands' on that basis alone."[10] To connect church leadership primarily to giftedness rather than to office necessarily diminishes the gap between clergy and laity, since all members of Christ's church are gifted to represent him and to minister his grace to the rest of the body. Miroslav Volf writes,

> Since the members of the church are interdependent, their life must be characterized by mutuality. The church is a community "of mutual giving and receiving" (Phil. 4:15). The "charismata of office" must be integrated into this mutuality. Officeholders do not stand opposite the church as those acting exclusively *in persona Christi*. Since the Spirit of Christ acts in them not by the power of their office, but rather in the execution of their ministry, their actions do not differ in principle from those of any other member of the church.[11]

What we see in the NT narrative is that Spirit filling and giftedness are prerequisites for positions of leadership. This pattern is illustrated in the choosing of servant leaders to deal with administrative problems in the church in Acts 6. Here, the choice of Spirit-filled men to lead the church in these issues illustrates how responsibility/leadership is given on the basis of appropriate Spirit gifting and character. Ronald Fung summarizes his research on the interplay between gift and office in the NT:

> We have repeatedly pointed out, in discussing [relevant] passages, the priority of
> the Spirit or his gifts in the mutual relations of function, gift, and office. It is the
> charisma, not the office, that creates the ministry: the office is but the channel
> through which the office-bearer may exercise the given charisma for a particular
> function; and the church's appointment to office (where such is involved) is but a
> sign of recognizing a person's spiritual gifts and a response to God's will made
> known in the bestowing of those gifts.[12]

Another illustration of the relationship of Holy Spirit gifting to authority in
the early church is the role of Pricilla as instructor of Apollos. As a woman,
she surely held no official office in the church (e.g., she was not an elder), yet,
as a Spirit-gifted teacher, she instructed Apollos in theology, even correcting
his errors so that he could teach more effectively (Acts 18:24–26). The implica-
tion of the story is that both Luke and Paul respected her teaching and gave it
a certain place of authority that had nothing to do with office.

By the Middle Ages the Catholic hierarchy had developed such that authority
became primarily a function of office. But even during this period, the issue
of Spirit filling and giftedness rose to prominence, even over the power of
religious office. One need only recall the influence of mystics like Catherine
of Siena, whose Spirit-inspired visions were revered to the point that she was
given personal audiences by popes. Other mystics of the period were held in
similarly high regard.

With such biblical and historical precedents in mind, the church should
always consider the role of the Spirit in its authority structure. This may be
taken into account in at least the following ways: If it is the consensus of the
church that an official leader does not show signs of Spirit filling and/or Spirit
gifting, his authority should not be unquestionable. Also, choosing persons for
leadership/authority should not be simply a matter of determining their skills
and experience (e.g., the idea that successful CEOs always make good elders),
but a matter of considering indications of Spirit filling and Spirit gifting. Of
course, the logical question that follows is, What or who determines when
a person is gifted for church leadership? The overwhelming evidence of the
New Testament is that the whole congregation must be involved in recognizing those gifted for leadership.

In Acts 6, the apostles look to the people to identify those who are Spirit-
filled and gifted for servant leadership. In Paul's epistles, the church recognizes
those who have the character necessary for leadership. In this sense, church
leaders, at least initially, are not made but recognized. No amount of training can instill a gift that God has not given. If this is true, it should have a
significant effect on the student populations of our seminaries, at least in
the case of those who seek to be pastors. As professors of theology, it is our
experience that there are some students in seminary preparing to be pastors
who may not be gifted to be pastors. Perhaps an important qualification that

every seminary should look for in those who desire to train specifically for pastoral ministry is a strong affirmation from the congregation of which the prospective pastor is a member, something that says, "This person is gifted for church leadership. When she leads, we want to follow. We just need you to train her so her gifts can be maximized." This kind of recognized giftedness, combined with godly character, creates leaders who do not need offices to have influence, but who will be appointed to offices by congregations who want to follow their lead.

## Church Polity and Authority

Throughout its history, the church has ordered itself in various ways. But all of these forms can be subsumed under three main church polities—episcopal, presbyterian, and congregational. The episcopal structure is the most hierarchical. The word *episcopal* is a transliteration of the Greek word *episcopos*, from which we get the word *bishop*. Churches with episcopal polity are connected to a larger denomination that is ruled by bishops. Each bishop is the senior authority figure over all the churches, including their priests/pastors in a particular region. The bishops together, then, become the ruling body for the entire denomination. In the case of the Roman Catholic Church, there is one bishop who holds authority over all the rest, the pope.

The word *presbyterian* is a transliteration of the Greek word *presbuteros*, which means "elder." In presbyterian polity, each church is ruled by elders, who make up a body called the session. Representatives from local church sessions then form a ruling body for a town/city called a presbytery. Representatives from various presbyteries form a ruling body for a region and are called a synod. Finally, representatives from the various synods form the General Assembly, the highest ruling body in most Presbyterian denominations.

In the congregational system, the highest human authority in each church is the whole body of voting members. Here the congregation generally must vote on the budget and the hiring of pastors, and can actually veto a decision by the pastors and/or elders. Many congregational churches are members of denominations and so submit to the leaders or national assembly of the denomination on such issues as ordaining pastors, church constitutions, and an agreed-upon doctrinal statement. Other congregational churches are completely independent, having no authority outside of the local congregation.

In the following pages we look at some of the support offered for each of the three main polities, both from the scriptures and from the perspectives of those traditions that hold to them. Then we suggest some strengths and weaknesses of each. It should be said that we do not argue for any of the three polities as "the biblical one" or the "God-ordained one," though many do.[13] We contend that the scriptures simply do not present a clear argument for any particular church polity. Thus, the most important issue for each church is not to reconsider the fidelity of its polity to scripture and church tradition, but to consider the strengths and weaknesses of its system as a means for ordering the people of God.

### Episcopal Church Polity

Briefly, the historical background of the episcopal system goes back to the early church, which had elders who were spiritual leaders of the local churches. As local churches multiplied and more oversight was needed, one elder was chosen to be bishop and eventually became the leader of the elders of several churches. We know that this structure was already in place by the end of the first century, for Ignatius, in his letter to Smyrna, contends that where the bishop is, there is the church of Jesus Christ.[14] As churches spread throughout a city, the bishop became known as a metropolitan bishop. These bishops then became the major leaders of Christendom, especially the bishops of the five patriarchates—Rome, Alexandria, Constantinople, Jerusalem, and Antioch. By the middle of the third century, the bishop of Rome began to be recognized by many as the premier bishop of the church, since he ruled in the traditional city of the martyrdom of Peter. This led to the establishment of the papacy.

Biblical support for the episcopal system would include Jesus's statement to Peter in Matthew 16 that he would build his church upon him and give him the keys of the kingdom of God.[15] While this passage has been highly debated over the years, with non-Catholics often arguing that Jesus did not mean here that he was building his church upon Peter, but upon Peter's confession or upon himself as the rock, the prevailing opinion among Protestant scholars now is that Jesus did indeed mean here that he would build his church upon Peter. The resistance among Protestants to this interpretation comes from the fact that the Roman church uses this passage to support the idea of Peter as the first pope. But even if Jesus does mean here that he will build his church upon Peter, that does not necessarily lead to the papacy. Two chapters later Jesus repeats his intention to bestow the keys of the kingdom, but here that bestowal is not to Peter alone, but to all the apostles (Matt. 18:18). But whether one understands this passage as pointing uniquely to Peter or to all the apostles, it is reasonable to argue that Jesus indicated a unique kind of authority in the church for the apostles, who form a kind of plurality of bishops to instruct, manage, and rule the early church.

In the episcopal system, the authority of this body of bishops is seen to be handed off to each succeeding generation of bishops in a concept known as "apostolic succession." Even for those churches that do not trace this succession back to Peter and opt for one supreme bishop, as does the Roman church, it is often understood to be a continuum of ruling and shepherding tradition that goes back to the apostles and is meant to continue throughout the church age until the return of the Great Shepherd. Another claim for biblical support for this system, though more anecdotal, is found in the fact that James seems to emerge as the lead bishop of the church in Jerusalem and presides over the Jerusalem council, where the other leaders seem to defer to him.

The hierarchy of the Roman Catholic Church is constituted through the theology of apostolic succession, arguing that the official pastoral ministry of the church was invested by Christ first and foremost in the apostle Peter, and subsequently in each successive bishop of Rome. Pastoral authority flows from Christ to the Bishop of Rome (the Pope), and from him to the other bishops and to the rest of the community of ordained priests.[16] Thus, we see that in the Catholic Church, both the role and the authority of the bishop are tied primarily to the office and not to the person or to the gifts given him by the Holy Spirit.[17]

The episcopal theology of the Orthodox Church differs from Rome in ascribing authority to the five patriarchs and the ecumenical councils (rather than the papal system). Orthodoxy does insist on the infallibility of the church as a whole but is built less around earthly authority structures and more around the mystical union of the church with Christ. Bishop Kallistos Ware argues that the relationship between God and the church is illustrated in the hierarchy. As the image of the Holy Trinity, the church is ordered after the unity in diversity of the Trinity; there is a coinherence that leads to freedom and authority, unity without totalitarianism. Thus, like the Father's position over the Son and Spirit, the bishop can hold a position of headship or authority over the rest of the church without expressing an inequality of personhood or value. In the church's hierarchy, the bishop is the living image of God on earth and fountain of the sacraments from which come salvation. The bishop is endowed with the threefold power of: (1) ruling: he is appointed by God to rule the flock ("He is a monarch in his own diocese"[18]); (2) teaching: he receives a gift from the Holy Spirit to act as teacher of the faith, and his highest act is the sermon at the Eucharist; (3) sacraments: the bishop is the fountain of the sacraments. Again, according to the Trinitarian ethos, the bishop is not set up over the church but holds office in the church. It is not the bishop alone who is the guardian of the faith, but the whole people of God fill that role. The bishop is the proclaimer of the truth, but all are stewards of the truth.

Laypersons are also crucial in Orthodox Church order, for the church is not only hierarchical, but also charismatic and Pentecostal. The Spirit is poured out on all God's people. So even though there are offices of bishop, priest, and deacon, all the people are prophets and priests. The "charismatic" side of the church means that each has gifts from the Spirit for the good of all. There is no ultimate conflict between the hierarchical and charismatic aspects of the church. A key concept of Orthodox structure is *sobornost,* which refers to the organic unity of the church.[19] Each member contributes to the common work of the church, doing his or her job with the help of others. There is both individuality and community. *Sobornost* expresses the idea that even though the church is hierarchical, governed by the bishop who represents God, there is also equality of all members. It is the Spirit who creates the church and its structure, and all believers are interrelated through the Spirit.

Still addressing episcopal polity, but switching to the perspective of the Roman Catholic Church, one of the fundamental issues that affects what it means for the church to be an ordered community consists in whether it is the gospel or the church that takes temporal priority in Christianity. For Protestants, the gospel is always primary. *Sola fides* is first about *sola scriptura*. One places faith in Christ through the message of the Bible and then enters the church. This is not the Roman Catholic view, which argues (as illustrated at the outset of the chapter in the quote by theologian Henri de Lubac) that the church takes priority. Lubac rejects the idea that the gospel existed before the church. The books from which the gospel comes, he says, were produced and verified by the church and thus cannot be separated from the tradition of the church. There has never been Christianity without the church. This fact means that the community, along with its structure, is foundational for all else. The gospel is not about a new relation of individuals to Christ, but about a new people of God. The church is not a group of individuals who have come together after having believed in Christ. There is no possibility of nonecclesial Christianity. Because Christ and his message are so tied to the church, "the essential structures of the Church are not 'ancient forms' which could be abandoned any more than the fundamental dogmas of our faith are out-of-date ideas in which a change of language would leave nothing subsisting."[20]

The doctrine of apostolic succession also argues that an episcopal system is not only biblical, but also crucial for God to dispense his grace to the church effectively. Lubac writes,

> The Body of Christ is not an invisible Church or an invertebrate people. It is always owing to the immediate mediation of pastors that this maternal function of all and of each one can be exercised, whether in relation to the Word of God in the individual soul or with regard to the community as a whole. For it is through them, successors of the first apostles, that the divine life continues to be transmitted, and it is they who have the responsibility of seeing to it that the "virginity" of the faith is preserved both intact and fruitful. They are the "co-workers of God" among us; they are the "dispensers of the mysteries of God" for us.[21]

Another conception of the episcopal system is that held by theologians like Anglican Paul Zahl. For him, the episcopal polity is good for the church but is not the essence of the church. Stated differently, "Episcopal church order is not constitutive of the church."[22] While the church may function best under a hierarchical system, it is not necessary for the church to be the church.[23]

### Strengths and Weaknesses of Episcopal Polity

There are several advantages of an episcopal form of church government. One is that a hierarchy tends to hold the church together in tough times and even amid disagreements. Especially when there is a sense of apostolic succession, such that the authority of the bishops is considered to be given by God, church splits are very unlikely. As a Presbyterian addressing two disagreeing Catholic scholars commented, "One of the amazing things about you Roman Catholics is that you can come here and take opposing sides on an important theological issue, yet, when the debate is over, you still remain Catholic. When we Presbyterians disagree on doctrine, we just form a new denomination."[24] While many congregationalists would object that the need to remain under the authority of a hierarchy can cause Christians to remain under the authority of those who teach heresy, a cursory examination of denominational splits would likely reveal that most such splits were not really the result of heresy. The doctrines of many Presbyterian and Baptist denominations are so similar to that of other denominations in their traditions that one wonders why they have to remain separated. Surely the inability of the church to work out its differences, resulting in a plethora of competing denominations, does not reflect Christ's hope for unity illustrated by his prayer in John 17, nor the love for each other by which the world is supposed to know that we belong to Jesus. Despite the downsides, episcopal systems do tend to keep the flock together and often protect it from heresy rather than fostering it.[25]

Another strength of episcopal systems is that they tend to value tradition. There is very little structural motivation for valuing tradition in a church where the local congregation, formed a few years or decades before, is the final authority in all matters. But the episcopal polity by nature understands authority to be passed on from generation to generation of bishops. Zahl notes that "the importance of tradition in the shaping of Episcopal Christianity is high. A besetting weakness of popular evangelicalism and Pentecostalism is the idea that the good news is new, that the gospel came to us just yesterday."[26] One of the problems of congregational systems, which tend not to value history and tradition, is that they fall prey to the fallacy that their interpretation of the scriptures is the most accurate and authoritative, with little awareness that their interpretation is always a product of their own culture. An appreciation of tradition listens to the voices of many interpreters who have struggled with how to express the tenets of the faith in eras when they were reacting to completely different issues. In this way tradition, properly understood and applied, becomes a filtering system. It helps the church to recognize and understand those doctrinal issues that really matter and have always been a concern to the church.

### Presbyterian Church Government

Presbyterian polity usually argues that there are two main offices in the church, elder and deacon. Elders are the main overseers of the church, responsible for its spiritual well-being, its doctrinal purity, and church discipline. Generally, two kinds of elders are recognized: ruling elders and teaching elders. Both serve on the session together, but teaching elders are those recognized as having a spiritual gift of teaching, while ruling elders are responsible for administrative leadership. Deacons compose the second office of the church and are generally responsible for the financial and physical issues of church life, often caring for the needy and managing church property.

Theologians who hold to the Presbyterian system of church government generally look to the early church for support, noting that the church adopted many of the practices and forms of the synagogue, which was ruled by a group of elders. Indeed, the early church congregations were run by elders, but as noted above, soon the elders of the various metropolitan congregations began the practice of choosing one elder to whom they would all be accountable. Thus, even if the earliest churches did have some measure of independence and were run by elders, this system soon gave way to a system of bishops that ruled the entire (Western) church until the Protestant Reformation. While the episcopal form took over in the subapostolic period, the Reformers, reacting to what they saw as the abuses of the Roman Catholic Church, generally established elder-rule churches, believing they were more supportable biblically. Early on, the move to Presbyterianism came from the influence of Calvin. Luther, while he eventually rejected the papacy, did not reject Episcopal polity. Chad Owen Brand and R. Stanton Norman write:

> In Geneva, Calvin organized the churches into a fourfold-ministry of pastors, elders, doctors (teachers), and deacons, though he tended to conflate the office of teacher with that of pastor . . . Calvin argued, against episcopacy, that there is only one level of ordained ministry (the elder), not two (elder and bishop), and that there are two kinds of elders in the New Testament—teaching elders and ruling elders—a conviction that arose from his interpretation of 1 Timothy 5:17.[27]

To this day, churches in the Reformed tradition generally operate via a Presbyterian system.

Biblical texts that support Presbyterianism are found throughout the New Testament. Luke's account of the early church mentions elders in Jerusalem, and Paul and Barnabas took funds for famine relief to the elders in that church. In Acts 14:23 and Titus 1:5, we read that elders were appointed to lead churches. And in 1 Peter 5, we see that the elders of each church have authority over the members. Numerous other passages speak of elder rule, including 1 Timothy 3:4–5; 1 Thessalonians 5:12; Hebrews 13:17. With the passing of the apostles, these elders were to continue to be the leaders of the local churches.

While the supporters of episcopal polity look to the Jerusalem Council in Acts 15 for support, so do Presbyterians. By the time of the council, there would have been a number of local congregations in Jerusalem. The council brought together the elders of those churches to decide an issue for the good of the whole church. For supporters of presbyterian polity, the issue at the council is not the singular authority of James, but the communal authority of the elders. They contend that ecclesiastical authority was shared by a plurality of elders, not just James or even the apostles.[28]

While supporters of Presbyterian polity do offer theological arguments, their main contention is that the scriptures clearly represent this polity as ordained by God. They see a plural leadership of representatives going all the way back to Moses, his group of elders, and the priestly body of Israel. And since Reformed theology sees a high degree of continuity between the testaments, it makes sense that God's ordained system of government for the church would reflect the plurality of that of Israel. While supporters of other polities may agree that there is significant evidence for other systems in the scriptures, Reformed theologians tend to argue that the scriptures clearly present presbyterianism as God's ordained polity. To depart from it or to add to it is to depart from or add to the scriptures.[29]

### Strengths and Weaknesses of Presbyterian Polity

One of the strengths of presbyterian polity is that even if, as we suggest, it is impossible to determine one form of church government that is clearly ordained by scripture, there is probably more narrative support for an elder-run church than for any other. There are numerous references to elders being appointed to churches (Acts 14:23; 1 Tim. 5:17; James 5:14; etc.), and the passages that enumerate the qualifications for elders imply that there is a plurality of them for each church (1 Tim. 3; Titus 1). On the other hand, it must be said that having multiple elders in the church does not preclude either an episcopacy or a congregational polity. Elder rule, by the very nature of its structure, also has the benefit of making leadership in the church a community affair. No single person can commandeer the church for his own purposes, and major decisions must be made with contributions from a variety of persons, helping to take personal agendas out of the equation of leadership and direction. Further, since the pastor is subject to the elder board, he not only can be kept from making mistakes, but can be protected from attacks and encouraged in difficult times by other leaders.

There are also downsides to presbyterian polity. In many elder-run churches, the elder board is a self-perpetuating body, choosing its members without any input or confirmation from the congregation. This can lead to the disconnection of the leadership from the congregation and also the perpetuation of a certain kind of personality, leading to a board that may not represent the congregation broadly. Further, in order to maintain church unity, elder-run churches need to work hard to make sure that the elders balance their authority to make official decisions with the importance of developing consensus on important decisions that affect the entire congregation.

### Congregational Polity

Historically, congregationalism surfaced in the post-Reformation period. A significant minority of English Puritans, rejecting the episcopal system of the Church of England as too reminiscent of Roman Catholicism, insisted on congregational polity.[30] Baptists, generally identifying with the Anabaptist movement, with its communal and democratic ethos, were also congregational. Later, the Scandinavian Free Church movement rejected the hierarchical system of the state churches and opted for congregationalism as well. Congregational polity became a significant part of the American landscape early on with the Baptists and later with the Scandinavian immigrations of the nineteenth century. Congregationalism also fit easily with America's democratic impulses.[31]

Support for the congregational form of government comes from various passages. In Matthew 18 and 1 Corinthians 5, for example, the whole church is responsible for church discipline. In Acts 6 and 2 Corinthians 8 we see that the whole church chooses its leaders. Further, at the Jerusalem council, it is not merely the apostles who establish its major decision, but the whole church (Acts 15:22). Moreover, the local church is the focus of Acts and the epistles, where there is little support for higher authorities beyond the local church.

Theologically, the Reformation principle of the priesthood of all believers is a central issue for those who argue for congregationalism. Paige Patterson contends that this priesthood is witnessed by the scriptures in numerous places, and in 1 Peter 2:5–9 is described regarding its nature. "In those verses the followers of Christ are said to constitute a 'spiritual house' made up of 'living stones' for the purpose of exercising a 'holy priesthood.'"[32] The upshot is that the congregation, made of up believing members, has direct access to God, without the need of any intermediary besides Christ himself. For Congregationalists, this "democratic" access to God affects not only salvation or worship, but becomes the defining factor in church structure and polity. Since the individual believer is responsible before God for his spiritual state, so also the congregation is the final locus of responsibility for the life of the local church.[33] Accordingly, Miroslav Volf argues that the general priesthood of the church is not a function of the officers of the church, but of all the individual members. He writes that "although one should in particular not underestimate the preeminent significance of officeholders, who have an indispensable role in the church, the whole life of the church is not ordered around them. Different persons can become soteriologically 'significant others' for other persons."[34] This being the case, the authority structure of the church should not be monocentric, as in episcopal polities, but polycentric, with the congregation playing a major role in the authority structure.

### Strengths and Weaknesses of Congregational Polity

At least by nature of its structure, congregationalism allows the most space for individual members to have a voice in the direction and life of the church. If individual members believe that the leadership is taking the church in unwise directions, they can vote against the policies and decisions of the leadership, even working together with other members, joining their voices to call upon the leadership to reevaluate or change course. On the positive side, congregationalists argue that their structure "is more capable than other polities of developing loyalty to and support of the congregation . . . Participating in decision-making helps Christians to be able to say meaningfully, 'our church.'"[35] Congregational polity is also most effective at connecting giftedness to influence. In this system, those with spiritual gifts of teaching and leadership, but who are not officers of the church, may still bring their gifts to bear on the decision-making process of the church.[36] Those who hold to congregationalism also often argue that it is the most effective system in keeping the congregation involved in the process of church discipline, which they believe is clearly mandated in Matthew 18.[37] The more church discipline is relegated to the control of bishops and elders, the less it becomes a community issue, and the less effective it is in calling the whole church to holiness.

As with other church polities, the strengths of congregationalism can also be the source of its greatest weaknesses. The caricature of a Baptist annual business meeting, where one obnoxious and vocal member can derail an important policy decision reached by a unified leadership and offered to the congregation for confirmation, is based on the experiences of many who have grown up in congregational churches. While the democratic ethos of congregationalism gives the most space for all members to be heard, it also allows for members who have influence beyond their actual wisdom and knowledge to undermine the work of the leadership of the church.

Another weakness of congregationalism, especially in the case of those churches that do not belong to a denomination, is that its emphasis on independence tends to weaken the local church's connection with the church universal. Episcopal churches, and especially the Catholic Church, where final human authority subsists in the papacy, have a built-in structure for ecclesial unity. Pope Benedict XVI has argued recently, for example, that the inclusiveness of the church, embracing communions outside the Roman Church, is not eliminated by, but is rooted in the unity created by apostolic succession through the Bishop of Rome back to Christ himself.[38]

L. Roy Taylor, a Presbyterian, has also expressed concern in this regard about congregationalism. He writes, "Throughout the centuries, the church has recognized herself as unique—one, holy, catholic, and apostolic. While independence fits well with rugged American individualism, and the entrepreneurial spirit, it is the least suitable form of church government to express the universality and oneness of the church."[39] Indeed, the exodus of thousands of churches from their denominations during the Bible Church Movement in the twentieth century has led to a structural disconnection of the one church of Jesus Christ in America as in no other place on earth. Congregationalism has doubtless played no small part in this scenario.

## Conclusion

Perhaps the most obvious downside to any system of church government is that they all put power and authority into the hands of broken, sinful people. And as with civil governments, the most efficient systems (dictatorships) are also those most susceptible to abuse; the most inclusive ones (absolute democracies) easily suffer from disunity and inefficiency. Even churches that argue that only one of the traditional forms of church government is truly biblical must still address these issues. For adopting the "right" church government is no guarantee of a proper use of authority. So we come back to the need not just for biblical *structures* of government, but also for biblical *principles*.

A biblical situation of church authority must exhibit the principles of both power and sacrifice. Elders are to rule the church (1 Pet. 5), but they are to do so with humility, exemplifying the self-sacrifice of Christ, the one true shepherd of the church. For all shepherds in the church are also sheep, dependent upon the rest of the flock for spiritual life, and equally in need of the guidance and grace of Christ. A biblical situation of church government will also focus on the principles of unity and connectedness. The spiritual unity of the church is not ultimately a product of the church's leaders, but of the life that comes from being the people of God in union with Christ through the Holy Spirit. Thus, biblical leaders and structures will foster inclusion and ownership, recognizing that the Spirit of God brings the life of Christ to the church through the gifts and service of all the church's members. Finally, in recognition of the fact that the abuse of power can be a function not just of individual persons, but also of whole communities, a church with a healthy leadership structure will always seek accountability from outside itself. As the church in Jerusalem, with James as its leader, listened to all the voices of the church in a time of controversy—to the congregation as well as to the apostles, to an apostle to the Jews (Peter) as well as to the apostle to the Gentiles (Paul)—so the eschatological community of God in any era, no matter what its governmental structure, must listen to voices from across the spectrum of the church, making sure to avoid a parochial leadership and any structure that has become blind to all but its own agendas and perspectives. For leaders in the contemporary church, this means listening to the voices of the church across denominational divisions, across cultural divisions, and across the span of church history. Will churches that operate through biblical and healthy governmental structures always agree on issues of church leadership? No, but that does not mean they cannot live at peace with one another.

## STUDY QUESTIONS

1. Why do so many people have such negative views of church authority figures today?
2. What difference does Christ's sacrificial lordship make for church leadership dynamics, including such matters as decision making as a church body?
3. What strengths and weaknesses does your church background bring to authority in the church?

# 12

# The Role of Women
# in the Ordered Community

Since the very nature of church order involves power and authority, the issue of gender has repeatedly surfaced in the church's discussions of polity and leadership. From the story of the fall in Genesis 3, where harmony between man and woman is broken, the role of women (and men) has been an issue in the biblical metanarrative. And passages like 1 Corinthians 11–14 and 1 Timothy 2 show that a woman's role in the church was controversial in the life of the early church. In this chapter, we look at church polity and leadership through the lenses of biblical eschatology as a way of considering the role of women in the ordered community of the church.

We recently heard Dr. Alice Matthews asked if she thought it would be possible for egalitarians and hierarchicalists to lead a church together.[1] She responded, "Well, it has to be, doesn't it?" While she may be right, one wonders if the church has a structure for such a possibility. Extensive exegetical studies of key passages on women's roles have been helpful, but nowhere near decisive. Every single major controverted passage can boast of scholars on both sides of the issue who contend that the best exegesis supports their conclusions. Perhaps the best we can expect from exegesis on this issue is that it demonstrates that neither perspective on a given passage is without credible support.[2]

But there are other ways of looking at the issue, and, given our juxtaposition of ecclesiology and eschatology in this book, we suggest that connecting these two streams of theology may give us at least one road around the impasse.

Indeed, the dialectic of the kingdom of God may be the best possibility for navigation between two positions that remain quite polarized. Our thesis is that if we view the church as a community that is fundamentally eschatological, drawing its future back into the present, we will necessarily move to a more egalitarian philosophy of leadership in the church, even if we remain hierarchical in our view of leadership in the family. A couple of necessary subsidiary elements of the thesis are that the eschatological image of the church is essentially egalitarian, and that the family is a temporal community whose leadership structure should not be uncritically adopted as the paradigm for leadership structure in an eschatological community. Regarding Paul, whose theology is clearly at the center of the debate, we will argue that he suggests a fundamental reconception of social structures in the church, moving clearly, albeit cautiously, in an egalitarian direction.

### The Egalitarian Future of the Church

First, we need to ask whether the eschaton reveals a structure for the church of the future that is hierarchical or egalitarian. And, if it is hierarchical, does it retain a family-based authority structure, transferred from the hierarchy of husband/wife? While it is impossible for us to understand a great deal about the structure of the economy of heaven/the eschaton, there are certain indications that give us a basic idea and also help to differentiate it from present hierarchical structures. One very interesting indication comes from Jesus himself when his detractors try to trap him in an insoluble dilemma of both cultural and theological significance (Matt. 22:23–32). The Sadducees suggest a scenario where a man marries a woman, then dies, leaving her without children. Then, following the levirate marriage law, each of his six remaining brothers successively marries her and dies, leaving her childless until, finally, the woman herself dies. Which husband, they ask, will this woman be married to at the resurrection? Jesus responds that in the eschaton, the community of God will not be structured on the basis of marriage between men and women, for human marriage will no longer exist. This means that even if there is a hierarchy implied in the creation order of Adam and Eve as husband and wife, that hierarchy does not apply to the eschatological people of God, the community of the resurrection. To be more specific, husbands will not be authoritative over their wives in heaven any more than there will be a seemingly unending line of fathers, going all the way back to Adam, who are authoritative over their children.

In Ephesians 5, we find another indication of the egalitarian nature of the eschaton and, indeed, the church of the eschaton. Paul's somewhat cryptic statement at the end of the passage, that what he is really talking about is the relationship between Christ and the church, is clearly eschatological.

Paul looks forward to the eschaton, when Christ, having fully redeemed the church by his self-sacrifice and resurrection and final victory over sin, will present the church to himself as his spotless bride. A key point here is that the ultimate husband/wife relationship is not the one between a man and a woman, but between Christ and the church. As such, the ultimate picture of the church, metaphorically speaking, is as one person—the bride of Christ. Thus, the eschatological structure of submission is between the church and Christ, not between husbands and wives, who together constitute the one bride of Christ.

But we must also ask a second question—even if the eschatological community of God will not function on the basis of the social structure of marriage between men and women, do we have evidence that this eschatological reality should be drawn into the church in some way now? Here again, Paul's theology helps us. As we noted above, he argues in Galatians and Ephesians for the elimination of social hierarchies in the community of salvation based on God's revelation. To him the church is the fulfillment, at least in anticipatory form, of the eschatological promise of the one community of the people of God, including both Jew and Gentile, both slave and free, both male and female. If Paul is calling for Jews and Gentiles, freemen and slaves to come together in the church on an equal footing, he is also calling for men and women to do so.

Obviously, Paul is not simply reporting that this is the way things are in the Galatian and Ephesian churches. In fact, they are not that way. His vision is based on seeing the church as a community of persons who are, individually and corporately, "in Christ." And while Paul recognizes that believers are truly "in Christ" now and raised up with him even in his heavenly existence at the right hand of God, the full application to life of this union with Christ awaits the day when Christ will appear in glory. But in the meantime, believers are to see themselves in view of the eschaton. They are to set their minds on their status as being seated with the resurrected Christ (Col. 1:1–4). For Paul, this practice of believers viewing their present lives through the future, in Christ, is never meant simply as an individual one, but also as a practice of the church. Thus, if the community of the future is one where social barriers between men and women are broken down, then they should begin to be broken down in the church now.[3]

We suggest that Paul advocates this kind of trajectory for the church in all of his discussions of house-code social structures, including parent/child and master/slave. While Ephesians 6 pictures a parent/child hierarchy, at least until the child is grown, Ephesians 4:14–16 suggests that, in Christ, through the gifts of the Spirit, the church ultimately comes to a point where no one is a "child" (infant) anymore, for all have "grown up into Christ," the head. Thus, in the church, there is a goal of equality based on spiritual maturity, a maturity that has nothing to do with age.[4] And it is clear that the church is to move toward this eschatological goal now. Further, the master/slave structure is revolutionized by the fact that, ultimately, there is only one Master (6:5–9), who will one day be clearly revealed as Lord of all (Phil. 2:10–11). Thus, the church should begin now to recognize that there is but one Master of all who belong to him.

## The Family, the Church, and Structures of Authority

This brings us to another important issue. The church has not typically looked to the biblical description of its eschatological identity for principles of leadership structure, but has looked to the family and, specifically, to a patriarchal image of the family.[5] This, of course, has led to a patriarchal paradigm of church leadership. Moreover, some theologians have argued, on the basis of passages like Ephesians 5, that since family metaphors are used for the church, church leadership must reflect the leadership structure of the family. Vern Poythress, for example, argues that since the Bible uses family authority language such as "father" and "husband" to describe the structure of the church, this means that just as men are in authority in the home as fathers and husbands, so men must be the authority figures in the church.[6] But this argument is unconvincing, because, among other reasons, Poythress simply assumes, without warrant, that the similarity of language necessitates interchangeability of leadership structure. Further, Poythress seems to ignore the fact that two persons can be related to each other through more than one family metaphor. For example, the New Testament says that Christ is actually our brother. But he is also our Lord. So, there are certain ways in which we relate to him as brother—as a "fellow heir"—while in other contexts we relate to him as our total authority. Poythress continues to argue for the authority structures of the family being transferred to the church when he says that Paul "advises Timothy to treat an older man 'as if he were your father. Treat younger men as brothers, older women as mothers, and younger women as sisters.'" This would indicate that, in certain contexts, Timothy should see older men as deserving of a certain respect and authority due to age. Yet in the very same book, Paul tells Timothy, "Command and teach these things. Don't let anyone look down on you because you are young" (1 Tim. 4:11–12), a text Poythress ignores.[7] Here, Timothy functions not as a son or as a young man in deference to older men, but as a brother and a pastor commanding older men from his position in the authority structure of the church. To apply this to the role of women in the church, hierarchicalists, even if they are right about a husband's authority over his wife, need to recognize that the Christian man is related to his wife not only as husband, but also as a brother in the church.

Still, even if we establish that the church of the eschaton does not function on the basis of such earthly, social categories as husband/wife, parent/child, and master/slave, and even if we can show that Paul intends that the church view itself through the lenses of the future, a question remains. Does Paul anywhere suggest how these structures should be transformed in the actual life of the church? Perhaps the book of Philemon gives us some clues. As Paul sends Onesimus, the runaway slave whom he has led to Christ, back to his master, Philemon, he encourages Philemon to receive him back, "no longer as a slave, but better than a slave, as a dear brother" (Philem. 16). Of course, Onesimus' "brotherhood" relationship with Philemon has nothing to do with blood or even marriage—it is an ecclesiological bond. As men who are now both in Christ, they have a new relationship, not necessarily in the household, but in the church. And as we know, Philemon was not addressed in this letter simply as a Christian man, but as the man in whose house the church met.

Thus, the letter to Philemon demonstrates how, in the church, social relationships are transformed—the master/slave relationship is overturned in the church in favor of the egalitarian relationship of brothers. Interestingly, while it cannot be proven that it is the same Onesimus, early church literature speaks of an Onesimus who became a bishop. If this is the same man, and, if he still remained the servant of Philemon, what we have is a situation where, in the church, one of the most powerful hierarchies of the ancient world is turned on its head such that while Philemon was in authority over Onesimus outside the church, inside the church the situation was just the opposite.

If then, Paul's theology of the transformation of social barriers in Christ argues for the movement of Onesimus the slave to a place of ecclesial equality with his master, does this not come to bear also on the situation of women, who are addressed by Paul in the same list of house codes as slaves and masters? In essence, what happens in the biblical narrative is that the church becomes the new family unit that for believers, takes priority over all other authority structures, even the birth/marriage family.[8] The family structure of the church is fundamentally one of brother/sister equality. What this means for the church of Paul's day is that certain hierarchies are transformed within the church even if they remain the same outside the church.

How might this paradigm transform the role of women in the church? Theologically, it means that in the church, a wife's primary and eschatological relationship to her husband is one of brother/sister, taking priority over the temporal husband/wife relationship. Applying this idea to a specific circumstance in the church, it means that a woman could remain in submission to her husband's authority in the home, yet function in the church as an elder/ leader, his ecclesiological equal or, perhaps, an authority over him. Some who argue for a hierarchical relationship of husband as the authority over his wife contend that it is impossible for a woman to have a place of authority in the church and still reflect submission to her husband in the marriage relationship.[9] We contend that this is no less workable than an employee being an elder at a church attended by his boss or a seminary student being the pastor of a church

attended by one of his professors. Might this be a place of possible rapproche-
ment for egalitarians and hierarchicalists? Even if one sees a temporal structure
of hierarchy existing in the home now, could it not be that in the church, as
the eschatological community, we can move toward egalitarian ministry that
more accurately reflects the ultimate values Christ for his bride?

## STUDY QUESTIONS

1. Whatever your view of women in church leadership, what are ways in
   which women can be empowered to bring their persons and gifting to
   bear on building up the whole church body?
2. How do you think your cultural background affects your view of the
   role of women in the church?

# 13

# The Church as a Cultural Community

## Christ, Culture, and the
## Sermon on the Mount Community

### Christ's Church's Multifaceted Relation to Culture

The church is a cultural community. It is Christ's eschatological kingdom community, itself a culture that engages other cultures from Christ's kingdom vantage point.[1]

There can be no monolithic view of the relation of Christ to culture, for there is no ideal culture. God's kingdom culture embodied in the church always takes particular form in concrete contexts. This chapter on the intersection and concrete engagement of Christ's church as a culture (which itself varies in diverse locations and over time) with other cultures involves an important claim. The claim is that the church as a culture in its relation to other cultures is to be multifaceted and dynamic, in no way static, always particular, never abstract, ever contemporary, never remote. A quote attributed to Martin Luther states it well: "If you preach the Gospel in all its aspects with the exception of the issues that deal specifically with your time, you are not preaching the Gospel at all."

We could do no better than to look to the Lord himself to see how to preach the gospel in a manner that deals specifically with our own time. For his story includes our own. We will approach the subject through analysis of Christian scripture, giving focused attention to the Sermon on the Mount. In the Sermon on the Mount and its surrounding context, we find indications of the Lord Jesus radically embracing *and* confronting the culture of his day. As the God-Man, Jesus is of his time and for his time, while transcending and transforming it. The church as Christ's kingdom community envisioned in the Sermon on the Mount takes its cue from its Lord; just as Jesus's engagement of culture is multifaceted, so too must ours be.

Within this framework, we will draw attention to the church's post–New Testament history. We will take a special look at one of our Lord's finest followers, Dietrich Bonhoeffer (1906–45), who sought to live out the Sermon on the Mount in the highly charged and challenging circumstances of Nazi Germany. The church's relationship to culture has been understood in dramatically different ways throughout its history, with models spanning a continuum from separation to transformation. We find various models exemplified in Bonhoeffer and the Christian community he envisioned. We will see that outside culture, there is no church. But outside the church of the Triune God's eschatological kingdom, there is no ultimate redemption of culture.

### Christ and Culture, the Beatitudes, Bonhoeffer, and Beyond

In what follows, we will survey various models, taking our cue from H. Richard Niebuhr's fivefold typology in *Christ and Culture*[2]: "Christ of Culture," "Christ against Culture," "Christ and Culture in Paradox," "Christ above Culture," and "Christ Transforming Culture." We use Niebuhr's types because of their widespread currency.[3] We will not follow Niebuhr's order, depiction, valuation, and illustration of these types in a slavish manner; each type serves a useful purpose and has a role to play as part of the church's overarching framework for engaging other cultures.

Positively framed, Jesus exemplifies each of the five types: Jesus is of culture as its *protagonist,* against culture as its *antagonist,* God's "yes" and "no" to culture as the divine and human *dualist*, above culture as the great *synthesist,* and the one who decisively transforms culture as the ultimate *transformationalist*. Given such exemplification, the church's aim in engaging culture is a straightforward one—to be about Christ-centered cultural encounters. However, what is signified by this aim defies simplistic forms of engagement. Bonhoeffer and his writing exemplify the multifaceted orientation required of every theologian and of every Christian community in interfacing with the cultural situation.

On the one hand, Bonhoeffer writes, "The *present* is not where the present age announces its claim before Christ, but where the present age stands before the claims of Christ."[4] On the other hand, he claims, "The word of the church to the world must . . . encounter the world in all its present reality from the deepest knowledge of the world, if it is to be authoritative."[5] While there is much more to be said, these introductory remarks suggest that we have our work cut out for us. What better place to turn first for assistance for tackling this mountain of a task than to the Bible and to what the Lord himself said in his longest and most famous sermon—the Sermon on the Mount.

### Christ of Culture—Christ as Protagonist

The Sermon on the Mount—Jesus's state of the union address—follows on the heels of Matthew's discussion of Jesus's baptism with the Spirit. The Spirit descends as a dove from the Father (Matt. 3:13–17), leads Jesus into the wilderness to be tempted by the devil (Matt. 4:1), and then grants Jesus the power to begin his public ministry (Matt. 4:17). Matthew provides a summary statement of the Lord's radical intervention on behalf of the people:

> Jesus went throughout Galilee, teaching in their synagogues, proclaiming the good news of the kingdom, and healing every disease and sickness among the people. News about him spread all over Syria, and people brought to him all who were ill with various diseases, those suffering severe pain, the demon-possessed, those having seizures, and the paralyzed; and he healed them. Large crowds from Galilee, the Decapolis, Jerusalem, Judea and the region across the Jordan followed him. (Matt. 4:23–25, TNIV)

The people gravitate to Jesus and his band of disciples (Matt. 5:1–2) because he speaks profoundly and acts redemptively in addressing their concrete situation. They flock to him and are in awe of him, for he speaks with authority (Matt. 7:28–29) and acts authoritatively (see Matt. 8–9)—unlike their religious leaders (Matt. 7:29). In other words, Jesus is "relevant." We will return to this word later, to clarify its meaning. For the time being, it is sufficient to note that Jesus is one who is a man of his times—he is from the people and for the people. To employ Niebuhr's categories, one might say that here the Lord exemplifies the "Christ of culture" model of cultural engagement.

Often, this phrase is taken negatively, as if to say that the person or group in question has compromised biblical convictions for cultural relevance. We will return briefly to discuss this phenomenon historically. Before doing so, however, it is important to stress that if one is *not* of culture, one is *also* compromising biblical faith. For the eternal Word left heaven's security to accommodate himself to our creaturely and worldly limitations in dependence on the written Word and Spirit, all to redeem the creation from its fall to decay and destruction. Jesus could transform humanity only by becoming one with us in our concrete cultural setting. For as Gregory of Nazianzus said, "the unassumed is the unhealed."[6]

Bonhoeffer's life bears witness to the Lord's incarnational orientation. Bonhoeffer was truly a man of his time, whose allegiance to Germany was so deep that he was willing to endure great sacrifice. During Hitler's reign, Bonhoeffer could have stayed in America to avoid the mounting pressures on the church and its leaders, but instead he determined to return to Germany to identify with the people, saying that he could not serve in the rebuilding efforts after the war if he did not endure the tragedies that had befallen the people. This is what it means to be "of the culture" in a positive sense.

The "German Christians," as they were called, typify the negative sense of what it means to be "of culture." They were church leaders who proclaimed an Aryan gospel apart from and beside the gospel of Jesus, and did so in service to the Führer—Lord Hitler—and to his Third (millennial) Reich (kingdom). The Barmen Declaration, written in protest of this capitulation, alludes to this Aryan gospel in the following denunciation:

> We reject the false doctrine, as though the church could and would have to acknowledge as a source of its proclamation, apart from and besides this one Word of God, still other events and powers, figures and truths, as God's revelation . . .
>
> We reject the false doctrine, as though there were areas of our life in which we would not belong to Jesus Christ, but to other lords—areas in which we would not need justification and sanctification through him.[7]

These German Christians provide us with a negative example of the "Christ of culture" model. Following the spirit of the age, they compromised their witness to the gospel of Jesus of Nazareth for power in the public square. The result was that they failed to proclaim the gospel in the power of the Spirit.

Similarly, the fundamentalist-evangelical church in North America (of which we are a part), like its liberal antagonist, is in danger of exchanging the gospel of Christ's kingdom for the gospel of American power. United Methodist bishop William Willimon argues regarding Jerry Falwell, Pat Robertson, the religious Right, and the religious Left:

> Pat Robertson has become Jesse Jackson. Randall Terry of the Nineties is Bill Coffin of the Sixties. And the average American knows no answer to human longing or moral deviation other than legislation.
>
> Again, I ought to know. We played this game before any Religious Right types were invited to the White House. Some time ago I told Jerry Falwell to his face that I had nothing against him except that he talked like a Methodist. A Methodist circa 1960. Jerry was not amused.[8]

Many conservatives and liberals have missed out on identifying the church's witness in terms of the power of the cross. All too often, we place our confidence in legislating this or that morality as if it—not Christ's justification of sinners through his cross and resurrection and his promised return—will save us here and now.

Being "relevant" does not necessarily entail that we let culture shape the gospel to make it appealing. The gospel creates its own relevance. Followers of Jesus are not salespeople, selling a product, but witnesses who are testifying to a kingdom, and are participating in the life of the king as his people who give and receive from his abundance. While it is important to be relevant to culture in terms of meaningfully communicating the gospel, even more important than the answer to the question "Is God relevant to culture?" is the answer to the question "Are the church and surrounding cultures relevant to the Triune God, who indwells, interrupts, and invites the society at large to participate in the church as the eschatological kingdom culture here and now?" The church is called to be a cultural community shaped first and foremost by the eschatological kingdom of the Triune God that Jesus proclaimed and embodied in the power of the Spirit. This trinitarian and eschatological shaping will undoubtedly make the church relevant to God and will also undoubtedly (on occasion) lead the church into conflict with the world at large. In fact, going against the surrounding society in a redemptive manner in view of God will make the church as a distinctive culture most relevant to the world round about it, for the church will be challenging the surrounding cultures in view of what they most need to hear.

### Christ against Culture—Christ as Antagonist

While Jesus identified with the surrounding culture in which he lived, he also confronted it head-on, in view of God's kingdom reality. Jesus challenged the dominant religious structures of his day, where legalists paraded righteousness but did not practice it, externalized spirituality, and ostracized those who did not live up to their self-imposed standards. In Matthew 6:1–8, Jesus confronts such hypocrisy. Although religious, these spiritual guides are human-centered—seeking after human glory, not God's (Matt. 6:2, 5). As John makes clear in his own Gospel, unlike the religious rulers, Jesus seeks God's glory (see John 2:24–25; 5:41–44).

It is interesting to note that the Lord prefaces his remarks on these hypocrites with an exhortation to enter through the narrow gate, for "small is the gate and narrow the road that leads to life, and only a few find it" (Matt. 7:14). No doubt Jesus's disciples were overwhelmed that the Lord told them, "I tell you that unless your righteousness surpasses that of the Pharisees and the teachers of the law, you will certainly not enter the kingdom of heaven" (Matt. 5:20). Those who think that moralistic religion is actually more demanding than the spirituality Jesus embodies and espouses should think again.

Those who aspire to a righteousness that exceeds that of the Pharisees will sense their brokenness or bankruptcy before God.[9] Jesus demands that we die to our attempts at justifying ourselves so that we might truly live. As the first of the beatitudes makes clear, "Blessed are the poor in spirit, for theirs is the kingdom of heaven" (Matt. 5:3). Such poverty in spirit is the result of the Spirit's movement in our lives. Just as the Spirit drove Christ forward into the wilderness to face temptation and embrace self-denial, the Spirit brings us to the end of ourselves, and forward as participants in God's kingdom. When the kingdom of God dawns and dwells in us, we perform righteous deeds; however, the flip side is not true, for a bad tree does not bear good fruit (Matt. 7:16–20).

Human power fails us when it comes to the transformation of the human heart. Only God can perform this work, and it is very costly. It cost the Triune God his Son, and it costs us our lives as well—taking us to the end of ourselves. We must die to ourselves and depend wholly on Christ for our life and righteousness, as Bonhoeffer himself reasons in his depiction of Luther. According to Bonhoeffer, Luther had gone to the monastery void of everything but his piety. But piety does not justify. God had to strip him even of his devotion.[10] Grace takes us to the end of ourselves, as well as to the end of obedience to Christ, no matter where it will lead us.

Bonhoeffer's Luther championed grace, not as cheap, but as costly.[11] Grace costs us our lives, whereas salvation by works leaves us intact. Works salvation is very otherworldly and worldly at the same time. It separates "saints" from simple Christians and "the humble work of discipleship," and turns "the self-renunciation of discipleship into the flagrant spiritual self-assertion of the 'religious.'"[12] "The monk's attempt to flee from the world turned out to be a subtle form of love for the world."[13] But it is not only pious self-assertion that is worldly. The attempt to obtain grace at the cheapest price is also worldly. God's grace will cost us our day-by-day existence as well as our lives.[14]

In commenting on Matthew 5:3 (the poor in spirit), Bonhoeffer writes,

> They are the "poor" *tout court* (Luke 6.20). They have no security, no possessions to call their own, not even a foot of earth to call their home, no earthly society to claim their absolute allegiance. Nay more, they have no spiritual power, experience or knowledge to afford them consolation or security. For his sake they have lost all. In following him they lost even their own selves, and everything that could make them rich. Now they are poor—so inexperienced, so stupid, that they have no other hope but him who called them.[15]

For Bonhoeffer, poverty or affluence is not in and of itself the goal. Rather, "everything depends on faith alone . . . It is possible to have wealth and the possession of this world's goods and to believe in Christ—so that a man may have these goods as one who has them not."[16] For Bonhoeffer, such self-abandoned faith has an eschatological component: "This is an ultimate possibility of the Christian life, only within our capacity in so far as we await with earnest expectation the immediate return of Christ."[17]

Bonhoeffer speaks to the difference between Jesus's disciples (old and new) and the system of affluence and influence: "Jesus knows all about the representatives and preachers of national religion, who enjoy greatness and renown, whose feet are firmly planted on the earth, who are deeply rooted in the culture and piety of the people and moulded by the spirit of the age."[18] A church that is "moulded by the spirit of the age" can never be led by the Spirit of freedom—the Spirit of the messianic age; nor can it offer hope of liberation to those so molded. Karl Barth wrote that if the church is to remain free, it must never demand rights and recognition from the state: "Whenever the Church has entered the political arena to fight for its claim to be given public recognition, it has always been a Church which has failed to understand the special purpose of the State, an impenitent, spiritually unfree Church."[19] It must concern itself with Christ's all-encompassing demand upon its own life. Only then can it offer hope to this decaying and darkening world. The church's hope is not in this world as such, but in the in-breaking of the Triune God's eschatological kingdom in this world. As an authentic witness to the Triune God's eschatological kingdom, the church offers hope to the world.

Bonhoeffer speaks of the church as a mediatory people called out from the world, yet for the world, by the reigning and returning Christ:

> Amid poverty and suffering, hunger and thirst, they are meek, merciful, and peacemakers, persecuted and scorned by the world, although it is for their sake alone that the world is allowed to continue, and it is they who protect the world from the wrath and judgement of God. They are strangers and sojourners on earth (Heb. 11.13; 13.14; I Pet. 2:11). They seek those things that are above, not the things that are on the earth (Col. 3:2). For their true life is not yet made manifest, but hidden with Christ in God. Here they see no more than the reflection of what they shall be. Here all that is visible is their dying, their secret daily death unto the old man, and their manifest death before the world. They are still hidden from themselves, and their left hand knows not what their right hand does. Although they are a visible society, they are always unknown even to themselves, looking only to their Lord. He is in heaven, their life is with him, and for him they wait. But when Christ, who is their life, shall be manifested, then they too shall be manifested with him in glory (Col. 3.4).[20]

The church is a kind of firstfruits that offers hope to the world of deliverance from God's judgment and wrath.

The preceding discussion demonstrates that Jesus and his disciple Bonhoeffer, as well as truly faithful Christian communities, cannot be identified simply with either pole—"Christ of culture" or "Christ against culture." Their means of engagement is just too complex; in light of their example, the contemporary church—no matter its location—should also engage the society at large in a multifaceted manner. Unfortunately, our own cultural heritage—the fighting fundamentalistic-evangelical movement—often fails to recognize the need for complexity. Its adversarial orientation fails to reflect Jesus's and Bonhoeffer's redemptive countercultural engagement of the society at large on behalf of that society's own redemption through the mediatory witness of the church. The same could be said of the religious Left. By the sound of the culture-war rhetoric, one might be led to believe that Jesus came to save us from liberals or conservatives—dependent, of course, on one's partisan political vantage point!

### A Transitional Note on the Christ and Culture Spectrum

As we have suggested, each of Niebuhr's models possesses some merit, for they are all reflected in some measure in the Gospels. The two noted at length so far—Christ as protagonist of culture and Christ as antagonist of culture—become extreme when not balanced with the others. Jesus's and Bonhoeffer's lives illustrate the truth that we flesh out various models of cultural engagement at various times and places, sometimes at the same place and time.

Niebuhr's remaining models—the dualist, the synthesist, and the trans-formationalist—stand somewhere on the spectrum between the protagonist and antagonist perspectives. Similarly, they stand somewhere between the eschatological extremes of the "now" and the "not yet." Geoffrey Wainwright argues that with the antagonist position, one finds an eschatology of the "not yet," perhaps even of the "never"[21]; with the protagonist position, the "now" overwhelms the "not yet."[22] According to Wainwright, both forms of spiritual-ity are "cripplingly deficient from the eschatological point of view. Either the Kingdom of God can never be achieved or its achievement was never necessary in the first place."[23] A dialectic between both poles—"now" and "not yet"—is required if we are to fully account for the biblical story.

This "now-and-not-yet" pattern is found at the outset of the Sermon on the Mount: a present-tense description or prescription is followed by a promise of future realization and reward. Note how each beatitude in Mat-thew 5:3–10 begins: "Blessed are the poor in spirit," ". . . those who mourn," ". . . the meek," ". . . those who hunger and thirst for righteousness," ". . . the merciful," ". . . pure in heart," ". . . the peacemakers," ". . . those who are persecuted because of righteousness." Each beatitude gives rise to promises of certain future blessings: "theirs is the kingdom of heaven," "they will be comforted," "they will inherit the earth," "they will be filled," "they will be shown mercy," "they will see God," "they will be called sons of God," "theirs is the kingdom of heaven." This kind of people—namely Christ's poor in spirit and persecuted community—*are* blessed, *for* they *will be* blessed. They follow in the footsteps of Jesus and the prophets and participate in the kingdom that is to come (Matt. 5:11–12).

Jesus speaks to his community of followers in the Sermon on the Mount (see Matt. 5:1–2), describing to them what the eschatological community of the Triune God looks like, what its values are, and how it lives out Jesus's mandate and mission. The church today is called to live out the Sermon on the Mount as Jesus's community in the present. The message we seek to proclaim in heart, word, and deed is a message of judgment and hope. It is a message for and against culture, accounting for the cross and the resurrection. The Christ of culture orientation, on its own, does not account for the judgment of the cross. The Christ against culture orientation, on its own, does not account for the transformative work of the resurrection. The following three models offer mediating possibilities.

### Christ and Culture in Paradoxical Relation—Christ as Dualist

The dualist position is the most difficult one to understand because it is paradoxical. Niebuhr describes the dualist position as follows:

> The dualist joins the radical Christian in pronouncing the whole world of human culture to be godless and sick unto death. But there is this difference between them: the dualist knows that he belongs to that culture and cannot get out of it, that God indeed sustains him in it and by it; for if God in His grace did not sustain the world in its sin it would not exist for a moment.[24]

Luther spoke of the Christian life in paradoxical terms. Believers are wholly righteous and wholly sinful, simultaneously and throughout their lives.[25] One also finds a paradox in Luther's view of the church's relation to the state:

> There are two kingdoms, one the kingdom of God, the other the kingdom of the world . . . God's kingdom is a kingdom of grace and mercy, not of wrath and punishment. In it there is only forgiveness, consideration for one another, love, service, the doing of good, peace, joy, etc. But the kingdom of the world is a kingdom of wrath and severity. In it there is only punishment, repression, judgment, and condemnation to restrain the wicked and protect the good . . . Now he who would confuse these two kingdoms—as our false fanatics do— would put wrath into God's kingdom and mercy into the world's kingdom; and that is the same as putting the devil in heaven and God in hell.[26]

Niebuhr argues that such a distinction is not a division. The kingdoms of God and the world are "closely related. The Christian must affirm both in a single act of obedience to the one God of mercy and wrath, not as a divided soul with a double allegiance and duty."[27]

Regardless of how one reads Luther, many Lutherans at the time of Hitler maintained that the two-kingdoms thesis meant for them that they submit to Hitler in the sphere of the state and to Christ in the sphere of the church. Barth's objection to Luther's translation of Romans 13 is relevant on this point. Barth argues that "Luther's translation speaks of 'being *subject*' . . . , which is something dangerously different from what is meant here. The last thing this instruction implies is that the Christian community and the Christian should offer the blindest possible obedience to the civil community and its officials."[28] Barth maintains that the church is to subject itself to Christ in the sphere of the state, for Christ's kingdom includes both the church and the secular domain. Neither the church nor the state, then, is an end in itself. Thus, the church must not subject itself to the state in blind obedience.[29] Both church and state are instruments of the kingdom, and they submit to each other only in their respective service to that one kingdom.

Dualists today among fundamentalist-evangelicals—and liberals, for that matter—often fail to recognize the church and state as mutually subject to Christ.[30] Earlier we stated that many conservatives and liberals have missed out on identifying the church's witness in terms of the power of the cross. Such moves on the part of fundamentalist-evangelicals and liberals are bound up with inadequate attention to ecclesiology and eschatology. Both movements often tend to individualize the faith rather than to conceive the faith in social or ecclesial terms.

Cynthia Moe-Lobeda's critique of H. Richard Niebuhr's brother, Reinhold Niebuhr, could be made against fundamentalist-evangelicalism as well. Moe-Lobeda states that liberalism and Reinhold Niebuhr embraced two conflicting claims: (a) "personal relationship with God" is "the centerpiece of faith" and (b) "personal relationship with God" is "*not* a centerpiece" of the Christian's political and public life. These two conflicting claims

> reflect the theological anthropology of liberalism's legacy . . . That anthropology is viewed clearly in the work of Reinhold Niebuhr who held that the individual is the primary human unit in relationship with God; the self—although a social being—stands before God as an individual. The result is a public–private dichotomy in which the moral knowledge and norms that faith offers are understood and enacted by individuals, rather than by social groups.[31]

Both the religious Right and the religious Left often make the individual—rather than the church—the primary human unit for the Christian's political and public life. Many today view the church as a voluntary association of religious individuals, whose true allegiance lies elsewhere. (The explicit or implicit endorsement of political candidates/parties from pulpits and opening of doors to them to share their wares, come election time, impact negatively the church's understanding of itself as a distinctive polis with its own political practices, such as baptism and the Lord's Supper.) Such emphasis on the private and/or individual has negative consequences. As Moe-Lobeda argues, "The social construction of human–divine intimacy as private has served the interests of established power structures, for singularly private relationship with God cannot issue in public challenge."[32]

The privatization-individualization-subjectivization of the faith in Bonhoeffer's day created a vacuum for a monster such as Hitler to arise,[33] and it serves as a serious warning to us in the States today. Bonhoeffer's close friend and colleague Eberhard Bethge found nothing benign about Reverend Falwell's church, with its emphasis on "American Christianity." While having a great admiration and affection for the United States, Bethge was deeply troubled when he entered Falwell's church:

> As we entered the foyer, an usher stepped forward and gave me two badges to fasten to my lapel: the one on the left said, Jesus First, and on the right, one with an American flag . . . I could not help but think myself in Germany in 1933 . . . Of course, Christ, but a German Christ; of course, "Jesus First," but an American Jesus! And so to the long history of faith and its executors another chapter is being added of a mixed image of Christ, of another syncretism on the American model, undisturbed by any knowledge of that centuries-long and sad history.[34]

If only the badge opposite Jesus had been the church! While a promoter of nationalistic Chistianity today may appear more benign than Hitler, there is nothing benign about public/private dualities and dichotomies. Such dichotomies weaken and threaten the church's pure witness as a public—Christ's kingdom community.

Let us be clear: while there is a distinction between church and state, there is no public/private dichotomy for Christian existence. The church is called to engage the state as a public facing another public, not as a subsidiary of the state. The failure of the church to see itself as a distinct public engaging other publics (such as the state) is likely "one reason it is susceptible to becoming the bearer of national and other identities and projects, securing for itself thus as a national or civil religion a measure of public relevance within the framework of the public arena of society at large," as Reinhard Hütter argues.[35] This failure of self-understanding and subservience to the state also signify that the church loses its prophetic voice to speak out in society at large.[36]

Biblically speaking, the church—not the individual or the state—is the primary human unit in effecting God's kingdom purposes; for the embodiment of Christ's kingdom mission is the church, not the isolated individual Christian, and certainly not the state. The privatization of faith to the realm of the individual is nontrinitarian, for the Triune God is by nature social and communal. Such privatization is also due to an imbalanced eschatology of the kingdom.

Emphasis on the individual and preoccupation with the distant future (without seeing that the church is the now of the not-yet kingdom) lead to the improper politicization of the faith, whereby the church becomes subservient to the state. Where there is inattention to this communal and contemporaneous trinitarian eschatological kingdom reality, those least suspected of politicizing the faith—dispensationalists—are sometimes most guilty of it. Given such inattention, supposed rapture-and-retreat fundamentalists following the lead of the late Jerry Falwell, Tim LaHaye of the *Left Behind* series fame, and Pat Robertson have aligned themselves with the Republican Party to take back centers of power for God and country. Their strange mixture of pretribulation theology and postmillennial practice fails to account for the fact that Christ's kingdom community must radically confront the world's kingdoms and parties with its proclamation and participation in Christ's story of cross and resurrection.[37]

The historical move by many mid-twentieth-century classic dispensationalists to limit the Sermon on the Mount's import to Israel and keep it off-limits for application to the church's engagement inadvertently keeps the church off-limits from the public sphere as Christ's kingdom community—a city on a hill. Capitol Hill ends up replacing it! The Sermon on the Mount makes clear that the Lord of the church publicly engages and confronts the fallen powers. Our Lord does not privatize the faith. He and his kingdom were viewed as a threat to the Romans. This is disclosed in the Sermon on the Mount where Jesus tells his community of disciples to turn the other cheek and carry the load a second mile, and at his trial when he tells Pilate that his kingdom is not of this world. His kingdom is a kingdom of grace, mercy, and love, as Luther maintains (see above), not that of retribution; and so, his kingdom threatens the very foundations on which "the Romans" have built theirs—then and now.

Jürgen Moltmann argues that while Pilate was mistaken in taking Jesus to be a "Zealot rebel," he clearly perceived Jesus with his divine "law of grace" to be an affront to "the *Pax Romana* and its gods and laws" of oppression and retribution.[38] Jesus was not a political revolutionary in the manner of the Zealots; in fact, for all his affinities to them, he stood in diametrical opposition to their vision and aims at key points. Thus, while both Jesus and the Zealots condemned the mistreatment of the poor, Jesus, contrary to the Zealots, "did not call upon the poor to revenge themselves upon their exploiters."[39]

Jesus's kingdom of grace and mercy is not one of passivity, however. Walter Wink says of turning the other cheek and walking the second mile that Jesus is instructing his followers: "Do not continue to acquiesce in your oppression by the Powers; but do not react violently to it either. Rather, find a third way, a way that is neither submission nor assault, flight nor fight, a way that can secure your human dignity and begin to change the power equation." Jesus's teachings are meant to "recover for the poor a modicum of initiative that can force the oppressor to see them in a new light." This approach makes it possible for the oppressed to oppose the enemy while holding out the possibility for the enemy to become just. "The logic of Jesus' examples in Matthew 5:39b–41 [turning the other cheek] goes beyond both inaction and overreaction to a new response, fired in the crucible of love, that promises to liberate the oppressed from evil even as it frees the oppressor from sin."[40] Jesus avoids the extremes of acquiescence and violent reaction by creating the church as an alternative politics—the theo-political communal presence of the not-yet eschatological kingdom that submits all judgment to God and loves the enemy, thereby destabilizing the kingdoms of this world.[41]

This reflects a certain dialectical two-kingdom approach. The church does not take up arms, but it does fight. The problem with many two-kingdom positions surfaces when people indeed acquiesce, saying that Jesus's politics of living in authentic community (in which we turn the other cheek and go the extra mile) has no bearing on the public Christian life. It is a text reserved simply for improving our state of mind and interior soul life. This is a common occurrence in the evangelical church and reflects a spiritual and hermeneutical abnormality. As a friend once said, he knew that something was wrong with evangelicalism when so much of his Gospels class in his Christian college consisted of being taught what Jesus didn't *really* mean by what he said.[42]

For Bonhoeffer, Jesus really *did* mean what he said. That is why Bonhoeffer found it so hard to join in the assassination plot against Hitler. He never sought to justify his actions; but he also could never justify the separation of powers where the Christian submits his soul to God and his body to the state.[43] While Bonhoeffer struggled with the Lutheran two-kingdom view as well as Jesus's words about turning the other cheek, he believed he must join the resistance movement in its assassination plot, regardless of the consequences. This shows that Bonhoeffer was no pure dualist; it also shows him to be a representative figure for all of us in dealing with the host of complexities surrounding cultural engagement and different approaches so many of us embody in our day-to-day lives, including the synthesist orientation to which we now turn.[44]

### Christ above Culture—Christ as Synthesist

With the synthesist model, while culture needs "to be purified and lifted," there are positive dimensions to it.[45] There is an end to which culture strives through supernatural enablement. On this model, grace does not destroy but perfects nature (*gratia non tollit sed perficit naturam*), as many Roman Catholics and other defenders of natural theology maintain.

Hints of the synthesist orientation may be found in several places in the Gospels. The synthesist model is incarnational and organic.[46] God's kingdom sprouts and grows in the world like a mustard seed and spreads like flour through dough (Matt. 13:31–33). Jesus often appealed to people's secular or earthy sensitivities in his images and parables of the life of the kingdom. He made use of birds and lilies (Matt. 6:25–34) and shrewd managers (Luke 16:8–9), and affirmed the faith and contriteness of pagan tax collectors while rebuking the religiosity and pride of the Pharisees (Luke 18:9–14). Jesus says in the Sermon on the Mount that "evil" parents know how to give good gifts to their children, going further to say that God gives even better gifts, and more abundantly (Matt. 7:9–11).

These hints of how the secular and pagan can have sacred ends calls to mind a story that John Doberstein recounts from Bonhoeffer's student days. While participating in one of Barth's seminars in Bonn, Bonhoeffer quoted the earthy saint Luther approvingly: "The curse of a godless man can sound more pleasant in God's ears than the Hallelujah of the pious."[47] This secular sentiment also surfaces in Bonhoeffer's *Letters and Papers from Prison*, written near the end of his life. Bonhoeffer speaks there of man come of age. Humanity no longer needs the hypothesis "God" to function in life. Faced with this state of affairs, as well as with the emptiness and absence of the all-powerful God who rescues us from gaps (*deus ex machina*)—who had not liberated Germany and the church from the Hitler menace—Bonhoeffer finds God's presence and fullness in the weakness and poverty and sorrow of the God-forsaken God on the cross. As he writes,

> God would have us know that we must live as men who manage our lives without him. The God who is with us is the God who forsakes us (Mark 15.34). The God who lets us live in the world without the working hypothesis of God is the God before whom we stand continually. Before God and with God we live without God. God lets himself be pushed out of the world on to the cross. He is weak and powerless in the world, and that is precisely the way, the only way, in which he is with us and helps us. Matt. 8.17 makes it quite clear that Christ helps us, not by virtue of his omnipotence, but by virtue of his weakness and suffering.[48]

Bonhoeffer is not calling for a Christ-less and churchless spirituality, but a "religionless Christianity" where Jesus is viewed as "the man for others" and the church as his body that "exists for others." As Bonhoeffer notes, "The Church is the Church only when it exists for others."[49] We must stop looking to God to intervene in our struggles and remove us from crises, and instead face those crises with the awareness that God suffers our affliction with us, and calls us to identify with others in their suffering.

While we do not deny that there are times in the church's history when God has intervened with his righteous right arm to redeem the church from oppression and suffering, we also realize that the church has often failed to see that God so profoundly and pervasively demonstrates his omnipotence through the weakness of the cross—in Christ and in his church. The church is growing most rapidly today in places where it is poor and oppressed, whereas in America most "growth" is through transfer of membership and attendance. When the church realizes that Jesus's identity is in and with and for others in the midst of affliction, and that it too is to exist for others in this way, it will gain ultimate affluence and influence with God.

We as the church have much to learn from secular humanity's coming of age, for it teaches us that we too, as God's church, need to come of age. This worldly age served as a stepping-stone if not a foundation stone for Bonhoeffer to recognize more and more clearly that

> it is only by living completely in this world that one learns to have faith. One must completely abandon any attempt to make something of oneself, whether it be a saint, or a converted sinner, or a churchman (a so-called priestly type!), a righteous man or an unrighteous one, a sick man or a healthy one. By this-worldliness I mean living unreservedly in life's duties, problems, successes and failures, experiences and perplexities. In so doing we throw ourselves completely into the arms of God, taking seriously, not our own sufferings, but those of God in the world—watching with Christ in Gethsemane. That I think is faith, that is *metanoia*; and that is how one becomes a man and a Christian (cf. Jer. 45!). How can success make us arrogant, or failure lead us astray, when we share in God's sufferings through a life of this kind?[50]

Worldly affluence and political influence—success by our standards—are often counterproductive by God's standards. Bonhoeffer's own abiding influence is in many respects the result of his having died to affluence and influence—giving up everything to gain Christ. Bonhoeffer understood well that it is the poor in spirit, the meek, those who mourn and who are persecuted because of their union with Christ, who are truly affluent and influential.

Bonhoeffer's form of discipleship and "religionless Christianity" did not take him out of the world, but further into it. While persecuted, he gave himself all the more fully to bringing about a more just society. In fact, he suffered at the hands of those who claimed to speak for the Christian God—Hitler and the German Christians—even while suffering for those Jewish people who did not share his Christian beliefs. He gave sacrificially of himself to take back Germany from the nationalistic Christians for the "unbelieving" people of God, seeking to build on new and better German foundations. As a result of reading Bonhoeffer's *Letters and Papers from Prison*, one such unbelieving Jewish person told Eberhard Bethge—the volume's editor—that he was now "beginning to see for the first time why Jesus could be regarded as divine."[51]

We American evangelicals have gained a lot of influence in centers of American power in recent years but have lost America's heart in the process. The appearance of taking back America for our own kind of people and Jesus for ourselves needs to be replaced by the reality of giving up our lives for America, just as Jesus, "the man for others," gave of himself unreservedly for the people of his day—irrespective of their relation to him. The "God of the gaps" and "Take Back America" way of thinking needs to give way to God in the gallows. This will involve getting our hands dirty and moving increasingly toward downward mobility and heterogeneity in our church life and outreach. Instead of going back to the religion of our founding constitutional fathers, who did not truly see all humans as created equal (Jefferson, for one, owned slaves), we will seek to go back to the religion founded by Jesus that has hardly taken root in our nation and religion. We will become slaves for Christ so that everyone else might become truly free in body and spirit through him, especially the poor and other "least of these" groups (and so that we ourselves might become truly free in the process).

The church can serve as a preservative and penetrating light in society only by facing persecution for its union with Jesus joyfully (see Matt. 5:11–16), and by not seeking to preserve itself, like the religious leaders of Jesus's day did by sacrificing Jesus to preserve the people, the temple, and their own position (see Matt. 27:18 and John 11:45–53). A transformation of the American church's spirituality is in order. Before it can take the sawdust out of the nation's eye, it must take the plank out of its own (see Matt. 7:3). Only then can it serve as a reforming and transforming force in the culture at large.

### Christ Transforming Culture—Christ as Transformationalist

Now we come to the last of the five categories—Christ as the transformer of culture. This view of Christ's engagement of culture requires culture's radical purification, but not its replacement. Here the positive reality of the creation and incarnation balances consideration of the negativity of the fall.[52] On this model, there appears to be no division of history into two autonomous spheres—sacred and profane, according to Wainwright.[53] The church is to be an "adumbration," "perhaps even an anticipation of the final Kingdom of God."[54]

The Sermon on the Mount certainly portrays Christ's community as an anticipation of the final kingdom of God, and Christ himself as the one who inaugurates and eventually consummates that kingdom. In fact, as we have noted in an earlier chapter, the Sermon on the Mount and its surrounding narrative signify that Jesus recapitulates or transforms Israel's history. After Jesus submits himself to John's baptism—a baptism of repentance—to identify with his people (Matt. 3:13–17), the Spirit drives Jesus into the wilderness to undergo temptation by the devil for forty days and forty nights (Israel had undergone temptations and trials for forty years) (Matt. 4:1–11). Upon his return, he begins his public ministry, proclaiming in word and deed that the eschatological kingdom is at hand in his person (Matt. 4:12–25). Then Jesus goes up the mountain to give the law of the kingdom (whereas Moses went up the mountain to receive the law) (Matt. 5:1–2). His disciples become the new teachers of the law, standing in the line of the Old Testament prophets (see Matt. 13:10–23).

Jesus is the ultimate prophet, priest, and king—summing up, perfecting, and transforming the whole of the Old Testament story so that it becomes part of his own. This calls to mind the opening lines of the letter to the Hebrews (1:1–3):

> In the past God spoke to our forefathers through the prophets at many times and in various ways, but in these last days he has spoken to us by his Son, whom

he appointed heir of all things, and through whom he made the universe. The Son is the radiance of God's glory and the exact representation of his being, sustaining all things by his powerful word. After he had provided purification for sins, he sat down at the right hand of the Majesty in heaven.

God speaks conclusively through his Son, the prophet Jesus, who is also the great high priest, who has provided purification for humankind's sin once and for all, and who now sits enthroned as God's ascended and reigning Messiah.

No wonder the writer of Hebrews can say that whereas Moses was faithful in all God's house, Jesus, God's Son, is faithful over all God's house. Christ's church is that house—holding firmly to the hope that is ours in Christ (Heb. 3:1–6). And no wonder Jesus says that he has come to fulfill or perfect the law and the Prophets in his person (see Matt. 5:17–20). Jesus counters the traditions that distort the law and deepens the law's significance, especially as it bears witness to him (see Matt. 5:17–6:8; 7:12, 24–29; see also Luke 24:25–27). John's Gospel reveals that Jesus casts his shadow over the law and Prophets as he serves as antitype for its various images. He is the ultimate bread of heaven (see John 6:30–35; cf. Exod. 16:1–22), the true light of the world (see John 8:12; cf. John 7:1–10 and Lev. 23:33–44),[55] the Good Shepherd (see John 10:1–18; cf. Ezek. 34:1–10), the resurrection and life (John 11), and the good and true vine (see John 15:1–8; cf. Isa. 5:1–7).

The law of Moses and the traditions of men certainly shaped the culture in which Jesus was embodied, which Jesus had come to confront, redeem, perfect, and transform. And yet, Jesus did not consummate the kingdom in his first coming. This point is often lost on the church. The founding fathers of Calvin's Geneva and the proponents of Manifest Destiny in the United States failed to recognize the line of demarcation between the "now" and "not yet" of Christ's kingdom. The church, not the state, is God's eschatological polis— the city set on a hill. While the gospel is the politics of Christ's kingdom, and intersects and impacts this world's polis and politics, the church must never be confused with the latter.

Whereas classic forms of dispensationalism have tended to subsume the "now" of the kingdom under the "not yet," theonomist versions of covenant theology have tended to subsume the "not yet" under the "now."[56] These moves parallel their respective approaches to Israel's relation to the church. Dispensationalism has often tended to divide Israel and the church,[57] whereas covenantal theology has often tended to displace Israel in favor of the church.[58] In contrast to both perspectives, there is a distinct though inseparable relation between Israel and the church according to which Christ is Lord over Israel and the church, and where the church is the fulfillment (not replacement) of Israel.

Calvinists such as John Winthrop and many other early colonists journeyed to America to create a Christian society.[59] They looked at the church as the

New Israel and at America as a new Promised Land, which they were destined by God to inhabit and rule. When nineteenth-century advocates of Manifest Destiny took up the call, it spelled disaster for the Native peoples of the land. Such proponents of Manifest Destiny treated the indigenous peoples like the Canaanites in Joshua's day.

Bonhoeffer gave much thought to what Germany would look like in the event of Hitler's overthrow. Though Bonhoeffer was too Lutheran to entertain any hope of a nation where the church becomes the state,[60] he did hope and plan for a better future for Germany and for the church. In *Letters and Papers from Prison*, he speaks against a "silly, cowardly kind of optimism," on the one hand, and those pessimists who "think that the meaning of present events is chaos, disorder, and catastrophe; and in resignation or pious escapism . . . surrender all responsibility for reconstruction and for future generations." Bonhoeffer will stop hoping and planning for a better earthly future only once the day of judgment dawns: "It may be that the day of judgment will dawn tomorrow; and in that case, though not before, we shall gladly stop working for a better future."[61]

The church in America today should work for a better future for the church and for America—as the church first and foremost—always seeking to bear witness through its own practices such as baptism, the Lord's Supper, and redistribution of resources on behalf of the poor to the politics and economics of the coming kingdom in light of which it engages the society at large. At the outset of this chapter, we indicated that the church is a cultural community that is shaped by the surrounding culture and that prophetically confronts that culture for the latter's own ultimate transformation. Outside culture, there is no church. But outside the church of the Triune God's eschatological kingdom, there is no ultimate redemption of culture. The church is joined to Jesus as his body and bride. As such it is called to embody his kingdom values and proclaim them in word and deed to the surrounding world.

## A City on a Hill

In 1630, John Winthrop preached a sermon titled, "A Model of Christian Charity," in which he warned the Puritan colonists of New England that the world would be watching them as they would "a city upon a hill." Drawing from the imagery of salt and light in the Sermon on the Mount, Winthrop wrote:

> For we must consider that we shall be as a city upon a hill. The eyes of all people are upon us. So that if we shall deal falsely with our God in this work we have undertaken, and so cause Him to withdraw His present help from us, we shall be made a story and a by-word through the world. We shall open the mouths of enemies to speak evil of the ways of God, and all professors for God's sake.

> We shall shame the faces of many of God's worthy servants, and cause their
> prayers to be turned into curses upon us till we be consumed out of the good
> land whither we are going.[62]

The church as a public, as a distinct culture engaging other particular publics
and cultures, must seek to be that city on the hill that sheds its light in such
a manner that those who see it would be led to glorify God rather than curse
it. The church can be this shining light only as it demonstrates charity toward
its members, and toward the world at large.

The Puritan community did not always practice the love toward one another that Winthrop's sermon on charity commended. Nor are the Puritans
usually remembered for exercising charity and tolerance toward those who
believed differently than they did. As a result, they opened the mouths of the
American church's enemies to speak evil of the ways of God. We no longer
live under Christendom or in a utopian Christian society, though many Christians still long for it and lobby on Capitol Hill for it. While the church will
always have its fair share of enemies, the church must ever live to bless those
communities with which it coexists, rather than seek to take back America
from its enemies or wall itself off from them as a separatist society. As Christ's
eschatological kingdom community, the church should not aspire to be taken
out of this world, but to exist as salt and light among this world's kingdoms
and their communities as firstfruits and as a witness to that kingdom that will
be consummated when Christ returns.

It is not the church's role to judge the world, but to serve it. It is not the
American church's place to take back America or its cities like Portland, Oregon, where we minister, but to "love on Portland," as Pastor Rick McKinley
of Imago Dei Community often says. And in place of a God-of-the-gaps-
who-will-come-to-rescue-us-from-this-evil-world theology of disengagement,
we need a God-in-the-gallows theology of engagement framed by the same
Jesus who did not come to take back Jerusalem from his enemies, but to give
up his life for his enemies on Golgotha outside the city's gates so as to win
them over to God.

Whereas Christ the transformer of culture has often presupposed Christendom and a church-state's use of force to impose its rule, the church in
America today can go forth as Christ's alternative kingdom culture in pursuit
of transformation of the surrounding cultures in our pluralistic society only
by bearing its cross. But bearing the cross alone is not sufficient to calm fears.
For the cross has often been used to promote Manifest Destiny's ambitions. As
Native American Vine Deloria Jr. said, "Where the cross goes, there is never
life more abundantly—only death, destruction, and ultimately betrayal."[63]
The American church today must not simply bear the cross but be willing to
be hung upon it on behalf of the surrounding world—and in the gallows too,
like Bonhoeffer before us. The transformationalist kingdom model espoused

here is Christ-centered, cruciform, and ecclesially framed.[64] Otherwise, we may transform Christ and his cross—distorting them—to serve as illustrations of the hardships we will face before we climb the mountain and set up our standard on the hill in the city of the New Jerusalem through which the Potomac River runs.

In "Armaments and Eschatology," John Howard Yoder wrote, "People who bear crosses are working with the grain of the universe,"[65] even while working against the grain and against the stream in a society dominated by the culture wars. The complex figure of Bonhoeffer serves as such a witness to this universal pattern, as he hung in the gallows on behalf of the endangered Jewish people and in view of his hope for a transformed Germany. Unless a kernel of wheat falls to the ground and dies, it can bear no fruit (John 12:24). Only as Christ's followers bear their persecution joyfully rather than bitterly can they serve as Bonhoeffer did as salt and light and as a brilliant city set upon a hill that leads others to glorify our Father in heaven (Matt. 5:11–16; cf. Heb. 11–13).[66]

## STUDY QUESTIONS

1. What is your view of the church's relation to the state?
2. Based on that understanding, how should the church engage culture?
3. For Christian politicians, how should their faith affect their roles as public figures?
4. For Christian politicians, how should their membership in the church affect their roles as public figures?

# 14

# Getting Past the Ghettoizing
# of the Gospel in Today's Culture

A friend of ours serves on staff at an emergent church that puts a lot of re-sources into the arts and social justice. Someone he knew commented that while this was all fine and good, wouldn't it be better to put a lot more focus on the gospel instead? Now, the church in question is very intentional about integrating its arts and social justice emphases into its proclamation of the gospel of Christ's kingdom. The question signifies a certain Christ-against-culture orientation, whereas our pastor friend and his church convey a Christ-as-transformer-of-culture model developed in chapter 13.

The misguided comment noted above is but another indication that we in the evangelical community have so often ghettoized the gospel, reducing it to a gospel tract. While it may be helpful, sharing tracts with people about get-ting right with God does not exhaust the gospel message. More will be said about the meaning and scope of the gospel in the next chapter ("The Church as a Missional Community"). For now, we will focus on how we can get out of the Christian ghettoizing of the gospel to a few spiritual laws accompanied by Christian songs and illustrated by art that bears the fish label (with or without the American flag). In their place, we need to gain God's kingdom perspective, where we envision the whole creation—human and nonhuman—as participating in salvation's drama (see Rom. 8:22–23, for example), and where we see that God the grand artist comes to restore and transform his ruined Rembrandt from the social ills that have defaced it.

The compartmentalizing of the gospel in terms of the arts and social justice can take several forms. Some churches value only Christian music and social ministry produced within and by the Christian subculture. Others engage in bait-and-switch tactics, using "secular" art and promoting social justice as marketing tools to show seekers how hip and relevant these churches are, drawing seekers in, and then introducing them to the real gospel.

The first orientation fails to recognize that it is not the Christian subculture that has cornered the market on art and social justice. The Triune God—the God of the universe—is the great artist who redeems his masterpiece from decay and destruction and social inequities, bringing about the new creation at the dawning of the new heavens and the new earth (see Rev. 21–22). God's redemptive and creative work in creation is not limited to the church's endeavors. Even the secular sphere participates in this grand production in profound and amazing ways. And so, there need be no such label as "Christian" music or "Christian" art. There is just art—good or bad. And Christians should engage in righting social wrongs no matter how they reflect on the Christian subculture's wholesome self-image.

The second orientation fails to recognize that since God is the great artist, there is no need to engage in bait-and-switch tactics—baiting people with the arts and social justice before switching over to share the gospel. For the gospel does not use art and social justice—the gospel is all about art and social justice. As the master playwright, God graphically depicts the way things are and also offers hope by disclosing to us the way things should and will be in view of the One who was, and is, and is to come.

God enters into our stories and weaves them into his epic saga through the Son and Spirit. As God's supreme icon or image, Jesus enters into the depths of creaturely and cultural life (see, for example, John 1:14, 18; and Heb. 1:1–3), and through the Spirit's manifold workings, takes shape in the vast host of cultures with the intent to redeem the vast array of cultures and make all things new. (See Acts 1 and 2, where Jesus continues to minister through the church, and where the Spirit particularizes Jesus's work to diverse peoples in their own languages; see also God's declaration in Rev. 21:5 that all things are being made new.) The church is called to participate in Christ's story through the Spirit in word and deed, reenacting the grand Christmas and Easter pageant through their own Christmas and Easter pageantry, in ways that communicate to the variety of cultures in which it finds itself.

Talk of Christmas and Easter pageantry and nativity sets calls to mind Jonathan Larson's play *Rent*. The story is raw and real, and it contextualizes many of the gospel's features to life in urban America at the turn of the new century. The play begins on Christmas Eve in New York City at the end of the second millennium. A group of young artists and their friends seek escape from the virtual reality of corporate America, the commercialized big city, and cyberspace. Some of the characters are suffering from homelessness (there is no room in the inn—Holiday Inn—on Christmas Eve, once again) and dying of AIDS and drug addictions. They are also suffering from the absence of lasting meaning. Everything is for rent, even love. They do have one another, though—at least for the moment. In the end, they find that they have more than the moment, for one of those who dies comes back to life, resurrecting life, hope, and meaning out of a culture of death and despair.[1]

It would be interesting if some church were to show the movie version of *Rent* at Christmastime or Easter, followed by a discussion of the redemptive themes the movie presents. While authentic community takes a backseat to virtual reality, urban renewal, commercialization, and technological sophistication in the dominant culture, there is a remnant in *Rent* that sees right through its impersonalizing lures. We also need to probe beneath the surface of the Christmas story to know that it is not ultimately a commercial aimed at getting people to buy stuff. Nor is it ultimately about nativity sets or shepherds with staffs and wise men bearing gifts. It is about God's gift to us—himself through the person of his Son. God's gift is not something, but someone. In light of the fact that God has given himself through the person of his Son to poor and despised shepherds, we can give of ourselves to others in similar situations.

In this light, Christians' battles to keep nativity sets in public parks strike us as odd and miss the whole point of Jesus's life and teaching. Jesus would have been much more concerned about helping the homeless—modern-day shepherds—watching out for their flocks (one another) in the parks at night. As an artist friend once said, we Christians often get caught up painting the flea and missing the dog.

*Rent* sheds more light on the heart of the gospel than many literal "Christian" gospel pageant productions do. Why is this? It is because we often turn the truth into fiction by failing to probe the story's depth to its core meaning; we turn Jesus's bloody, sweaty, and tear-infested birth into a gift-wrapped, porcelain-faced Christ child peacefully asleep on a silent night. Also, we often fail to incarnate the gospel truth in our own lives as well as fail to use artistic media that are true to who we are as messengers of the message. We need to concern ourselves with the truthfulness of the message, the messenger, and the medium in our gospel productions.

Here we turn from Jonathan Larson to John Steinbeck and Johnny Cash, beginning with Steinbeck's discussion of the truthfulness of the biblical message. In *East of Eden* (which reenacts the story of Cain and Abel), one of Steinbeck's characters—Lee, the Chinese servant of Adam Trask—says that the story of Cain and Abel is "the best-known story in the world because it is everybody's story. I think it is the symbol story of the human soul . . . I think this old and terrible story is important because it is a chart of the soul—the secret, rejected, guilty soul."[2] Elsewhere, Lee says that "no story has power, nor will it last, unless we feel in ourselves that it is true and true of us."[3] And again, "And here I make a rule—a great and lasting story is about everyone or it will not last. The strange and foreign is not interesting—only the deeply personal and familiar."[4] Someone listening to Lee finally remarks: "Lee, you better keep your complications out of the machinery of the set-up churches or there might be a Chinese with nails in his hands and feet. They like complications but they like their own."[5] The "set-up churches" on every street corner claim to have a corner on the truth, but they often fail to delve into the dark corners of the human soul, as Steinbeck so masterfully does.

While the biblical message or story is true regardless of whether we believe it or not, one reason why it has such enduring power and lasts from generation to generation, and why its themes appear time and time again in a vast array of artistic forms from *Rent* to *East of Eden*, is that we feel in ourselves that it is true, and true of us. It is true of us because we derive our being from the one who wrote the script. Not only *Rent* and *East of Eden*, but also those stories void of biblical symbolism, can illuminate the gospel story from particular angles. Tales upstream and downstream in history from Christ may point to God's story—like Greek tragedies and fertility cult legends of gods coming to earth, dying and rising again.

While one finds resonance between the biblical story and other tales, it is not an illustration of the ongoing quest of the human spirit for immortality, one myth among many. For as C. S. Lewis claimed, this story is not myth alone, for "if ever a myth had become fact, had been incarnated, it would be just like this."[6] It is the myth become fact, for it is God's primal story with humanity from which all other stories derive their redemptive pattern and significance. But such recognition is not enough. It must also become factual and significant in our lives as its messengers.

This brings us to Johnny Cash and the movie *Walk the Line*, which chronicles much of Cash's life. There is a beautiful scene early on in the movie where a young Cash and his band are auditioning at a record studio, hoping to cut their first album. They're singing a Jimmie Davis gospel tune about Jesus saving them, having peace within, and wanting to shout it out. The man for whom they're auditioning—Sam Phillips—stops them and tells them gospel like that doesn't sell. When pressed, Phillips says he doesn't believe Cash. He later adds:

> If you was hit by a truck and you were lying out there in that gutter dying, and you had time to sing one song, one song people would remember before you're dirt, one song that would let God know what you felt about your time here on earth, one song that would sum you up, you're telling me that's the song you'd sing, that same Jimmie Davis tune we hear on the radio all day about your peace within and how it's real, and how you're going to shout it? Or would you sing something different, something real, something you felt? Because I'm telling you right now, that's the kind of song people want to hear, that's the kind of song

that truly saves people. It ain't got nothing to do with believing in God, Mr. Cash. It has to do with believing in yourself.[7]

While we would qualify the last statement to read, "It has nothing to do with beliefs. It has everything to do with whether or not you really believe in this stuff or not," the point on the need to keep it real still stands. In the movie, Cash then goes on to sing one of the songs he wrote while in the Air Force, "Folsom Prison Blues." After watching this scene, one of our sons remarked that he didn't like the first number because it was dull and dry, but really liked the second because it had soul. Based on the movie's rendition, it's no good talking or singing or writing about saving souls if our own souls haven't been saved.

The movie also chronicles Cash's recovery from drug addiction and his conviction that God had given him a new lease on life. After his recovery, Cash looks over his fan mail, and realizes how many of his fans are behind bars in prison. Testimony after testimony reveals that his songs such as "Folsom Prison Blues" really touched the souls of those imprisoned. That's what led him to do a concert at Folsom. The record producer mentioned earlier was right. The only songs we sing that will save others are those songs that have saved us, whether they have Christian lyrics or not. As one of our students remarked after watching the Cash–Phillips audition scene, "Are we smoking what we are selling?" The message is important. So too are the messenger and medium.

In the evangelical community, we have spent so much time burning and banning rock albums for back-masking, the drumbeat, and the like, and have invested hardly any time banning the singing of "Christian" songs that mask and imprison our hearts, or which fail to free those behind bars. The medium must fit the messenger's response to the message. What is Bach without the harpsichord and baroque? And what is Cash without the guitar, rock, country, and the blues? The message and medium are one.

As already noted in our worship chapter, when we were growing up we heard such claims as "Volume plus pulsation equals manipulation."[8] In other words, people who listen to rock 'n' roll at high decibels succumb to the rock 'n' roll pied piper's not-so-subliminal advances. If so, wouldn't it make sense to return the favor with Christian alternatives? As Larry Norman, the father of "Christian rock," cried out, "Why Should the Devil Have All the Good Music?" Moreover, if volume plus pulsation equals manipulation, why not ban John Philip Sousa's marches and Promise Keepers' rally renditions of Martin Luther's "A Mighty Fortress Is Our God," fearing that they too could become manipulative?

The debate is not isolated to rock 'n' roll in the Anglo-dominated evangelical subculture. Today, in Native American Christian circles, there is a debate about the use of native drums in worship. Some—even Native Christians—

claim that native drums are from the devil and so cannot be used. One can only wonder where Native Christians came upon this idea. Without drums, our Native American Christian brothers and sisters might as well tap their feet to the beat of some polka accompanied by the accordion. Fortunately, Lakota Sioux Christian leader Richard Twiss brings sound theological judgment to bear on the situation:

> Because we are all so prone to be culturally egocentric, the temptation is to consider our worldview *the* biblical and correct one, shunning all others as unbiblical and wrong. Worse yet is our habit of judging cultural ways—songs, dances, rituals, etc.—to be sinful when there is no clear violation of Scripture.[9]

Twiss also claims, "Because music is flexible and able to be reinterpreted, old Indian music styles can become sacred or Christian, not by reason of form but through context and meaning."[10]

If Luther could turn bar tunes into hymns, we can certainly do the same today—no matter the instrument or melody. Bound up with context and meaning, it's all about what's going on inside the one singing or playing.[11] Without singing songs that have touched us in the way they have touched us, we will never touch others and reform the church.[12] It has nothing to do with banning and burning albums, but everything to do with whether or not our own souls are set on fire by the songs we sing.

Of course, we must concern ourselves with bearing authentic witness to the biblical drama centered in Christ. Such authentic witness will highlight one or more of the following aspects: "the goodness of the original creation," the creation in bondage to the fall, "its liberation," or its future glorification.[13] Cash's song "Folsom Prison Blues," as well as his remake of the Nine Inch Nails song "Hurt," certainly highlights creation's bondage. And by identifying with the plight of those in bondage, it also sets the stage for their own hoped-for redemption. Cash's profound honesty and heartfelt conviction that God had radically redeemed him comes through in his music and speaks volumes to multitudes of people, bearing witness to God revealed in Christ.

What does "Christian" music or Christian art in general in the evangelical subculture communicate to people? While the response will certainly be varied, one of our friends once remarked that so much of what passes for Christian art is like pornography. For example, the surreal, otherworldly, and nostalgic outlook of so much Christian art promises us—at least many of us—something we cannot have.[14] Perhaps such art receives some of its inspiration from fundamentalism's otherworldly eschatology, as well as from its rejection of culture, which resulted in its not being able to hear God speak through the fallen and broken, as noted in the chapter on worship.[15]

*Rent*'s Jonathan Larson, Steinbeck, and Cash, on the other hand, provide us with avenues into our souls, and the tragic side of life, through their attention to the fallen and broken. It is only as we face life head-on that we can find redemption. For Christ did not avoid the pain and plight of creation's travail, but gave himself over to be swallowed up in darkness and death in order to bring new life to the creation, transforming it from the inside out.

While much of Christian art in evangelical circles fails to engage reality authentically, and so is ultimately un-Christian, the French Catholic artist Georges Rouault's pictures of clowns and prostitutes bear witness to Christ. In fact, his clowns were often Christlike in appearance. Rouault painted clowns and prostitutes because he saw in them "a certain religious aspect." Like Christ, they "were humiliated and had to bear their humiliation."[16] And yet, the fact that his suffering is interwoven with theirs means that their hoped-for redemption is interwoven with the salvation he authors. Rouault's Christ engages reality authentically, being incarnated in the world of blood, sweat, and tears.

Hans Urs von Balthasar speaks of the connection between Christ and the clown in Rouault's work: "If the clown is the representative and summing up of all that is humanly grotesque, his portrait is bound, imperceptibly and in a continuous process, to turn into the image of Christ."[17] Balthasar points to such works as *Christ with the Crown of Thorns* and the *Old Clown* as examples of this connection.[18] *Don't We All Wear Makeup?* also bears witness to the similarity between the classic clown and Christ.

Certainly, like Christ, the clown sums up "all that is humanly grotesque," embodying the tragic element in humanity. The caption to Rouault's work *The Old Clown, 1917–1920*, reads, "Behind our glittering masks, we all hide a tormented soul, a tragedy." One commentator notes, "This is the message that Rouault sought to convey in his pictures of clowns."[19] Balthasar says that "it is in the clown that the most open image of human existence is to be found: wanderer without a homeland, unarmed and exposed, in the very ridiculousness of his costume revealed in all simplicity."[20]

It is worth noting that in Rouault's work, for all its emphasis on tragedy, there is profound hope. In fact, there is a translucent quality to his work, reflecting his training as an apprentice to a stained-glass maker in his youth.[21] This translucent quality adds iconic significance to his work, including his paintings of clowns, offering us a window into the divine.

Rouault's iconic clowns serve as parabolic witnesses to Christ and his kingdom, for Christ is the archetypal human representative and cosmic clown. Balthasar speaks of Christ as the cosmic clown at the close of his discussion on folly, idiots, and the like, where the individual clown is superseded by the cosmic antitype:

Here the clown image and the whole metaphysics of that "principal reason" (Myshkin), which in this chapter we have seen as honest, foolish, indeed idiotic reason, is superseded. The games of the fools from Parzival to Don Quixote and Simplicius were a merry prelude to the seriousness of the Idiot, but now the destiny of that lonely individual has become the destiny of mankind, a destiny which, at the point where human existence was proclaiming its senselessness and idiocy, has been taken up by the gentle divine Idiot on the cross. He silently contains everything in himself and imprints on everything His form, the form of the divine mercy, for which it is a matter of sublime indifference whether its glory is manifested invisibly in earthly beauty or in ugliness.[22]

Christ—the cosmic clown—is the destiny of humankind, imprinting his divine mercy on all, manifested in beauty as well as ugliness. The church serves as a doorway through which the nations may enter, offering itself as an iconic window into Christ's glory made manifest in the grime and filth of daily life.

The emergent church mentioned at the outset of this chapter uses icons in worship, enhancing their sense of participation in the ancient drama of salvation as it unfolds in the contemporary world.[23] As participants in this drama, these contemporary saints function iconically, missionally—providing people a window into how God is at work in our world, celebrating the divine beauty disclosed in the messiness and brokenness of life.

The integration of the arts into this church's mission is one reason for the creation of its Worship and Arts department. The Worship and Arts department oversees various art communities, including those for visual artists, musicians, writers, songwriters, photographers, dancers, filmmakers, and response groups to popular movies and books. These communities within the church serve as catalysts to help these artists bring their gifts to bear on edifying the body at large. The pastoral leaders in this department mentor the various artists, helping them integrate their art and faith, which in turn assists in the edification of the body and its proclamation of the gospel to the surrounding community.[24]

Not only is it important for Christian leaders to mentor artists, but also it is important for Christian leaders to mentor all believers in the arts, since the arts relate to a fundamental part of our being as humans and as Christians. We are wired to search for the true, the good, and the beautiful; and careful attention to the arts helps us on our journey. The arts can be of service to us as we bear witness to all people—Christian and pre-Christian alike—of the profundity of the gospel story, which is the ultimate story to which all other stories bear witness. Besides the use of various forms of artistry such as sculpture and dance and painting in evangelistic ministry, it is equally important that intentional efforts be made to incorporate these various forms into Christian worship. All too often, we settle exclusively for music. As important as music is to worship, it engages only one part of the human person. Audible and visible forms of artistic expression alike are needed if we hope to worship God with our whole being. Not only should we be concerned for the incorporation of the arts into Christian worship, but also we should be concerned for the incorporation of the arts into Christian education programs. Thus, those responsible for Christian education in local churches could develop classes on the gospel and literature, referencing Shakespeare's and Steinbeck's works among others in their depiction of the gospel story through the arts. The same goes for the gospel and film, whereby educators make use of films like *Rent*, *Magnolia*, and *Les Misérables* in their classes.

To return to the discussion of mentoring artists, as with any profession it is important for the pastoral leadership of a given church to help artists integrate their art with their faith. Taking responsibility for mentoring artists is especially important today, and for several reasons. First, the arts have so often been neglected in the church, being viewed as ornamental and not as constitutive of the Christian faith. But the arts do have a significant role to play and are constitutive of the faith, for as has already been noted, God is the grand artist, and creation and church are his masterpieces.

Second, given that the Triune God is the grand artist, whose supreme masterpiece is the church, artists have a very significant role to play in church life. Artists who were filled with the Spirit were instrumental in the building of the tabernacle (and temple) and the ensuing worship there (see Exod. 35:30–36:1; cf. 1 Chron. 22). Further to this same point, as the temple of the Holy Spirit and bride of Christ, the church is to adorn herself in preparation for the marriage supper of the Lamb (Rev. 19:6–9). Given the profound intimacy of the marriage feast, it is very important that artists skilled in their trade and mature in faith help to prepare Christ's community for worship and the celebration of the Lord's Supper as a foretaste of what's to come.

Third, as the body of Christ, we are the embodiment of the divine life in the world. In view of Christ's incarnation and his headship, art that emerges from Christ's church must be incarnational and missional. These artists must embody their faith in the surrounding community, serving as extensions of Christ's body. The role of artists as missional witnesses is especially significant today. Rationalistic accounts of the faith no longer have staying power. Rationalism has often served to fragment human identity, reducing people to thinking machines, suppressing their passion, sense of hope, meaning, and purpose.

In this light, one of the most compelling proofs of the Christian faith today is its beautiful, holistic hope founded upon the good news that as the grand artist the Triune God restores his ruined Rembrandt. God is not reactive, but creative. God does not discard his defaced and disfigured masterpiece, starting from scratch. Rather, God enters the creation through his Son and Spirit, pouring his very being into its restoration, transforming it from the inside out. And so, the church as Christ's body bears witness to the Triune God's artistic genius and passion as it displays God's mercy and manifold glory to those around it, offering hope in the midst of darkness, a foreshadowing and foretaste of wondrous things to come.

## STUDY QUESTIONS

1. How can the arts serve as a manifestation of the gospel?
2. How would you respond to the following question: "Why should the devil have all the good music?"

# 15

# The Church as a Missional Community

## *The Being*-Driven *Church*

### The Missional Movement of Christ's Church

We now come to the final two chapters of the book; we also come full circle to the place where we began. In the first chapter, we spoke of the church as a trinitarian community, which is *being*-driven. Its purpose and activity flow forth from the church's identity, which is constituted through its communion with the Triune God. In this chapter, we speak of the church as being-*driven*, as missional: its being is identified as that which turns upward, outward, and downward in communion with God, its own members, and the world.

God's own being *is* the Father, Son, and Spirit turning outward toward one another in the divine life, and expressed in the Father's sending the Son and Spirit into the world. Through the Spirit, the Father sends the Son into the world. Through this same Spirit, the Son is driven into the wilderness, lifted upon a cross, and raised from the dead. In turn, with his ascent, the Father and Son send the Spirit into the world to birth, indwell, and empower the church. This same Spirit who unites the church to Christ sends the church into the world to bear witness to Christ in word and deed until the end of the age.

The aim of this chapter is to trace God's missional movement in and through the church. Along the way, we seek to answer the following questions, and in this order: What are the meaning and significance of the missional church? What are its direction and destination? What is its message, including the relation of word to deed? And what is the scope of salvation that it proclaims?

## The Meaning and Significance of the Missional Church

The church is God's people on the move—a community of sojourners destined for the Promised Land. God led the people of Israel out of bondage in Egypt to freedom in Canaan (Exod. 13:21–22). So too, the Lord goes before the church by day and by night as it journeys forward as a witness to God among the nations, ever in search of its eternal home. As the Lord himself commands and promises, "Go and make disciples of all nations . . . , and surely I am with you always, to the very end of the age" (Matt. 28:19a, 20b).

It is important to differentiate the missional church from a church with a missions program. "A church with a missions program" may suggest that bearing witness is one aspect of the church's identity, purpose, and activity. This limited view compartmentalizes missions to something the church does outside its walls, rather than seeing missions as expressing the church's missional being poured out through the Spirit into the world. "Missional church" signifies that bearing witness is constitutive or reflective of the church's being or identity and, as a result, its entire purpose and activity. The church's being is not static but dynamic, as it is driven by God into the world. The church's missional being results from its union by faith with the God of Triune love, whose loving being is communal and co-missional.[1]

God's loving triune being is communal and co-missional, for God is three persons in communion turning outward toward one another and downward toward the world in holy love. As God's people, the church ascends by faith in Christ through the Spirit of love and downward with Christ by the outpoured Spirit of love toward its neighbor—the world at large.[2] Thus, the church participates in the Triune God's own missions—the Father's sending the Son and Spirit into the world.

As the Father forms the church, through the Son and Spirit, in worship and loving service, into a distinct cultural community, the church turns outward toward the world. The formation of the church's communal and co-missional being or identity gives rise to its distinctive purpose and activity as a community that bears witness to God among the nations. This missional and witnessing orientation has always been true of God's people.

While people often seek to make a name for themselves rather than bearing witness to God's name, as in the case of Babel (Gen. 11:1–9), we find in the person of Abram, or Abraham, a faithful witness. God calls this Gentile to leave his people and homeland, and to go to the place God will give him (Gen. 12:1). God makes him the first Jew and the father of the Jewish nation (Gen. 17:9–14), as well as the father of all people of faith—Jew and Gentile (Rom.

4:11). Following God's example, Abraham and his family were a people on the move, bearing witness to God's faithfulness among the nations. All who have the faith of Abraham belong to this missional people—looking for a city and homeland that is to come (Heb. 11:8–10; 13:14).

God's name-bearing people—Israel—were on the move when Moses led them out of Egypt. God continues to call and lead his children out of Egypt through his Son (Matt. 2:15; Rev. 7), just as he called Israel—his son—out of bondage at the exodus (see Hos. 11:1). We should never put down roots in an ultimate sense—telling God we are staying put! When we do, we cease being obedient and missional. Our missional orientation is bound up with our belonging to another city and kingdom, whose foundations are from God (Heb. 13:14).

A church whose orientation is to put down roots and remain stationary is often a church whose members seek only to minister to their "own kind of people." God intended not only to bless Abraham and his descendants, but also to make him a blessing to all nations (Gen. 12:1–3). Not only did Christ intend to build his church in Jerusalem, but also he purposed to send his followers out through the Spirit to be his witnesses in Judea, in Samaria, and throughout the whole earth as well (Acts 1:8).

Unfortunately, as with mission-less churches today, Israel and the early church often lost sight of their missional purpose. When God led Israel out of Egypt, many Egyptians went with them (Exod. 12:38). Moses and Israel did not try to keep Egyptians—whose ruler had oppressed them—from experiencing God's glory, power, and love. But later Israel was more closed to outsiders, as in the case of the prophet Jonah. Jonah was upset that the Assyrians repented of their wicked ways when he warned them of God's impending judgment. He wanted God to judge Israel's enemies (Jonah 4:1–3).

The same problem continues on in the New Testament. While Jesus was raised in Nazareth, began his ministry in Galilee of the Gentiles, and reached out to prostitutes, tax collectors, and Roman soldiers, his disciples were surprised to find Jesus talking to a Samaritan woman (John 4:27) and calling little children to himself (Luke 18:15–17). Samaritan women and little children held little value in that culture—no doubt, they contributed very little to the GNP. It was not until persecution hit the Jerusalem church that the believers began spreading out as gospel witnesses throughout the greater region (Acts 8:1–4).

Peter's own particular Jewish upbringing made it painfully difficult for him to comprehend the news that God had removed the wall of division between Jews and Gentiles (Acts 10:9–16). After the Cornelius episode, Peter realized that God's grace in Christ by the Spirit comes to the Gentiles in the same way that it comes to the Jews (Acts 10:44–11:18). However, due to peer pressure, he refused to have table fellowship with Gentile believers when Jewish believers came to Antioch from the church in Jerusalem. His actions led Paul to rebuke him (Gal. 2:11–14).

For his own part, the former Pharisee—Paul—became all things to all people to reach them for Christ. In his former life as a Pharisee, Paul quite possibly crossed land and sea to convert people, and yet shut them out of the kingdom—making them twice the sons and daughters of hell as he was—he through strict enforcement of the legal codes (Matt. 23:13–15). However, after his conversion on the Damascus Road, Paul became a Jew to the Jews and a Gentile to the Gentiles, so that by all possible means he might save some (1 Cor. 9:19–23). Paul would not allow cultural forms to be imposed upon gospel content. Paul did not want a legalistic reading of the law to be a stumbling block, nor to be a stumbling block himself. For Paul, Christ was the stumbling block to Jews and Gentiles as the cornerstone of God's house in which Jews and Gentiles were now full and equal members (Eph. 2:11–22). Paul would allow for cultural particularities such as circumcision and un-circumcision to remain. But he would not sit back quietly and tolerate Peter's breaking table fellowship with Gentile Christians, since through the Spirit Jewish and Gentile believers were one flesh as members of Christ's body and called to sit at the same table as members of God's household (Eph. 2:11–22).

The church made up of Jews and Gentiles is a mobile home, whose cornerstone is the incarnate Son of God. It is a community in pursuit of Christ and will not find what it is looking for until Christ—their cloud and pillar of fire—establishes his people in the Promised Land. The church goes out into the world and reaches out to all people so that people from every nation might become members of God's household and royal nation. The church goes forth throughout the earth until the end of the age, when Christ's kingdom will arrive in its fullness.

## The Direction and Destination of the Missional Church

We can learn a lot about people from where they are headed in life. Their direction or trajectory in life and final destination influence their purposes and activities. The same goes for the communal and co-missional God. As communal and co-missional, God promises to come and live *among* the community he names as his own people (1 Pet. 2:10), to make his people *one with* his Son as a mature body and spotless bride (Eph. 5:25–32), and to build his people into a glorious temple *in* which God lives by his Spirit (1 Cor. 3:16). Everything God does is to this end. As communal and co-missional, God purposes to live among his people, to be one with his people, and to indwell his people. The church's identity is rooted in covenantal communion with the Triune God as the people of God, the body and bride of Christ, and the temple of the Holy Spirit. These images are determinative of the church's missional purpose and activity.

*As the people of God*, the church represents the transcendent and eternal Trinity, who exists in eternal, interpersonal communion beyond creation, but who turns outward to create fellowship with humanity. This personal God calls us to himself to be his people—a people for his name's sake. *As the body and bride of Christ*, the church engages culture through incarnational presence and witness as Christ ministers through his people in the world. This personal God touches the world through the church. *As the temple of the Holy Spirit*, the church invites the world to know and experience God through his presence in the community of believers. As God's named people, the church is relational, identifying others by name and identifying with them. As Christ's body and bride, the church "incarnates" God's presence to others. As the temple of the Holy Spirit, the church invites others to enter into God's presence. We will take up each item in turn.

### A Place Where Everybody Knows Your Name

The theme song for the television show *Cheers* says the pub (Cheers) is a place where everybody knows your name. Would it not be wonderful if the same thing could be said of our local churches? While alcohol has a way of making many people become more transparent, letting their guard down, those filled with God's Spirit truly become more transparent and authentic and relate to others interpersonally, identifying with them and calling them by name. It all follows from the fact that the Triune God is irreducibly personal, and that the Father graciously discloses himself to us through the personal presence of the Spirit of his Son in our lives.

We cannot reduce *God's* tri-personal identity to three roles or functions, for they are irreducibly Father, Son, and Spirit, who reach out relationally, and express and manifest their persons through their distinctive activities and roles. The personal God who enters into our lives by his Spirit calls each of us by name. God's personal address and determination to make us his people signify that God values us as human persons, not as mere functionaries to be exploited for profit.

In America, those of us who belong to the dominant Anglo culture tend to categorize and value people in terms of their gifting and vocations. In this light, we tend to identify ourselves by our respective job titles and descriptions when we introduce ourselves to others. In Native American settings, on the other hand, people tend to identify and value themselves and others by way of their respective families and extended family networks. The latter resonates much more readily with scripture than the former.

As was stated in a previous chapter, we must be careful to guard against attributing value to people based solely on their gifting and service in the church; people express themselves through their gifts for building up one another. Their gifting and acts of service *express rather than establish and exhaust* who they are. This follows from the fact that we are created in the image of the Triune God as persons in communion. This orientation safeguards against commodifying people, whereby we turn human persons into impersonal cogs that keep the goods and services assembly line of free-market American spirituality going.

Lesslie Newbigin argues that the "post-Enlightenment project" absorbs "all human activity" into "labor." Human activity becomes "an unending cycle of production for the sake of consumption." Against this backdrop, "what does not enter the market is ignored." Thus, homemakers (as well as small children and the elderly) are not perceived as having much significance. Their work does not assist the market—while the "gambling syndicate, arms salesman and drug pusher" do.[3]

A true familial community is a place where the strong *and* the weak, the healthy *and* the diseased, the young *and* the old, the wise *and* the simple live. So many of our churches bearing the name *community* in their titles need to be very intentional so as not to succumb to the pressures of free market spirituality and target only the strong, the healthy, the young, the wise, and the successful so as to survive and thrive. Such "success" comes at the expense of building true community and bearing witness to God's own targeting practices revealed in scripture.

God chose Israel from among the nations—a small and insignificant slave people by the world's standards—to be his people and bear his name. Then God chose from within Israel the twelve apostles to build Christ's church. Most of them were unschooled and ordinary (Acts 4:13). Not many of us were significant before God chose us and brought us into his family (1 Cor. 1:26). God does this so that others will take note that we have been with Jesus (Acts 4:13), and that our own boast would be in God, and not ourselves (1 Cor. 1:27–31). For we are bearers of *his* name—the LORD ("Let him who boasts boast in the LORD"). Bearing his name should be the source of our security and significance as the people of God, not the respective names of our various churches—the First Church of Cephas, Apollos, or Paul.

God makes his home with us as his named people. He does so through his Son and Spirit, who bear his name. As the church goes forth as the people who bear God's name and are called to be a community "where everybody knows your name," it invites the surrounding world to come along and experience God's named presence in their midst. God's identity and missional activity of interpersonal communion in our midst make it possible for us to name our churches "community churches." As the body and bride of the incarnate Christ, God also makes it possible for us to reach out toward the world as participants in Christ's incarnate presence through our union with Christ in the Spirit.

### A Place Near You

Luke tells us in Acts 1:1 that he had written about "all that Jesus began to do and to teach" in his previous book (the Gospel of Luke). Here he is suggesting that Jesus's ministry continues through his church. As the body and bride of Christ, the church participates in Christ's incarnate presence in the world through the Spirit. Thus, like Christ before them, the church community must live among the people—in the flesh. We see evidence of this approach to ministry in Acts 5:

> The apostles performed many miraculous signs and wonders among the people. And all the believers used to meet together in Solomon's Colonnade. No one else dared join them, even though they were highly regarded by the people. Nevertheless, more and more men and women believed in the Lord and were added to their number. As a result, people brought the sick into the streets and laid them on beds and mats so that at least Peter's shadow might fall on some of them as he passed by. Crowds gathered also from the towns around Jerusalem, bringing their sick and those tormented by evil spirits, and all of them were healed. (Acts 5:12–16)

It was certainly the case that, as with Jesus before them, the apostolic community's presence would have been missed if they were to have closed up shop and left town.

If we were to leave town, would anyone know? While our buildings would stay put, are our facilities placed in strategic locations to impact the community at large? While megachurches' presence is felt in terms of the space they occupy, these churches must ask themselves whether they serve as salt and light in the surrounding communities. Gretchen Buggeln writes, "In what congregations build and where they build it, they say something about their relationship to the surrounding culture. They also demonstrate what is important in their rituals and beliefs." She also notes, "Intentionally or not, buildings communicate what really matters to their builders."[4] Auditorium churches in the nineteenth century were designed and situated in key metropolitan areas to play a significant public role in culture, not to serve as spiritual oases.

No doubt, the locations of many evangelical auditorium churches on the outskirts of town bear witness not simply to the lack of spacious vacant lots in cities but also to the impact of the fundamentalist-evangelical church's retreat from the public urban square following the "Scopes Monkey trial" in the early twentieth century. As a result of its forced exodus, the fundamentalist-evangelical church developed a fortress mentality, where the holy remnant sought refuge from the onslaught of an ungodly culture by retreating to the outskirts of the city (the city was often viewed as the den of wickedness, since the dominant liberal political and religious institutions were often stationed there).

*Harper's Magazine*'s Jeff Sharlet comments that "contemporary fundamentalism has become an exurban movement." In keeping with this move, he writes that it has reframed the question of theodicy—if God is good, then why does He allow suffering?—as a matter of geography. Some places are simply more blessed than others. Cities equal more fallen souls equal more demons equal more tempta-tion, which, of course, leads to more fallen souls. The threats that suffuse urban centers have forced Christian conservatives to flee—to Cobb County, Georgia, to Colorado Springs. Hounded by the sins they see as rampant in the cities (homo-sexuality, atheistic school-teaching, ungodly imagery), they imagine themselves to be outcasts in their own land. They are the "persecuted church"—just as Jesus promised, and just as their cell-group leaders teach them.[5]

While the evangelical church has regained political influence in recent years, as witnessed by the 2004 presidential election, in which megachurches played a key role in the reelection strategy,[6] its influence is often felt most strongly in Washington, DC, and overseas, not in urban centers closer to home, especially in communities of disrepair.

Related to the problems noted above is the predominance of the commuter church phenomenon, tied to the breakdown of the family and the bankrupt prosperity gospel movement. Here is what John M. Perkins has to say to these matters:

> The breakdown of the family, the commuter church, and the prosperity gospel erode the foundations of our society. The split-apart family, the back-and-forth commuter church, and the leave-the-poor-behind prosperity gospel success story do nothing to stem the poverty, crime, and violence that we see played out on the evening news. In contrast, families who stay together, churches that main-tain a vital presence in a community, and those who abandon their upwardly mobile ways to identify with others less fortunate than they are preserve society and guard against the deterioration of local communities across America. The evangelical church has to recreate family and community by becoming an in-carnate presence in society rather than remaining transient and self-consumed, by proclaiming the gospel of reconciliation rather than the gospel reduced to church growth and success. If we truly incarnate the church in a community, then we are better able to participate in God's redemption of the poor from oppression and act out divine jubilee justice.
>
> All too often, we think of the church simply as a building with programs aimed at making sure the church survives and thrives. On this model, people do everything possible to keep the show going. This view of the church is not missional. And as far as the poor in the surrounding community are concerned, they are viewed simply as a side issue—simply the beneficiaries of our charity. In some cases, we may actually go so far as to invite these beneficiaries of our charity to church. But charity does not build community. It fosters dependence on the one hand and separation on the other hand—keeping the poor at the far end of our outstretched hand.[7]

Evangelicals often point to the breakdown of the family and call for safeguard-ing family values, but as already suggested and noted in Sharlet's piece, the family values campaign often gives the appearance of calling for the protection of Christian families from a pagan world, not calling for Christian families to serve that same world.

God's incarnation in a broken world has import for the church's witness today as his body. Christ gave himself "for the least of these." As Christ's body in the world today through its union with Christ's Spirit, the church must reach out *as* Christ's compassionate embrace to those in need. The church must be a place—a haven of rest—near and for the least of these. While much attention over the years has been given to the church as Christ's body in church growth circles, the focus has largely been internal: know and exercise your spiritual gifts so as to make the church function most effectively. Of course, it is vitally important that we help people use their gifts and resources as well-functioning parts in service to the whole body; but it is also vitally important that the church see itself as Christ's body sacrificially serving the world.

One of our friends directs a ministry for the homeless in northern California. He has an increasingly significant sphere of influence in his county, working with political and business leaders to help address the social ills that plague the region. He is an outspoken evangelical Christian who does not compromise his biblical convictions. But his missional life and holistic, compassionate service create space for his views to be heard. Our friend longs for his evangelical brothers and sisters to give themselves as Christ's hands and feet to the community at large rather than putting their hands in their pockets and incubating themselves in the Christian bubble.

Giving ourselves to others entails being where they are. We cannot expect them to come to us. We have to go where they are. God relocated from heaven to earth to reach a lost world. So too we must relocate, living among those who do not yet confess Christ. Not only must we make space for others, but also we must make time for them. In Jesus, God makes space and time for us.[8]

We know how hard it is to make time for people outside Christian confines. As professors at a Christian school and leaders in churches, we spend much of our time rubbing shoulders with believers. We have to be intentional about getting out of those friendly confines time and time again to make friends with those who do not share our uniquely Christian convictions. The social causes we ourselves embrace (such as concern for the homeless and the environment) bring us into contact with beautiful people who are created in the image of the Triune God, yet who often inhabit other worldview universes. While we are peculiarly Christian, many of our social instincts shaped by our biblical perspectives overlap with those from other traditions. We go through (not around) our convictions in search of bridge-building opportunities in the public square.

Church leaders must be intentional about making sure they and their congregations are not consumed by church activities aimed at edification. Attention to outreach is equally important. Perhaps this will entail encouraging members to join softball teams with no church affiliation, or to join reading or arts and crafts groups at community centers. It may also entail encouraging members to consider putting their children in public schools and getting involved in parent–teacher organizations. Parents committed to home schooling must make sure that their children are engaged somehow in the community at large. Whole churches can minister missionally by identifying needs in the community and reaching out to address those needs.

Just as God ministers in the world through his two hands—the Son and Spirit—we are his hands and feet through our union with Christ in the power of the Spirit. As the body of Christ, the church with its buildings goes out to the world, serving as Christ's hands and feet and as a shelter from life's storms. As the church is in the world, we will have ample opportunity to invite the world inside. Like Jesus, we must live among the people, tabernacling in their midst, while also inviting them to tabernacle with us as God's temple community.

### No Place like Home

In the Hebrew Scriptures, the tabernacle and later the temple served as the places where God's glory dwelt, and where the nations could come and seek God. King Solomon bears witness to this reality during his prayer at the dedication of the temple in Jerusalem. He cries out,

> As for the foreigner who does not belong to your people Israel but has come from a distant land because of your name—for men will hear of your great name and your mighty hand and your outstretched arm—when he comes and prays toward this temple, then hear from heaven, your dwelling place, and do whatever the foreigner asks of you, so that all the peoples of the earth may know your name and fear you, as do your own people Israel, and may know that this house I have built bears your Name. (1 Kings 8:41–43)

Against this backdrop, it is little wonder Jesus was incensed when he cleared the temple in Jerusalem—his own people had turned God's house of prayer for the nations into a market at the expense of the nations (Mark 11:15–17).

In Luke's account, Jesus clears the temple and weeps over Jerusalem's approaching destruction (Luke 19:41–46). Even so, scripture reveals God's promises to restore Jerusalem's and its temple's fortunes. God will vindicate Jerusalem in the sight of the kings of the earth, giving Zion a new name, and adorning the sanctuary with the wealth of the nations (Isa. 60:13; 62:2). God will marry Jerusalem (Isa. 62:4–5). Revelation tells us that the city of the New Jerusalem—the bride of Christ the Lamb—will descend from heaven (Rev. 21:9–11). The bride will bear the names of the twelve tribes of Israel and the twelve apostles (Rev. 21:12–14) as the one people of God. There will be no temple, for the Lord Almighty and the Lamb will be the temple (Rev. 21:22). The kings of the earth will bring their splendor into the New Jerusalem (Rev. 21:24). So too the leaves of the Tree of Life—which stands on either side of the River of Life flowing down the middle of the great street of the city—will bring healing to the nations (Rev. 22:1–2). The Spirit and the bride will invite all who are thirsty to come and take the free gift of the water of life from that river (Rev. 22:17).

In light of that day, the church must open its doors wide today. It is one thing to be in the world. It is quite another to open the church's doors to the nations. We often hear Christians say that the communities in which they live are very homogeneous. This is rarely the case, even in very wealthy communities. The question is how open are our eyes and our hearts. In one of the wealthier suburbs in the Portland area, there are growing numbers of Hispanic families—some of whose breadwinners are migrant workers. Also, due to gentrification in Portland, many poorer families are leaving the city and moving into apartment complexes in the surrounding suburbs.

While we could give numerous examples of churches opening their doors, we will briefly draw attention to one in particular. One church in the Portland area that has been quite intentional about reaching out to diverse communities shares its facilities with an Asian congregation, makes certain that its leadership team is inclusive of diverse ethnicities, and has birthed a church on its premises that ministers to the skateboarding population. The church has continued to serve as salt and light in its neighborhood and region even as its surroundings have become increasingly diverse. Of course, there have been some tensions. Some members have recommended that the church locate elsewhere, and others have left the church. But the leadership has determined (in our estimation rightly) to remain. Sometimes being missional will require of us as God's temple community that we stay put.

Sometimes being missional will also require of us as God's temple community that we reappraise our priorities. We cannot allow our rightful concern for protecting our families and preserving church facilities to keep us from reaching out and welcoming those who do not belong to our target audiences. One of us recalls a concerned layperson remarking that homeless people would start coming to church if the leadership kept on talking about caring for the downtrodden. Their presence would pose a risk for church members' children's safety. While our children's safety should certainly be a priority given Jesus's own concern for little children who are so often neglected, such rightful attention to our children's well-being should not keep us from being concerned for others who are also so often neglected. We should not speak in either/or here, but in terms of both/and. Besides, if our children have no exposure to society's fringe elements, how will they be prepared to engage them missionally and redemptively when they do cross paths?

Concern for church premises has kept at least one church we know from opening its doors to those "less fortunate." The leadership of the church in question had no difficulty sending short-term missionaries to Mexico and having them stay with the Mexican believers while they built church facilities. But they were not willing to let these same Mexican believers come and stay in their own church facilities when the opportunity presented itself. The leadership feared that the Mexican believers would get the facilities dirty. If that is how they relate to fellow believers with whom they have had fellowship, just imagine how they must relate to nonbelievers of the same kind! Not only has the church leadership in question mistakenly equated external cleanliness with godliness, but also they have mistakenly equated short-term missions programs with being missional, proving themselves to be the least fortunate of all.

Once again, though, there is hope. Above mention was made of a church with a skateboarder ministry among unchurched youth. When the ministry began, these youth could often be found skateboarding on the cement floor of the church's cavernous basement. Many of the older church people complained about the dust swirling about and carrying over into the kitchen. All their complaining stopped, however, as soon as the first set of skateboarding youth came forward to make public their new confession of faith in Christ and to be baptized. In fact, some of the older congregants set about to construct a building on the premises with state-of-the-art skateboarding ramps for the youth. Today, news of Skate Church has spread far and wide. While not every church will build a skateboarding facility, a missional orientation may lead many to use their facilities for providing ESL (English as a second language) classes, job-training seminars, neighborhood association meetings, and nomadic shelters for the homeless.

As the temple of the Holy Spirit, the missional church is called to welcome sinner and saint alike (and by the way, every Christ-follower is a sinner and a saint alike), those who possess much and those long dispossessed. When we fail to act upon our missional calling as God's temple community existing for the nations (which will include any group whom we deem foreign) and as God's healthcare provider for sinners, it suggests that we have lost direction and sight of our destination.

In this light, concern for the missional state of our buildings and facilities must give way to a more fundamental concern—the state of our own souls. Often, we lock ourselves in our buildings, shutting the world out because our own souls are enslaved.[9] God needs to free us from ourselves if we are to be of service in the liberation of others. When our souls are freed, we will respond with compassionate concern for those being released from various forms of imprisonment.

Groups ministering to those recently released from prison or who have finished rehab programs for sexual or substance abuse addictions tell us how difficult it is to find communities in which their people can be spiritually nurtured. We as the church community must see that there is no such thing as normal sin. All sins are abnormal, and we are all in desperate need of the divine physician's healing touch. Only when we see that apart from Christ we are as desperately lost as the prostitutes, demon-possessed, and tax collectors to whom Jesus ministered will we experience full redemption. Only then can we bear witness to Jesus as the good news so that others might experience redemption too. Only when we have heard Jesus calling *us* to leave behind our red-light districts, only when we have heard his summons to *us* to come out from among the tombs, only when we have heard his invitation to *us* to come down from our trees of self-imposed isolation will salvation at last come to our house, and through our houses of prayer to the nations.

### In Sum—Seeking and Saving the Lost

Our direction and destination as God's missional church entail being a missional people bearing God's personal name in whose communal midst this personal God dwells. Our direction and destination also entail our participating in Christ's incarnate presence as his body and bride in the community at large. Lastly, our direction and destination entail our being the temple of the Holy Spirit, welcoming others into our fellowship as a sanctuary for saints and a hospital for sinners. We identify personally with others, "incarnate" God's presence to others through union with Christ in the Spirit, and invite them to enter into God's presence as members of his community, seeking and saving the lost.

Jesus's encounter with Zacchaeus exemplifies this missional orientation of seeking out the lost so that they might be saved. In Luke 19, Jesus and his followers were on the move—passing through Jericho on what would be his final journey to Jerusalem. The crowds surrounded Jesus. This made it impossible for a little man and chief tax collector named Zacchaeus to get close. So Zacchaeus climbed a tree to get a good look at Jesus. Zacchaeus was very wealthy as a result of his trade as an employee of the Roman government, which also made him an enemy of his own people (Luke 19:1–4). Perhaps this was one reason he climbed the tree. When Jesus passed beneath the tree, he looked up and called to Zacchaeus by name. Jesus instructed Zacchaeus that he would be coming to his house for dinner. This caused a great stir, leading the crowds to grumble. How could Jesus eat with sinners? (Luke 19:5–7). But as Jesus himself said, "The Son of man came to seek and to save what was lost" (Luke 19:10).

Jesus always went where the religious establishment would not go. He went to where the "sinners" were. But he did not leave it there. As the incarnate presence of God, Jesus turned people back to God. In this case, Zacchaeus repented of having cheated people, and he promised to repay them four times the amount along with giving half his possessions to the poor. And so, he fulfilled the law of Moses, which required making restitution before a priest (Lev. 6:1–5). Salvation had come to Zacchaeus's house, as the great high priest himself declared (Luke 19:9). Jesus identified Zacchaeus, and identified with him. As the incarnate Lord, Jesus incarnated God's presence to him, while others refused to go near him. Lastly, Jesus drew Zacchaeus back into fellowship with God. Like Jesus, we must be on the move, bearing the message of repentance and forgiveness in his name.

Christians can become more intentional about identifying with others as God's people, "incarnating" Christ's presence, and inviting others to become members of the Holy Spirit's temple community by being active in church small groups and home communities. Such intentionality makes it possible for us to know one another's names—especially if we belong to large churches. As members of small groups and home communities, we can get involved in social outreach in the community at large. As we minister to people spiritually, emotionally, and physically, they may choose to become members of our home communities and, eventually, vital participants in the church at large. This is what happened in Acts 5, noted above as Peter and the rest of the believers ministered to the sick and those tormented by evil spirits. As a result of the apostles' performing "many miraculous signs and wonders among the people" in Solomon's Colonnade, "more and more men and women believed in the Lord and were added to their number" (Acts 5:12, 14).

Having addressed our calling as the church to go forth as the people of God, the body and bride of Christ, and the temple of the Holy Spirit, we now turn to the gospel message itself and the relation of word to deed in gospel proclamation.

## The Gospel Message of the Missional Church

The message of the missional church is the hope-filled gospel of the eschatological kingdom. The gospel of this kingdom is the good news that God the Father loves us—even us, who have turned our backs on him and who have risen up against him—and invites us to enter by repentant faith into saving relationship with himself through his Son in the Spirit, in which we receive forgiveness of our sins. Not only, though, have we turned against God, but also we have turned against one another and against the rest of God's creation. Thus, our salvation involves the ultimate transformation of body, soul, and spirit in Christ's redeemed community in a renewed cosmos, to which the church itself presently bears witness.

The whole gospel that we proclaim is for the whole person in the whole community in the whole world. Salvation is all-encompassing, involving our relationship with God, with one another, and with the creation in its entirety. Salvation also involves the redemption of our entire being. The early chapters of Genesis bear witness to the personal, corporate, and cosmic dimensions of sin and hoped-for salvation.

As this epic story reveals, God placed our first ancestors—Adam and Eve—in a garden to nurture and care for the creation and to be fruitful and procreate, multiplying across the whole earth (Gen. 1:28–30). As those created in the image of the Triune God, they existed to live in loving communion with God and one another on earth (Gen. 1:26–27). However, they rebelled, determining to displace God rather than to exist in loving communion (Gen. 3:1–7).

Their rebellion against God severely impacted their relationship with one another and the rest of creation. Adam blamed Eve for their first act of rebellion, and Eve blamed the serpent. As a result of their rebellion, God foretells that the man would rule over the woman, the woman would undergo severe agony in bearing children, and the whole creation would experience travail (see Gen. 3:12–21). The very next chapter tells of how their firstborn son is the first murderer, killing his own brother (Gen. 4:8), resulting in his restless wandering on the earth, which will no longer bear fruit for him (Gen. 4:11–12).

The aftermath of humanity's sinful ways spells the utter dissolution of the entire creation. However, God promises to redeem his fallen creation even as he pronounces judgment. The first gospel promise recorded in scripture is found in Genesis 3:15: "And I will put enmity between you and the woman, and between your seed and her seed. He will crush your head, and you will strike his heel." So begins the cosmic warfare between the serpent, or dragon, and God's promised deliverer, the Messiah, that climaxes with his crucifixion and resurrection as Lion of Judah and Lamb of God, and which culminates in the last battles recorded in Revelation (see Rev. 19–20). The Tree of Life in Eden's garden that is transplanted to the New Jerusalem is the tree on which the Messiah dies outside Jerusalem in order to bring life to all.

God purposes Israel to be a people for his triune name's sake that will prepare the way for the Messiah, whom the Spirit will unite to his people— the new Israel, the church—as head and husband to body and bride in the new heavens and earth. The Spirit and bride invite all who are thirsty to come and drink from the water of life and to make preparations for the eternal kingdom. In that kingdom's principal city—the New Jerusalem—to which the nations will bring their wealth, there will be no bloodshed, no tears, no pain; the lamb will lie down with the lion, and the Lion who is the Lamb, who takes away the sin of the world, will reign with God and his people in the fullness of the Spirit.

The gospel message is hope-filled and holistic, encompassing every area of life. It also requires holistic proclamation—in word and deed—by a people whose faith is formed by the divine love. Its scope is also all-encompassing— having a bearing upon all people. Having reflected upon the content of the gospel message, we now turn to consider the holistic nature of gospel proclamation in word and deed by a people whose faith is formed by divine love.

In closing, we will speak to the matter of the all-encompassing scope of the gospel address.

### The Holistic Proclamation of the Gospel Hope

The church is called to bear witness to Christ's kingdom in the world in word and deed (Matt. 28:18–20, esp. 20a; Acts 2:40–47; Acts 3:1–4:4), just as Jesus proclaimed the kingdom in word and deed (Matt. 4:23; 9:35; Luke 4:16–21; 5:17–26; 7:18–23). In fact, Christ's word is deed: Jesus speaks, and things happen; people are healed and demons are cast out.

Jesus spoke with authority (Matt. 7:28–29), and lived with it too (Matt. 8:1–4). It is necessary to do both. However, in our day, the church has in many respects lost its authority and right to speak. The only way we can regain this right and authority is not by power politics but by creating the space with sacrificial lives for our views to be heard. Key to our struggle is fighting against the disease of "affluenza."

Conservative evangelical Christian theology often *removes* issues of justice and this life from Jesus and his kingdom. Jesus is our substitute, who died to save us from sin and to bless only those who are poor in spirit. On this view, sin and righteousness are viewed simply in spiritual terms. Liberal Christian theology often *reduces* Jesus to a social revolutionary and his kingdom to a fulfillment of this life. On this view, Jesus died as the representative of the poor, identifying with them in their plight. Here the tendency is to reduce the poor in spirit to the poor.[10]

In contrast to these extremes, Jesus died for the sins of the world as our substitute and representative, seeking to save us from sin, which impacts every area of our lives—spiritual, social, physical, and psychological. Thus, for example, Jesus is concerned for the poor in spirit *and* the poor (Matt. 5:3; Luke 6:20). It is a both/and, not an either/or. As Gordon Fee and Douglas Stuart write,

> In Matthew the poor are "the poor in spirit"; in Luke they are simply "you poor" in contrast to "you that are rich" (6:24). On such points most people tend to have only half a canon. Traditional evangelicals tend to read only "the poor in spirit"; social activists tend to read only "you poor." We insist that *both* are canonical. In a truly profound sense the real poor are those who recognize themselves as impoverished before God. But the God of the Bible, who became incarnate in Jesus of Nazareth, is a God who pleads the cause of the oppressed and the disenfranchised. One can scarcely read Luke's gospel without recognizing his interest in this aspect of the divine revelation (see 14:12–14; cf. 12:33–34 with the Matthean parallel, 6:19–21).[11]

Of course, one would pray that all—rich and poor—would be poor in spirit. In fact, the poor are more often poor in spirit than the rich, as Jesus suggests in his statement about the rich young ruler in Luke 18:25. Moreover, those disciples to whom Jesus speaks in Matthew's Sermon on the Mount and Luke's Sermon on the Plain include his closest band of followers, who had left everything to follow him (see Luke 18:28).

Jesus came to save whole people—body, mind, and spirit. At the outset of his public ministry recorded in Luke's Gospel, Jesus applied Isaiah 61:1–2 to himself: "The Spirit of the Lord is on me, because he has anointed me to preach good news to the poor. He has sent me to proclaim freedom for the prisoners and recovery of sight for the blind, to release the oppressed, to proclaim the year of the Lord's favor" (Luke 4:17–19). With the inception of Jesus's public ministry filled and empowered by the Spirit (see Luke 4:14), the great year of Jubilee, the messianic age, has dawned. While justice, peace, and healing will not be complete until the messianic age is consummated, the messianic age of justice, peace, and holistic health has dawned in Jesus. And so, his community must proclaim the gospel of Christ's kingdom's advance holistically—in word and deed.

As stated above, Jesus proclaimed the gospel in word and deed. When John the Baptist sent his disciples to Jesus to ask him if he were truly the Christ and if the eschatological kingdom had truly come, Jesus was casting out many demons and healing many people of various diseases and illnesses, as well as blindness (Luke 7:18–21). Jesus responded:

> Go back and report to John what you have seen and heard: The blind receive sight, the lame walk, those who have leprosy are cured, the deaf hear, the dead are raised, and the good news is preached to the poor. Blessed is the man who does not fall away on account of me. (Luke 7:22–23)

When Jesus spoke, the dead were raised, the lame walked, the blind saw. The one through whom God created all things as the living, active Word is the same one through whom God will redeem all things—as the incarnate Word, who is the firstborn of the new creation and from the dead. Jesus's words and deeds constituted the eschatological kingdom's presence in his first advent, and the church is called to bear witness and participate in Christ's kingdom presently through the Spirit in word and deed.

While John had expected Israel's total deliverance from the Roman oppressors and complete restoration of Israel's fortunes with Jesus's coming, and while oppression did not cease, profound deliverance in a variety of ways did come to God's people with Jesus's inauguration of the eschatological kingdom. The church continued to bear witness to God's eschatological kingdom having dawned in Jesus, as the rest of the New Testament makes clear.

We have already drawn attention to Acts 5:12–16 in this chapter. In Acts 3, Peter heals a crippled man—who, by the way, was not a member of the church. The man had asked for a handout, but came away with much more—his legs and feet restored. Peter did not have any silver or gold, but he did not leave gospel proclamation in the realm of word only. Peter proclaimed healing to him:

> Then Peter said, "Silver or gold I do not have, but what I have I give you. In the name of Jesus Christ of Nazareth, walk." Taking him by the right hand, he helped him up, and instantly the man's feet and ankles became strong. He jumped to his feet and began to walk. Then he went with them into the temple, courts, walking and jumping, and praising God. (Acts 3:6–8)

The proclamation of the gospel in word and deed led this man to give glory to God, and those who beheld him in the temple were filled with amazement (Acts 3:9–10).

Later, when the decision was made for Peter, James, and John to focus on the Jews, and Paul and Barnabas on the Gentiles, those reputed to be pillars of the church gave one stipulation: to take care of the poor, which Paul said was the very thing he and Barnabas were eager to do (Gal. 2:9–10). Jesus's own brother, James, gives warning to rich oppressors (James 5:1–6) and says that the religion that God "accepts as pure and faultless" is "to look after orphans and widows in their distress and to keep oneself from being polluted by the world" (James 1:27). James places much emphasis on faith in action. So too does John. While addressing believers' relations with one another, he writes, "If anyone has material possessions and sees his brother in need but has no pity on him, how can the love of God be in him? Dear children, let us not love with words or tongue but with actions and in truth" (1 John 3:17–18). Although John is talking specifically about Christian fellowship, the other texts already noted reveal that such care and concern must extend to Christians' engagement of the world at large.

Such proclamation must not end with Jesus and the first Christians. As his body here on earth, the church must ever seek to live in light of what will be when Jesus comes again, proclaiming the gospel in word and deed. While we are wary of speaking of a "Social Gospel," the gospel is social. Whether or not we would use the phrase "liberation theology," theology is liberating. While the church can never be reduced to a social program that exists to promote civil society, its inherent communitarian sociality means that it will fight injustices waged against humanity in word and deed. It will resist the reductionistic commodification of humans' identity from people created in the image of God for communion to units of productivity and production whose sole purpose is market expansion—regardless of whether the market be "religious" or "secular."

The church's own identity is an unconditional given, enacted in God's gracious disclosure, wherein God comes to us in Christ and the Spirit and unites us to himself forever. Thus, the church's identity is not based on the legalistic contractual arrangements dependent upon the ever-fluctuating whims of market preference. With this in mind, as the church proclaims the gospel in word and deed, it must remain ever mindful that its identity is not reduced to words and deeds. The collapsing of the church's identity to its purpose and activity makes it difficult to guard the church from being reduced to a market or social program. As stated in the first chapter, the church's identity must shape its missional purpose and activity. And so, its proclamation in word and deed is ultimately founded in faith formed by divine love. There is no autonomy. As with Israel, the church can do nothing apart from its participation in God's story in Christ through the Spirit. It must remain in the divine vine (see John 15; see also Isa. 5), by faith formed by the divine love.

### By Faith Formed by Divine Love

In his first encyclical letter, *Deus Caritas Est* ("God Is Love"), Pope Benedict XVI speaks to these matters. The pope chose "to speak of the love which God lavishes upon us and which we in turn must share with others" because God's name is often wrongly "associated with vengeance or even a duty of hatred and violence."[12] After reflecting upon "the unity of love in creation and salvation history," the pope turns to discuss the church's practice of love.

The pope guards against reducing the church to a social program by rooting the church with its practices in the Trinity. The church's practice of charity is itself "a manifestation of Trinitarian love."[13] Charity is not something the church should neglect, leaving it to others, for it "is a part of her nature, an indispensable expression of her very being" through the church's union with the Triune God.[14] While engaging in a life of charity and concern for justice, the church's role is not "to bring about the most just society possible." This is the state's task.[15] And while the church's charitable ministries work alongside other organizations, the pope is careful not to reduce the church's charitable activity to "just another form of social assistance." The pontiff safeguards against such reduction in part by emphasizing that the church's love of neighbor is a "consequence deriving from" believers' "faith" and is "independent of parties and ideologies" or the attempt to impose the faith on others.[16]

Fellow Roman Catholic theologian Hans Urs von Balthasar speaks of how such love is founded in the Ultimate Love in whom believers trust, who allowed others to impose upon him. Absolute faith is reserved only for the ultimate deed of love revealed in and as Jesus Christ; such divine love gives rise to a response of absolute faith.[17] It follows from this that "Christian action is therefore a being taken up into God's action through grace, being taken up into God's love so that one can love with him."[18]

Over against moralism and antinomianism, such love calls for a response of love—nothing more and nothing less. As Balthasar writes, "Love desires no recompense other than to be loved in return; and thus God desires nothing in return for his love for us other than our love. 'Let us not love in word or speech, but in deed and in truth' (1 John 3:18)."[19]

Whereas moralism involves the love of law, and antinomianism the love of lawlessness, pluralism signifies the love of a nameless deity who places no limits on competing loves (for there can be no competing loves when the object of love is amorphous, nebulous, and objectless). In contrast, the Bible calls on us to respond in faith and faithfulness, in deed and in truth, to the One who is a jealous lover, who loves us absolutely through his eternal covenant in Christ. Balthasar looks at Old Testament Israel as a warning to the church when he writes:

> The jealous God, who makes a gift of himself in the covenant, desires in the first place nothing other than his partner's zealously faithful love—for him. Indeed, we must love absolute love and direct our love to the Lover, setting aside all other relative and competing objects of love. To the extent that we do not remain absolutely faithful to absolute love, these objects turn into idols. The bridegroom and the bride in the Song of Songs have no children; they are everything and sufficient for one another, and all their fruitfulness lies enclosed within the circle of their mutual love.[20]

Later, he writes, "Unconditional priority must be accorded to the placing of oneself entirely at the disposal of divine love."[21] All other action follows from this prior act of responding with the whole of one's being to God as the absolute love.[22]

God is absolute love—the absolute lover, who is jealous for his people and for their love. Our hope who is this God who loves us jealously and who pours out his love in Christ into our hearts through the Holy Spirit does not disappoint. He will destroy those Pharaohs and Caesars who oppress his people. He also invites all peoples—Egyptian, Roman, Greek, barbarian, and Scythian—to enter into his covenant community with believing Israel through Christ in the Spirit; in faith, hope, and love, in word and in deed, in action and in truth. This last point leads us to a discussion of the scope of salvation, which entails such questions as the "target audience" of the church.

### The All-Encompassing Scope of the Gospel Message

As stated above, God is jealous for his people, and God invites all peoples to enter into his covenant community through Christ Jesus in the Spirit. It is crucial for the church to proclaim the gospel in word and deed and through faith formed by divine love to all people, for as Peter himself declares, "Salvation is found in no one else, for there is no other name given under heaven by which we must be saved" (Acts 4:12, TNIV). This is the same name to which

Jesus refers when he declares, "All authority in heaven and on earth have been given to me. Therefore go make disciples of all nations, baptizing them in the name of the Father and of the Son and of the Holy Spirit, and teaching them to obey everything I have commanded you. And surely I am with you always, to the very end of the age" (Matt. 28:19–20). And this is the same name that God discloses to Moses at the burning bush, the name that Moses is to make known to Israel when he declares God's word to Pharaoh: "Let my people go" (Exod. 3–5).

In Acts 2, we are told that God-fearing Jews from every nation under heaven heard Peter declare the good news of salvation in Jesus's name and responded in faith. Thousands more responded to the apostles' message of salvation through faith in Christ Jesus in Acts 4. The rulers' response to the apostles' message in Acts 4 was not unlike the reception Moses received in Pharaoh's court—one of complete rejection. Both Pharaoh in Exodus 5 and the rulers of Israel in Acts 4 were troubled over the commotion Moses and the apostles were creating among the people. In each episode, we find that the commotion is the result of God's messenger reaching out compassionately—to the enslaved people of Israel in Moses's case (Exod. 5), and to a crippled man in Peter's case (Acts 3; see Peter's words in Acts 5:8–12). The deliverance of Israel and of this man results from the proclamation of God's message in God's name in word and deed.

Moses proclaimed the kingdom of the LORD in word and deed. The words, "Let my people go," were accompanied by deeds of judgment—from Moses's staff/serpent swallowing Pharaoh's court magicians' snakes to the outpouring of plagues on Egypt. The Lord Jesus proclaimed the kingdom of God as the living word enacted in history, bringing God's people out of bondage to Pharaoh-Caesar—a deliverance that has begun but will not reach its fulfillment until the consummation of all things. As "LORD" (see Rom. 10:9–13), Jesus *is* the named God through whom Moses led the people out of Egypt into the wilderness, and in view of whom Peter established the church in the Diaspora, both moving God's missional people toward the Promised Land.

Both Moses and Peter invited the nations to participate in this missional journey. They even welcomed those hailing from those nations that had long oppressed them—Egyptians and Romans alike joined them (Exod. 12:38; Acts 10:44–48). Peter's words spoken in the centurion Cornelius's house are apt here: "I now realize how true it is that God does not show favoritism but accepts men from every nation who fear him and do what is right" (Acts 10:34–35).

Unlike Pharaoh, who scoffed at Moses's report that God had spoken and would act on behalf of his oppressed people, the centurion Cornelius feared God and came to trust in Jesus as "the one whom God appointed as judge of the living and the dead" (Acts 10:42). As a God-fearer, Cornelius rejected the ancient and widespread doctrine of the essential namelessness of God presupposed by the adherents of the Roman pantheon of the gods. Pharaoh, on the other hand, may have presupposed this doctrine in his dismissal of Moses's report: "Who is the LORD, that I should obey him and let Israel go? I do not know the LORD and I will not let Israel go" (Exod. 5:2).[23]

Such a deity is useful to Pharaohs and Caesars, who would unite various peoples under their imperial rule. As Edward Gibbon remarks, during the time of the Caesars all forms of worship were "considered by the people equally true, by the philosophers equally false, and by the magistrates equally useful."[24] Nameless deities are equally useful to magistrates who would use and abuse people for extending their rule and building their empires, as Pharaoh did in the case of Israel. A people whose deity is ultimately nameless, and who have forgotten their history, language, and name, are never an imposing threat to the fallen powers' imperial rule. While Israel had not forgotten its history, language, or name, Pharaoh was not aware of Joseph (Exod. 1:8), and until Israel's deliverance under Moses, neither Pharaoh nor Israel knew of God's name as the LORD. An oppressed people who are convinced that their named God is the all-sovereign deity are always a threat to the fallen powers, whose own sovereignty is thereby called into question.

Further to a previous point, a nameless god and a nameless people can be commodified, as in the case of Caesar, who employed the pantheon to serve his empire centered in the great Babylon and extended through her kings and merchants throughout the world to profit from the peoples of the earth (Rev. 18). The named people of the named God, however, cannot be commodified.[25] This God's people cannot be reduced to numbers. While the 144,000—God's righteous remnant—can be slain, they can never be eradicated; for they bear God's name and await God's deliverance and judgment. God's righteous remnant overcome the fallen powers by the blood of the Lamb and by the word of their testimony, not shrinking from death, for they bear the name of the Triune God (Rev. 3:10–12; 12:11; 14:1–5) and will reign with this named God forever (Rev. 3:21–22).[26] No wonder the church that takes its calling as witness to this deity seriously has always been a threat to the fallen principalities and powers.

While the church has often used God's name in vain by practices of domination, exploiting "God" for its own ends, it could only use God's name in vain by refusing to act in light of that name as revealed in Jesus of Nazareth. The God of Israel makes himself known in Jesus of Nazareth (Heb. 1:1–3). As John writes, "No one has ever seen God, but God the one and only who is at the Father's side has made him known" (John 1:18). The church that bears witness to the Living Word and Lamb of God who takes away the sin of the world will not sacrifice others for its sake but will sacrifice itself for the world's sake in bearing witness to its Lord.

The answer to imperialism's rule is not pluralism's nameless deity, no matter how right the concern of those who have espoused this doctrine to safeguard against oppression.[27] The answer to imperialism's rule is the church's witness to the named deity—revealed in the center of salvation history as the crucified and risen Jesus—through the church's own missional and sacrificial witness on behalf of the world.

While we are not certain of his Christology, Martin Luther King Jr.'s practice resonates profoundly with a truly orthodox conception of the co-missional God's acts throughout salvation's history. Steeped in the biblical narrative, King functioned as a modern-day Moses with his missional campaign to protest the fallen principalities and powers' oppression of his people: "Let my people go." In view of Jesus's love ethic and Gandhi's method of civil disobedience, King writes,

> We will match your capacity [that of Whites] to inflict suffering with our capacity to endure suffering. We will meet your physical force with soul force . . . Do to us what you will and we will love you. Bomb our homes and threaten our children; send your hooded perpetrators of violence into our communities and drag us out on some wayside road, beating us and leaving us half-dead, and we will still love you. But we will soon wear you down by our capacity to suffer.[28]

King drew strength from the biblical narrative, from the outpouring of God's Spirit of love, from his community's own resolve, and from his hope that God will someday fully redeem his people, leading them into the Promised Land.

We no longer live under Jim Crow laws of segregation, where God's authentic witnessing church suffers physical abuse. But we do live under commodity-oriented consumer-based segregation and all the suffering this commodity-oriented consumer culture creates, with people's identities reduced to their tastes and talents/abilities, and how much they are able to purchase and consume. The commodity-oriented consumer culture drives much of the church growth movement today, and leads to the separation of ethnicities and economic classes in churches because of these churches' predominant focus on taste, abilities/talents, and individualistic preference. The church that caters to the commodity-oriented consumer culture also reduces people's identities to their drives and choices, purposes and activities, whereby they become mere tasters with gifts, enslaved and used for the advance of free-market religion and ecclesial empires.

The God of the gospel of Jesus Christ engages all people as people, not as slaves to an empire's expansion, whether that empire is a state or market or church. The God of the gospel of Jesus Christ engages the whole person, not reducing people's identities to their purposes, activities, tastes, and abilities. That is one reason why we speak first and foremost of the church as *being*-driven. When we replace people's names with numbers and reduce their identities to purposes, activities, tastes, and abilities, we tend only to target our outreach based in tastes and abilities to those whose tastes and abilities give our churches the most bang for their buck (namely, the most tasteful and able—the "preferred target audience"), thereby separating people along race and class lines.

Evangelical Civil Rights and Community Development leader John M. Perkins challenges the commodity-oriented, consumer culture and all that it entails for communities in disrepair noted earlier in this chapter. His robust Christology and missional reading of the Bible provide him with the theological resources to promote a biblically based model of community development— over against commodity development—of relocation (living with people who are different from us—those of different races and classes), reconciliation (being made right with God and these other people), and redistribution (shar-ing talents, skills, resources, and lives with these same people who, like us, are created in the irreducibly interpersonal image of the named God) centered in the church. The God revealed in Jesus and worshipped in the church makes possible authentic community development and restoration of communities of dysfunction—making rich and poor, black and white, male and female function as the one communal people (not individually packaged products) they are called to be as bearers of the same family name—that of the God revealed in Jesus Christ.

The God revealed in Jesus Christ is the necessary condition for the possibil-ity of human existence as communal—where we are irreducibly personal and interpersonal, not commodified and segregated. The church must proclaim this named deity, not setting forth disclaimers that the Trinity is the greatest mystery of the Christian faith and so we should leave this doctrine alone. A church that leaves this God alone not only fails to see that the Triune God is revealed mystery, but also unwittingly replaces this God with an unnamed deity, functionally or explicitly. The explicit replacement comes from the religious pluralist, who says that God is beyond naming. The functional replacement comes from the evangelical pragmatist, who says (explicitly or implicitly) that reflection on the Triune God—the God whose name is Father, Son, and Spirit—is irrelevant for Christian practice.

Espousing a nameless deity—explicitly or functionally—opens the door to the commodification of religion and the commodification of human identity. The choice (activity) of the customer is sovereign and free, whatever it might be. The church made up of a community of tasters and consumers, picking and choosing the deity it demands, and falling prey to the demands placed on it by the consumer culture and free-market economic empire of which it is a part, becomes a shopping mall of base consumption. This evolution of the church entails the commodification of human and ecclesial identity and the eroding of the biblical ideal of a community of profound communion centered in the self-sacrificing authority of Jesus Christ.[29]

Jeff Sharlet's 2005 *Harper's Magazine* article exposes this problem. Sharlet interviewed the former head of the National Association of Evangelicals and former senior pastor at New Life Community Church, Ted Haggard. In what follows, it is by no means our intent to ridicule Rev. Haggard, who during his tenure as president of the NAE supported several key initiatives such as promoting environmental stewardship among evangelicals as well as religious and cultural tolerance in America among those from across the ideological spectrum. However, it should be noted that Haggard did not need to leave either position based on his views of free-market spirituality, but because of marital infidelity. The NAE or Haggard's church did not see a problem with the former; our point is a criticism ultimately of evangelicalism as a whole, for Haggard simply articulated in an explicit and straightforward manner the heart of the dominant evangelical church's missional or not-so-missional paradigm.

According to Sharlet's Haggard,

> "Free-market globalization" has made us so free, he realized, that an American cell-group system could be mature enough to function just like a market. One of Pastor Ted's favorite books is Thomas Friedman's *The Lexus and the Love Tree*, which is now required reading for the hundreds of pastors under Ted's spiritual authority across the country. From Friedman, Pastor Ted says he learned that everything, including spirituality, can be understood as a commodity. And unregulated trade, he concluded, was the key to achieving worldly freedom.[30]

Christian leaders must "'harness the forces of free-market capitalism in our ministry.' Once a pastor does that, his flock can start organizing itself according to each member's abilities and tastes."[31] After quoting Haggard as saying that "evangelical" stands for being pro-free market and pro-private property, Sharlet quotes from and discusses Haggard's book *Dog Training, Fly Fishing, & Sharing Christ in the 21st Century*, where Haggard reflects on the kind of church he believes "good Christians" desire:

> "I want my finances in order, my kids trained, and my wife to love life. I want good friends who are a delight and who provide protection for my family and me should life become difficult someday . . . I don't want surprises, scandals, or secrets . . . I want stability and, at the same time, steady, forward movement. I want the church to help me live life well, not exhaust me with endless 'worthwhile projects.'" By "worthwhile projects" Ted means building funds and soup kitchens alike. It's not that he opposes these; it's just that he is sick of hearing about them and believes that other Christians are, too. He knows that for Christianity to prosper in the free market, it needs more than "moral values"—it needs customer value.[32]

One can only hope that the reason Sharlet's Haggard does not speak about soup kitchens is because he thinks (albeit mistakenly) that the free market enterprise left to itself will inevitably do away with poverty.

*Christianity Today*'s Tim Stafford quotes Haggard as saying, "Free markets have done more to help poor people than any benevolent organization ever has." It appears that for the former head of the NAE, the best way to fulfill the biblical mandate to care for the poor is to promote the free-market society. While acknowledging that Jesus never mentioned free markets, but instead told the rich young ruler to sell all and give to the poor, Haggard responds in *Christianity Today* by saying, "Jesus was in the 1st century . . . and we're in the 21st century."[33]

Soup kitchens or not, the free-market enterprise that Haggard espouses can enslave people and keep us from reaching out and freeing those long oppressed. In contrast, John Perkins is a capitalist of a higher order, who, while going beyond soup kitchens, also goes beyond the not-so-free market by promoting economic development that strategically elevates the poor out of poverty. His three principles of relocation, reconciliation, and redistribution mentioned earlier are intended to help the poor and dispossessed take ownership of their communities. True freedom requires equal footing. Freedom as in autonomy leads to abuses and the sole survival of the economic fittest. A *laissez-faire* approach to the market is both *lazy* and *unfair*. In opposition to the advocate of the autonomous market, Perkins seeks to change the underlying structures that enslave people to welfare in the U.S. and to ensure that the capitalistic venture proceeds on level ground.[34]

Over against Haggard's view and in keeping with Perkins's model, God frees the church to embrace an economic order that runs counter to the dominant culture's economic enterprise. As Lois Barrett points out, "The alternative economics of the church has . . . spread beyond its members to various programs of helping the poor, establishing hospitals and mental health institutions, building homes, and sharing food. The church is called to an alternative economics that puts needs ahead of wants."[35]

The church that is united to the Triune God must not commodify human identity or espouse free market spirituality (with its instrumentalist reduction of people to their abilities and tastes) and all that it entails for economics generally; for the church belongs to the alternative economic order of the kingdom, which is founded in the interpersonal and communal identity, purpose, and activity of the Triune God, who although he was rich, became poor so that we might become the riches of God (2 Cor. 8:9). The church is its reconciling and redistributing members, which follows from the fact that its own being is contingent upon and reflects the interpersonal, communal being of the outwardly oriented and downwardly mobile God.[36]

Churches should focus on living in keeping with their being as the communion of persons newly created in the image of the outwardly oriented and downwardly mobile Triune God, united with God and one another through Christ in the Spirit. Here one values relational identity descriptions and economic practices that flow from communion with the Triune God and God's people and guards against reducing individual churches and individual members' significance to what they can produce and consume.

Further to the preceding points, the former head of the NAE should have rethought commodification of spirituality, given his participation in the Judeo-Christian tradition and role in championing the plight of the human unborn. Regarding the former item, Jonathan Sacks, chief rabbi of the United Hebrew Congregations of the British Commonwealth, says that

> the fatal conceit for Judaism is to believe that the market governs the totality of our lives, when it in fact governs only a limited part of it, that which concerns the goods we think of as being subject to production and exchange. There are things fundamental to being human that we do not produce; instead we receive from those who came before us and from God Himself. And there are things that we may not exchange, however high the price.[37]

Regarding the latter item, Kendall Soulen claims,

> The market, of course, promises to make the consumer king, and encourages us to think that we are in charge. But the market charges a high price in return, namely, the increasing commodification of human life itself. To take just one example, as genetic knowledge becomes more complete and available to consumers through law, prospective parents will be subject to pressure to screen their pregnancies in order to screen out inefficiencies such as mental retardation, genetic disorder, etc.[38]

While authentic witness to the Triune God will arise from outside the walls of the church, such as through Rabbi Sacks of the British Commonwealth and the Hindu revolutionary Gandhi in India, or through our Unitarian Universalist activist friends in the States, whose concern for the dispossessed often puts orthodox Christians such as ourselves to shame,[39] the church *of the Triune God* bears direct witness to this God through its close proximity to scripture and the sacraments. Outside the Trinity, there is no salvation, no redemption, not even for the church. Outside the church of the Triune God, there is no salvation.[40]

Having said this, the missional church is neither stationary nor exclusionary. It is called to be a community on the move, attacking the gates of hell, releasing captives, and giving of itself for the sake of the least of these for the greatest of all—Jesus. Just as Martin Luther King Jr. envisioned taking his Ebenezer Baptist Church in Atlanta (which stood as a visible witness against the fallen principalities and powers[41]) with him on his civil rights campaigns,[42] the church is a community of people called to relocate, reconcile, and redistribute its wealth on behalf of all people—inside and outside the church, especially the downtrodden—for Jesus's sake. The church that relocates, reconciles, and redistributes wealth in this way moves out as a missional witness to the communal and co-missional God, who wages war against the whore of Babylon and the merchants with whom she committed adultery, and against Pharaoh and Caesar, who impose their nameless deity and imperial rule on peoples for their own economic gain. This missional church prefigures the day when the city of the New Jerusalem—Christ's holy bride—will be a place where

> the nations will walk by its light, and the kings of the earth will bring their splendor into it. On no day will its gates ever be shut, for there will be no night there. The glory and honor of the nations will be brought into it. Nothing impure will ever enter it, nor will anyone who does what is shameful or deceitful, but only those whose names are written in the Lamb's book of life. (Rev. 21:24–27)

## STUDY QUESTIONS

1. What kind of dialogue should the church establish with non-Christian faith traditions?
2. What is the relation of the gospel to social justice?
3. What does it mean for the church to be missional today?
4. How can consumerism affect negatively the church's missional orientation?

# 16

# From Building Programs
# to Building God's Missional Kingdom

## Jesus Loves All the Little Children—but Do We?

We grew up singing, "Jesus loves the little children, all the children of the world. Red and yellow, black and white, they are precious in his sight. Jesus loves the little children of the world." Jesus does love all the children of the world. But do *we* love *all* the children who live near us? Evangelical Christians have rightly emphasized sending missionaries to foreign fields. But all too often we evangelical followers of Jesus do not exist missionally among those who appear foreign to us in the cities, suburbs, and towns where we live.

One of our students serving on staff at a church in the Portland area described that church's outreach strategy in the surrounding community. Soon after she had joined the church staff, she was told that the decision had been made to bypass reaching out to a lower-income apartment complex and to "target" a well-to-do subdivision (which was probably very homogeneous, given that race and class tend to track one another in the United States).[1] The rationale was that the church would get more "bang for the buck" from well-to-do converts and transfer members, and that this move would help them with their facilities and building program. The student was appalled, to which another staff member replied, "I'm sorry we told you."

In fact, we do not only the poor but also the rich a disservice when we go this route. In our affluenza-stricken culture, one of the best ways to reach the rich is through ministry among the poor and with the poor. Even people disillusioned by Christianity marveled at Mother Teresa and were fascinated in hearing what she had to say about Jesus. Her life of service among "the least of these" created the space for her views to be heard even among the greatest. And no doubt, we have all heard the testimonies of American Christians returning from short-term mission projects in Mexico. Mexican believers who were so rich in Christ yet so poor by the world's standards profoundly impacted them.

### Taking Aim at Common Church Growth Strategies: "Target" Practice

Our missions programs must bear witness to the missional God at work in the world. So too must our building programs and strategic plans for missions outreach in the community. God is always reaching out. While Jesus died for the whole world, and there are many rich people who love God and give sacrificially to his kingdom work, the Bible tells us that God has determined to fill his kingdom with the weak and foolish, the poor and despised (1 Cor. 1:18–31; James 2:5). In fact, the rich are often the hardest to reach; their riches can keep them from being rich toward God, as in the case of the rich young ruler (Luke 18:18–30). If this is so, why do we put an inordinate amount of resources into targeting people in more well-to-do communities?[2] Many of America's most highly publicized churches are located in affluent suburbs.

One youth minister serving in an affluent Seattle suburb said that it is easy to reach inner-city youth for Christ, because they sense their great need. He added that it is a far greater challenge to reach out to wealthy youth in the suburbs, because they believe all their needs are already met. So his church pours money into fun programs designed to reach these wealthy (and sometimes jaded) youth in order to try and convince them otherwise. In our estimation, his church would be much better off if the leaders were to take much of that money and put it toward ultimate adventure weekends for these youth—service projects among the homeless, the poor, and the sick. Such encounters help all of us come face-to-face with our own spiritual wandering, poverty of soul, and sickness unto death—leading us to new and renewed life in Christ.

Once, when one of us was exhorting a group of Christian youth workers to reach out to the poor, one of them responded, "But God loves the rich too." Who would question this point? If evangelical outreach is any indication, it is obvious that God loves the rich. Apart from notable exceptions like Shane Claiborne, it is less obvious that God loves the poor.[3] So often, we target the rich because we want to climb the social ladder and be successful. But God gives special attention to the poor.[4] James rebukes his readers for targeting the rich, saying, "Listen, my dear brothers: has not God chosen those who are poor in the eyes of the world to be rich in faith and to inherit the kingdom he promised those who love him?" (James 2:5).

This does not preach well in a culture driven by consumerism and the accumulation of stuff. People are encouraged to seek to get whatever they want when they want it at the least cost to themselves, and to climb the social ladder. And so, they associate with those who will help them advance and succeed in acquiring a greater share of the good life. Those who are spiritually inclined bring this mind-set into the religious realm. We want relational security, wonderful families, and good jobs. How would dealing with race and class issues help us put in place the programs that will help us get what *we* want? And if we want to build churches fast, we are tempted to focus all of our energies on engaging high achievers, who will reach out to their high-achieving friends. To reach them, though, we figure that it will likely mean downplaying downward mobility and heterogeneity.

We all face this struggle, no matter where we are on the social ladder. The poor do not want to be poor. Who would? Even the poor are tempted to disengage from those around them in order to succeed in life, and the prosperity gospel only encourages them along these lines. John Perkins puts it this way:

> The prosperity movement is heavily accepted among the poor but has done very little in terms of real community development at the grass roots level. It takes people's attention away from the real problem, and if those people succeed it encourages them to remove themselves from the very people they ought to be identifying with and working among.[5]

The prosperity gospel teaches that the children of the world whose families succeed financially are precious in God's sight. It teaches that these golden and greenback children bear the mark of God's favor, not those who are poor in spirit, or who identify with the poor.

Now what does the biblical gospel say about the favor of the Lord? Does not the favor of the Lord rest upon those who lovingly identify with and work among the downtrodden? For as scripture says,

> If you do away with the yoke of oppression, with the pointing finger and malicious talk, and if you spend yourselves in behalf of the hungry and satisfy the needs of the oppressed, then your light will rise in the darkness, and your night will become like the noonday. The LORD will guide you always; he will satisfy your needs in a sun-scorched land and will strengthen your frame. You will be like a well-watered garden, like a spring whose waters never fail. Your people will rebuild the ancient ruins and will raise up the age-old foundations; you will be called Repairer of Broken Walls, Restorer of Streets with Dwellings. (Isa. 58:9b–12)

Talk about a truly significant church building program—building ancient ruins and raising up age-old foundations!

Certainly, God wants the church to minister to people to help them build meaningful relationships with their neighbors and cultivate wholesome families. For God's greatest commands are to love God with all one's heart and one's neighbor as oneself (Mark 12:30–31), and the command to honor one's parents is the first command that comes with a blessing (Eph. 6:1–3). But God redefines neighbor to include our enemies, the downtrodden, and those who fall outside our affinity groups, as evidenced in the parable of the Good Samaritan (Luke 10:25–37). And while Jesus certainly cared for his mother, he also said that his true mother and family members were those who obeyed God's word (Luke 8:19–21). Lastly, scripture never demeans hard work. But the goal of such work should never be the sheer accumulation of wealth; it should be the right use of wealth, good stewardship, and redistribution of resources (Luke 12: 13–34). We must reshape our relational, familial, and vocational values in light of Christ's countercultural and upside-down kingdom values. Christ himself became poor so that we could become rich toward God. As Paul declares, "For you know the grace of our Lord Jesus Christ, that though he was rich, yet for your sakes he became poor, so that you through his poverty might become rich" (2 Cor. 8:9).

Now what about those who say that the poor, blacks, and women are better off reaching their groups than the rest of us are? Isn't it better if we just support such niche groups and let them reach their own kind? To the contrary, in light of scripture, it is in the best interest of our nuclear as well as our church families that we reshape our family values to reflect Christ's kingdom values and reach out missionally to those outside our own subcultures.

This brings to mind a Christian lawyer friend of ours who moved his family out of the suburbs into the inner city. He and his wife have a grown son and a couple of teenage daughters. Friends of theirs asked them how they could do this to their daughters—moving them into the godforsaken inner city. Our friend said that their son—now a successful businessman—is the one who has lost out. Their son has not been the beneficiary of the social exposure and kingdom perspective that their daughters have been. While we do not live in the inner city, we think it important that our children become vitally connected to those who live outside our affinity group structure. Our children *need* such exposure for kingdom living in the twenty-first century. For us to move forward along these lines, we need to redefine success and reframe mission so that we will begin living out a more profound dream and uncommon kingdom vision.

### Redefining Success and Reframing Mission: Living Out the Dream

We need to redefine success. We can so inoculate our children against the world that they lose all kingdom perspective and become irrelevant to God.

We must look beyond the prosperity gospel and its definition of success to the good news of God. The prosperity gospel in whatever form encourages us to associate with those who will help us climb the social ladder. The gospel of the kingdom, on the other hand, encourages us to journey with Jesus by becoming outwardly and downwardly mobile and reaching out to those who look, act, think, and smell different from us.

Jesus builds his kingdom community by breaking down affinity group divisions between people groups (Gal. 3:28), including racial, class, and gender divisions. Living for Jesus means that we are to die to our sins, not cater to our fleshly desires. Consumerism keeps us in bondage to our fleshly desires. Just when we think it is time to die to our selfish desires, the consumer gospel tells us that we should get whatever we want, and as much of it as possible. After all, God placed us in America, and so we are to chase the American dream.

Consumerism teaches us to want things we would not otherwise want, kind of like the story of humanity's fall in the Garden (Gen. 3). The creation stories (Gen. 1 and 2) tell us that Adam and Eve were doing just fine, content in God's ordering of their lives. But then the serpent came and planted a thought and a desire in their minds and souls: "Your lives lack meaning because you're so naïve. You will only be fulfilled by becoming wise in the ways of the world. It's quick and easy, and can be accomplished in just two easy steps: first, pick the fruit; second, eat it. It will change your lives!"

Not only does the consumerist ideology trick us into thinking we need things we do not need, but also it inspires the fear of scarcity within us. The two are connected. While we do not need more than what we need, and should shape our desires to reflect our needs, fear creeps in and tells us that there is not enough to go around for today, or for tomorrow. While the people of Israel were told to take only the amount of manna they would need for the day (except for the Sabbath preparations on the sixth day, when they were instructed to take double), many of them sought to hoard as much as they could for the future. All the excess manna rotted (see Exod. 16:14–30).

We find the same problem with the rich fool. He built more barns to hoard away the wealth he had made rather than become rich toward God and share his possessions with the poor. As a result, he rotted. In contrast to the rich fool, Jesus exhorts his followers to be faithful servants who give to the poor because God has given them the kingdom. We can give because God has given to us (see Luke 12:13–34). Are our churches storehouses for the poor or for the rich? Are we storing up wealth to give away to others, especially the poor, or to keep things to ourselves and "our kind of people"?

So, what would our churches look like if they were to become more missional? They would use their building complexes to serve the complex needs of their surrounding communities. Such services might include housing medical clinics and using their church fellowship halls for nomadic homeless shelters.

A friend of ours who runs a nomadic homeless shelter in partnership with local churches in Solano County, California (Mission Solano), has recently been building a multimillion-dollar complex with the help of churches, the city, and local businesses. Many partnering churches, afraid that the new facility might mean they were no longer needed to provide shelter, requested that they still be allowed to house homeless people in their church facilities. They did not want to miss out on the blessing of receiving for giving.

For those churches without buildings or those in need of acquiring more space, they may consider entering into long-term rental agreements with public schools for use of their facilities for Sunday worship so as to put much-needed resources into the school systems. They may also wish to purchase or lease buildings for church office spaces and the like in diverse areas of their towns, so as to increase their visible presence in the communities at large. Imago Dei Community in Portland models this approach. Churches must be very intentional about blessing the surrounding communities, asking themselves if these surrounding communities would miss them if they were to close their doors and leave town.

Missional outreach might also include (for example) paying the expenses of some Mexican pastors and some of their people to come and assist them on short-term mission projects to reach out more effectively to the increasing numbers of Hispanic families in their own communities. To do so, they will need to see that missions outreach goes both ways, and that we all need one another as members of the body of Christ. Thus, the American church must see that it needs to be on the receiving as well as the sending end.

Missional outreach requires great intentionality, patience, and modeling. "Intentionality" suggests that the church in question at the beginning of this chapter reach out to the lower-income apartment complex *as well as* to the well-to-do subdivision. "Patience" suggests that it requires significant time and instruction to help people see that such expansive outreach is biblical and resonates with God's heart and kingdom perspective. "Modeling" suggests that leaders live it out themselves in their people's midst. Just as we need to model such intentionality, patience, and exemplary lives, we need models who will encourage us.

We find great intentionality, patience, and modeling in the life of the apostle Paul. Paul reached out to Jews and Gentiles and rich and poor, and was very intentional about making sure these various groups all worshiped and had table fellowship together. Such outreach and church growth initiatives were by no means easy. The letter to the Romans and first epistle to the Corinthians indicate as much. In Rome, the Jewish believers looked down on the Gentile Christians (Rom. 2), and the Gentile Christians looked down on Jews (Rom. 11:13–24). In Corinth, the rich did not share their abundance with the poor at the agape feast (1 Cor. 11:17–34). Paul was patient with these various groups, even while urging them on to maturity—no doubt because of God's long-suffering love of Paul, who prior to his conversion had despised the poor and powerless Christ, and prized Jewish people over the Gentiles. Paul also modeled God's kingdom perspective when he rebuked Peter for succumbing to Judaizing peer pressure by refusing to have table fellowship with Gentile Christians in Antioch (Gal. 2:11–14). The same modeling is evident in Paul's refusal to have Titus circumcised, and in his defense of Gentile Christians' equality in Acts 15. Both moves could have jeopardized Paul's standing in the apostolic community. The same possible fate may be in store for us.

The fate of the late Archbishop Romero of El Salvador was certainly tragic, yet heroic. He was martyred for his courageous solidarity with the poor indigenous people, who suffered numerous injustices at the hands of the ruling class. Romero's solidarity carried over into his administration of baptism and Holy Communion. The movie *Romero* documents how he refused to provide a separate baptismal service for the baby of one of his wealthy friends of Spanish descent. She did not want her baby baptized with Indian babies. Romero's refusal angered her, and she told him that he had abandoned his own people. William Cavanaugh tells of how on another occasion Romero brought the rich and poor together to celebrate the mass. Although the wealthy were infuriated, Romero drew courage and comfort from the theo-political significance of the Lord's Supper and resolved "to collapse the spatial barriers separating the rich and the poor." Many North American evangelicals lack such resolve, for they think the rich and poor are united as members of the universal church, and so do not have to worship together. They fail to understand that they are called to bear witness here and now to this eschatological reality. Romero did not bring the rich and poor together "by surveying the expanse of the Church and declaring it universal and united, but by gathering the faithful in one particular location around the altar, and realizing the heavenly Catholica in one place, at one moment, on earth."[6]

For all our talk of being practical, we leave church unity in the realm of generalities and abstractions when we refuse to bring Christians from diverse backgrounds together in worship. The words of Martin Luther King Jr. ring true today—Sunday morning at 11:00 a.m. is still the most segregated hour in America.

> There is another thing that disturbs me to no end about the American church. You have a white church and you have a Negro church. You have allowed segregation to creep into the doors of the church. How can such a division exist in the true Body of Christ? You must face the tragic fact that when you stand at eleven o'clock on Sunday morning to sing "All Hail the Power of Jesus' Name" and "Dear Lord and Father of All Mankind," you stand in the most segregated hour of Christian America. They tell me that there is more integration in the entertaining world and other secular agencies than there is in the Christian church. How appalling that is.[7]

Such appalling generalities and abstractions suggest to the world that there is more reconciling power in the world than in the church. Such a specter impacts negatively our claim that the good news of Jesus Christ is life-transforming, and makes it look as if the wine of the Lord's Supper is nothing more than an opiate of the masses.

Many North American Christians fail to understand that we are called to bear witness here and now in particular places at particular times to Christ's eschatological kingdom's realization of equality and inclusiveness in our worship, including our baptismal practice and celebration of the Lord's Table. We also fail to recognize that Romero and King's strategic confrontation of segregation broke down the cultural barriers that keep many people from entering into the church. The church in El Salvador grew as the masses flocked to hear Romero and like-minded priests speak. Even to this day, King is America's most-recognized preacher. His sermons and service to the black masses inspire scores of diverse peoples to this day. Like our Lord before them, Romero and King proclaimed in word and deed the year of Jubilee. While many were incensed by their message and lives, the multitudes revered them (see Luke 4:14–44).

Pastors like Bill Hybels of Willow Creek Community Church—one of the most well-known proponents of targeting "niche communities" to grow the church—are beginning to get this message. There is hope. Just attend to Hybels's words:

> Willow Creek started in the era when . . . the church growth people were saying, "Don't dissipate any of your energies fighting race issues. Focus everything on evangelism." It was the homogeneous unit principle of church growth. And I remember as a young pastor thinking, "That's true." I didn't know whether I wanted to chance alienating people who were seekers, whose eternity was on the line, and who might only come to church one time. I wanted to take away as many obstacles as possible, other than the Cross, to help people focus on the gospel.
>
> So now, 30 years later, . . . I recognize that a true biblical functioning community must include being multi-ethnic. My heart beats so fast for that vision today. I marvel at how naïve and pragmatic I was 30 years ago.[8]

Like Hybels, we have a dream that one day Jesus's church will not only love all the children of the world, but also love all the children who live near us. We have a dream that one day little children will not be judged by their parents' skin color or bank accounts, but by the fact that Jesus loves them. We have a dream that one day in our community little red and yellow boys and girls will join hands with little black and white boys and girls, and those children from gated communities with those from trailer parks, as brothers and sisters to sing, "Jesus loves the little children of the world."

Prepare the way for the Lord's visitation in the consumer wasteland by reaching out to all people with the gospel. Make straight the highway for our God. The Lord will raise every valley and lay low every mountain and hill. The Lord will level the rough ground and rugged places so that the church will no longer put obstacles before the people, keeping many of them out with their targeting practices. On that day, the glory of the Lord will be revealed, and all humankind will see it together. May the coming kingdom of the nonhomogeneous and downwardly mobile God inspire us to hew out of those towering building programs of despair cornerstones of living hope to bear witness to God's triune name.

## STUDY QUESTIONS

1. What are the upsides and downsides of building churches based on "target" audiences?
2. How do trinitarian and eschatological images impact the way we think of diversity in the church today?
3. How can middle-class churches reach out to the poor in a way that draws them into the church community as equals?
4. What would you make of the following statement? "The best way to reach the rich is to help the rich be reached by the poor."

# A Postmodern Postscript

Postmodernity has heightened our awareness of the cultural forces that shape us. Theologians writing about the church must demonstrate a heightened awareness of those cultural forces that shape the church in the postmodern age. Moreover, it is important for theologians writing about the church to speak of specific ways in which the gospel of the Triune God's eschatological kingdom must shape the church if the church is to serve as an authentic witness to the gospel in the postmodern era.[1] These are two reasons that we have included cultural reflection chapters in this book. In what follows, there are specifically three themes we wish to highlight on how to envision ecclesiology culturally in the current cultural milieu. These themes are particularity, purity, and peace, and they bear directly on the well-being of the church and ecclesiology in a postmodern era.

## Particularity

Each church and each ecclesiology reflects a distinctive culture or cultures. This point is often lost on the fundamentalist-evangelical church. Dating back to the "Scopes Monkey trial," the fundamentalist-evangelical movement has commonly seen itself as existing outside culture, given that it was forced out of the public square. Regardless of its relationship to the prevailing culture around it, a given church is itself a cultural community with its own language, spoken or unspoken rules of conduct, expectations, and the like.

While it is possible to discern authentic and inauthentic expressions of the gospel and church in a given culture, it is impossible to separate the gospel and the church from culture. What Lesslie Newbigin says about the gospel bears directly on our understanding of the church, especially since the church is the "hermeneutic" of the gospel.[2] As Newbigin sees it, "The idea that one can or could at any time separate out by some process of distillation a pure gospel unadulterated by any cultural accretions is an illusion."[3] Newbigin is surely correct in his assertions, given the inseparable relation of Christ's deity to his concrete humanity, and Christ to the church. Just as it is impossible to separate Christ's deity and humanity—he is forevermore Jesus of Nazareth—so too it is impossible to separate Christ from the church, for the church is his body and bride. What is true for Christ must be true for his church as well.

Both church culture and the culture surrounding it always take particular form. As stated in chapter 13, the intersection and concrete engagement of Christ's church as a culture (which itself varies in diverse locations and over time) with other cultures involves the claim that the church as a culture in its engagement with other cultures is to be multifaceted and dynamic, in no way static, always particular, never abstract, ever contemporary, never remote. Thus, the culture of the church in Portland, Oregon, will be different from that of the church in Portland, Maine. So too the respective Baptist and Lutheran church cultures in the inner city of Chicago will be distinctively different from their Baptist and Lutheran church counterparts in rural Illinois. The same holds true for ecclesiology. Theology must always bear witness to the gospel's universal truth claims in particular cultural forms, including analysis of ecclesiology.

There is no such thing as an abstract culture, just as there is no such thing as an abstract Christ, an abstract church, or an abstract proclamation of Christ's Word. Christ himself took cultural form in a particular place and time. John writes: "The Word became flesh and made his dwelling among us" (John 1:14). Paul exclaims: "But when the fullness of the time had come, God sent forth his Son, born of woman, born under the law" (Gal. 4:4, NKJV). Just as Jesus becomes human in a particular place and time, so Christ's body as the church always takes particular form in concrete cultural contexts through the particularizing work of God's Spirit. The whole church is present in particular cultural locales, such as Corinth (1 Cor. 1:2). Christ, in the power of the Spirit, uniquely addresses each of the seven distinctive churches designated in Revelation 2 and 3 according to their cities.

The question, then, is not whether a given church or ecclesiology is encultur-ated, but what that particular church's culture is. Fears arise at this point for many conservatives: they may see us as coming dangerously close to reducing the gospel and the church to a predicate of a given culture, taking away from the gospel's and the church's universal claims. Such concerns, while understand-able, are premature and unbalanced. Such concerns are premature in that we are adamant in maintaining that the *eternal* Word becomes creaturely flesh; as enculturated, the Word *remains* transcendent. Such concerns are unbal-anced in that we must also maintain that while transcendent, the eternal Word always remains enculturated; there is no such thing as a bodiless and culture-less Jesus. Along these lines, belief that the true gospel is unenculturated is dangerous, in that it betrays blindness to one's own cultural reception of the gospel and, following from this, to the possible suppression and eradication of other (legitimate) gospel enculturations.

Concern for bearing authentic witness to the gospel involves giving careful consideration to legitimate and illegitimate gospel enculturations. While we do not share the rejection of an overarching biblical metanarrative, as some postmoderns contend, we do reject the Western and modern monopoly on the reading of that biblical metanarrative. Hermeneutical monopolies—privileging one culture's reception of the gospel over others—give the appearance of being concerned for absolutes. However, such absolutizing moves distort the gospel, giving rise to syncretistic aberrations.

With this in mind, there is a need for hermeneutical suspicion and humility. One way in which the church in the West can practice such hermeneutical humility is to listen attentively to non-Western church traditions, so as to learn of the gospel anew. Newbigin exhorts the Western church to become sensitive to its own particular tendencies in the direction of syncretism and to listen more attentively to the gospel proclamation as presented through non-Western world categories. By listening and learning from these other presentations of the gospel, the Western church will become more aware of its own gospel enculturation and perceive more keenly how to proclaim the gospel to its own audience. The Western church will also realize that the gospel, while enculturated in Western forms, is not limited to those forms, but transcends them.[4]

The non-Western church could certainly assist the Western church in several areas. We will mention only two here. The first concerns individualism, and the second concerns consumerism. We have discussed each of these problems in the course of this volume. Let us begin with individualism. In chapter 2, we mentioned how one of us learned a great deal about community life from a church made up of Middle Eastern Christians living in the States. Whereas in the West, we often define human identity in terms of what we as individuals do and accomplish, those in the non-Western world often define human identity in terms of who we are in relation to others in our immediate or extended communities. The latter orientation—communal identity—must come to serve as the foundation for how we as Christians and churches and theologians grade our purposes, activities, and accomplishments. The making of money, building of churches, and writing of books should serve people, not the other way around. We must guard against leveraging the church and spirituality as religious means to serve our own advancement as church leaders, religious scholars, and tent-making Christians.

This brings us to materialism and consumerism. Those who view human identity in terms of production often tend to reduce human worth to what we have accumulated as individuals. No doubt, this is one reason why we in the West consume more than those from the non-Western and developing world. In consumerist America, he who dies with the most toys wins, or, put differently, those who consume the most are more valuable than the rest. One of our friends—a Native American Christian leader—once said that while he often faces the syncretistic charge for use of native drums in worship, Anglo Christians have no trouble receiving the money in the offering plate from those corporate executives who have made their money through greed (at times, we would add, at the expense of indigenous peoples around the world). Our compartmentalized view of spirituality in the West makes it possible for Sunday Christians to exist—even to the point that we can take dirty money acquired during the week and launder it in time to put it in the offering plate on Sunday to legitimate illegal trade. No wonder Native Americans could never quite understand the white man's god's greed—why this god lusted so for the gold, trees, and fur, raping the land to fulfill his desires under the doctrine of Manifest Destiny (noted in chapter 13). Having raped the land from shore to shore, this god has turned his attention to other lands' shores—and their mountains and forests too.

The affluent Western church can learn a thing or two from the church in the developing world, which has not yet fallen prey to the Western god and its materialistic disease—affluenza. How often have we heard the testimonies of short-term missionaries returning from foreign fields, and about how churches in impoverished nations are often much better off spiritually than we are in the West? It is only by engaging adequately the particular enculturation of the gospel and church within one's own cultural forms and the forms of other cultures that one is able to safeguard against cultural and ecclesial imperialism and its bearing on wealth, among other things. The truly international gospel and ecumenical church are those that take account of the incarnation and particular presence of the Word in the plethora or plurality of cultures through the Spirit, not seeking after an amorphous gospel and church.

Kanzo Uchimura, a leading Japanese Christian scholar of Japan's Meiji era (1868–1912), takes aim at those in the West who contend for an amorphous Christianity:

> A Japanese by becoming a Christian does not cease to be a Japanese. On the contrary, he becomes more Japanese by becoming a Christian. A Japanese who becomes an American or an Englishman, or an amorphous universal man, is neither a true Japanese nor a true Christian.[5]

Uchimura goes on to speak of Paul, Luther, and Knox as those who "were not characterless universal men, but distinctly national, therefore distinctly human, and distinctly Christian."[6] He adds that those Japanese who convert to Christianity as "'universal Christians' may turn out to be no more than denationalized Japanese, whose universality is no more than Americanism or Anglicanism adopted to cover up their lost nationality."[7] We must deconstruct calls for an amorphous Christianity, gospel, and church by particularizing our churches and ecclesiologies and by accounting for the plurality of ways Christ is manifest through the church in diverse cultural settings.

While the Lord becomes "incarnate" in given cultures through his church in the power of the Spirit, he remains free to become enculturated in new forms. The Lord himself became incarnate in a given culture while ever remaining Lord in relation to that culture. The distinction between the "now" and "not yet" of the kingdom helps to safeguard against the divinization of a particular cultural form. While a particular church and church age participate in the kingdom, they do not exhaust the kingdom. Rightly conceived, contextualization does not spell domestication. As Newbigin again writes, "The word of God is to be spoken in every tongue, but it can never be domesticated in any."[8]

Particularity and plurality do not in themselves spell the domestication and relativizing of the church. All too often, though, the church has been domesticated and relativized when the ambition exists to make the church profitable by reducing it to a functionary of the state or a mere participant in the nurturing of civil society, or by transforming it into a business selling religious products. The church can profit society only when it remains the church—purely and simply. The only way to safeguard against such abuses is for the church to remain constant in its witness to the Triune God, who breaks into time and space through the Son and Spirit to establish the eschatological kingdom here on earth. This brings us to the second theme we wish to discuss for the development and doing of ecclesiology in a postmodern age.


## Purity

A growing number of younger evangelicals are sensitized to the gospel being reduced to this or that political platform or a formula used to make a profit.[9] In addition to being alert to these and other cultural trends, many of them long to see the gospel concretized in the life of the church as the Triune God's eschatological community. Unfortunately, individualistic spirituality and futuristic eschatology have created a vacuum for inauthentic expressions of community and politics to surface.

Attention was drawn to Stanley Hauerwas and Mark Sherwindt's claim in chapter 13 that "without the Kingdom-ideal, the church loses her identity-forming hope; without the church, the kingdom loses its concrete character."[10] From their perspective, the abstracting of the kingdom ideal from the church can lead to the underwriting of any notion of a just society.[11] For these authors, the church is the "now" of the "not yet" kingdom. Once this frame of reference is lost, the church so readily becomes a predicate of not-so-heavenly kingdoms.

Purity, not profitability in terms of affluence and influence, must mark the church. Only a pure church is a truly profitable church. Only then does

it serve the world as salt and light, as God's Sermon on the Mount community. With this in mind, sanctification pertains not simply to the individual
and invisible. It also pertains to the corporate and visible church. Bonhoeffer claims that "sanctification is . . . possible only with the visible church."
The visible church is set apart from the world in the world. The church (not
America)

> is the city set on the hill and founded on earth by the direct act of God, it is
> the "*polis*" of Matt. 5.14, and as such it is God's own sealed possession. Hence
> there is a certain "political" character involved in the idea of sanctification
> and it is this character which provides the only basis for the Church's political
> ethic. The world is the world and the Church the Church, and yet the Word of
> God must go forth from the Church into all the world, proclaiming that the
> earth is the Lord's and all that therein is. Herein lies the "political" character
> of the Church.[12]

Bonhoeffer lived downstream from the demise of the *Corpus Christianum*
and the marriage of church and empire in Europe. Today we are witnessing
the demise of Christendom in America: we no longer (not that we ever did!)
live in a Christian nation. While the religious Right is engaged in last-gasp
efforts to take back America, a church that is culturally sensitive to being a
beacon of light yet founded firmly as that city on a hill (Matt. 5:14–16) will
speak missionally and prophetically as a witness to that coming kingdom
in which it participates as that kingdom's community here on earth here
and now.

Ecclesiologies written in the postmodern climate would do well to take to
heart this post-Christendom context and realize that the demise of this unholy
marriage between Christianity and the American nation makes it possible for
the church to be a pure and truly profitable witness to the unadulterated gospel.
The fundamental problem with Christendom—old and new—is its belief that
European or American society is throughout a Christian world; this belief
makes it very difficult to see the non-Christian world and impedes "a genuine
encounter of the Gospel and man," as Karl Barth said.[13] The "strange" and
foreign gospel's confrontation of nominal Christendom is required if there is
to be a true and vital encounter between gospel and world.[14]

Such vital encounters will mean that ecclesiologies from this perspective
will call for the church to be less worldly and more worldly at the same time:
less worldly in that the unholy alliance between church and state/American
society is destroyed; more worldly in that the church can engage the state and
society more authentically as God's polis *in* the world—the communal and
co-missional people of the Triune God's eschatological kingdom. Only then
can it be a pure church. But purity and authentic particularity also involve the
demonstration of peace and a profound sense of unity in the visible church—
inside and outside the walls of our respective churches.

## Peace

We live in a post-Christian age that is often hostile toward the church. Since this is the case, why are we at war with one another? We must come to terms with the fact that we—the variety of members within a given church and the variety of churches—need one another to survive. We will never work together until we sense our need for one another and make peace. This point was brought home to us several years ago. A Christian minister laboring in one of America's depressed inner cities said to us that it was only when the various ethnic churches in his urban community realized that they could not survive without one another that they got beyond their petty differences and turf battles and worked together. With this example in mind, we need to move beyond comfort zones based on ethnicity and economics, along with competition over an increasingly smaller religious slice of the American cultural pie and contentious debates over doctrine, to seek after unity in the body. Otherwise, we will continue sending a very clear message to the surrounding, cynical world that our God's gospel is powerless to break down divisions among his people.

The church is a now-and-not-yet eschatological community birthed by the nonhomogeneous Triune God, who is the same yesterday, today, and forever. Since this is the case, why do we have visions for our respective churches that compete with God's ultimate, eschatological vision for his church? As the eschatological community of the Triune God, we need to live now in light of what will be. Our outreach must become as vast as God's expansive missional program, whereby we engage the world at our doorstep, not simply those who appear most like us.

We evangelicals have much to offer the greater body of Christ in terms of our emphasis on reconciliation and relationships. But our individualistic and antistructural bent also proves problematic when it comes to addressing pressing race and class problems (among others) in the American church and broader culture.[15] This bent disables us and makes it difficult for us to see how our homogeneous structuring of the church caters to individual personal preference and comfort levels. As a result, certain groups and their concerns are marginalized, while others (often those belonging to the dominant culture) advance. J. I. Packer puts it this way:

> Evangelical Christianity starts with the individual person: the Lord gets hold of the individual; the individual comes to appreciate certain circles—the smaller circle of the small group, the larger circle of the congregation. These circles are where the person is nurtured and fed and expanded as a Christian. So, we evangelicals are conditioned to think of social structures in terms of what they do for us as individuals. That's all right, but it does lead us to settle too soon for certain self-serving social structures. And we are slow to pick up the fact that

some of the social units that we appreciate for that reason can have unhappy spinoff effects on other groups.[16]

In light of these dynamics, it is important for us to move beyond promoting relationships and community with those with whom we feel most comfortable to promoting relationships based on the biblical model of community and neighbor love.

Philip Yancey's development of a point made by Henri Nouwen noted in chapter 2 deserves repeating here:

> Henri Nouwen defines "community" as the place where the person you least want to live with always lives. Often we surround ourselves with the people we most want to live with, thus forming a club or a clique, not a community. Anyone can form a club; it takes grace, shared vision, and hard work to form a community.[17]

Such "shared vision" involves the eschatological vantage point that people from every tongue and tribe will worship together at the throne. Evangelical ecclesiologies must attend to this eschatological vision in seeking to assist the church in bearing authentic witness to the gospel of the Triune God in our increasingly cynical and hostile culture.[18] In the face of such hostility, we must look increasingly to Christ, who is our peace and who has the authority and power to make peace between warring and hostile factions in our world today.

Paul speaks to this matter when he addresses Christ's authority and power to remove the ancient and deep-seated division between Jews and Gentiles:

> For he himself is our peace, who has made the two one and has destroyed the barrier, the dividing wall of *hostility*, by setting aside in his flesh the law with its commands and regulations. His purpose was to create in himself one new humanity out of the two, thus making peace, and in one body to reconcile both of them to God through the cross, by which he put to death their hostility. He came and preached peace to you who were far away and peace to those who were near. For through him we both have access to the Father by one Spirit. (Eph. 2:14–18, TNIV; italics added)

This passage has bearing not only on the Jew–Gentile divide, but upon all other divisions in Christ's community, so that God might construct a holy temple in which God dwells through his Spirit with Christ as its cornerstone (see Eph. 2:19–22).

The evangelical emphasis on personal relationship also has much to offer and much to hinder ecumenical partnerships. Positively speaking, evangelicals have much to contribute to ecumenical partnerships. It is encouraging, for example, to read the assessment of evangelical contributions in the Princeton Proposal for Christian Unity: evangelicals have much to offer to the greater church community given "their vitality, their zeal for evangelism, and their commitment to Scripture." The statement goes on to say that evangelicals "demonstrate a spirit of cooperation with each other and sometimes with others that breaks down old barriers, creates fellowship among formerly estranged Christians, and anticipates further unity. The free church ecclesiologies of some evangelicals bring a distinct vision of unity to the ecumenical task." This is an encouraging sign, given how often the broader ecclesial and theological community has looked askance at the evangelical tradition, including the supposed contributions it might bring to bettering ecclesial life and ecclesiology.[19]

Evangelicals have often been guilty of the same tendency, looking askance on the contributions of those from other traditions. The Princeton Proposal suggests that evangelicals often fail to discern living faith beyond their walls. Out of concern for the whole body, it is important that evangelicals "accept invitations to participate" in ecumenical dialogues, "discern and celebrate living faith beyond their boundaries," "practice hospitality and pursue catholicity" (as in unity with the whole church), and use "their resources" not only to benefit their own causes and concerns but also to "work for the health of all Christian communities."[20]

Evangelical scholars have been so concerned with defining who we are as evangelicals *in contradistinction from* other members and parts of Christ's body that we have been largely negligent in defining ourselves *in relation to* them. While doctrinal distinctives are important and must not be minimized, we must never allow our respective distinctives to keep us from seeking after unity.

Part of the problem stems from the historic fundamentalist–modernist divide, when evangelicals left mainline Protestant denominations and their seminaries in droves to found independent Bible schools and church traditions. The wounds associated with the religious-theological culture wars between left and right that were part and parcel of this migration are still often open, visible, and painful today. We must pray together that God would heal these wounds and make us one. Instead of various traditions trying to triumph over one another, they should put down their swords and take up their chisels, shovels, and picks to build a stronger community made up of formerly disparate but now reconciled parts, realizing that we are stronger together than we are separate, and that no church tradition makes up the entire house. At best, each tradition could claim for itself that it manifests best the definitive skeletal structure, requiring other traditions to flesh it out. No church tradition should exaggerate the role it has in building up Christ's body or denigrate the role of other traditions. Just as there are various members in every church fellowship, making up the one body, so each church has a role to play in building up the universal church.

A theology of unity and peace must undergird our desire for theological accuracy. Thus, we must not stop short at our differences or go around them, but go through them to ecumenical dialogue and partnerships. The same zeal that has led evangelical evangelists of the fundamentalist–modernist era to create broad platforms at their crusades and prayer rallies for those from various traditions to participate and take ownership must carry over into ministerial alliances and theological explorations, as in the writing of evangelical ecclesiologies in the postmodern and post-Christian era.

This is by no means an easy task. Without a living and firm eschatological hope in the Triune God removing all divisions in the body, we evangelicals and non-evangelicals alike will not have the strength to fight for unity and peace in the here and now. But with such hope in this God of holy love whom all of us as God's people are called in faith to worship lovingly in the Spirit and in the Word of truth, we will have the strength and sustenance to serve the church sacrificially and lovingly in the diversity of cultures, as God's missional people in the world. As we move forward in view of our wedding day, may we look to our God, who by his Spirit reorders the church as one through Word and sacrament in view of Christ's life. In like manner to husbands being called to love their wives in view of Christ's love for the church, so too we as God's people should love Christ's body as we do our own lives as members of that same body in view of our Lord's example to whom the apostle bears witness: "Christ loved the church and gave himself up for her to make her holy, cleansing her by the washing with water through the word, and to present her to himself as a radiant church, without stain or wrinkle or any other blemish, but holy and blameless" (Eph. 5:25–27, TNIV). As Christ's witnesses, may we give ourselves to this same end until that day. For while the church may have stains and wrinkles, blemishes and warts here and now, it is still Christ's bride and, as such, will be more beautiful than we could ever imagine then and there.

## STUDY QUESTIONS

1. How does your particular culture shape your understanding of the church?
2. What specific ways would you like to see the gospel of the Triune God's eschatological kingdom shape the church's witness in our postmodern setting?

# Recommended Readings

## Introduction

Donald Bloesch. *The Church: Sacraments, Worship, Ministry, Mission*. Christian Foundations. Downers Grove, IL: InterVarsity, 2005.

Tony Campolo. *Letters to a Young Evangelical: The Art of Mentoring*. New York: Basic Books, 2008.

Edmund P. Clowney. *The Church*. Contours of Christian Theology. Downers Grove, IL: InterVarsity, 1995.

Kenneth J. Collins. *The Evangelical Moment: The Promise of an American Religion*. Grand Rapids: Baker Academic, 2005.

Everett Ferguson. *The Church of Christ: A Biblical Ecclesiology for Today*. Grand Rapids: Eerdmans, 1996.

Thomas N. Finger. *A Contemporary Anabaptist Theology: Biblical, Historical, Constructive*. Downers Grove, IL: InterVarsity, 2004.

Veli-Matti Karkkainen. *An Introduction to Ecclesiology: Ecumenical, Historical and Global Perspectives*. Downers Grove, IL: InterVarsity, 2002.

Dan Kimball. *They Like Jesus, but Not the Church: Insights from Emerging Generations*. Grand Rapids: Zondervan, 2007.

John Meyendorff. *The Orthodox Church: Its Past and Its Role in the World Today*, with selected revisions by Nicholas Lossky. 3rd ed. Crestwood, NY: St. Vladimir's Seminary Press, 1996.

Donald Miller. *Blue Like Jazz: Nonreligious Thoughts on Christian Spirituality*. Nashville: Thomas Nelson, 2003.

Mark Noll and Carolyn Nystrom. *Is the Reformation Over? An Evangelical Assessment of Contemporary Roman Catholicism*. Grand Rapids: Baker Academic, 2005.

Thomas P. Rausch. *Towards a Truly Catholic Church: An Ecclesiology for the Third Millennium*. Collegeville, MN: Liturgical, 2005.

Robert Saucy. *The Church in God's Program*. Chicago: Moody, 1972.

John G. Stackhouse Jr., ed. *Evangelical Ecclesiology: Reality or Illusion?* Grand Rapids: Baker Academic, 2003.

————, *Evangelical Landscapes: Facing Critical Issues of the Day.* Grand Rapids: Baker Academic, 2002.

D. Elton Trueblood. *The People Called Quakers.* Richmond, IN: Friends United Press, 1985.

Timothy Ware. *The Orthodox Church.* New ed. London: Penguin, 1993.

Robert Webber. *Ancient-Future Faith: Rethinking Evangelicalism for a Postmodern World.* Grand Rapids: Baker Academic, 1999.

## Chapters 1 and 2

Avery Dulles. *Models of the Church.* New York: Image, 2002.

Stanley J. Grenz. *The Social God and the Relational Self: A Trinitarian Theology of the Imago Dei.* The Matrix of Christian Theology. Louisville: Westminster John Knox, 2001.

Colin E. Gunton. *The Promise of Trinitarian Theology.* 2nd ed. London: T&T Clark, 2004.

Joseph Hellerman. *The Ancient Church as Family.* Minneapolis: Fortress, 2001.

Paul Louis Metzger, ed. *Trinitarian Soundings in Systematic Theology.* London: T&T Clark, 2005.

Paul S. Minear. *Images of the Church in the New Testament.* Louisville: Westminster John Knox, 2004.

Lesslie Newbigin. *Household of God.* London: SCM, 1953.

Miroslav Volf. *After Our Likeness: The Church as the Image of the Trinity.* Grand Rapids: Eerdmans, 1997.

John Howard Yoder. *The Priestly Kingdom: Social Ethics as Gospel.* Notre Dame, IN: University of Notre Dame Press, 1985.

John D. Zizioulas. *Being as Communion: Studies in Personhood and the Church.* New ed. London: Darton, Longman & Todd, 2004.

## Chapters 3 and 4

Scott Bader-Saye. *The Church and Israel after Christendom: The Politics of Election.* Eugene, OR: Cascade, 2005.

Craig Blaising and Darrell Bock. *Progressive Dispensationalism.* Grand Rapids: Baker Academic, 1993.

Stephen Bouma-Prediger. *For the Beauty of the Earth: A Christian Vision of Creation Care.* Engaging Culture. Grand Rapids: Baker Academic, 2001.

Brian Daley. *The Hope of the Early Church: A Handbook of Patristic Eschatology.* New York: Cambridge University Press, 1991.

Oliver Davies, Paul D. Janz, and Clemens Sedmak. *Transformation Theology: Church in the World*. Edinburgh: T&T Clark, 2008.

Everett Ferguson. *The Church of Christ: A Biblical Ecclesiology for Today*. Grand Rapids: Eerdmans, 1996.

Stanley Hauerwas. *The Peaceable Kingdom*. Notre Dame, IN: University of Notre Dame Press, 1983.

George Eldon Ladd. *The Presence of the Future*. Grand Rapids: Eerdmans, 1974.

———, *A Theology of the New Testament*, edited by Donald A. Hagner. Grand Rapids: Eerdmans, 1993.

Jürgen Moltmann. *The Church in the Power of the Spirit: A Contribution to Messianic Ecclesiology*. Minneapolis: Fortress, 1993.

Paul Santmire. *Nature Reborn: The Ecological and Cosmic Promise of Christian Theology*. Minneapolis: Fortress, 2000.

N. T. Wright. *The New Testament and the People of God*. Minneapolis: Fortress, 1992.

John Howard Yoder. *The Royal Priesthood: Essays Ecclesiological and Ecumenical*. Grand Rapids: Eerdmans, 1994.

## Chapters 5 and 6

Simon Chan. *Liturgical Theology: The Church as Worshiping Community*. Downers Grove, IL: InterVarsity, 2006.

Rodney Clapp. *A Peculiar People: The Church as Culture in a Post-Christian Society*. Downers Grove, IL: InterVarsity, 1996.

Marva Dawn. *Reaching Out without Dumbing Down: A Theology of Worship for the Turn-of-the-Century Culture*. Grand Rapids: Eerdmans, 1995.

Aidan Kavanaugh. *On Liturgical Theology*. Collegeville, MN: Liturgical, 2002.

Ralph Martin. *Worship in the Early Church*. Grand Rapids: Eerdmans, 1964.

Henri Nouwen. *With Burning Hearts: A Meditation on the Eucharistic Life*. Maryknoll, NY: Orbis, 1994.

Robin Parry. *Worshipping Trinity: Coming Back to the Heart of Worship*. Bletchley, UK: Paternoster, 2005.

Alexander Schmemann. *For the Life of the World: Sacraments and Orthodoxy*. Crestwood, NY: St. Vladimir's Seminary Press, 1973.

James B. Torrance. *Worship, Community, and the Triune God of Grace*. Downers Grove, IL: InterVarsity, 1996.

Bernd Wannenwetsch. *Political Worship: Ethics for Christian Citizens*. Oxford Studies in Theological Ethics. Oxford: Oxford University Press, 2004.

Robert E. Webber. *Ancient-Future Worship: Proclaiming and Enacting God's Narrative*. Grand Rapids: Baker Books, 2008.

John Witvliet. *Worship Seeking Understanding: Windows into Christian Practice*. Grand Rapids: Baker Academic, 2003.

## Chapters 7 and 8

Kurt Aland. *Did the Early Church Baptize Infants?* Eugene, OR: Wipf and Stock, 2004.

Roland H. Bainton. "The Wild Boar in the Vineyard," in *Here I Stand: A Life of Martin Luther*. Nashville: Abingdon, 1978.

*The Catechism of the Catholic Church*. Liguori, MO: Liguori Publications, 1994.

William T. Cavanaugh. *Theopolitical Imagination: Discovering the Liturgy as a Political Act in an Age of Global Consumerism*. Edinburgh: T&T Clark, 2002.

————, *Torture and Eucharist: Theology, Politics, and the Body of Christ*. Challenges in Contemporary Theology. London: Blackwell, 1993.

Cyril of Jerusalem. *Promise and Presence: An Exploration of Sacramental Theology*. Bletchley, UK: Paternoster, 2006.

John E. Colwell. *Lectures on the Christian Sacraments: The Procatechesis and the Five Mystagogical Catecheses*. Edited by F. L. Cross. Crestwood, NY: St. Vladimir's Seminary Press, 1986.

Christopher J. Ellis. *Gathering: A Theology and Spirituality of Worship in Free Church Tradition*. London: SCM, 2004.

Walter A. Elwell, ed. *Evangelical Dictionary of Theology*. Grand Rapids: Baker Academic, 1984, s.v. "Baptism, Believers'" and "Baptism, Infant" by G. W. Bromiley.

Joachim Jeremias. *Infant Baptism in the First Four Centuries*. Eugene, OR: Wipf and Stock, 2004.

Aidan Kavanaugh. *The Shape of Baptism*. Collegeville, MN: Liturgical, 1991.

Martin Luther. *The Babylonian Captivity of the Church* in *Three Treatises*. Philadelphia: Fortress, 1966.

Maximus the Confessor. *The Church, the Liturgy and the Soul of Man: The Mystagogia of St. Maximus the Confessor*. Translated by Dom Julian Stead, OSB. Still River, MA: St. Bede's, 1982.

Alexander Schmemann. *The Eucharist: Sacrament of the Kingdom*. New York: St. Vladimir's Seminary Press, 1988.

James White. *Sacraments as God's Self-Giving*. Nashville: Abingdon, 2001.

————, *The Sacraments in Protestant Practice and Faith*. Nashville: Abingdon, 1999.

John Howard Yoder. *Body Politics: Five Practices of the Christian Community before the Watching World*. Scottdale, PA: Herald Press, 2001.

## Chapters 9 and 10

David Bartlett. *Ministry in the New Testament*. Minneapolis: Fortress, 1993.

Dietrich Bonhoeffer. *Life Together*. In *Dietrich Bonhoeffer Works*, vol. 5. Edited by Geffrey B. Kelley. Translated by Daniel W. Bloesch and James H. Burtness. Minneapolis: Fortress, 1996.

Marva J. Dawn. *Powers, Weakness, and the Tabernacling of God*. Grand Rapids: Eerdmans, 2001.

Hans Küng. *The Church*. Garden City, NY: Image, 1976.

Stephen Seamands. *Ministry in the Image of God: The Trinitarian Shape of Christian Service*. Downers Grove, IL: InterVarsity, 2005.

William Willimon. *Proclamation and Theology*. Horizons in Theology. Nashville: Abingdon, 2006.

John Howard Yoder. *The Fullness of Christ: Paul's Revolutionary Vision of Universal Ministry*. Elkhart, IN: Brethren, 1987.

## Chapters 11 and 12

Chad Owen Brand and R. Stanton Norman, eds. *Perspectives on Church Government: Five Views of Church Polity*. Nashville: Broadman and Holman Academic, 2004.

Raymond Brown. *Priest and Bishop: Biblical Reflections*. Eugene, OR: Wipf and Stock, 1999.

Steven Cowan, ed. *Who Runs the Church? 4 Views on Church Government*. Grand Rapids: Zondervan, 2004.

Stanley J. Grenz and Denise Muir Kjesbo. *Women in the Church: A Biblical Theology of Women in Ministry*. Downers Grove, IL: InterVarsity, 1995.

Henri de Lubac. *The Motherhood of the Church*. San Francisco: Ignatius, 1989.

Ronald Pierce, Rebecca Merrill Groothuis, and Gordon D. Fee, eds. *Discovering Biblical Equality: Complementarity without Hierarchy*. Downers Grove, IL: InterVarsity, 2004.

John Piper and Wayne Grudem, eds. *Recovering Biblical Manhood and Womanhood: A Response to Evangelical Feminism*. Wheaton: Crossway, 1991.

Joseph Cardinal Ratzinger. *God's Word: Scripture—Tradition—Office*. San Francisco: Ignatius, 2008.

Alexander Strauch. *Biblical Eldership: An Urgent Call to Restore Biblical Church Leadership*. Littleton, CO: Lewis and Roth, 1995.

Miroslav Volf. *After Our Likeness: The Church as the Image of the Trinity*. Grand Rapids: Eerdmans, 1997.

William Webb. *Slaves, Women, and Homosexuals: Exploring the Hermeneutics of Cultural Analysis*. Downers Grove, IL: InterVarsity, 2001.

## Chapters 13 and 14

Jeremy S. Begbie. *Resounding Truth: Christian Wisdom in the World of Music*. Engaging Culture. Grand Rapids: Baker Academic, 2007.

———, *Voicing Creation's Praise: Towards a Theology of the Arts*. Edinburgh: T&T Clark, 1991.

D. A. Carson. *Christ and Culture Revisited*. Grand Rapids: Eerdmans, 2008.

Craig A. Carter. *Rethinking Christ and Culture: A Post-Christendom Perspective*. Grand Rapids: Brazos, 2007.

Rodney Clapp. *Border Crossings: Christian Trespasses on Popular Culture and Public Affairs*. Grand Rapids: Brazos, 2000.

Andy Crouch. *Culture Making: Recovering our Creative Calling*. Downers Grove, IL: InterVarsity, 2008.

Craig Detweiler and Barry Taylor. *A Matrix of Meanings: Finding God in Pop Culture*. Engaging Culture. Grand Rapids: Baker Academic, 2003.

Colin E. Gunton. *The One, The Three and the Many: God, Creation and the Culture of Modernity*. The Bampton Lectures 1992. Cambridge: Cambridge University Press, 1993.

Robert K. Johnston. *Reel Spirituality: Theology and Film in Dialogue*. Engaging Culture. Grand Rapids: Baker Academic, 2006.

D. Stephen Long. *Theology and Culture: A Guide to the Discussion*. Eugene, OR: Cascade, 2008.

George M. Marsden. *Fundamentalism and American Culture: The Shaping of Twentieth-Century Evangelicalism, 1870–1925*. New York: Oxford University Press, 1980.

Paul Louis Metzger. *The Word of Christ and the World of Culture: Sacred and Secular through the Theology of Karl Barth*. Grand Rapids: Eerdmans, 2003.

John Milbank. *Theology and Social Theory: Beyond Secular Reason*. 2nd ed. London: Blackwell, 2006.

Lesslie Newbigin. *The Gospel in a Pluralist Society*. Grand Rapids: Eerdmans, 1989.

H. Richard Niebuhr. *Christ and Culture*. New York: Harper and Brothers, 1951.

Jaroslav Pelikan. *Jesus through the Centuries: His Place in the History of Culture*. New Haven: Yale University Press, 1999.

Glen Stassen, D. M. Yeager, and John Howard Yoder. *Authentic Transformation: A New Vision of Christ and Culture*. Nashville: Abingdon, 1996.

John R. W. Stott. *The Message of the Sermon on the Mount (Matthew 5–7)*. Edited by J. A. Moyer and John R. W. Stott. Downers Grove, IL: InterVarsity, 1978.

Paul Tillich. *Theology of Culture*. New York: Oxford University Press, 1959.

Robert E. Webber. *The Secular Saint: A Case for Evangelical Social Responsibility*. Eugene, OR: Wipf & Stock, 2004.

## Chapters 15 and 16

William J. Abraham. *The Logic of Evangelism*. Grand Rapids: Eerdmans, 1989.

Hans Urs von Balthasar. *Love Alone Is Credible*. Translated by D. C. Schindler. San Francisco: Ignatius, 2004.

Lois Barrett, ed. *Treasure in Clay Jars: Patterns in Missional Faithfulness*. The Gospel & Our Culture. Grand Rapids: Eerdmans, 2004.

Pope Benedict XVI. *Deus Caritas Est: God Is Love*. San Francisco: Ignatius, 2006.

David Bosch. *Transforming Mission: Paradigm Shifts in Theology of Mission*. Maryknoll, NY: Orbis, 1991.

Paul W. Chilcote and Laceye C. Warner, eds. *The Study of Evangelism*. Grand Rapids: Eerdmans, 2008.

Darrell L. Guder. *The Continuing Conversion of the Church*. The Gospel & Our Culture. Grand Rapids: Eerdmans, 2000.

————, ed. *Missional Church: A Vision for the Sending of the Church in North America*. The Gospel & Our Culture. Grand Rapids: Eerdmans, 1998.

Stanley Hauerwas and William H. Willimon. *Resident Aliens: Life in the Christian Colony*. Nashville: Abingdon, 1989.

Philip D. Kenneson and James L. Street. *Selling Out the Church: The Dangers of Church Marketing*. Nashville: Abingdon, 1997.

Paul Louis Metzger. *Consuming Jesus: Beyond Race and Class Divisions in a Consumer Church*. Grand Rapids: Eerdmans, 2007.

Harold Netland. *Dissonant Voices: Religious Pluralism and the Question of Truth*. Grand Rapids: Eerdmans, 1991.

————, *Encountering Religious Pluralism: the Challenge to Christian Faith and Mission*. Downers Grove, IL: InterVarsity, 2001.

Lesslie Newbigin. *Foolishness to the Greeks: The Gospel and Western Culture*. Grand Rapids: Eerdmans, 1986.

Bruce Nichols, ed. *In Word and Deed: Evangelism and Social Responsibility*. Exeter, UK: Paternoster, 1985.

John M. Perkins. *Beyond Charity: The Call to Christian Community Development*. Grand Rapids: Baker Books, 1993.

————, *Let Justice Roll Down*. 3rd ed. Ventura, CA: Regal Books, 2006.

————, *With Justice for All*. 3rd ed. Ventura, CA: Regal Books, 2007.

Soong-chan Rah. *The Next Evangelicalism: Freeing the Church from Western Cultural Captivity*. Downers Grove, IL: InterVarsity, 2009.

## Postscript

Carl E. Braaten and Robert W. Jenson, eds. *In One Body through the Cross: The Princeton Proposal for Christian Unity*. Grand Rapids: Eerdmans, 2003.

Stanley J. Grenz. *A Primer on Postmodernism*. Grand Rapids: Eerdmans, 1996.

Craig Ott and Harold A. Netland, eds. *Globalizing Theology: Belief and Practice in an Era of World Christianity*. Grand Rapids: Baker Academic, 2006.

James K. A. Smith. *Who's Afraid of Postmodernism? Taking Derrida, Lyotard, and Foucault to Church*. The Church and Postmodern Culture. Grand Rapids: Baker Academic, 2006.

# Appendix

## Types of Ecclesiology

**High church ecclesiology:** High view of church history and tradition. Emphasizes the liturgy and, above all, the Eucharist. Churches are generally structured episcopally (i.e., through a hierarchy of bishops who stand in communion with one another). Emphasizes salvation as membership in the church through participation in the sacraments. Generally holds to infant baptism. Close connection between baptism and initiation into the broad community of faith.

**Low church ecclesiology:** Generally suspicious of history and tradition. Emphasizes the Bible as the church's ultimate authority, and preaching is more central than the Eucharist or the liturgy. Churches tend to be structured congregationally (i.e., governed by the local congregation itself or through one or more elders appointed by congregations). Emphasizes salvation as the subjective appropriation and confession of faith in Christ. Generally holds to believers' baptism. Close connection between salvation, baptism, and committed discipleship in community.

**Strong ecclesiology:** Holds a high view of the role of the church in the economy of salvation. Understands that the church is the means by which God is at work in the world. A strong view of the church as the ongoing embodied presence of Christ in the world. The church participates in the mission of God to redeem the world. Membership in the visible church community is indispensable to Christian life and the shape of Christian salvation.

**Weak ecclesiology:** Holds a humble and limited view of God's role for the church in his plan of salvation. The church exists to strengthen and instruct the believer and to witness to God's work of salvation that takes place solely through God's action. The church does not participate in God's action but points away from itself to God's action outside of human effort. The emphasis is on the invisible church, the universal body of all people who believe in Christ throughout the world. All Christians are members of this church, and that is what is primary. Membership in a local congregation is for edification and growth, but is not central to salvation.

# Notes

## Introduction

1. Dan Kimball addresses people's attraction to Jesus and disillusionment with the church in *They Like Jesus, but Not the Church: Insights from Emerging Generations* (Grand Rapids: Zondervan, 2007). The overwhelmingly popular reception of Donald Miller's book *Blue Like Jazz: Nonreligious Thoughts on Christian Spirituality* (Nashville: Thomas Nelson, 2003) bears witness to spirituality's increasing appeal in contemporary culture and the decline of appeal in organized religion.

2. See the article "My Mother, the Church" by Nancy Kennedy and her references to a recent Gallup poll on this subject: http://www.chronicleonline.com/articles/2007/06/19/columns/grace_notes/grace770.txt.

3. Tony Campolo attributes to Augustine the statement that "the church is a whore, but she's my mother." Campolo refers to this claim in his appeal to young evangelicals not to leave organized religion and the local church because of its whoredom, but to passionately commit their lives to the church because it is their maternal lifeline to God. Tony Campolo, *Letters to a Young Evangelical: The Art of Mentoring* (New York: Basic Books, 2006), 68.

4. John Calvin, *Institutes of the Christian Religion*, ed. John T. McNeill (Philadelphia: Westminster, 1960), Bk. IV, Ch. 1, 1016.

5. Martin Luther, *The Freedom of a Christian,* in *Martin Luther's Basic Theological Writings,* ed. Timothy F. Lull (Minneapolis: Fortress, 1989), 604.

6. Kimlyn J. Bender, "The Church in Karl Barth and Evangelicalism—Conversations across the Aisle," 5. The paper was presented at the conference "Karl Barth and American Evangelicals: Friends or Foes?" June 27, 2007, Princeton Theological Seminary, Princeton, New Jersey. Bender refers the reader to Kenneth J. Collins, *The Evangelical Moment: The Promise of an American Religion* (Grand Rapids: Baker Academic, 2005), 33.

7. John G. Stackhouse Jr., *Evangelical Landscapes: Facing Critical Issues of the Day* (Grand Rapids: Baker Academic, 2002), 28.

8. The statement, while brief, addresses the Bible, the Trinity, the person and work of Christ, the Holy Spirit, salvation, sanctification for a godly life, and the resurrection to heaven or hell, but not the church, other than to affirm that there is a spiritual unity among believers. See www.nae.net/index.cfm?FUSEACTION=nae.statement_of_faith.

9. Mark Noll and Carolyn Nystrom, *Is the Reformation Over? An Evangelical Assessment of Contemporary Roman Catholicism* (Grand Rapids: Baker Academic, 2005), 145.

10. Bruce Hindmarsh, "Is Evangelical Ecclesiology an Oxymoron?" in *Evangelical Ecclesiology: Reality or Illusion?* (Grand Rapids: Baker Academic, 2003), ed. John G. Stackhouse Jr., 15–37. Hindmarsh himself believes that evangelicalism has its own "ecclesial consciousness," if not a developed specific ecclesiology per se.

11. Instead of saying that evangelicals don't have an ecclesiology, it may be better to say that the majority of evangelicals have a weak ecclesiology. A weak ecclesiology is characterized by a minimalist view of God's role for the church in his plan of salvation. It tends to emphasize the individual Christian and sees the church as existing primarily to nurture the believer. A weak ecclesiology also highlights the "universal" and "invisible" nature of the church to the detriment of the "local" and "visible" church. By contrast, a strong ecclesiology emphasizes that vital participation in a local and visible church community is indispensable to the cultivation of Christian life and shaping of salvation, and that the church as the ongoing embodied presence of Christ in the world is the Triune God's primary means for advancing his kingdom mission, not the individual Christian or another agency or organization. The reader is encouraged to look to the appendix at the close of this volume titled, "Types of Ecclesiology," formulated by Halden Doerge. One of the aspirations for this book is that evangelicals will come away with a greater desire to foster a strong ecclesiology that nonetheless resonates with their largely non-hierarchal and non-liturgical orientation and sensibilities.

12. Many Dispensationalists typically would not affirm that the church is promised in the Hebrew Scriptures, but that the church is there only in mystery form. Moreover, certain Reformed would maintain that the church is not simply promised in the OT, but actually present there as well.

13. We recognize that many Reformed churches and most Pentecostal and charismatic churches may identify themselves as evangelical. But they are also rooted in movements separate from the American evangelical movement and so are considered separately in this argument.

14. It has been typical for preachers in evangelical churches to preach verse by verse through whole books of the Bible rather than to preach topically and use biblical passages to support their points. Nevertheless, over the last few decades, topical preaching has been on the rise significantly. Also, in some evangelical churches, the "praise chorus" section of the worship service now rivals the sermon in terms of time and emphasis.

15. This antipathy for traditional liturgy is an example of how evangelicalism, while moving beyond fundamentalism, remained connected to its fundamentalist roots.

## Chapter 1  The Church as a Trinitarian Community: The *Being*-Driven Church

1. In her discussion of God's "intrinsically relational and communicative nature" in Jonathan Edwards's thought, Amy Plantinga Pauw speaks of Edwards's agreement with Richard Sibbes's notion of the spreading goodness of God. Amy Plantinga Pauw, *The Supreme Harmony of All: The Trinitarian Theology of Jonathan Edwards* (Grand Rapids: Eerdmans, 2002), 126–27. Note also her references to Sibbes and Maximus the Confessor on 127.

2. For an example of this approach, see Rick Warren, *The Purpose Driven Church: Growth without Compromising Your Message & Mission* (Grand Rapids: Zondervan, 1995). While Warren's five purposes are certainly biblical (see 103–7), and while he is right in claiming that all too often our work for God crowds out our worship of God (103), he needs to make clear that our purposeful worship and love for God flow out of God's loving us into being as his people.

3. See chapter 6 of Paul Louis Metzger, *Consuming Jesus: Beyond Race and Class Divisions in a Consumer Church* (Grand Rapids: Eerdmans, 2007), for a discussion of the co-missional God. See also George R. Hunsberger's discussion of this theme in "Missional Vocation: Called and Sent to Represent the Reign of God," in *Missional Church: A Vision for the Sending of the Church in North America,* ed. Darrell L. Guder (Grand Rapids: Eerdmans, 1998), 82.

4. For an in-depth treatment of various New Testament images of the church, see Paul S. Minear, *Images of the Church in the New Testament* (Louisville: Westminster John Knox, 2004).

5. Irenaeus writes that God did not need help in "accomplishing of what He had Himself determined with Himself beforehand should be done, as if He did not possess His own hands. For with Him were always present the Word and Wisdom, the Son and the Spirit, by whom and in whom, freely and spontaneously, He made all things, to whom also He speaks, saying, 'Let Us make man after Our image and likeness'; He taking from Himself the substance of the creatures [formed], and the pattern of things made, and the type of all the adornments in the world." James Donaldson and Alexander Roberts, eds., *Ante-Nicene Christian Library*, vol. 1, *The Writings of Irenaeus*, by St. Irenaeus, trans. Alexander Rovers and W. H. Rambaut (Edinburgh: T&T Clark, 1867), 487–88.

6. Dietrich Bonhoeffer, *Creation and Fall: A Theological Interpretation of Genesis 1–3* (New York: Macmillan, 1959), 37.

7. Ibid.

8. See Karl Barth's discussion of the divine plural in Genesis 1:26 in *Church Dogmatics*, III/1, *The Doctrine of Creation*, ed. G. W. Bromiley and T. F. Torrance (Edinburgh: T&T Clark, 1958), 191–92. In addition to rejecting with others the interpretation that the divine plural is merely "a formal expression of dignity," Barth also rejects the modern dismissal of the early church's exegesis. He writes that "it may be stated that an approximation to the Christian doctrine of the Trinity—the picture of a God who is the one and only God, yet who is not for that reason solitary, but includes in Himself the differentiation and relationship of I and Thou—is both nearer to the text and does it more justice than the alternative suggested by modern exegesis in its arrogant rejection of the Early Church (cf. for instance, Gunkel)." Quoting Genesis 1:26, the early-second-century theologian Irenaeus writes: "Now man is a mixed organization of soul and flesh, who was formed after the likeness of God, and moulded by His hands, that is, by the Son and Holy Spirit, to whom also He said, 'Let Us make man.'" *Writings of Irenaeus*, 463.

9. Bonhoeffer, *Creation and Fall*, 36.

10. The terms *transitive* and *intransitive* apply to verb types. A transitive verb is one that requires a direct object, while an intransitive verb does not require a direct object. We are employing these terms to refer to different kinds of love—that love that requires another, versus that love that is self-focused. God's love always requires a direct object: God loves another. Sinful, self-centered love is the kind of love that does not have an object other than itself. It is in this sense that we refer to it as intransitive.

11. This position stands in marked contrast to John Piper's adaptation of the Westminster Confession in his book *Desiring God: Meditations of a Christian Hedonist*, 2nd ed. (Sisters, OR: Questar, 1996). For a fuller treatment of this position, see Paul Louis Metzger, "The Half-way House of Hedonism: Potential and Problems in John Piper's *Desiring God*," in *CRUX* 41, no. 4 (2006): 21–27.

12. See, for example, Vladimir Lossky, *The Mystical Theology of the Eastern Church* (Crestwood, NY: St. Vladimir's Seminary Press, 1976), 10.

13. God recapitulates the creation, taking it beyond its original state. As the recapitulated cosmos, God transforms the creation, taking it forward to a state beyond what Adam and Eve could ever have imagined. To recapitulate a story is to revise it and transform it in its retelling. Irenaeus taught that in Christ the story of Adam was recapitulated, but this time as a defeat of sin rather than a defeat by it. God had intended for Adamic humanity to mature and grow beyond its initial condition, but that process was interrupted by the fall into sin. Christ's refusal and overcoming of sin makes it possible for the human story to resume its dramatic movement toward maturity and wholeness.

14. Barth states it well in his discussion of Colossians 1:15–18 and its relation to Genesis 1: Paul "has no abstract Christological interest in this equation. Or rather, this Christological

equation has at the root an inclusive character, so that it is also an ecclesiological and therefore even an anthropological equation." Barth, *Church Dogmatics,* III/1, 205.

15. It is well worth noting at this point that at the giving of Christ's Spirit at Pentecost to build the church we find the reversal of Babel. Everyone present at Pentecost hears God's glad tidings to bless humanity in Christ spoken in their native tongues (Acts 2:5–12). Because God's glory is communal and communicative, God shares it with his people so that they might be one and might reflect God's love in Christ to the world (John 17:22–23). See the perceptive comments of J. Kameron Carter on recapitulation as the "pentecostalization of the world" in "Race, Religion, and the Contradictions of Identity: A Theological Engagement with Douglas's 1845 Narrative," in *Modern Theology* 21, no. 1 (2005): 58–59.

16. On the subject of the Jewish people not commonly referring to God as "Father," see D. A. Carson, *The Sermon on the Mount: An Evangelical Exposition of Matthew 5–7* (Grand Rapids: Baker Books, 1978), 62.

17. Joseph Hellerman, *The Ancient Church as Family* (Minneapolis: Fortress, 2001), 221.

18. Many theologians throughout the history of the church have understood the Angel of the Lord to be the pre-incarnate Christ.

19. In the Hebrew Scriptures prior to the building of the temple, the tabernacle (which was a holy tent) represents God's presence and the way in which he dwells with his people. In this volume, we often use the term "Hebrew Scriptures" to refer to the thirty-nine books of the "Old Testament." We use these terms ("Old Testament" and "Hebrew Scriptures") interchangeably, because "Old Testament" on its own could wrongly be taken to signify that these writings are no longer applicable.

20. While it was not Cyprian of Carthage (d. 258) who began the discussion of this issue, it is to his name that *Extra Ecclesiam nulla salus* ("Outside the church there is no salvation") is attached historically. Cyprian's concern was for those heretics and schismatics who found themselves outside the church, primarily because of their own voluntary separation from it. He writes: "Whoever breaks with the Church and enters on an adulterous union, cuts himself off from the promises made to the Church; and he who has turned his back on the Church of Christ shall not come to the rewards of Christ: he is an alien, a worldling, an enemy. You cannot have God for your Father if you have not the Church for your mother . . . Whoever breaks the peace and harmony of Christ acts against Christ; whoever gathers elsewhere than in the Church, scatters the Church of Christ . . . If a man does not keep this unity, he is not keeping the law of God; he has lost his faith about Father and Son, he has lost his life and his soul." Cyprian of Carthage, *The Unity of the Catholic Church,* in Robert L. Ferm, *Readings in the History of Christian Thought* (New York: Holt, Reinhart and Winston, 1964), 435.

21. See Heiko Augustinus Oberman, *Luther: Man Between God and the Devil* (New Haven: Yale University Press, 1989), 183–84.

22. Martin Luther, *The Freedom of a Christian,* in *Martin Luther's Basic Theological Writings,* ed. Timothy F. Lull (Minneapolis: Fortress, 1989), 604.

23. Righteousness on this account is more than forensic. God declares us righteous because we are one flesh with Christ through the Spirit. Thus, righteousness is ultimately participational and relational. See Paul Louis Metzger, "Mystical Union with Christ: An Alternative to Blood Transfusions and Legal Fictions," in *Westminster Theological Journal* 65 (2003): 201–13. See also Veli-Matti Karkkainen, *One with God: Salvation as Deification and Justification* (Collegeville, MN: Liturgical, 2005).

24. Luther, *Freedom of a Christian,* 604. Hosea is addressing Israel, but Paul claims that God's people, to whom Christ is married, includes Israel and the church. From our perspective, the "church" is a New Testament reality. Having said that, believing Old Covenant Israel is in Christ and therefore part of the church now.

25. John R. W. Stott, *The Message of the Sermon on the Mount (Matthew 5–7)* (Leicester, UK: InterVarsity, 1978), 39.

26. Luther claims that the believer in Jesus does not live "in himself, but in Christ and in his neighbor. Otherwise he is not a Christian. He lives in Christ through faith, in his neighbor through love. By faith he is caught up beyond himself into God. By love he descends beneath himself in to his neighbor. Yet he always remains in God and in his love." Luther, *Freedom of a Christian,* 623.

27. The *Catechism of the Catholic Church* states: "Since Christ entrusted to his apostles the ministry of reconciliation [a footnote at this point in the text refers the reader to Jn. 20:23 and 2 Cor. 5:18], bishops who are their successors, and priests, the bishops' collaborators, continue to exercise this ministry. Indeed bishops and priests, by virtue of the sacrament of Holy Orders, have the power to forgive all sins 'in the name of the Father, and of the Son, and of the Holy Spirit.'" *Catechism of the Catholic Church* (Liguori, MO: Liguori Publications, 1994), sec. 1461, 367.

28. It is important to safeguard the balance between the church as a visible and invisible reality. The Catholic catechism speaks of the church as both "visible and spiritual." *Catechism,* sec. 771, 203. The Reformer John Calvin gave special consideration to the church as invisible, in part so as to guard against the excesses of Roman Catholic institutionalism in his day, on the one hand, and nominal Christianity on the other. However, Calvin sought to maintain balance between consideration of the church as visible and invisible. See John Calvin, *Institutes of the Christian Religion,* ed. John T. McNeill (Philadelphia: Westminster, 1960), Bk. IV, Ch. 1, 1016, 1021–24. In view of the fundamentalist–modernist controversy, many evangelicals left mainline denominational structures in the early to middle part of the twentieth century to found *independent* Bible churches. Fundamentalist-evangelicals tended to emphasize the invisible over the visible, though they also certainly saw the need for some form of organization and structure as well as the importance of making visible their faith in community. In our day, due to certain forms of religious pluralism, the excesses of American individualism, disillusionment with the local church, and the consumerist ideology (church shopping), some believers have gone even further, completely abandoning active participation in local, visible, concrete manifestations of the invisible church. While it is important to safeguard against the excesses of ecclesial institutionalism and nominal Christianity—thus, the need for emphasizing the invisible church—it is equally important to stress that the invisible church ever takes concrete form in local, visible assemblies.

29. Millard J. Erickson, *Christian Theology,* vol. 3 (Grand Rapids: Baker Books, 1985), 1033.

30. See the discussion of the American religious enterprise and free market spirituality in Roger Finke and Rodney Stark, *The Churching of America, 1776–1990: Winners and Losers in Our Religious Economy* (New Brunswick: Rutgers University Press, 1992), 17.

31. Carl E. Braaten and Robert W. Jenson, eds. *In One Body through the Cross: The Princeton Proposal for Christian Unity* (Grand Rapids: Eerdmans, 2003), 42–43.

32. We are not suggesting the elimination of denominations or ecclesiastical traditions. We are concerned for the cultivation of grace wed to truth and partnerships between groups. One example is the partnership between evangelicals and Catholics. See "Evangelicals & Catholics Together: The Christian Mission in the Third Millennium," in *First Things* 43 (May 1994): 15–22.

33. According to John Zizioulas, the Spirit conditions and constitutes Christ and the church. The Spirit also makes of Christ the eschatological human. See John D. Zizioulas, *Being as Communion: Studies in Personhood and the Church* (Crestwood, NY: St. Vladimir's Seminary Press, 1997), 111, 130, 139.

34. Such consummation in eternity is not static. The relational union, while perfect, will continue to deepen. Gregory of Nyssa also conceives of our eternal state in dynamic terms. See his section titled "Eternal Progress," in *Gregory of Nyssa: The Life of Moses* (New York: Paulist Press, 1978), 111–20.

35. Colin E. Gunton, *Act and Being: Towards a Theology of the Divine Attributes* (London: SCM, 2002), 146.

36. Ibid., 118.

37. The reader can find a picture of the icon at http://www.valley.net/~transnat/trinlg .html.

38. Boris Bobrinskoy, *The Mystery of the Trinity: Trinitarian Experience and Vision in the Biblical and Patristic Tradition,* trans. Anthony P. Gythiel (Crestwood, NY: St. Vladimir's Seminary Press, 1999), 12.

39. Ibid., 141.

40. Robert W. Jenson, *Systematic Theology,* vol. 2, *The Works of God* (Oxford: Oxford University Press, 1999), 19. The quotation from Jonathan Edwards is found in the *Miscellanies,* (entry nos. a–z, aa–zz. 1–500), *The Works of Jonathan Edwards,* vol. 13, ed. Thomas A. Schafer (New Haven, CT: Yale University Press, 1994).

## Chapter 2  The Trinitarian Church Confronts American Individualism

1. Bertrand Russell, *Why I Am Not a Christian: And Other Essays on Religion and Related Subjects,* ed. Paul Edwards, with an appendix on the "Bertrand Russell Case" (New York: Simon and Schuster, 1952), 42.

2. See for example George M. Marsden, *Fundamentalism and American Culture: The Shaping of Twentieth-Century Evangelicalism, 1870–1925* (New York: Oxford University Press, 1980), 153–98.

3. See Rudolph Nelson, "Fundamentalists at Harvard: The Case of Edward J. Carnell," *Quarterly Review* 2, no. 2 (1982), for an example of this orientation. While rejecting liberal institutions and starting their own theological schools, fundamentalist-evangelical scholars desired to receive credible degrees, and so they attended these bastions of liberal scholarship. According to Nelson, these early fundamentalist-evangelical leaders were also motivated to attend Harvard and similar schools because of their desire for "encountering the Beast of Scholarly Unbelief in its own labyrinth and emerging with new confidence and new powers" (84).

4. The notes in the margins of *The Serendipity New Testament for Groups* place much emphasis on the individual. Under "Reflect" for the discussion based on salvation in Romans 3:21–31, four out of five of the questions read: "If you had to explain the gospel from this passage alone, what would you say? When did the message of God's grace become real to you? What difference is it making in your life right now?" The next question deals with groups: "What prejudices and barriers exist in the church today?" It concludes, though, with, "How could you help to break them down?" Lyman Coleman, ed., *Serendipity New Testament for Groups,* 2nd ed., *New International Version* (Littleton, CO: Serendipity House, 1987), 306.

5. Brian D. McLaren, *A New Kind of Christian: A Tale of Two Friends on a Spiritual Journey* (San Francisco: Jossey-Bass, 2001), 130.

6. See David F. Wells's discussion and critique of "Self-Piety," chapter 4 of *No Place for Truth, or, Whatever Happened to Evangelical Theology?* (Grand Rapids: Eerdmans, 1993).

7. In a former era, churches competed with one another based on doctrines and sacraments: who had the best beliefs and best practices? Today, competition often takes the form of which churches are the best family-services providers.

8. Pastors today often note how many families in their churches do not come to church during sports seasons. Sports teams no longer give deference to Sundays and Christian worship. Nor do many families in the church. These families would do well to take to heart the writer of Hebrews' exhortation in Heb. 10:24–25.

9. Rick Warren, *The Purpose Driven Life: What on Earth Am I Here For?* (Grand Rapids: Zondervan, 2002), 17.

10. According to George Hunsberger, "both members and those outside the church expect the church to be *a vendor of religious services and goods.*" See George R. Hunsberger, "Missional Vocation: Called and Sent to Represent the Reign of God," in *Missional Church: A Vision for the Sending of the Church in North America,* ed. Darrell L. Guder (Grand Rapids: Eerdmans,

1998), 84. Roger Finke and Rodney Stark speak to the matter of the survival of the fittest in the free-market religious system in America: "Religious organizations must compete for members and . . . the 'invisible hand' of the marketplace is as unforgiving of ineffective religious firms as it is of their commercial counterparts." See Roger Finke and Rodney Stark, *The Churching of America, 1776–1990: Winners and Losers in Our Religious Economy* (New Brunswick: Rutgers University Press, 1992), 17.

11. Robert E. Webber critiques the individualized notion of salvation—"enlightenment evangelism"—in *Ancient-Future Faith: Rethinking Evangelicalism for a Postmodern World* (Grand Rapids: Baker Academic, 1999), 143–46. See also Everett Ferguson, *The Church of Christ: A Biblical Ecclesiology for Today* (Grand Rapids: Eerdmans, 1997), chapter 3.

12. Dietrich Bonhoeffer, *Letters and Papers from Prison,* rev. ed., ed. Eberhard Bethge (New York: Macmillan, 1967) 203–4.

13. Maximus the Confessor spoke of the church in microcosm terms. See St. Maximus the Confessor, *The Church, the Liturgy and the Soul of Man,* trans. Dom Julian Stead, OSB (Still River, MA: St. Bede's, 1982), 66–67, 69. So too did Martin Luther King Jr. See Richard Lischer, *The Preacher King: Martin Luther King, Jr. and the Word That Moved America* (New York: Oxford University Press, 1995), 16–17.

14. Philip Yancey, "Why I Don't Go to a Megachurch," *Christianity Today,* May 20, 1996, 80.

## Chapter 3 The Church as an Eschatological Community

1. Stanley Grenz, *Theology for the Community of God* (Grand Rapids: Eerdmans, 2000), 479.

2. Eschatology technically means "last things," not "future things." So biblical eschatology is not merely about events that are future from where the church finds itself in history. Eschatology, from the standpoint of the biblical prophets, is about the events that fulfill God's plan to redeem his creation from the fall and to bring his people into everlasting, perfect relationship with him. Thus, some eschatological events, such as the cross, burial, and resurrection, have already happened. Others, such as the second coming of Christ, remain future.

3. Several books that explain and chronicle the development toward this consensus are: George Eldon Ladd, *The Presence of the Future* (Grand Rapids: Eerdmans, 1974); George Eldon Ladd, *A Theology of the New Testament* (Grand Rapids: Eerdmans, 1974); Darrol Bryant and Donald Dayton, *The Coming Kingdom: Essays in American Millennialism and Eschatology* (Barrytown, NY: Rose of Sharon Press, 1983); Shirley Jackson Case, *The Millennial Hope* (Chicago: University of Chicago Press, 1958); W. G. Kummel, *Promise and Fulfillment: The Eschatological Message of Jesus,* trans. Dorothea Barton (London: SCM, 1971); Timothy Weber, *Living in the Shadow of the Second Coming: American Premillennialism: 1875–1982,* 2nd ed. (Grand Rapids: Academic Books, 1983); and Craig Blaising and Darrell Bock, eds. *Dispensationalism, Israel and the Church* (Grand Rapids: Zondervan, 1992).

4. For examples of first-century Jewish messianic expectations, see intertestamental literature such as *Psalms of Solomon* 17, *The Testament of Judah* 24, *1 Enoch* 48, and *IV Ezra* 13.

5. George Eldon Ladd, *A Theology of the New Testament,* rev. ed. (Grand Rapids: Eerdmans, 1993), 336.

6. Typically, dispensational premillennialists, while they understand Revelation to describe an actual future period of human history known as the "great tribulation" immediately preceding the second coming of Christ, do not see the church as being present during this period, having been "raptured" at the beginning of this seven-year tribulation. Thus, John's image of the church as the suffering people of God is not a part of dispensationalists' interpretation of Revelation. However, the rest of the images presented here still apply, since they are images of the victorious church that returns with Christ at his second coming to begin the millennial period. Nondispensational premillennialists and those who hold to nonfuturist or nonhistorical interpretations of Revelation understand the entire book as being descriptive of the church.

7. There are numerous issues in the way we have approached this chapter—the relationship of the church to the kingdom of God, the church as the promised people of God, the ultimate image of the church as a multiethnic world community, etc.—which raise the question of the relationship between the church and Israel. The history of this discussion has resulted in a general polarity. Either Israel has been replaced by the church, which is the "new Israel," meaning that the nation of Israel is no longer a unique factor in the future of the people of God, or the church is a community separate from Israel in God's plan. In this second scenario God will, in the last resort, fulfill his historic promises to Israel, bring the nation as a whole to faith in Christ in the last days, and return to earth to rule the millennium from the nation of Israel. Numerous mediating positions have also been suggested. Our position, briefly, is that we do not subscribe to a replacement theology that makes Israel of no account in the future of the people of God. Rather, we find evidence to believe that God may still work with Israel in a unique way at some time in the future, perhaps as a factor in the events of Christ's second advent and millennial rule (Rom. 9–11). But neither do we subscribe to the view that sees the church as a kind of parenthesis in history, essentially fading into the background of the biblical narrative of the eschaton, while Israel again becomes the focus of the biblical idea of the people of God. The ultimate biblical vision of the people of God is the vision of the church, one people, Jew and Gentile, living together forever in union with Christ and each other in the worship and service of God. For further discussion of the church and Israel, see Scott Bader-Saye, *The Church and Israel after Christendom: The Politics of Election* (Eugene, OR: Cascade Books, 2005).

8. The scholar most influential in bringing American evangelicals to this position in the middle of the twentieth century was George Eldon Ladd. His work, originally published in his *Jesus and the Kingdom*, later retitled *The Presence of the Future*, became the basis for what has become the consensus position among dispensationalists and nondispensationalists as well.

9. Historical surveys of the eschatology of the early church are rare. One excellent exception is Brian Daley's *The Hope of the Early Church: A Handbook of Patristic Eschatology* (New York: Cambridge University Press, 1991. See also J. N. D. Kelly, *Early Christian Doctrines* (San Francisco: Harper Collins, 1978), 459–89.

10. Cyril Richardson, *Early Christian Fathers* (New York: Macmillan, 1970), 93.

11. Ibid.

12. Early church adherents include Papius, Pseudo-Barnabus, Justin Martyr, Irenaeus, Tertullian, and Hippolytus.

13. Influential teachers of dispensationalism in America include C. I. Scofield, Lewis Sperry Chafer, John Walvoord, Dwight Pentecost, and Charles Ryrie. All of these were connected to Dallas Theological Seminary, which remains the most prominent institutional proponent of dispensationalism in America.

14. William E. Blackstone, *Jesus Is Coming* (New York: Fleming H. Revell, 1908), 82–84. Our contention is that when Paul speaks in Ephesians of the church as a "mystery," he does not mean that the Hebrew Scriptures did not anticipate it or even speak of it. Rather, the church fulfills God's promises about a future kingdom for his people, Israel, without eliminating the idea that God may still have future plans for ethnic/national Israel as part of his kingdom promises.

15. In this chapter, when we speak of evangelism vs. social action/engagement, we have the following definitions in mind. By *evangelism* we refer to the practice of verbal proclamation of the gospel by Christians to non-Christians for the purpose of introducing them to the saving message and person of Jesus Christ and calling them to faith. By *social action/engagement* we mean those actions taken by the church for the betterment of human beings and society. This is to be understood in the broadest terms and could be represented by the church working for such things as better living conditions for the poor, better health care, better race relations, racial and gender equality, etc. We understand and agree that these actions can be and are seen by many to be forms of evangelism. But in this discussion, we will address evangelism and social action as different but complementary endeavors.

16. This oft-repeated line was spoken by the famous radio preacher J. Vernon McGee but is usually attributed to D. L. Moody.

17. Brian Daley, *The Hope of the Early Church: A Handbook of Patristic Eschatology* (Peabody, MA: Hendrickson, 2003), 78.

18. Augustine, *City of God,* 20.9, in *Nicene and Post-Nicene Fathers,* vol. 2, ed. Philip Schaaf (Grand Rapids: Eerdmans, 1979), 430.

19. Perry Miller, *Errand into the Wilderness* (Cambridge: Harvard University Press, 1956), 5.

20. Ernest Lee Tuveson, *Redeemer Nation: The Idea of America's Millennial Role* (Chicago: University of Chicago Press, 1968), 99.

21. Jonathan Edwards, "Some Thoughts concerning the Revival of Religion in New England," *The Works of Jonathan Edwards,* 2 vols., ed. John E. Smith (New Haven: Yale University Press, 1772), 2:353.

22. For further information on this idea, see Conrad Cherry, *God's New Israel: Religious Interpretations of American Destiny* (Chapel Hill: University of North Carolina Press, 1998); and Paul Boyer, *When Time Shall Be No More* (Cambridge: Belknap Press of Harvard University Press, 1992).

23. See Donald Dayton, "Millennial Views and Social Reform in Nineteenth-Century America," in *The Coming Kingdom.* For an excellent study on the relationship of millennial movements to social crises, see Michael Barkun's *Disaster and the Millennium* (New Haven: Yale University Press, 1974). Among his descriptions of the sensitivities of these communities to crisis, he remarks that members of such movements perceive themselves moving into a new form of religious piety and from error to truth. They also see themselves reacting against inequities perceived in traditional institutions. These sensitivities would be represented in the reactions of dispensational fundamentalists against society and mainline Christianity.

24. Austin Flannery, OP, ed., *Vatican Council II: The Conciliar and Post Conciliar Documents,* rev. ed., *Lumen Gentium* (Boston: St. Paul Editions, 1987), 48. See also Henri de Lubac, *The Splendor of the Church* (San Francisco: Ignatius Press, 1986), 156–59, 238–39.

25. See Craig Blaising and Darrell Bock, *Progressive Dispensationalism* (Grand Rapids: Baker Academic, 1993).

26. Cyprian of Carthage, *On the Unity of the Church,* 13–14, in *Ante-Nicene Fathers,* vol. 5, eds. Alexander Roberts and James Donaldson (Peabody, MA: Hendrickson, 1994), 425–26.

27. Two key problems common to the critique of the Reformers were that the institution of the church had become more authoritative than the scriptures and that the church had become more instrumental in distributing the grace of God than the Spirit of God himself.

28. See, for example, Avery Dulles, *Models of the Church* (Dublin: Gill and Macmillan, 1988); Dennis Doyle, *Communion Ecclesiology: Vision and Versions* (Maryknoll, NY: Orbis, 2000).

29. John Calvin, *Institutes,* 4.1.7. Note Calvin's departure from medieval Catholicism here. All baptized members are not necessarily true members of the church, since they might actually be unbelievers. Thus, Calvin's definition of the church is more individualistic than institutional. On this point see John Howard Yoder, *The Royal Priesthood: Essays Ecclesiological and Ecumenical* (Grand Rapids: Eerdmans, 1994), 57ff, where Yoder traces this separation of the visible and invisible church to Constantine. Also, see Robert Webber's discussion of this idea in his *Ancient-Future Faith: Rethinking Evangelicalism for a Postmodern World* (Grand Rapids: Baker Academic, 1999).

30. We will discuss this further below as we examine the theology of Paul in the chapter "The Church as a Serving Community."

31. Ladd, *Presence of the Future,* 268.

32. G. L. Alrich, "Our Comforting Hope," *Our Hope* 21.8 (February 1915): 180.

33. The positive side of this emphasis on evangelism was a renewed effort in missionary activity. Dispensationalists were important in the foundation of the Student Volunteer Movement and other such missions organizations. As a result, premillennialists became *the* force in overseas missions at the end of the nineteenth and into the twentieth century. Great emphasis

was placed on bringing the good news of Christ to as many people as possible, as quickly as possible, before the Lord's return.

34. J. E. Conant, "The Growing Menace of the 'Social Gospel,'" in *Fighting Fundamentalism: Polemical Thrusts of the 1930s and 1940s,* ed. Joel Carpenter (New York: Garland, 1988), 61.

35. For a brief discussion of Luther's theory, see Robert Webber, *The Secular Saint* (Grand Rapids: Zondervan, 1979). See the more extensive discussion of Luther's theopolitical views in Bernd Wannenwetsch, *Political Worship: Ethics for Christian Citizens* (Oxford: Oxford University Press, 2004), 59–71.

36. See his chapter on the church in Carl Braaten and Robert Jensen, eds., *Christian Dogmatics,* vol. 2 (Philadelphia: Fortress, 1984), 179–248.

37. Ibid., 2:247.

38. Donald Bloesch, *The Church: Sacraments, Worship, Ministry, Mission* (Downers Grove, IL: InterVarsity, 2002), 69–81.

39. For an excellent article on this work, see D. Bentley Hart, "The 'Whole Humanity': Gregory of Nyssa's Critique of Slavery in Light of his Eschatology," *Scottish Journal of Theology* 54, no. 1 (2001): 51–69.

40. Ibid., 55.

41. For a summary of the place of women in the ancient world, see Klyne Snodgrass, *Ephesians: The NIV Application Commentary* (Grand Rapids: Zondervan, 1996).

42. Walter Kaiser, *Toward an Old Testament Theology* (Grand Rapids: Zondervan, 1978).

43. The emphasis here is on the community rooted in the presence of the King with his people. Similarly, in Exodus 33, Moses argues that the only way the nations will know that Israel is the people of God is if God is with them.

44. Irenaeus of Lyons, *Against Heresies,* Bk. 3, Ch. 24, *Ante-Nicene Fathers,* vol. 1, 458.

45. Flannery, ed., *Lumen Gentium,* 48. See also Simon Chan, *Liturgical Theology: The Church as Worshipping Community* (Downers Grove, IL: InterVarsity, 2006).

46. See Karl Barth, *The Preaching of the Gospel* (Philadelphia: Westminster, 1963).

47. Given the nature of Christ as the ultimate sacrifice, we would argue that, for the church, this aspect of reconciliation of believers around the altar is represented in the Eucharist. See the chapter below on the church as a sacramental community.

48. See Thomas N. Finger, *Christian Theology: An Eschatological Approach* (Scottdale, PA: Herald Press, 1989), 2:247–69, for an extended discussion of the "already/not yet" in the apostolic church.

49. Note that Ephesians 2:11–22 is a restatement of this same basic argument by Paul. Gentiles, who were once outside of the promise given to national/ethnic Israel, are now brought near to God through the blood of the cross. But again, Paul's vision here is not merely one of individual salvation of Gentiles but of the reconciliation of alienated segments of society, Jews and Gentiles, into one body, one building, with Jesus Christ as the cornerstone. On this point see N. T. Wright, *The Climax of the Covenant: Christ and the Law in Pauline Theology* (Minneapolis: Fortress, 1994).

50. Irenaeus of Lyons, *Against Heresies,* 21.

51. For a full discussion of the place of the church's eschatological battle against the demonic in the theology of Paul, see Clinton E. Arnold, *Powers of Darkness: Principalities and Powers in Paul's Letters* (Downers Grove, IL: InterVarsity, 1992). See also Walter Wink, *The Powers,* 3 vols. (Minneapolis: Fortress, 1984–92).

52. Cyril of Jerusalem, *Mystagogical Catechesis I: On the Rites before Baptism,* 3–6.

## Chapter 4 Eschatology, the Church, and Ecology

1. Tom Sine, "Who Is Tim LaHaye?" *Sojourners* (September/October 2001): 2.

2. Jonathan Wilson, "Evangelicals and the Environment: A Theological Concern," *Christian Scholars Review* 28, no. 2 (1998): 301.

3. Lynn White, "The Historical Roots of Our Ecologic Crisis," *Science* 155, no. 3767 (1967).

4. It must be noted that premillennialists, both in the early church and in twentieth-century dispensational thought, have had a clear theology of the perfection of creation in the kingdom of God. But classic dispensationalists, since they tended to see the kingdom as essentially future, did not draw its environmental implications back into the present.

5. Richard Young, *Healing the Earth: A Theocentric Perspective on Environmental Problems and Their Solutions* (Nashville: Broadman and Holman, 1994), 139.

6. Paul Santmire, *Nature Reborn: The Ecological and Cosmic Promise of Christian Theology* (Minneapolis: Fortress, 2000), 133.

7. David Garland, *Colossians/Philemon: The NIV Application Commentary* (Grand Rapids: Zondervan, 1998), 94.

8. At this point, a comment is in order on the tension created by 2 Peter 3, which presents an image oriented more toward destruction and re-creation than to renewal and transformation. It must be conceded that Peter's language leans toward destruction rather than renewal with his use of the word "destruction" and his reference to the basic elements of the cosmos. On the other hand, the textual evidence leads most scholars to conclude that the word at the end of verse 10 should be "laid bare" rather than "burned up," which sounds like purification rather than destruction.

Peter himself used renewal-type language in his speech in Acts 3. In verse 21 he says that the Messiah must remain in heaven until the time comes for God to restore everything. Peter's imagery also relies heavily on Isaiah, who often mixes imagery of destruction/newness with those of renewal/transformation. The NT also uses both kinds of imagery in the same passages. Revelation 21:1 indicates the passing away of heaven and earth, while verse 5 talks of God making all things new, which sounds like renewal. In contrast to Peter, Paul's eschatology of the cosmos in Romans 8 simply cannot be read in terms of destruction. Paul clearly has healing and transformation in mind.

In summary, the Bible speaks in paradoxical terms on this issue, while not contradicting itself. The fact is, that both renewal/transformation and destruction/replacement are present in the text, so both must be embraced. The text speaks of something that is obviously impossible for us to understand. So it uses various images from our current frame of reference, doing the best it can in human terms to explain a reality beyond the bounds of our comprehension. For a comprehensive exegetical consideration on this text, see Douglas Moo, *2 Peter/Jude: The NIV Application Commentary* (Grand Rapids: Zondervan, 1996), 200–202.

9. Francis Schaeffer, "Pollution and the Death of Man," in *The Complete Works of Francis Schaeffer: A Christian Worldview*, vol. 5 (Westchester: Crossway, 1982), 37–76.

10. Ernest Lucas, "The New Testament Teaching on the Environment," *Transformation* 16 (1999): 98.

11. For further discussion on how creation has a voice, see Rodney Clapp's comments on how nature praises God by being itself: Rodney Clapp, *Tortured Wonders: Christian Spirituality for People, Not Angels* (Grand Rapids: Brazos, 2004), 128–30.

12. We are not environmental scientists, but common knowledge of environmental issues would suggest a number of concrete ways in which the church can be involved in creation care. An obvious issue is recycling. Church offices should recycle or use as scratch paper the reams of corrected or unused documents that often end up in the trash. Aluminum soda cans from large church picnics should be gathered and turned in to metal recyclers. Churches can get involved in cleaning up the environment near the church property, perhaps adopting a highway or organizing trash removal crews. Churches can also volunteer to help with reforestation where the land has been stripped by logging or by natural disaster. Church building managers can get their power companies to do energy audits, perhaps not only helping them use less energy, but bringing a cost savings that could be turned into money for missions. Churches can intentionally

use ecologically friendly methods of landscaping and gardening. Finally, preaching is important in creation care as well. Pastors need to make their parishioners aware when the Bible affirms God's care for his creation. They also need to teach that damaging the environment often damages people, often affecting the poor more than others. For more information on creation care, consider the following organizations: Restoring Eden, the Christian Environmental Network, and the National Association of Evangelicals (all of which can be reached online). Also consider watching Bill Moyers's excellent PBS documentary *Is God Green?*

## Chapter 5  The Church as a Worshipping Community

1. Donald Bloesch, *The Church: Sacraments, Worship, Ministry, Mission* (Downers Grove, IL: InterVarsity, 2002), 117.

2. Similar statements come from theologians across the spectrum of Christian traditions. Reformed theologian Donald Bloesch argues that theology is both dogmatic and doxological (ibid.). Charismatic theologian Rodman Williams writes that worship is the primary function of the church. See Rodman Williams, *Renewal Theology: The Church, the Kingdom and Last Things* (Grand Rapids: Zondervan, 1992), 87. Anglican theologian Rowan Williams suggests that theology should be divided into celebratory, communicative, and critical dimensions. Rowan Williams, *On Christian Theology* (Oxford: Blackwell, 2000), xiii.

3. Westminster Larger Catechism, Question 1.

4. Irenaeus of Lyons, *Against Heresies,* 1.22.1.

5. Robin Parry, *Worshipping Trinity* (Bletchley, UK: Paternoster, 2005), 102–21.

6. Cf. Augustine, *On the Trinity,* Book 9; Jonathan Edwards, "Treatise on Grace," in *The Works of Jonathan Edwards. Vol. 21: Writings on the Trinity, Grace, and Faith,* ed. Sang Hyun Lee (New Haven: Yale University Press, 2003), 186–89.

7. See Parry, *Worshiping Trinity,* 112–15.

8. Philip Schaff, ed., *The Creeds of Christendom,* 6th ed., vol. 3 (Grand Rapids: Baker Books, 1993), 59.

9. James B. Torrance, *Worship, Community, and the Triune God of Grace* (Downers Grove, IL: InterVarsity, 1996), 39.

10. We see this in Harnack, for instance, where religion is essentially turned into ethics. For him, Christ is not the God who engages us relationally, but only an example of God's character. See also G. K. Chesterton's provocative discussion of this theme in *Orthodoxy* (New York: Image Books, 1959), 141–42.

11. The latter of these was the result of much of late-nineteenth- and early-twentieth-century liberal Christianity, illustrated by theologians such as Adolf von Harnack and Henry Nelson Wieman.

12. Our thanks to Dr. Ray Lubeck, professor of Hebrew Bible at Multnomah University, who helped us understand the theology of worship in the Psalms.

13. Cf. Kallistos Ware, "The Earthly Heaven," in *Eastern Orthodox Theology: A Contemporary Reader,* ed. Daniel B. Clendenin (Grand Rapids: Baker Academic, 1995), 12. See also Alexander Schmemann, *For the Life of the World: Sacraments and Orthodoxy* (Crestwood, NY: St. Vladimir's Seminary Press, 1973).

14. This idea is in conflict with the practice of the homogeneous unit principle, elucidated by Donald McGavran, Peter Wagner, and others in the 1970s. The homogeneous unit principle has become a guiding principle for much church growth in the megachurch era. The idea is that if a church targets a particular segment of society and shapes its programs to attract just those people, it will create an affinity group and the church will grow faster. Does it work? It would appear so, from the explosive growth of many megachurches, especially those that are white and upwardly mobile. But a question we find rarely asked is, "What kind of church does this strategy create?" Our own sense is that this strategy will almost always fail to create a church that looks anything like the one at the end of the biblical metanarrative. The church today needs

to seriously rethink this approach. Interestingly, Bill Hybels, who used such narrow targeting strategies to build the iconic Willow Creek Community Church, has begun to consider some of the downsides in his interaction with minority pastors. See the interview published in *Christianity Today* 49, no. 4 (April 2005). Also see Paul Louis Metzger, *Consuming Jesus: Beyond Race and Class Divisions in a Consumer Church* (Grand Rapids: Eerdmans, 2007).

15. Cf. Walter Kaiser, *Toward an Old Testament Theology* (Grand Rapids: Zondervan, 1978), and J. Barton Payne, *The Theology of the Older Testament* (Grand Rapids: Zondervan, 1962).

16. Rudolph Otto, *The Idea of the Holy: An Inquiry into the Non-Rational Factor in the Idea of the Divine and Its Relation to the Rational* (New York: Oxford University Press, 1958).

17. Ralph Martin, *Worship in the Early Church* (Grand Rapids: Eerdmans, 1964), 14.

18. Otto, *Idea of the Holy,* 140.

19. Marva Dawn, *Reaching Out without Dumbing Down: A Theology of Worship for the Turn-of-the-Century Culture* (Grand Rapids: Eerdmans, 1995).

20. Søren Kierkegaard, *Devotional Classics,* eds. Richard Foster and James Bryan Smith (San Francisco: HarperCollins, 1993), 107.

21. It is clear in Acts 10 that worship/praise was a component of the manifestation of the Holy Spirit. Because this event is just one example of a paradigm illustrated in chapters 2, 8, 10, and 19, it is assumed that worship/praise was a part of each of these events, even if praise is not specifically mentioned.

22. Paul gets at this idea as well in Ephesians 4, explaining that the grace of Christ, even Christ himself, is mediated to us through one another in the church through the practicing of the gifts of the Spirit.

23. An obvious practical response to this theology is that worship leaders should strive to use worship forms that foster community rather than individuality, that invite the congregation into participation rather than mere observation. One example of a common worship-leading practice that discourages community is the presence of music leaders who stand in front of the audience singing with their eyes closed. This posture does not engage the community but disengages the leader from everyone around him or her, giving others the impression that this person is having his or her own "me and Jesus" moment, and that no one else is included.

24. The subject of the relationship between the priesthood and the laity in the Catholic and Orthodox communion is a complicated one. Both continue to contend for a substantive difference in the role, authority, and position of the priest as mediator. In the Catholic Church, there is a significant amount of latitude among theologians as to how distinct this separation actually is. And to be sure, Vatican II, especially in the *Decree on the Apostolate of the Laity,* raised the level of involvement of the laity in all areas of church ministry, including the celebration of the sacraments. For a brief explanation of the Catholic view, see Richard McBrien, *Catholicism* (Oak Grove, MN: Winston Press, 1981), 679–80, 808–11. For a brief comment on the Orthodox view, see John Karmiris, "Concerning the Sacraments," in Clendenin, *Eastern Orthodox Theology,* 22–23. For a more extended treatment, consult Schmemann, *For the Life of the World.*

25. See, for example, Millard Erickson, *Christian Theology* (Grand Rapids: Baker Academic, 1985), 1056–57; Wayne Grudem, *Systematic Theology* (Grand Rapids: Zondervan, 1994), 1003; and James Montgomery Boice, *Foundations of the Christian Faith* (Downers Grove, IL: Inter-Varsity, 1986), 589.

26. The glory-focused theology of John Piper, author of *Desiring God,* has become very popular in evangelical circles in the last decade, but it is not without its detractors. To encourage glorifying God, even with the added attraction of enjoying him, before loving God always raises the danger of a duty-based glorification, which departs from the relational ethos of the God who initiates encounter with humanity by loving humanity. To put it succinctly, "Though one can glorify God without loving God, one cannot love God without also desiring to glorify God. Put differently, the person who loves God longs to glorify God, while the person who glorifies

God does not necessarily love God." Paul Louis Metzger, "The Halfway House of Hedonism: Potential Problems in John Piper's *Desiring God*," *CRUX* (Winter 2005) 41:4, 21–27. See also Arthur McGill's trinitarian account of divine glory in *Death and Life: An American Theology* (Eugene, OR: Wipf and Stock, 1987), 66–69.

27. Deuteronomy 5:10; 6:5; 7:9, 12, 13; 10:12, 19; 11:1, 13, 22; 13:3, 6; 19:9; 21:15–16; 30:6, 16; 20; 33:3.

28. Stanley Grenz, *Theology for the Community of God* (Grand Rapids: Eerdmans, 1994), 491.

29. Cf. texts like Isaiah 1 and 58, Malachi 2, etc.

30. Robert Webber, *Ancient-Future Faith: Rethinking Evanglicalism for a Postmodern World* (Grand Rapids: Baker Academic, 1999), 99.

31. Note that Pope Benedict XVI's recent encouragement for parishes to provide a Latin mass is not a return to pre–Vatican II ideas. He is simply allowing for the traditional mass for those who desire it.

32. For the historical background of the fundamentalist/modernist controversy, cf. George Marsden, *Fundamentalism and American Culture* (New York: Oxford, 1982), and Mark Noll, *American Evangelical Christianity: An Introduction* (Oxford: Blackwell, 2001).

33. Considered a segment of evangelicalism, churches of the Pentecostal and charismatic traditions would argue correctly that they have always been characterized by a high level of congregational participation in worship. It has not, however, been a participation through the means of historic Christian liturgy, but instead has created a liturgy largely its own. For historical background, cf. Grant Wacker, *Heaven Below: Early Pentecostals in American Culture* (Cambridge: Harvard University Press, 2001), and Vinson Synan, *The Century of the Holy Spirit: 100 Years of Pentecostal and Charismatic Renewal, 1901–2001* (Nashville: Thomas Nelson, 2001). See also the fascinating contribution of Pentecostal theologian Simon Chan, who seeks to bring into conversation the participatory aspects of Pentecostal worship and the riches of the Catholic and Orthodox liturgical traditions. *Liturgical Theology: The Church as Worshipping Community* (Downers Grove, IL: InterVarsity, 2006), esp. 147–66.

34. It is our contention that the "breaking of the bread" here is the Lord's Supper. This breaking of bread seems to be an actual part of the worship service, as opposed to the communal meal that took place apart from that service. Also, Luke uses the concept of breaking bread to refer to the Eucharist, both in the passion narrative and in the story of the disciples on the road to Emmaus in Luke 24. See also Marva Dawn, *Powers, Weakness, and the Tabernacling of God* (Grand Rapids: Eerdmans, 2001), 98–100.

35. Cf. his *Letter to the Ephesians* 20:2, and *Letter to the Smyrnaeans* 7:1.

36. Justin Martyr, *First Apology,* chapter 67 in Richardson, *Early Christian Fathers,* (New York: Macmillan, 1970), 287–88.

37. *The Apostolic Tradition* is an early manual for church life, which includes forms of worship. It comes from the third century and is the earliest extrabiblical example of worship and service forms in the church.

38. Some groups have been reticent to use forms they do not see in the Bible. The Church of Christ, for example, has traditionally not used musical instruments. And some very conservative Reformed churches practice what is known as the regulative principle of worship, which uses only those worship forms seen in the scriptures, reasoning that God has ordained the only proper forms of worship and that no one should be forced to worship in a way that God has not ordained. For examples of a strong regulative principle of worship, see John Murray, *Collected Writings of John Murray*, vol. 1 (Edinburgh: Banner of Truth, 1976), 165–68; and the Westminster Confession of Faith, 20.2. For a more moderated view, see Edmund Clowney, *The Church* (Downers Grove, IL: InterVarsity, 1995), 117–36.

39. Carl E Braaten and Robert W. Jenson, eds. *Christian Dogmatics*, vol. 2 (Philadelphia: Fortress, 1984), 231.

40. Ibid., 232.

41. Ibid., 233.

42. All references in this section are taken from the *Catechism of the Catholic Church.* (Ligouri, MO: Ligouri Publications, 1994), sections 1066 and following.

43. Ibid., 1082.

44. Ibid., 1091.

45. *Christian Theology* by Erickson, *Foundations of the Christian Faith* by Boice, and *Systematic Theology* by Grudem. Boice and Grudem each use the term once, Erickson not at all.

46. Grudem, *Systematic Theology*, 1012, note 14.

47. Robert Saucy, *The Church in God's Program* (Chicago: Moody, 1972), 177–90.

48. Webber, *Ancient-Future Faith*, 109. See also Wannenwetsch, *Political Worship: Ethics of Christian Citizens* (Oxford: Oxford University Press, 2004), 68–69.

49. Webber, *Ancient-Future Faith*, 107.

50. Adalbert Hamman, ed. *The Mass: Ancient Liturgies and Patristic Texts* (Staten Island, NY: Alba House, 1967), 20. For another important early church testimony to the importance of the scriptures in worship, see the *Apostolic Tradition of Hippolytus,* Part IV, 35. Here the believers are urged to get to church as much as possible to hear the instruction from God's Word, through which the believer will hear God speaking and encounter the Holy Spirit. Thus, the scriptures are understood to be an important way of encountering God relationally, not just learning about him intellectually.

51. This is seen in the typical evangelical practice of celebrating the Lord's Supper only monthly or quarterly instead of weekly.

52. For an explanation of the various views of the Eucharist, see below in "The Church as a Sacramental Community."

53. For discussions on this idea, see Eddie Gibbs, *Church Next: Quantum Changes in How We Do Ministry* (Downers Grove, IL: InterVarsity, 2000); Dan Kimball, *The Emerging Church: Vintage Christianity for New Generations* (Grand Rapids: Zondervan, 2003); Tom Beaudoin, *Virtual Faith: The Irreverent Spiritual Quest of Generation X* (San Francisco: Jossey-Bass, 1998).

54. This imagery of Christ as the host of the table is often lost on those church traditions that pass the bread and the cups through the pew-seated rows of worshippers. This practice makes it difficult for believers to sense that they are coming to the table to meet Christ there. For an extended discussion of this imagery in the Eucharist, cf. Henri Nouwen, *With Burning Hearts: A Meditation on the Eucharistic Life* (Maryknoll, NY: Orbis, 1994).

55. Saucy, *Church in God's Program,* 184.

56. Grenz, *Theology for the Community of God,* 492.

57. This pattern of prayer has commonly taken the form of the acronym "ACTS," for "adoration, confession, thanksgiving, and supplication" as a way for Christians to memorize a biblical pattern of prayer. To see how prayers have fit into the liturgy of the church throughout its history, cf. Frank C. Senn, *Christian Liturgy: Catholic and Evangelical* (Minneapolis: Fortress, 1997).

58. There are many sources for traditional church prayers. One of the most common and accessible is the *Book of Common Prayer.* In the United States it is published by the Episcopal Church as a representative of the Anglican communion worldwide. The most recent edition is from 1979, and it is available online in its entirety.

59. Good sources for examples of prayers of the church from its early years to the present include Hamman, ed., *The Mass*; R. C. D. Jasper and G. J. Cuming, eds., *Prayers of the Eucharist: Early and Reformed* (New York: Oxford, 1980); and *The Book of Common Prayer.* Excellent ancient sources include *The Apostolic Tradition* of Hippolytus (third century) and *The Apostolic Constitutions* (fourth century).

60. Richard Leonard, "Service of the Word," in *The Complete Library of Christian Worship,* vol. 1, *The Biblical Foundations of Christian Worship,* ed. Robert E. Webber (Nashville: Star Song, 1993), 304.

61. Nicholas Ayo, *The Lord's Prayer: A Survey Theological and Literary* (Notre Dame, IN: University of Notre Dame Press, 1992), 121.

62. The value of corporate recitation of well-known prayer can also be experienced by corporate proclamation of the historic creeds, a practice largely abandoned by evangelicals in the twentieth century. Reciting the Nicene or Apostles' creeds, for example, can give a congregation a sense of unity with the entire church throughout the ages and also provides a valuable way for people to memorize the key theological foundations of the Christian faith.

## Chapter 6 The Worshipping Church Engages Culture

1. An ex–rock drummer argued for this formula in a local church attended by one of the authors in the early 1970s. There are other evangelicals who have recently argued more positively concerning rock music. See Craig Detweiler and Barry Taylor, *A Matrix of Meanings: Finding God in Pop Culture* (Grand Rapids: Baker Academic, 2003).

2. Stanley Grenz, "(Pop) Culture: Playground of the Spirit or Diabolical Device?" *Cultural Encounters: A Journal of the Theology of Culture* 1, no. 1 (2004): 17.

3. In the 1960s, it would have been typical in evangelical churches to hear people speak disapprovingly of Martin Luther King because he was suspected of connections to communism. More recently, it is his sexual infidelities that are mentioned as cause for doubt.

4. *Confessions of St. Augustine*, 1.1.

5. Tom Beaudoin, *Virtual Faith: The Irreverent Spiritual Quest of Generation X* (San Francisco: Jossey-Bass, 1998), xiv.

6. Grenz, "(Pop) Culture," 15.

7. John Witvliet, *Worship Seeking Understanding: Windows into Christian Practice* (Grand Rapids: Baker Academic, 2003) 115.

8. Ibid., 118.

9. Donald Bloesch, *The Church: Sacraments, Worship, Ministry, Mission* (Downers Grove, IL: InterVarsity, 2002), 131.

10. Ibid., 135.

11. Marva Dawn, *Reaching Out without Dumbing Down: A Theology of Worship for the Turn-of-the-Century Culture* (Grand Rapids: Eerdmans, 1995), 98.

12. Witvliet, *Worship Seeking Understanding*, 119.

13. Dawn, *Reaching Out without Dumbing Down*, 59.

14. Witvliet, *Worship Seeking Understanding*, 119.

15. One of the most dangerous examples of culture co-opting the church for its own self-image is when churches put the American flag on the platform next to the symbols of Jesus and his church. The church is to bear witness to the biblical trinitarian God and to his good news of redemption in Jesus Christ. To connect those things to America through the flag is to baptize the role and activity of the United States in the world as if it represents the agenda of God. To do this is to seriously undercut the church's witness in a world where American policies and activity are often despised as arrogant and immoral.

16. Another form of this same issue pertains to ethnic churches. For example, should a church made up of Vietnamese immigrants remain a Vietnamese church indefinitely? This is a difficult question. Clearly, there is a need for immigrant churches that worship in the language of the worshippers, for only then can they worship with understanding. But three generations later, when most of the members of the church are Americans and native English speakers, should the church work to preserve itself as a Vietnamese church? The upsides include the preservation of ethnic culture and the ability to reach out effectively to other Vietnamese. But the downsides are significant. Such a church will be virtually unable to connect to anyone outside its own ethnicity. Also, as successive generations begin to identify more as Americans than as Vietnamese (we do not suggest that this is either a good thing or a bad thing), they will find it increasingly difficult to worship in a Vietnamese church. The sad reality today is that many churches in this situation

are splitting, the young people leaving to form a new American church, thus losing the wisdom of age and ethnic culture. A better solution would entail some maintenance of ethnicity along with the adoption of more culturally relevant forms.

17. Walter Brueggemann, *Biblical Perspectives on Evangelism: Living in a Three-Storied Universe* (Nashville: Abingdon, 1993), 121.

18. We would contend, obviously, that baptism is the same kind of unchangeable symbol. For water, and even the practice of pouring it, being immersed in it, and passing through it, represents so many important theological realities in the biblical narrative, there is just no way to duplicate that meaning with any other symbol.

19. Creative worship leaders have done a number of things to draw young people into authentic worship while still using more traditional forms. Examples include: taking classic hymns and rearranging the music, making its feel more contemporary while still maintaining the traditional words; and telling the history behind certain hymns (e.g., Horatio Spafford's composition of *It Is Well with My Soul* after learning of the drowning of his children in a shipwreck), investing the hymn with a power and relevance that transcends its cultural form.

20. Dawn, *Reaching Out without Dumbing Down*, 59.

### Chapter 7 The Church as a Sacramental Community

1. The term *theo-political* conveys our understanding of the church as God's (theo-) polis (political)—a kind of city with its own governmental and political structure. This structure is shaped by the church's identity as Christ's kingdom community. The sacraments of baptism and the Lord's Supper are events that signify incorporation and continuation in Christ's polis and its governance. 1 Peter instructs the Christian community to show respect to all authorities established by God for Christ's sake (1 Pet. 2:13–17). Having said that, 1 Peter also distinguishes the Christian community from all other groups and domains in the same context, specifying that the church is "a chosen people, a royal priesthood, a holy nation, a people belonging to God" (1 Pet. 2:9). Thus, while it is important that the church exist in this world as an agent of God's peace among the nations, it is also vitally important that the church maintain its distinctiveness from all other powers, given its singular existence as the Triune God's kingdom community.

2. Before we get going, it is important to note that consideration will focus on the sacraments of baptism and the Lord's Supper. For much of its history, the Roman Catholic Church has claimed that there are seven sacraments: baptism, confirmation, the Lord's Supper, marriage, ordination, penance, and extreme unction. Protestantism has recognized two: baptism and the Lord's Supper. Given the ecumenical nature and scope of this volume, our intent is not to discuss the five debated "sacraments," but to focus consideration on the two that have been recognized by the three major branches of the church—Catholic, Orthodox, and Protestant (apart from a few exceptions in the case of the latter). There are enough debates concerning just these two sacraments to keep us busy! Our ultimate purpose in discussing these two sacraments—baptism and the Lord's Supper—is to help the reader reflect seriously on what it means to think of the church as a sacramental community.

3. Many Protestants do not see John 6 as a eucharistic passage, while Roman Catholics and Orthodox do. But given that John does not narrate the Last Supper (whereas the Synoptic Gospels do), we believe that John 6 conveys John's understanding of the Lord's Supper.

4. Cyril of Jerusalem, *Lectures on the Christian Sacraments: The Procatechesis and the Five Mystagogical Catecheses,* ed. F. L. Cross (Crestwood, NY: St. Vladimir's Seminary Press, 1986), 54.

5. Ibid., 54–56.

6. Ibid., 59.

7. Ibid., 59–60.

8. Ibid., 61–62.

9. Ibid., xxx. As a result of Cyril's teaching, and later Augustine's, Roman Catholics and Lutherans, for example, hold that water baptism actually saves. This is one of the reasons why Catholics and Lutherans baptize infants. As they see it, water baptism remits original sin. Typically, those traditions coming from Calvin and the Anabaptists reject baptismal regeneration. The Reformed tradition arising from Calvin affirms that baptized infants are made participants in the covenant community, much like circumcised infants in the Hebrew Scriptures. For the Reformed, infant baptism is efficacious as a sign and symbol of grace, but is not regenerative. The baptism of infants confers on them grace that will assist these infants toward salvation and godliness later in life but will also confer judgment on the baptized if they do not eventually believe and grow in the knowledge and grace of the Lord. Baptists do not see baptism as salvific, or even as a means of grace, but rather as an external sign of an inner reality that comes through personal faith in Christ. For those in the Baptist tradition, only those able to assent in faith and who believe (thus, not infants) should be baptized. Thus, baptistic churches perform baby dedications but reject the practice of infant baptism.

10. William T. Cavanaugh, *Theopolitical Imagination: Discovering the Liturgy as a Political Act in an Age of Global Consumerism* (Edinburgh: T&T Clark, 2002), 122.

11. Stanley Hauerwas, *Against the Nations: War and Survival in a Liberal Society* (Notre Dame, IN: University of Notre Dame Press, 1992), 124.

12. See Hans W. Frei, *The Eclipse of Biblical Narrative: A Study in Eighteenth and Nineteenth Century Hermeneutics* (New Haven: Yale University Press, 1980).

13. See Robert E. Webber's discussion of the neutralizing of sacred space in the 1980s in *Ancient-Future Faith: Rethinking Evangelicalism for a Postmodern World* (Grand Rapids: Baker Academic, 1999), 108.

14. Maximus the Confessor, *The Church, the Liturgy and the Soul of Man: The Mystagogia of St. Maximus the Confessor,* trans. Dom Julian Stead, OSB (Still River, MA: St. Bede's, 1982), 68.

15. Ibid., 69.

16. See Richard Lischer, *The Preacher King: Martin Luther King, Jr. and the Word That Moved America* (New York: Oxford University Press, 1995), 17.

17. Ibid., 16.

18. Ibid., 17–18.

19. Ibid., 17.

20. Ibid.

21. Cyril of Jerusalem, *Lectures on the Christian Sacraments*, 53–54.

22. Ibid., 54–55.

23. Ibid., 57–58.

24. Ibid., 60–61.

25. Ibid., 61.

26. Martin Luther, *The Babylonian Captivity of the Church* in *Three Treatises* (Philadelphia: Fortress, 1966), 158.

27. *The Catechism of the Catholic Church* (Liguori, MO: Liguori Publications, 1994), 344 (italics added).

28. See ibid., subsection 1103, 286 (italics added).

29. Ibid., 344 (italics added).

30. Each tradition—Catholic and Protestant—wishes in its own way to safeguard the doctrine of God's sovereignty. Each succeeds, and each fails. Catholics are right to emphasize God's sovereign working in the church, and Protestants are right to emphasize God's sovereign working in the individual believer's life. However, pre–Vatican II Catholics were wrong in saying that the church mediates Christ's presence, in that they tended to make the Roman Catholic Church alone sovereign (while some argue that the present pope has gone a long way to correct this abuse, others raise concern over the recent statement put forth by the Congregation for the

Doctrine of the Faith: http://www.vatican.va/roman_curia/congregations/cfaith/documents/rc_con_cfaith_doc_20070629_responsa-quaestiones_en.html). Protestants have gone in the opposite direction by making the individual believer sovereign through his or her faith (although Luther sought to guard against this tendency by arguing that God creates the faith). In contrast to both extremes, God is sovereign through his Son and Spirit in uniting himself to the church and in creating faith.

31. Luther, *The Babylonian Captivity of the Church*, 143–52.

32. Council of Trent (1551): DS 1642; quoted in *Catechism of the Catholic Church*, 347. While the Orthodox Church has often employed the term *transubstantiation*, Kallistos Ware claims that the term "enjoys no unique or decisive authority" in the Orthodox Church. Nor does its use in the Orthodox Church "commit theologians to the acceptance of Aristotelian philosophical concepts" (as it has in the Roman Catholic Church). Ware also notes that while the Orthodox have always "insisted on the *reality* of the change" from bread and wine into the body and blood of Christ at the consecration of the elements, the Orthodox have "never attempted to explain the *manner* of the change." See Kallistos (Timothy) Ware, *The Orthodox Church* (Baltimore: Penguin, 1963), 290–91. What Ware says of the sacraments' significance for the Orthodox Church can also be said for the Roman Catholic Church and possibly even the Lutheran Church: "The chief place in Christian worship belongs to the sacraments or, as they are called in Greek, the *mysteries*" (281).

33. See Roland H. Bainton, *Here I Stand: A Life of Martin Luther* (Nashville: Abingdon, 1978), 108.

34. Ibid., 249. See also "The Marburg Colloquy and The Marburg Articles, 1529," in *Luther's Works: Word and Sacrament*, IV, vol. 38, trans. Martin E. Lehmann (Philadelphia: Fortress, 1971), 58–61.

35. See the following works for a discussion of this christological theme: Richard Muller, "communicatio idiomatum/communicatio proprietatum," in *Dictionary of Latin and Greek Theological Terms: Drawn Principally from Protestant Scholastic Theology* (Grand Rapids: Baker, 1985); Heinrich Schmid, *The Doctrinal Theology of the Evangelical Lutheran Church*, 3rd ed., rev. trans., Charles A. Hay and Henry E. Jacobs (Minneapolis: Augsburg, 1899), 331; Heinrich Heppe, *Reformed Dogmatics: Set out and Illustrated from the Sources*, with a foreword by Karl Barth, ed. Ernst Bizer, trans. G. T. Thomson (Great Britain: George Allen & Unwin, 1950; reprint, Grand Rapids: Baker, 1978), 432–33; Karl Barth, *The Göttingen Dogmatics: Instruction in the Christian Religion*, vol. 1, trans. Geoffrey W. Bromiley (Grand Rapids: Eerdmans, 1990), 159.

36. See Richard Muller's entries "sursum corda" and "unio sacramentalis," in *Dictionary of Latin and Greek Theological Terms*. Calvin writes: "For, in order that pious souls may duly apprehend Christ in the Supper, they must be raised up to heaven . . . Scripture itself also not only carefully recounts to us the ascension of Christ, by which he withdrew the presence of his body from our sight and company, to shake from us all carnal thinking of him, but also, whenever it recalls him, bids our minds be raised up, and seek him in heaven, seated at the right hand of the Father [Col. 3:1–2]." John Calvin, *Institutes of the Christian Religion*, ed. John T. McNeill (Philadelphia: Westminster, 1960), vol. II, Bk. IV, Ch. XVII, part 36.

37. For a nuanced example, see Christopher J. Ellis, *Gathering: A Theology and Spirituality of Worship in Free Church Tradition* (London: SCM, 2004). Whereas the Catholic understanding of memorial signifies that Christ's work is re-presented at the table, the widespread Baptist understanding of memorial signifies that Christ is not re-presented but simply remembered. For the majority in the Baptist heritage, Christ's finished work at the cross remains an event of history, and his work's present significance is reserved to its existential impact on the believer's life. On this view, Christ is present at the table gathering in the same manner that he is present to any other spatial event. It is worth noting here that an evangelical Baptist who holds to Christ's real presence in the sacraments is John E. Colwell. See his work, *Promise and Presence: An Exploration of Sacramental Theology* (Bletchley, UK: Paternoster, 2006).

38. It is worth noting that in Luke 24 the very words of institution used at the Last Supper are used again here. For Luke, this is a model for the church in its post-resurrection encounter with the risen Christ at the table. It is also worth noting that only when the Lord breaks the bread while restating the words of institution that the disciples who were present recognized him (and not when he had earlier disclosed to them all that the scriptures said of the Messiah on the road to Emmaus).

39. If we follow this logic to its illogical conclusion, we would pray only once a month and read the Bible once a month to preserve prayer and scripture reading as special events.

40. For a helpful introduction to the Quaker view of the sacraments, see D. Elton Trueblood's chapter "A Sacramental World," in *The People Called Quakers* (Richmond, IN: Friends United, 1971). For a thorough overview of the variegated Anabaptist theologies and practices, see Thomas N. Finger, *A Contemporary Anabaptist Theology: Biblical, Historical, Constructive* (Downers Grove, IL: InterVarsity, 2004), esp. 184–97.

41. John Howard Yoder, *Body Politics: Five Practices of the Christian Community before the Watching World* (Nashville: Discipleship Resources, 1992), 17.

42. John Howard Yoder, *The Politics of Jesus*, 2nd ed. (Grand Rapids: Eerdmans, 1994), 150.

43. Luther, *Babylonian Captivity of the Church*, 142.

44. Bainton, *Here I Stand*, 108.

45. Ibid., 110.

46. See ibid., 108–9. Three current theologians whose theologies and ecclesiologies are vitally shaped by their appreciation for the Eucharist are the Roman Catholic William Cavanaugh, the Greek Orthodox John Zizioulas, and the Lutheran Robert Jenson.

47. See Bainton's discussion in *Here I Stand*, 110. It is worth noting though that, as in the case of the Lord's Supper, Luther believed that faith was critical for water baptism to prove efficacious (first by the notion of implicit faith in the child and then later by the faith of a child's sponsor).

48. See Geoffrey Bromiley's articles on infant and believer baptism in Walter A. Elwell, ed., *Evangelical Dictionary of Theology* (Grand Rapids: Baker Academic, 1984), s.v. "Baptism, Believers'" and "Baptism, Infant." For further discussion of this question, see Joachim Jeremias, *Infant Baptism in the First Four Centuries* (Eugene, OR: Wipf and Stock, 2004); and Kurt Aland, *Did the Early Church Baptize Infants?* (Eugene, OR: Wipf and Stock, 2004).

49. Elwell, *Evangelical Dictionary of Theology*, s. v. "Baptism, Infant," by Bromiley.

50. For a well-articulated defense of God's providential designs for America as a nation under God, see Stephen H. Webb, *American Providence: A Nation with a Mission* (New York: Continuum, 2004). See also his debate with William T. Cavanaugh in *Cultural Encounters: A Journal for the Theology of Culture* 2, no. 2 (2006): 7–29; Cavanaugh's article "The Empire of the Empty Shrine: American Imperialism and the Church," Webb's response to Cavanaugh, and Cavanaugh's reply.

51. On this point, see N. T. Wright's discussion of the function of symbols within the cultural worldview of Jesus's time in *Jesus and the Victory of God* (Minneapolis: Fortress, 1994), 369–442. Wright's analysis is quite helpful in diagnosing our own need to radically subvert and challenge the dominant symbols that order the Christian life in America today.

## Chapter 8  Sacraments and the Search for the Holy Grail

1. Arnold T. Olson, *Believers Only* (Free Church Press, 1964). While the free church tradition must guard against so universalizing the body that it fails to localize it at a given place, those church traditions that practice closed communion (no matter their emphasis on the visible church being the universal church) end up facing the same danger.

2. Gordon D. Fee, *The First Epistle to the Corinthians*, The New International Commentary on the New Testament, vol. 7 (Grand Rapids: Eerdmans, 1987), 533–34. Craig Blomberg argues

that Paul's vision for the church in 1 Corinthians bears relevance for homogeneous groupings in the church-growth movement today. Craig L. Blomberg, *1 Corinthians,* The NIV Application Commentary, 6 (Grand Rapids: Zondervan, 1995), 239.

3. Fee, *First Epistle to the Corinthians,* 544.

4. John Howard Yoder, *Body Politics: Five Practices of the Christian Community before the Watching World* (Nashville: Discipleship Resources, 1992), 17.

5. Walter Brueggemann, "The Liturgy of Abundance, the Myth of Scarcity," *Christian Century,* March 24–31, 1999, 342.

6. By no means do we wish to suggest that the solution to the problem of the loss of the "common table" is a simple one. Catholics and Orthodox believe that the Sacrament of Orders is required for a true Eucharist. If Catholics and Orthodox came to the table with Protestants, they would in effect be renouncing Catholicism and Orthodoxy. For Protestants to come to the table with Catholics or Orthodox, they would have to renounce their Protestant traditions and become Catholic or Orthodox.

7. Brueggemann, "The Liturgy of Abundance, the Myth of Scarcity," 344–45.

8. Ibid., 346.

9. Ibid.

10. Ibid.

11. The quote is taken from Lee Strobel, "Making the Case for Christmas," found at Faithful Reader.com. See http://www.faithfulreader.com/authors/au-strobel-lee.asp. The article is based on *The Case for Christmas: A Journalist Investigates the Identity of the Child in the Manger* (Grand Rapids: Zondervan, 2005).

12. More will be said of these matters in chapter 16.

## Chapter 9 The Church as a Serving Community

1. Howard Snyder, *Community of the King* (Downers Grove, IL: InterVarsity, 1978), 75.

2. Dietrich Bonhoeffer, *Life Together*, in *Dietrich Bonhoeffer Works*, vol. 5, ed. Geffrey B. Kelley, trans. Daniel W. Bloesch and James H. Burtness (Minneapolis: Fortress, 1996), 33.

3. Sister Nonna Harrison writes, "It is wrong to think that in the Trinity self-emptying and deference to another person belong specifically to the Son and the Holy Spirit. The Self-emptying that is everything else, begins with the Father. The Son and the Holy Spirit respond to His humble love by offering the same back to Him, so Their relationship is mutual." "The Holy Trinity: A Model for Human Community," *St. Nina Quarterly* 3, no. 3 (April 2005): 5, http://www.stnina.org/journal/art/3.3.2.

4. Timothy Ware, *The Orthodox Church* (London: Penguin, 1997), 208.

5. See Timothy Ware, "The Human Person as an Icon of the Trinity," unionwithchrist.org.

6. Miroslav Volf, "The Trinity and the Church," in *Trinitarian Soundings in Systematic Theology*, ed. Paul Louis Metzger (London: T&T Clark, 2005), 170.

7. Vatican Council II, *Dogmatic Constitution on the Church,* 361. For an excellent pre–Vatican II discussion of the priestly involvement of the laity, see Yves Congar, *Lay People in the Church* (London: Geoffrey Chapman, 1965).

8. Martin Luther, "The Freedom of the Christian," in *Martin Luther: Selections from His Writings,* ed. John Dillenberger (Garden City, NY: Doubleday, 1961), 53.

9. Ibid., 75.

10. Thomas à Kempis, *The Imitation of Christ* (Garden City, NY: Image, 1955), 54.

11. Hans Küng, *The Church* (Garden City, NY: Image, 1976), 247–48.

12. Snyder, *Community of the King,* 79.

13. Austin Flannery, OP, ed., *Vatican Council II: The Concilier and Post Conciliar Documents*, rev. ed. (Boston: St. Pacel Editions, 1987), 363. We understand that there are differences in the Catholic and Protestant understandings of grace. The Catholic idea of infusion is problematic, in our view. But the typical evangelical Protestant idea of legal imputation is also problematic,

in that it is too narrow. For more on this, see Paul Louis Metzger, "Mystical Union with Christ: An Alternative to Blood Transfusions and Legal Fictions," *Westminster Theological Journal* 65 (2003): 201–14.

14. Another area of interest for the theology of spiritual gifts as a means of creating redemptive community pertains to ministry in the church as either gift-based or office-based. This topic will be addressed in the chapter "The Church as an Ordered Community." Also, since both the descriptions of the various gifts and the debate about whether the so-called charismatic gifts are still active are subjects addressed by many authors, we will not cover them here. Several of the most recent sources for these discussions are: Kenneth Berding, *What Are Spiritual Gifts? Rethinking the Conventional View* (Grand Rapids: Kregel, 2006); Bruce Bugbee, *What You Do Best in the Body of Christ: Discover Your Spiritual Gifts, Personal Style, and God-Given Passion* (Grand Rapids: Zondervan, 2005); Stuart Calvert, *Uniquely Gifted: Discovering Your Spiritual Gifts* (Birmingham: New Hope, 1993); J. I. Packer et al., *The Kingdom and the Power: Are Healing and the Spiritual Gifts Used by Jesus and the Early Church Meant for the Church Today?* (Ventura, CA: Regal, 1993).

15. David Wells, *No Place for Truth, Or, Whatever Happened to Evangelical Theology?* (Grand Rapids: Eerdmans, 1993), 4.

16. An Internet perusal of Christian bestseller lists just confirms this assertion.

17. See David Wells for these and similar observations.

18. Comment made by Dr. James Hitchcock to a group of evangelicals in St. Louis, Missouri, in 1994.

19. See John Perkins's critique of the prosperity gospel among the poor: John M. Perkins, *Beyond Charity: The Call to Christian Community Development* (Grand Rapids: Baker Books, 1993), 71.

20. Consider, for example, Jesus's proclamation to a crippled man that his sins are forgiven, addressing his relational healing with God before considering his need for physical healing.

21. Jean-Paul Sartre, *No Exit and Three Other Plays* (New York: Alfred A. Knopf, 1989), 45.

22. See Wells, *No Place for Truth,* and Donald Bloesch, Donald G. Bloesch, *The Church: Sacraments, Worship, Ministry* (Downers Grove, IL: InterVarsity, 2002).

23. Augustine, *Confessions*, 1.1.

24. Francis Schaeffer, *The Church at the End of the Twentieth Century,* in *The Complete Works of Francis Schaeffer: A Christian Worldview,* vol. 4, *A Christian View of the Church* (Westchester, IL: Crossway, 1982), 64.

25. Carmel Pilcher, RSJ, "A Culture of Sharing: Truthful Eucharist," *Dies Domini: Year of the Eucharist,* 2005, www.cathnews.com/eucharist/reflections.php.

26. John L. Ronsvalle and Sylvia Ronsvalle, *The State of Church Giving through 2000* (Champaign, IL: Empty Tomb, 2002), 40.

27. George Barna, *Barna Research Archives: Money,* Barna Research Group, www.barna.org.

## Chapter 10 Church Discipline—The Lost Element of Service

1. While there are surprisingly few books written on church discipline, the following resources should be considered. In addition to books on the subject, most denominations have standards and practices for church discipline, especially in the case of pastoral sin, which can be accessed by contacting those denominations directly. J. Carl Laney, *A Guide to Church Discipline* (Minneapolis: Bethany House, 1985); Don Baker, *Beyond Forgiveness: The Healing Touch of Church Discipline* (Portland, OR: Multnomah, 1984); Marlin Jeschke, *Discipling in the Church: Recovering a Ministry of the Gospel* (Scottdale, PA: Herald Press, 1988); *Church Ethics and Its Organizational Context: Learning from the Sex Abuse Scandal in the Catholic Church,* ed. Jean M. Bartunek, Mary Ann Hinsdale, and James F. Keenan (Lanham, MD: Rowman & Littlefield, 2006).

2. Jeschke, *Discipling in the Church,* 30.

3. See Laney's chapter on the purpose of church discipline for more on this (Laney, *Guide to Church Discipline*).

4. H. B. Swete, "Penitential Discipline in the First Three Centuries," in *Studies in Early Christianity*, vol. 16, *Christian Life: Ethics, Morality and Discipline in the Early Church*, ed. Everett Ferguson (New York: Garland, 1993), 249.

5. *Ephesus* 10.1, *Philadelphia* 3.2, 8.1, *Smyrna* 4.1, 5.3.

6. *Philadelphia* 6.1.

7. Swete, "Penitential Discipline in the First Three Centuries," 257.

8. This story took place in a Midwest church where one of the authors joined the pastoral staff toward the end of the events. The names of those involved have been changed for privacy. While the author was a firsthand witness to some of the events, the recounting of the story comes from a sermon by Rev. Michael P. Andrus, the senior pastor who shepherded the process of discipline, on the day the sinning believers were welcomed into church membership by the entire congregation.

9. Some would argue that the biblical thing to do in a situation like this would be for this husband and wife to divorce and go back to their previous spouses. We believe this is misguided. First, the result would be to break yet another one-flesh relationship to go back to another one. Second, God has demonstrated that in his grace he brings redemption to those who carry on in such a marriage after having come to a place of confession and repentance. This is illustrated in God's beautiful irony of ultimately bringing the Messiah into the world through David's sinful relationship with and marriage to Bathsheba.

## Chapter 11 The Church as an Ordered Community

1. Henri de Lubac, *The Motherhood of the Church* (San Francisco: Ignatius, 1982), 8.

2. Paul F. M. Zahl, "The Bishop-Led Church: The Episcopal or Anglican Polity Affirmed, Weighed, and Defended," in *Perspectives on Church Government: Five Views of Church Polity*, ed. Chad Owen Brand and R. Stanton Norman (Nashville: Broadman and Holman Academic, 2004), 210.

3. Thus, both Pope Benedict and theologian John Zizioulas, representing Catholic and Orthodox traditions, argue for a hierarchical church structure based on a hierarchical model of the Trinity. On the other hand, Miroslav Volf understands the Trinity to be more egalitarian and thus argues that congregational polity is more reflective of the trinitarian essence. See Volf's arguments against Joseph Ratzinger and John Zizioulas in *After Our Likeness: The Church as the Image of the Trinity* (Grand Rapids: Eerdmanns, 1997), 236.

4. Perhaps at this point it would be helpful to add a note of explanation regarding the five-hundred-year-old disagreement between Catholics (and Orthodox as well) and Protestants on the issue of authority in the church. Since the Reformation, Protestants have contended that the Bible is the premier authority in the church, which connects the church to its ultimate authority, Jesus Christ. This is the essence of *sola scriptura*. And as a result of centuries of animosity and misunderstanding, Protestants have accused the Catholic Church (and thus the Orthodox by association) of making church tradition and the Magisterium (teaching office held by the bishops) authoritative over the scriptures. Catholics and Orthodox, on the other hand, have argued that the lack of any unified interpretive authority leaves Protestants without the means to judge the propriety of any person's own understanding of the Bible. Both of these accusations are unfair. Simply put, the Catholic understanding of authority never puts tradition or the teaching office over the Bible. Rather, all three work together with tradition and the teaching office accurately explaining, reflecting, and guarding the truth of scripture. For a detailed explanation of this process, see the Vatican II document *Dogmatic Constitution on Divine Revelation, Dei Verbum,* Austin Flannery, OP, ed., *Vatican Council II: The Concilier and Post Conciliar Documents*, rev. ed. (Boston: St. Pacel Editions, 1987). Equally, in mainstream Protestant thought, *sola scriptura* has never meant that the Bible needs no authoritative interpretation for the church. The very

existence of guiding documents such as the Lutheran and Reformed catechisms, the Augsburg Confession, and the Westminster Confession witnesses to the awareness Protestants have that the Bible must be properly interpreted and understood in order for its authority as the Word of God to be implemented in the church. A brief but helpful explanation of the Protestant idea of biblical authority can be found in the chapter titled, "The Power of God's Word: Authority," in Millard Erickson's *Christian Theology* (Grand Rapids: Baker, 1985).

5. For example, congregationalist James Leo Garrett cites English Baptist Alex Gilmore: "The Church is not, and must never be regarded as, a democracy, for the power is not in the hands of the *demos* but of the *Christos*: it is a Christocracy." James Leo Garrett, "The Congregation-Led Church" in *Perspectives on Church Government*, 179. Similarly, *The Dogmatic Constitution on the Church,* from Vatican II, argues regarding the church, "It is also a flock, of which God foretold that he would himself be the shepherd, and whose sheep, although watched over by human shepherds, are nevertheless at all times led and brought to pasture by Christ himself, the Good Shepherd and prince of shepherds, who gave his life for his sheep." Flannery, *Vatican II*, 353. Thus, in the episcopal system, the authority of bishops, and even of the pope, is always subservient to and representative of the complete and unique authority of Jesus Christ as Lord of the church.

6. For example, Protestants would cite the papal proclamation of the immaculate conception of Mary, seeing it as an example of an overreaching episcopal authority, able to establish dogma with little or no biblical evidence. Those in the episcopal tradition might refer to incidences like the rise of cult leaders Jim Jones and David Koresh and their ability, within the congregational system disconnected from interpretive tradition or episcopal authority, to claim that they alone are the true interpreters of scripture, and therefore completely authoritative in all they teach.

7. The perspicuity of the scriptures is the idea that the Bible, in its fundamental affirmations, is clear and therefore understandable. It is not necessary for it to be mediated or explained by some other authority.

8. For example, the Catholic catechism explains regarding the role of the bishops: "The mission of the Magisterium is linked to the definitive nature of the covenant established by God with his people in Christ. It is this Magisterium's task to preserve God's people from deviations and defections and to guarantee them the objective possibility of professing the true faith without error." *The Catechism of the Catholic Church* (Liguori, MO: Liguori Publications, 1994), 890.

9. Bengt Holmberg, *Paul and Power: The Structure of Authority in the Primitive Church as Reflected in the Pauline Epistles* (Lund: CWK Gleerup, 1978), 198.

10. Gordon Fee, "The Priority of Spirit Gifting for Church Ministry," in *Discovering Biblical Equality: Complementarity without Hierarchy,* ed. Ronald Pierce and Rebecca Groothuis (Downers Grove, IL: InterVarsity, 2004), 249.

11. Volf, *After Our Likeness*, 231.

12. Ronald Y. K. Fung, "Function or Office? A Survey of the New Testament Evidence," *Evangelical Review of Theology* 8, no. 1 (April 1984): 39.

13. We do believe that scripture ordains offices (elder, deacon, pastor), but not a particular system of authority. Also, some would argue that many churches today use systems that are really hybrids of the traditional models. We will not address these.

14. Ignatius of Antioch, *Letter to Smyrna,* 6.

15. Interestingly, in medieval and Renaissance art, the pope is often known by the fact that he has keys hanging from his belt.

16. The *Catechism* states: "The Lord made Simon alone, whom he named Peter, the 'rock' of his Church. He gave him the keys of his Church and instituted him shepherd of the whole flock. 'The office of binding and loosing which was given to Peter was also assigned to the college of apostles united to its head.' This Pastoral office of Peter and the other apostles belongs to the Church's very foundation and is continued by the bishops under the primacy of the Pope. The

*Pope,* Bishop of Rome and Peter's successor, 'is the perpetual and visible source and foundation of the unity both of the bishops and of the whole company of the faithful.' 'For the Roman Pontiff, by reason of his office as Vicar of Christ, and as pastor of the entire Church has full, supreme, and universal power over the whole Church, a power which he can always exercise unhindered.'" *Catechism,* 881–82.

17. This idea is not new to the church but goes back at least to Augustine who, in his arguments against the Donatists, contended that God dispenses his grace through ordained clergy by virtue of their office and this grace is not undercut even by the existence of some sin in the life of the bishop/priest.

18. Timothy Ware, *The Orthodox Church* (London: Penguin, 1997), 249.

19. Veli-Matti Karkkainen, *An Introduction to Ecclesiology* (Downers Grove, IL: InterVarsity, 2002), 22.

20. Lubac, *Motherhood of the Church,* 30–31.

21. Ibid., 85.

22. Zahl, "Bishop-Led Church," 213.

23. This issue of the hierarchy as fundamental to a faith community being called a church is addressed by the former Joseph Cardinal Ratzinger, now Pope Benedict XVI, in the document *Dominus Iesus,* published in August of 2000 under the authority of Pope John Paul II. Groups without a hierarchy are called "ecclesial communities," rather than churches proper.

24. This remark was made by Dr. Beldon Lane, Professor of Historical Theology, St. Louis University, at a conference where one of the authors was in attendance.

25. For example, the Catholic catechism remarks that it is the Magisterium's task "to preserve God's people from deviations and defections and to guarantee them the objective possibility of professing the true faith without error. Thus, the pastoral duty of the Magisterium is aimed at seeing to it that the People of God abides in the truth that liberates." *Catechism,* 235.

26. Zahl, "Bishop-Led Church," 237.

27. Brand and Norman, *Perspectives on Church Government,* 18.

28. See L. Roy Taylor, "Presbyterianism," in *Who Runs the Church? 4 Views on Church Government,* ed. Steven B. Cowan (Grand Rapids: Zondervan, 2004), 81.

29. Taylor, Reymond, Berkhof, and Boice, for example, all argue this point.

30. This kind of separatist Puritanism is exemplified in Robert Browne's *Reformation without Tarrying for Any* (1582), and the Savoy Declaration (1658), which was a separatist response to the Westminster Confession of Faith.

31. See Cowan, ed., *Who Runs the Church?* 135–38 for history.

32. Paige Patterson, "Single Elder Congregationalism," in ibid., 139.

33. James Leo Garrett argues that Luther's doctrine of the priesthood of believers led to his argument that the Christian congregation has the right to judge all teaching, to call pastors, and to dismiss them if they are heretical. See "Congregation-Led Church," 174.

34. Volf, *After Our Likeness,* 226.

35. Garrett, "Congregation-Led Church," 193.

36. This idea of connecting giftedness directly to influence in the structure of the church and its leadership is a key issue in the significant debate among American evangelicals on the issue of women in leadership. To see examples of the connection between gifts and women in leadership, see the website of Christians for Biblical Equality (cbeinternational.org/new/index.shtml).

37. See Garrett, "Congregation-Led Church," 188, and Wayne Grudem, *Systematic Theology* (Grand Rapids: Zondervan, 1994), 934.

38. For his most extensive discourse on this topic, see his *Dominus Iesus: On the Unicity and Salvific Universality of Jesus Christ and the Church,* published in August of 2000.

39. Taylor, "Presbyterianism," 236.

### Chapter 12  The Role of Women in the Ordered Community

1. Dr. Matthews is Lois W. Bennett Distinguished Associate Professor of Educational Ministries and Women's Ministries at Gordon Conwell Theological Seminary in Massachusetts. Also, for this work, egalitarians are defined as those who contend that women have the right to an authority equal to that of men in both marriage and the church, or at least in the church. Hierarchicalists are those who believe that the Bible argues that men are to take the ultimate human authority roles in both the home and the church.

2. It is also interesting to notice how exegetical interpretation of the key passages has changed in the last couple of centuries in light of women's movements. Linda Mercadante, in a summary of her master's thesis on changes in the interpretation of 1 Corinthians 11, noted correctly that Calvin was illustrative of his paternalistic era. His commentary contends that the prophecy Paul refers to in the passage is authoritative teaching, which means that women could not have done it, with or without a head covering. Moreover, he contends that not only wives, but also all women, are created inferior to all men and are to be in subjection to them. Today of course, even most traditionalist interpreters of this passage would interpret it quite differently, allowing that women were permitted to prophesy, precisely because the prophecy mentioned is not a proclamation akin to authoritative teaching. Moreover, few would venture to contend for Calvin's radical subjection of the entire female gender to men. Mercadante is careful to note that egalitarian interpretations are also subject to their cultural settings. Cf. Linda Mercadante, "The Male–Female Debate: Can We Read the Bible Objectively?" *CRUX* 15, no. 2 (June 1979): 20–25.

3. This is not to suggest that there are no proper hierarchy structures in the present church or even in the church of the eschaton. But authority structures in the present church are based on such things as community-recognized gifting, and character (Acts 6; 1 Tim.; elders/deacons, etc.), or a specific commission by Christ, such as Paul's call to be an apostle to the Gentiles and their churches. Moreover, authority in the church of the future, such as we are able to understand it, seems to be based on faithfulness to Christ in the present, not on gender (Rev. 3:21; 20:6; Matt. 19:28–30).

4. Paul appears to apply this issue to Timothy when he advises him to continue in his authoritative teaching role, not to allow anyone to look down upon him simply because he is young.

5. Cf. examples of this trend in articles by Vern Poythress and George Knight in *Recovering Biblical Manhood and Womanhood: A Response to Evangelical Feminism*, ed. John Piper and Wayne Grudem (Wheaton, IL: Crossway, 1991).

6. Vern Poythress, "The Church as Family: Why Male Leadership in the Family Requires Male Leadership in the Church," in Piper and Grudem, eds., *Recovering Biblical Manhood and Womanhood*.

7. Schreiner also ignores this verse in his similar commentary on the same passage. Cf. *Two Views on Women in Ministry*, ed. James Beck and Craig Blomberg (Grand Rapids: Zondervan, 2001), 211.

8. See Joseph Hellerman's excellent work *The Ancient Church as Family* (Minneapolis: Fortress, 2001) for an extensive discussion of the church as ultimate family structure.

9. Note that we are not arguing here for or against marital hierarchy in the home.

### Chapter 13  The Church as a Cultural Community: Christ, Culture, and the Sermon on the Mount Community

1. "Culture" may be defined as the totality of human activity in all spheres, both work and leisure, and includes language and social norms—whether spoken or unspoken—that shape people's lives and worldviews and guarantee rites of passage in society. Culture is also taken to refer to the heights of human achievement in the realms of the sciences, the arts, ethics, or sports. Lastly, culture may be seen to refer to the whole of a particular society or civilization, which may be viewed either as inclusive of the church or as distinct from a society's religious or spiritual

counterpart. In this essay, we are thinking specifically of culture as a community with a given language and social norms, which shape that community's values, actions, and practices.

2. H. Richard Niebuhr, *Christ and Culture* (New York: Harper and Brothers, 1951).

3. For other helpful treatments of Christ's relation to culture through the centuries, see the following works: Robert Webber, *The Secular Saint: A Case for Evangelical Social Responsibility* (Eugene, OR: Wipf & Stock, 2004); Jaroslav Pelikan, *Jesus through the Centuries: His Place in the History of Culture*, with a new preface by the author (New Haven: Yale University Press, 1999). The latter book shows Christ's impact on culture through the various epochs; each age's predominant image of Christ presented here provides a lens for viewing that particular era. Two important critiques of Niebuhr's paradigm are: Glen Stassen, D. M. Yeager, and John Howard Yoder, "How H. Richard Niebuhr Reasoned: A Critique of Christ and Culture," in *Authentic Transformation: A New Vision of Christ and Culture* (Nashville: Abingdon, 1996); and Craig A. Carter, *Rethinking Christ and Culture: A Post-Christendom Perspective* (Grand Rapids: Brazos, 2007).

4. Dietrich Bonhoeffer, *No Rusty Swords,* edited and with an introduction by Edwin H. Robertson et al. (London: Collins, 1970), 306.

5. Dietrich Bonhoeffer; quoted in Larry Rasmussen, *Dietrich Bonhoeffer: Reality and Resistance* (Nashville, TN: Abingdon, 1972), 25.

6. Gregory of Nazianzus, Epistle 101, "To Cledonios," in *Patrologia Græca,* vol. XXXVII, col. 181C; quoted in Erwin Fahlbusch and Geoffrey William Bromiley, eds., *The Encyclopedia of Christianity* (Grand Rapids: Eerdmans, 2005), s. v. "Salvation, The Orthodox Tradition," by Dan-Ilie Ciobotea.

7. Karl Barth, "The Barmen Declaration"; quoted in Arthur C. Cochrane, *The Church's Confession under Hitler* (Philadelphia: Westminster Press, 1962), 239–40.

8. William H. Willimon, "Been There, Preached That: Today's Conservatives Sound like Yesterday's Liberals," *Leadership: A Practical Journal for Church Leaders* 16, no. 4 (Fall 1995): 76.

9. John R. W. Stott speaks of poverty in spirit as "spiritual bankruptcy" in *The Message of the Sermon on the Mount (Matthew 5–7),* The Bible Speaks Today, ed. J. A. Moyer and John R. W. Stott (Downers Grove, IL: InterVarsity, 1978), 39.

10. Dietrich Bonhoeffer, *The Cost of Discipleship,* 2nd ed. (New York: Macmillan, 1959), 50–51.

11. Ibid., 50–53.

12. Ibid., 50–51.

13. Ibid., 51.

14. Ibid., 52–53.

15. Ibid., 120.

16. Ibid., 90–91.

17. Ibid., 91.

18. Ibid., 120.

19. Karl Barth, "The Christian Community and the Civil Community," in *Against the Stream: Shorter Post-War Writings, 1946–1952,* ed. R. G. Smith, trans. E. M. Delacour and S. Godman (London: SCM, 1954), 31.

20. Bonhoeffer, *Cost of Discipleship,* 303–4.

21. Geoffrey Wainwright, "Types of Spirituality," in *The Study of Spirituality,* ed. Cheslyn Jones, Geoffrey Wainwright, and Edward Yarnold, SJ (New York: Oxford University Press, 1986), 595.

22. Ibid., 596.

23. Ibid., 597–98.

24. Niebuhr, *Christ and Culture,* 156.

25. Luther writes that "a Christian man is righteous and a sinner at the same time, holy and profane, an enemy of God and a child of God. None of the sophists will admit this paradox,

because they do not understand the true meaning of justification." Martin Luther, *Luther's Works*, vol. 26, *Lectures on Galatians*, 1535, chapters 1–4, ed. Jaroslav Pelikan (Saint Louis: Concordia Publishing House, 1963), 232–33.

26. Martin Luther, "An Open Letter on the Harsh Book against the Peasants," in *Luther's Works*, vol. 46, *The Christian in Society*, ed. Robert C. Schultz (Philadelphia: Fortress, 1967), 69–70. See also Bonhoeffer's dialectical depiction of the relation of Christ, church, and state in *Christ the Center*, trans. Edwin H. Robertson (San Francisco: HarperSanFrancisco, 1978), 63–64.

27. Niebuhr, *Christ and Culture*, 172.

28. Karl Barth, "The Christian Community and the Civil Community," 24.

29. See ibid., 29.

30. We use the term *fundamentalist* here as a qualifier to signify that not all evangelicals are fundamentalistic in their engagement of culture.

31. Cynthia D. Moe-Lobeda, *Healing a Broken World: Globalization and God* (Minneapolis: Fortress, 2002), 106.

32. Ibid.

33. See also Alan J. Torrance's discussion of the situation at the time of Hitler in his introduction to *Christ, Justice and Peace: Toward a Theology of the State in Dialogue with the Barmen Declaration*, by Eberhard Jüngel, trans. D. Bruce Hamill and Alan J. Torrance (Edinburgh: T&T Clark, 1992). Torrance speaks of how nationalism's rise in Germany led to the subjectivizing of spirituality and the relativizing of the "imperatives of the Gospel" (xi). See also Paul Louis Metzger, *The Word of Christ and the World of Culture: Sacred and Secular through the Theology of Karl Barth* (Grand Rapids: Eerdmans, 2003), 165–66.

34. Bethge's remarks are found in John W. de Gruchy, *Daring, Trusting Spirit: Bonhoeffer's Friend Eberhard Bethge* (Minneapolis: Fortress, 2005), 200–201.

35. Reinhard Hütter, *Suffering Divine Things: Theology as Church Practice* (Grand Rapids: Eerdmans, 1999), 11.

36. See Kristen Deede Johnson, "'Public' Re-Imagined: A Reconsideration of Church, State, and Civil Society," in *A World for All? Trinity, Church and Global Civil Society*, ed. William F. Storrar, Peter J. Casarella, and Paul Louis Metzger (forthcoming with Eerdmans), 14–15.

37. Falwell was a very complex figure. As an antagonistic fundamentalist distancing himself from secular America, he promoted the model of Christ against culture. As a reconstructionist trying to take back America, he promoted the model of Christ as the transformer of culture. He also inadvertently promoted Christ and culture in paradox, given his subjugation of the church to the state in promoting culture's transformation. Falwell functioned as a kind of dualist in that he did not see the church as the primary agent for bringing about society's transformation; for this he turned to the state. The church was awarded a subservient role to the state in bringing about society's transformation.

38. Jürgen Moltmann, *The Crucified God: The Cross of Christ as the Foundation and Criticism of Christian Theology* (Minneapolis: Fortress, 1993), 143–44.

39. Ibid., 141.

40. Walter Wink, *The Powers That Be: Theology for a New Millennium* (New York: Doubleday, 1998), 110–11.

41. Suffice it to say that Jesus's claim that he is king, and that his kingdom is here though not yet fully realized, and will be realized at his second coming, has always made the Caesars apprehensive. Barth was ousted from Germany in the early 1930s for claiming in the Barmen Declaration that there is no other Führer (or Lord) than Jesus Christ. Japanese pastors during World War II were imprisoned for preaching the return of Christ. The problem for Führers and Tojos, Caesars and Caiaphases alike, is that the resurrected and reigning Jesus serves as a check on their ambitions and spoils their garden parties.

42. See Bonhoeffer's discussion of interpretive sophistry when dealing with Christ's claims, in *Cost of Discipleship,* 87–91.

43. Regardless of how Luther intended them, his remarks that while the body is under Caesar's authority, the soul is under God's alone certainly opens the door for Christians to offer blind and reckless submission to the state. See Martin Luther, "Temporal Authority: To What Extent It Should Be Obeyed," in *Luther's Works,* vol. 45, *The Christian in Society,* ed. Walther I. Brandt (Philadelphia: Fortress, 1962), 111. Ultimate authority over our souls and bodies belongs to the One who alone can throw both soul and body into hell (Matt. 10:28). See William T. Cavanaugh's discussion of the problem of separating authority over the body/temporal and the soul/spiritual in Roman Catholic circles in the section, "The Minimum of Body," in *Torture and Eucharist: Theology, Politics, and the Body of Christ* (Oxford: Blackwell, 1998), 157–65.

44. Chapter 14 will provide a distinctive entry point to consideration of the synthetic approach that differs from the discussion set forth in the immediately following section.

45. Wainwright, "Types of Spirituality," 598.

46. Wainwright claims that the incarnation and resurrection receive particular attention in the synthesist model; this orientation bears the marks of the biological and the infused, which impact the entire race of humanity (ibid., 598). Wainwright presents 2 Tim. 1:10 (the infusion of divine life into the whole race through Christ) as representative of this form of spirituality (598–99).

47. Dietrich Bonhoeffer; quoted in John W. Doberstein, "Introduction," in Dietrich Bonhoeffer, *Life Together* (New York: Harper & Row, 1954), 9.

48. Dietrich Bonhoeffer, *Letters and Papers from Prison,* ed. Eberhard Bethge, rev. ed. (New York: Macmillan, 1967), 188.

49. Ibid., 203.

50. Ibid., 193–94.

51. Eberhard Bethge, "Foreword," in Dietrich Bonhoeffer, *Letters and Papers,* xv.

52. See Wainwright, "Types of Spirituality," 603.

53. See ibid., 604.

54. See ibid., 605.

55. It is quite possible that Jesus proclaimed, "I am the light of the world," against the backdrop of the lights from the booths scattered on the hills surrounding Jerusalem during the Feast of Tabernacles.

56. Theonomists maintain that the church is to strive to make America a Christian nation where God's law set forth in the Hebrew Scriptures is enforced. For a representative work, see Gary North and Gary DeMar, *Christian Reconstruction: What It Is, What It Isn't* (Tyler, TX: Institute for Christian Economics, 1991).

57. See the critique of classic forms of dispensationalism as it concerns the separation of Israel and the church in Craig Blaising and Darrell Bock, *Progressive Dispensationalism* (Grand Rapids: Baker Academic, 1993), 50–51.

58. See the discussion of supersessionism (the church displacing Israel) in Scott Bader-Saye's *Church and Israel after Christendom: The Politics of Election* (Eugene, OR: Cascade, 2005), 67, 74, 76.

59. See Perry Miller's discussion of Winthrop in *Errand into the Wilderness* (Cambridge: Belknap Press of Harvard University Press, 1956), 4–6.

60. Thus, he was no theonomist. But he was no Anabaptist either. Unlike Anabaptists, Bonhoeffer was not reticent to get involved in confronting and/or promoting governmental or social structures as a Christian. Usually when Anabaptists get involved socially, they speak as a community. It would be out of character for them to seek public office. While Bonhoeffer does not see the church as a voluntary association of religious individuals whose ultimate public allegiance is to the state, he did see that he as an individual Christian had a public role beyond

participation in Christ's polis, the church. Thus, he involved himself in various efforts nationally and internationally in the fight against the Nazi menace.

61. Bonhoeffer, *Letters and Papers,* 16.

62. The quotation is taken from John Winthrop (1630), "A Model of Christian Charity," http://religiousfreedom.lib.virginia.edu/sacred/charity.html.

63. Vine Deloria Jr., *God Is Red* (Golden, CO: Fulcrum, 1994), 261.

64. Niebuhr's typology is neither Christ-centered, nor cruciform, nor ecclesially framed. Concerning Jesus, he writes: "[Christ] is not a center from which radiate[s] the love of God and of men, obedience to God and Caesar, trust in God and nature, hope in divine and human action. He exists rather as the focusing point in the continuous alternation of movements from God to man and from man to God." Niebuhr, *Christ and Culture,* 29. When Christ in his particularity as the crucified and risen Messiah is not taken seriously in our reflections on the church's engagement of culture, the danger exists that the church will take matters into its own hands when facing the world's opposition, rather than entrusting judgment to God. Christ's cross instructs us to undergo judgment and persecution, and Christ's resurrection encourages us to hope in God to deliver and redeem us in his time and in his way. Furthermore, Christ's particular embodiment in the church does not figure significantly in Niebuhr's reflections on Christ's relation to culture either. Without seeing the church as key to the matrix, Christ is abstracted from his concrete embodiment in culture. And when Christ is abstracted from the church, there is nothing to safeguard the Christian individual from being conformed to the patterns of the fallen powers, including the state or market. Christ and his kingdom are crucial to the church as its transcendent ground, providing firm hope. The church is also of critical importance in that the church is the concrete manifestation of Christ's kingdom, providing the context for the demonstration of this hope as contemporary witness. As Stanley Hauerwas and Mark Sherwindt write, "Without the Kingdom-ideal, the church loses her identity-forming hope; without the church, the kingdom loses its concrete character." Stanley Hauerwas and Mark Sherwindt, "The Kingdom of God: An Ecclesial Space for Peace," *Word & World* 2, no. 2 (1982): 131.

65. John Howard Yoder, "Armaments and Eschatology," quoted in Stanley Hauerwas, *With the Grain of the Universe: The Church's Witness and Natural Theology* (Grand Rapids: Brazos, 2001), 6.

66. According to Paul Minear, salt was essential to the temple liturgy and worship in the ancient world. Paul Minear, "The Salt of the Earth," in *Interpretation* 51 (January 1997): 34. The sacrifices themselves were salted. According to Jesus, persecution-suffering-sacrifice is a key trait of faithful discipleship. Jesus's disciples' saltiness was and is indissolubly related to their suffering for the faith. As Minear notes, when disciples avoid suffering for the gospel, they lose out on the power (saltiness) of the gospel (see 36).

## Chapter 14  Getting Past the Ghettoizing of the Gospel in Today's Culture

1. Jonathan Larson, *Rent* (Finster & Lucky Music, 1996).

2. John Steinbeck, *East of Eden,* Steinbeck Centennial ed. (New York: Penguin, 2002), 268–69.

3. Ibid., 266.

4. Ibid., 268.

5. Ibid., 269.

6. C. S. Lewis, *Surprised by Joy: The Shape of My Early Life* (London: Geoffrey Bles, 1955), 222.

7. The quotation is taken from the 2006 DVD for 20th Century Fox's *Walk the Line*, directed by James Mangold.

8. See Brad Harper's "Response" to Stanley J. Grenz's essay "(Pop) Culture: Playground of the Spirit or Diabolical Device?" in *Cultural Encounters: A Journal for the Theology of Culture* 1, no. 1 (Winter 2004): 27–30. In addition to Grenz's article, along with the responses offered to

it, the reader is encouraged to look to the following sources on God's redemptive engagement of pop culture: Robert K. Johnston, *Reel Spirituality: Theology and Film in Dialogue* (Grand Rapids: Baker Academic, 2000); Craig Detweiler and Barry Taylor, *A Matrix of Meanings: Finding God in Pop Culture* (Grand Rapids: Baker Academic, 2003).

9. Richard Twiss, *One Church, Many Tribes: Following Jesus the Way God Made You* (Ventura: Regal Books, 2000), 113.

10. Ibid., 125.

11. A great example of this is found in comparing Depeche Mode's, Marilyn Manson's, and Johnny Cash's respective renditions of "Personal Jesus." Cash uses the same basic tune and words as the other two, but infuses the tune and words with new meaning through his intent.

12. It is one thing for people who have used native drums for demonic purposes as non-believers to say that they themselves cannot use such drums in Christian worship because of their numerous past personal associations. It is quite another for them to say that other Native Christians who worship God authentically and truthfully through the use of native drums cannot use them. Anything not done from faith is sin, and anything done according to biblical faith is righteous.

13. See Karl Barth, *Church Dogmatics*, IV/3.1, *The Doctrine of Reconciliation*, ed. G. W. Bromiley and T. F. Torrance (Edinburgh: T&T Clark, 1961), 123.

14. See, for example, the discussion of Thomas Kinkade's art in Marco R. della Cava, "Thomas Kinkade: Profit of Light," in *USA Today,* March 12, 2002. An artist friend of ours saw an exhibit of Kinkade's work and was pleasantly surprised to find in one corner of the exhibit paintings of Christ and of life in general that reflected an edgier and messier side to human existence. He spoke with one of Kinkade's representatives, asking why we don't see more of these kinds of works from Kinkade. The agent said that while Kinkade loves these works, they don't sell. The consumer demands his more surreal-looking art.

15. Also, as argued in the chapter on worship, while culture certainly distorts God's revelation, God also speaks through cultural forms. And so, while we need to be careful, we must also be creative. It is important that we make use of cultural forms in the church, for even the language we speak is part and parcel of the given culture. We can never speak truthfully if we do not speak meaningfully to those around us. How can we expect those in the surrounding culture to listen and hear us in the church if we are not listening to them?

16. Gerhard Perseghin, "Georges Rouault Emphasizes the Religious in His Works at the Phillips," in *Catholic Standard*, July 8, 2004, 13.

17. Hans Urs von Balthasar, *The Glory of the Lord: A Theological Aesthetics*, vol. v, *The Realm of Metaphysics in the Modern Age* (Edinburgh: T&T Clark, 1991), 203.

18. Ibid.

19. José María Faerna, ed., *Rouault*, trans. Alberto Curotto, Great Modern Masters (Cameo/Abrams, Harry N. Abrams, 1997), 25.

20. Balthasar, *Glory of the Lord,* 202.

21. See Perseghin, "Georges Rouault Emphasizes the Religious," 13.

22. Balthasar, *Glory of the Lord*, 204. It should be noted that indifference, according to Balthasar, is positive; it involves love for another and a disregard for one's own desires. See also David Bentley Hart, *The Beauty of the Infinite: The Aesthetics of Christian Truth* (Grand Rapids: Eerdmans, 2003), especially 336–38.

23. While icons can certainly be abused, icons can enhance our worship experience. One of the roles of icons is to enhance our sense of communion with the great cloud of witnesses throughout church history, and to help us see ourselves as participants in the ongoing drama of salvation. The incarnation serves as the ultimate justification for icons in the Eastern church. For Christ is the supreme window into God's glory offered in the creation. As the ultimate image or icon of God, Christ's representation stands for the Ancient of Days on the ceiling of St. Nicholas Orthodox Church in Portland, Oregon. In Rublev's *Icon of the Holy Trinity,* the

three angelic messengers who visited with Abraham by the tree of Mamre stand in place of the divine persons. Contrary to popular Protestant opinion, the Orthodox clergy do not teach their people to worship icons, but to use them as windows and guides in worship. There is a theological science to iconography, which also serves to guard against abuse. In addition to the limit placed on representing naked deity, icons possess a translucent quality, guiding the viewer through them into the realm of the divine. Moreover, iconographers alter perspective and dimension in their work to guard against confusing their icons with ultimate reality itself. Now we look through a glass dimly, so to speak; then we shall see face to face.

24. We wish to thank Josh Butler of Imago Dei Community, Portland, Oregon, for his insights and reflections in the course of writing chapter 14.

## Chapter 15  The Church as a Missional Community: The Being-*Driven* Church

1. The discussion of communal and co-missional reflects the influence of George R. Hunsberger in "Missional Vocation: Called and Sent to Represent the Reign of God," in *Missional Church: A Vision for the Sending of the Church in North America,* ed. Darrell L. Guder (Grand Rapids: Eerdmans, 1998), 82. See also David Bosch, *Transforming Mission: Paradigm Shifts in Theology of Mission* (Maryknoll, NY: Orbis, 1991).

2. This view reflects the influence of Martin Luther, *The Freedom of a Christian,* in *Martin Luther's Basic Theological Writings,* ed. Timothy F. Lull (Minneapolis: Fortress, 1989), 623.

3. Lesslie Newbigin, *Foolishness to the Greeks: The Gospel and Western Culture* (Grand Rapids: Eerdmans, 1986), 30–31.

4. Gretchen T. Buggeln, "Sacred Spaces: Designing America's Churches," *Christian Century,* June 15, 2004, 25.

5. Jeff Sharlet, "Inside America's Most Powerful Megachurch," *Harper's Magazine* 310, no. 1860 (May 2005): 50.

6. A 2005 *New York Times Magazine* article on a megachurch in Surprise, Arizona, claims that as with "many fast-growing exurbs," the typical Surprise resident "is a young, white, married couple of modest means. These are people that the Republican Party has always run well with—its conventional wisdom among political analysts that young, middle-class couples raising children tend to be conservative—and in 2004 the G.O.P. made a strong play for exurbanites. Megachurches were a key part of the strategy." Jonathan Mahler, "The Soul of the New Exurb," *New York Times Magazine,* March 27, 2005, 37.

7. John M. Perkins, "Afterword," in Paul Louis Metzger, *Consuming Jesus: Beyond Race and Class Divisions in a Consumer Church* (Grand Rapids: Eerdmans, 2007), 174–75.

8. We are indebted to Karl Barth at this point for this spatial and temporal incarnational framework.

9. The fine arts and pop culture bear witness to the view that many perceive the church to be without doors or that the church locks its doors—keeping people in or out. The reader is encouraged to reflect upon Vincent Van Gogh's *Church of Auvers* and the movie *Chocolat* as possible instances of this perception.

10. For a good summary of various models of evangelism's relation to social action, see Tokunboh Adeyemo, "A Critical Evaluation of Contemporary Perspectives," in *In Word and Deed: Evangelism and Social Responsibility,* ed. Bruce Nichols (Exeter: Paternoster, 1985). See also John Perkins's excellent discussion of the holistic nature of the gospel—moving beyond the conservative and liberal impasse—in chapter 13, "The Whole Gospel," in John M. Perkins, *Let Justice Roll Down,* with a new foreword by Shane Claiborne (Ventura: Regal Books, 1976), 98–108.

11. Gordon D. Fee and Douglas Stuart, *How to Read the Bible for All It's Worth: A Guide to Understanding the Bible,* 2nd ed. (Grand Rapids: Zondervan, 1993), 125.

12. Pope Benedict XVI, *Deus Caritas Est,* 1. See http://www.vatican.va/holy_father/benedict _xvi/encyclicals/documents/hf_ben-xvi_enc_20051225_deus-caritas-est_en.html.

13. Ibid., 11.

14. Ibid., 13.

15. Ibid., 14–15.

16. Ibid., 17–18.

17. Hans Urs von Balthasar, *Love Alone Is Credible,* trans. D. C. Schindler (San Francisco: Ignatius Press, 2004), 100–102.

18. Ibid., 116.

19. Ibid., 107.

20. Ibid., 107–8.

21. Ibid., 108. See also Balthasar's *The Heart of the World* (San Francisco: Ignatius Press, 1980) for further development of this theme.

22. Balthasar and Luther speak of faith and love's relation in very similar terms. Whereas medieval Catholicism often spoke of union with God through our acts of love (faith formed by love), and Protestant Scholasticism often speaks of justification by an act of faith apart from consideration of God's active love poured out into our hearts through the Spirit, Balthasar and Luther before him maintained that God's absolute love ushers forth in a response of faith. For Luther's view, see *The Freedom of a Christian,* in *Martin Luther's Basic Theological Writings,* ed. Timothy F. Lull (Minneapolis: Fortress, 1989), 585–629.

23. For a discussion of this theme, see R. Kendall Soulen's essay, "'Go Tell Pharaoh,' Or, Why Empires Prefer a Nameless God," in *Cultural Encounters: A Journal for the Theology of Culture* 1, no. 2 (Summer 2005): 51–52.

24. Edward Gibbon, *History of the Decline and Fall of the Roman Empire* (London: Jones and Co., 1826), 1:18.

25. Soulen's essay (noted above) has served as a source of inspiration for this section of the chapter. See also Lesslie Newbigin, *Truth to Tell: The Gospel as Public Truth* (Grand Rapids: Eerdmans, 1991).

26. Robert Mounce maintains that the 144,000 are the entire body of saints. He writes: "In chapter 7, 144,000 were sealed against the woes that lay ahead (7:4–8). Now the same number stands secure beyond that final ordeal. The repetition of the number is not to ensure an exact identification between the two groups but to point out that not one has been lost. John's symbols are fluid, and, in fact, the number 144,000 of chapter 14 corresponds with the innumerable multitude found in the second vision of chapter 7. Both portray the full complement of the redeemed throughout history." Robert H. Mounce, *The Book of Revelation,* rev. ed., The New International Commentary of the New Testament (Grand Rapids: Eerdmans, 1998), 265.

27. Gordon Kaufman maintains that the apostle Paul turned Jesus's story of total sacrifice of the self "into ultimate prudence and self-aggrandizement; it also laid the foundation for later Christian imperialism" with the development of the doctrines of Christ's deity and the Trinity. The claim that salvation was found only in Christ led to the church having complete control over salvation, and in turn to such horrors as the Crusades and Inquisition. See Gordon D. Kaufman, *God-Mystery-Diversity: Christian Theology in a Pluralistic World* (Minneapolis: Fortress, 1996), 115. See also Gordon D. Kaufman, *In Face of Mystery: A Constructive Theology* (Cambridge: Harvard University Press, 1993), 378–79; and *Theology for a Nuclear Age* (Philadelphia: Westminster Press, 1985), 50. Paul Molnar responds to Kaufman's critique of orthodox Christology by saying, "It does not seem to occur to Kaufman that events like the inquisition and crusades, as well as the idea that salvation can be controlled by the Church, result whenever Christians do not take seriously enough Jesus' uniqueness as the one Lord of life." Paul D. Molnar, "Myth and Reality: Analysis and Critique of Gordon Kaufman and Sallie McFague on God, Christ, and Salvation," in *Cultural Encounters: A Journal for the Theology of Culture* 1, no. 2 (Summer 2005): 33. Kendall Soulen argues that in actual fact religious pluralism's proposal is the age-old theology of empire. See Soulen, "'Go Tell Pharaoh,'" 54.

28. Martin Luther King Jr., *Stride toward Freedom* (New York: Ballantine Books, 1958), 217. For King, "Christ furnished the spirit and motivation while Gandhi furnished the method" for the civil rights movement. *The Autobiography of Martin Luther King, Jr.*, ed. Clayborne Carson (New York: Warner Books, 1998), 67.

29. For an important work on the market model's negative impact on the church, see Philip D. Kenneson and James L. Street, *Selling Out the Church: The Dangers of Church Marketing* (Nashville: Abingdon, 1997). See also Rodney Clapp's significant discussion of consumer capitalism in "Green Martyrdom and the Christian Engagement of Late Capitalism," in *Cultural Encounters: A Journal for the Theology of Culture* 4, no. 1 (Winter 2008): 7–20, and his analysis of consumer capitalism's development in "The Theology of Consumption and the Consumption of Theology," in *Border Crossings: Christian Trespasses on Popular Culture and Public Affairs* (Grand Rapids: Brazos, 2000), 136–56, and in *Families at the Crossroads: Beyond Traditional & Modern Options* (Downers Grove, IL: InterVarsity, 1993), 48–66.

30. Sharlet, "Inside America's Most Powerful Megachurch," 48.

31. Ibid., 47.

32. Ibid.

33. Tim Stafford, "'Good Morning, Evangelicals!' Meet Ted Haggard: The NAE's Optimistic Champion of Ecumenical Evangelism and Free-Market Faith," *Christianity Today,* November 2005, 44.

34. See the following work for Perkins's treatment of the 3 R's of community development: John M. Perkins, *With Justice for All,* with a foreword by Chuck Colson (Ventura: Regal Books, 1982), chapters 6 through 18. See his treatment of owning the pond and community development in John M. Perkins, *Beyond Charity: The Call to Christian Community Development* (Grand Rapids: Baker Books, 1993), 119.

35. Lois Barrett, "The Church as Apostle to the World," in *Missional Church: A Vision for the Sending of the Church in North America,* ed. Darrell L. Guder (Grand Rapids: Eerdmans, 1998), 122. See also Eugene McCarraher, "The Enchantments of Mammon: Notes toward a Theological History of Capitalism," in *Modern Theology* 21, no. 3 (2005): 429–61.

36. In addition to the problems already noted, it is worth adding that whenever we separate the church from its people as well as focus on people's abilities and tastes rather than upon them as persons in communion with God and others, we end up promoting the commodification of spirituality and ultimately competition between churches in the free market of religion. This less-than-personal worldview conveys a contractual model of relations between an individual church member and the church he or she attends. As long as the church delivers the goods and services to satisfy the member's tastes, and the member delivers on abilities so that the church can continue appealing to customer tastes, the partnership continues. The union dissolves once some*thing* better comes along. The union is only as deep as the quality of the goods and performance of services provided.

37. Jonathan Sacks, "Markets and Morals," *First Things,* no. 105 (August–September, 2000): 28.

38. Soulen, "'Go Tell Pharaoh,'" 55.

39. Both of us have participated with Unitarian Universalists in forums concerning creation stewardship and care for the poor, and have been moved by their intellectual and moral resolve and empathy toward such pressing issues, longing to see more of such conviction and compassion in the evangelical community we call home.

40. The reader is encouraged to refer to the following missional resources that affirm on the one hand the particularity and supremacy of Jesus Christ to which the church bears ultimate responsibility for authentic witness and, on the other hand, the possibility of authentic witness to Christ occurring outside the walls of the church: Karl Barth, *Church Dogmatics,* IV/3.1, *The Doctrine of Reconciliation,* ed. G. W. Bromiley and T. F. Torrance (Edinburgh: T&T Clark, 1961); Paul Louis Metzger, *The Word of Christ and the World of Culture: Sacred and Secular through*

*the Theology of Karl Barth* (Grand Rapids: Eerdmans, 2003), chapter 4; Newbigin, *The Gospel in a Pluralist Society*; Pope John Paul II, *Dominus Iesus:* http://www.vatican.va/roman_curia/congregations/cfaith/documents/rc_con_cfaith_doc_20000806_dominus-iesus_en.html; Bosch, *Transforming Mission.*

41. See the discussion in chapter 7 of King's imaginative construal of the significance of Ebenezer Baptist Church's sacred space.

42. See Richard Lischer, *The Preacher King: Martin Luther King, Jr. and the Word That Moved America* (New York: Oxford University Press, 1995), 17.

## Chapter 16  From Building Programs to Building God's Missional Kingdom

1. Sociologists Michael O. Emerson and Christian Smith argue that race impacts every sphere, including economics, politics, education, and "social" and "religious systems." They define a racialized society—that is, a society defined along racial lines—in the following terms: "A racialized society is *a society wherein race matters profoundly for differences in life experiences, life opportunities, and social relationships*" (italics original). Emerson and Smith add, "A racialized society can also be said to be 'a society that allocates differential economic, political, social, and even psychological rewards to groups along racial lines; lines that are socially constructed.'" Michael O. Emerson and Christian Smith, *Divided by Faith: Evangelical Religion and the Problem of Race in America* (New York: Oxford University Press, 2000), 7. The quote within the quotation is taken from Eduardo Bonilla-Silva and Amanda Lewis, "The 'New Racism': Toward an Analysis of the U.S. Racial Structure, 1960s–1990s," unpublished manuscript, 1997.

2. Church growth people always ask: "Who's your target audience?" For example, Rick Warren tells the reader to target the "typical unchurched person your church wants to reach." See p. 169 of his chapter, "Who Is Your Target?" in *The Purpose Driven Church: Growth without Compromising Your Message & Mission* (Grand Rapids: Zondervan, 1995). While Warren encourages churches to "target" people, we are not claiming that he calls on churches to target the rich over against the poor. All of us must be careful not to give preferential treatment to some over against others.

3. See Shane Claiborne's *The Irresistible Revolution: Living as an Ordinary Radical* (Grand Rapids: Zondervan, 2006). See also the *Christianity Today* feature essay on Claiborne and the emergence of ordinary though radical monastic communities in depressed urban settings. Rob Moll, "The New Monasticism," *Christianity Today*, September 2005, 38–46. For a thorough exposition of the nature and practices of this movement, see Rutba House, ed., *School(s) for Conversion: 12 Marks of a New Monasticism* (Eugene, OR: Cascade Books, 2005).

4. Besides the fact that many churches that employ "targeting" terminology focus on more well-to-do communities, "targeting" is problematic for a variety of other reasons. In *Consuming Jesus,* the claim is made that "demographic targeting is not the same as deliberate contextualization. 'Targeting' as cultivating intentional contact is basically benign; but 'targeting' as a marketing strategy is problematic. The set of practices built into demography militate against whole-person and whole community analysis. In contrast, contextualization (as I am using it here) involves thick description and life-on-life involvement from one person to another person in a given community, and it accounts for sensitivity to that community's language and location." Paul Louis Metzger, *Consuming Jesus: Beyond Race and Class Divisions in a Consumer Church* (Grand Rapids: Eerdmans, 2007), 53. "Targeting" also connotes shooting, impacting from afar, remaining in control, and making others subject. We are grateful to Rodney Clapp for bringing these connotations to our attention.

5. John M. Perkins, *Beyond Charity: The Call to Christian Community Development* (Grand Rapids: Baker Books, 1993), 71.

6. William T. Cavanaugh, *Theopolitical Imagination* (Edinburgh: T&T Clark, 2002), 122.

7. Martin Luther King Jr., "Paul's Letter to American Christians," in *A Knock at Midnight: The Great Sermons of Martin Luther King, Jr.,* ed. Clayborne Carson and Peter Holloran (London: Little, Brown, 1998), 30–31.

8. Bill Hybels; quoted in Edward Gilbreath and Mark Galli, "Harder than Anyone Can Imagine," in *Christianity Today,* April 2005, 38.

## A Postmodern Postscript

1. Three helpful books on the relation of Christian faith to postmodernity are Stanley J. Grenz, *A Primer on Postmodernism* (Grand Rapids: Eerdmans, 1996); James K. A. Smith, *Who's Afraid of Postmodernism? Taking Derrida, Lyotard, and Foucault to Church*, The Church and Postmodern Culture (Grand Rapids: Baker Academic, 2006); and Robert E. Webber, *Ancient-Future Faith: Rethinking Evangelicalism for a Postmodern World* (Grand Rapids: Baker Academic, 1999).

2. Lesslie Newbigin, *The Gospel in a Pluralist Society* (Grand Rapids: Eerdmans, 1989), 222.

3. Lesslie Newbigin, *Foolishness to the Greeks: The Gospel and Western Culture* (Grand Rapids: Eerdmans, 1986), 4.

4. Ibid., 146–47. One sustained attempt at moving beyond such Western hegemony is *Globalizing Theology: Belief and Practice in an Era of World Christianity,* edited by Craig Ott and Harold A. Netland (Grand Rapids: Baker Academic, 2006).

5. Kanzo Uchimura, "Japanese Christianity," in Sources of Japanese Tradition, vol. 2, ed. Ryusaku Tsunoda, Wm. Theodore de Bary, and Donald Keene (New York: Columbia University Press, 1958); reprint, H. Byron Earhart, ed. Religion in the Japanese Experience: Sources and Interpretations, The Religious Life of Man Series, ed. Frederick J. Streng (Belmont: Wadsworth Publishing Company, 1974), 113.

6. Ibid., 113.

7. Ibid., 114.

8. Newbigin, *Foolishness to the Greeks,* 147.

9. See Donald Miller, *Searching for God Knows What* (Nashville: Thomas Nelson, 2004).

10. Stanley Hauerwas and Mark Sherwindt, "The Kingdom of God: An Ecclesial Space for Peace," *Word & World* 2, no. 2 (1982): 131.

11. Ibid., 131.

12. Dietrich Bonhoeffer, *The Cost of Discipleship,* rev. ed. (New York: Collier Books, 1963), 314.

13. Karl Barth, *Church Dogmatics,* vol. IV/3.1, *The Doctrine of Reconciliation* (Edinburgh: T&T Clark, 1961), 20.

14. Ibid.

15. See Michael O. Emerson and Christian Smith, *Divided by Faith: Evangelical Religion and the Problem of Race in America* (New York: Oxford University Press, 2000); and chapter 2 of Paul Louis Metzger, *Consuming Jesus: Beyond Race and Class Divisions in a Consumer Church* (Grand Rapids: Eerdmans, 2007).

16. J. I. Packer, quoted in "We Can Overcome," *Christianity Today,* October 2, 2000, 43.

17. Philip Yancey, "Why I Don't Go to a Megachurch," *Christianity Today,* May 20, 1996, 80.

18. Two important texts dealing with theory and practice as to how to foster multiethnic churches are: Mark DeYmaz, *Building a Healthy Multi-ethnic Church: Mandate, Commitments and Practices of a Diverse Congregation,* J-B Leadership Network Series (SanFrancisco: Jossey-Bass, 2007); Curtiss Paul DeYoung, Michael O. Emerson, George Yancey, and Karen Chai Kim, *United by Faith: The Multiracial Congregation as an Answer to the Problem of Race* (Oxford: Oxford University Press, 2003).

19. Carl E. Braaten and Robert W. Jenson, eds., *In One Body through the Cross: The Princeton Proposal for Christian Unity* (Grand Rapids: Eerdmans, 2003), 55–56.

20. Ibid.

# Subject Index

Advent Conspiracy, 152
affinity group, 132, 268–69, 306n14
affluenza, 153, 252, 265, 278
Alcoholism, 170–71
Alrich, G. L., 62
American, 20, 34, 45, 57–58, 110, 115, 118, 143, 144, 163, 169, 197, 210, 217, 221, 227, 242, 261, 271, 280, 281, 310n15. *See also* Christians; Patriotism
    dream, 41, 269
    Middle Eastern, 277
Anabaptist, 138–39, 197, 312n9, 314n40, 323n60
*Anamensis*, 136
Andrus, Mike, 9, 180, 317n8
Anglicanism, 108, 148, 309n58. *See also* Zahn, Paul
Antinomianism, 255–56
*Apostolic Constitutions*, 104–5
apostolic succession, 17, 191–93, 198
architecture, 47
    Church, 17
arts, 111, 114, 227, 228, 234–35, 236, 246
Augustine, Saint, 56–57, 115, 171, 295n3, 306n6, 312n9, 319n17

*Babylonian Captivity of the Church*, 135, 139, 143–44
Bainton, Roland, 139–40, 314n47
bait-and-switch, 228
baptism, 32, 57, 75, 119, 123, 124–25, 127–30, 133, 138–39, 145
    believer, 57, 101, 134–35, 141, 293, 314n48
    modes of, 141–44
    spirit, 140–42

water, 126, 128, 140
baptismal regeneration, 140–41, 312n9
Baptist, 15, 137, 141, 148, 176, 194, 197, 198, 312n9, 313n37
Barmen Declaration, the, 210, 322n41
Barrett, Lois, 262
Barth, Karl, 71, 213, 216, 220, 280, 297n8, 297–98n14, 326n8
Bender, Kimlyn, 15
Benedict XVI, 198, 308n31, 319n23
Bertrand, Russell, 39
Bethge, Eberhard, 217, 221
biblical drama, 86, 124, 127, 140, 142, 232
Bloesch, Donald, 13, 64, 117, 306n2
Bonhoeffer, Dietrich, 21–22, 44, 156, 208, 210, 212–14, 217, 219–21, 224, 226, 280, 322n26, 323n42, 323n60
*Book of Common Prayer*, 108–9, 309n58, 309n59
born again, 11, 40–41, 45, 117
Brand, Chad Owen, 195
Bromiley, Geoffrey, 142
Brown, Dan, 147, 153
Brueggemann, Walter, 81, 119, 150, 152
Bucer, Martin, 136
Buggeln, Gretchen, 243

Calvin, John, 11, 61, 137, 172, 195, 223, 299n28, 313n36, 320n2
Calvinism, 115, 137, 224, 312n9
Capitalism, 261, 328n29
Cash, Johnny, 229, 230, 315n11
Catechism, 101, 136

Cavanaugh, William, 130, 271, 314n46, 323n43
charismatic movement, 16, 103, 296n13, 308n33
charity, 102, 158, 172, 225, 244, 255
Christ and culture, 17, 41, 52, 65, 160, 164, 207–26, 227–29, 232–35, 259–60, 276
    antagonist, 208, 210, 211–14
    dualist, 208, 214, 215–19
    protagonist, 208–11, 214
    synthesist, 208, 214, 219–22
    transformationalist, 222–26
Christendom, 191, 225, 279–80
Christians
    American, 34, 99, 114, 118–19, 166, 221, 231–32, 266, 270, 271, 272
    German, 208, 210, 217, 221
    Middle Eastern, 43, 277
    Native American, 231–32, 278
Christology, 259, 260, 327n27
    union with Christ, 29–32, 35–36, 44, 54, 67, 70, 94, 96–97, 145, 192, 199, 203, 222, 242, 245–46, 249, 255
Church
    in heaven, 17, 51, 70–71
    hospital for sinners, 37, 171, 249
    membership, 61, 138, 159, 180, 220, 226, 293, 294
    sanctuary for saints, 249
    wholeness of, 166
Church growth movement, 244, 259, 315n2
    transfer growth, 220
civil society, 217, 254, 278–79
Claiborne, Shane, 266–67
Clapp, Rodney, 328n29, 329n4
Communion
    closed, 147, 153
    community oriented, 133
    open, 148–49

# Scripture Index